Creative Spaces for Qualitativ

PRACTICE, EDUCATION, WORK AND SOCIETY
Volume 5

Other books in this Series:

1. Higgs, J., Horsfall, D., & Grace, S. (2009). *Writing qualitative research on practice*. Rotterdam, The Netherlands: Sense Publishers.

2. Higgs, J., Cherry, N., Macklin, R., & Ajjawi, R. (2010). *Researching practice: A discourse on qualitative methodologies*. Rotterdam, The Netherlands: Sense Publishers.

3. Higgs, J., Fish, D., Goulter, I., Loftus, S., Reid, J., & Trede, F. (2010). *Education for future practice*, Rotterdam, The Netherlands: Sense Publishers.

4. McAllister, L., Paterson, M., Higgs, J., & Bithell, C. *Innovations in allied health fieldwork education: A critical appraisal*. Rotterdam, The Netherlands: Sense Publishers.

Creative Spaces for Qualitative Researching:
Living Research

Edited by

Joy Higgs
Charles Sturt University, Australia

Ang
Inde

Deb
Uni

Dor
Cha

SENSE PUBLISHERS
ROTTERDAM/BOSTON/TAIPEI

A C.I.P. record for this book is available from the Library of Congress.

ISBN: 978-94-6091-759-2 (paperback)
ISBN: 978-94-6091-760-8 (hardback)
ISBN: 978-94-6091-761-5 (e-book)

Published by: Sense Publishers,
P.O. Box 21858,
3001 AW Rotterdam,
The Netherlands
http://www.sensepublishers.com

Printed on acid-free paper

TABLE OF CONTENTS

JOY HIGGS

SERIES INTRODUCTION

Practice, Education, Work and Society

This series examines research, theory and practice in the context of university education, professional practice, work and society. Rather than focussing on a single topic the series examines areas where two or more of these arenas come together. Themes that will be explored in the series include: university education of professions, society expectations of professional practice, professional practice workplaces and strategies for investigating each of these areas. There are many challenges facing researchers, educators, practitioners and students in today's practice worlds. The authors in this series bring a wealth of practice wisdom and experience to examine these issues, share their practice knowledge, report research into strategies that address these challenges, share approaches to working and learning and raise yet more questions.

The conversations conducted in the series will contribute to expanding the discourse around the way people encounter and experience practice, education, work and society.

Joy Higgs, Charles Sturt University, Australia

FOREWORD

This book reflects the intersecting journeys of a group of qualitative researchers – Joy Higgs, Angie Titchen, Debbie Horsfall and Donna Bridges. And it celebrates our encounters with various groups and networks of researchers and research participants across these journeys.

In this book we extend, burnish and revise previous research discussions and experiences in the 2007 book *Being Critical and Creative in Qualitative Research* (Hampden Press) edited by Joy Higgs, Angie Titchen, Debbie Horsfall and Hilary Armstrong. Plus we draw into this critical and creative space, new narratives and innovative research practices.

We present this book to readers who are, or want to the possibility of doing critical and creative qualitative research that seeks to illuminate or transform human life and activity.

SECTION 1: RESEARCHING LIVING PRACTICES

STEPHEN LOFTUS, JOY HIGGS AND FRANZISKA TREDE

1. RESEARCHING LIVING PRACTICES

Trends in Creative Qualitative Research

Qualitative research has come a long way since its origins in anthropology well over a century ago (Loftus & Rothwell, 2010). Numerous influences have shaped the development of qualitative research, which has flourished and branched off in many different directions such as grounded theory, narrative inquiry, the many approaches shaped by phenomenology, critical inquiry, and action research.

There was a long period in which qualitative research had to justify its existence as a valid form of inquiry in many disciplines, the so-called "paradigm wars". Qualitative researchers were challenged because what they were doing did not seem to be rigorous or methodical in the same way that quantitative researchers claimed for their projects. There were convenience samples as opposed to random samples. There were no attempts at accurate measurements of phenomena that enabled cause/effect mechanisms to be explained. Above all, there was the acceptance within qualitative research of subjectivity as inevitable and actually desirable, whereas quantitative science prized objectivity and detachment. It is now more widely accepted that qualitative research has come of age. It does not set out to test theory, rather it generates theory. Qualitative research is more about understanding phenomena than explaining or predicting them. Subjectivity is present in all research to some degree and subjective experience is itself a source of valuable insights. So where is qualitative research going? And, as we consider creative spaces for qualitative research in this book, where are we going in terms of creating spaces for doing creative qualitative research? In this book we examine these questions through several key themes or trends: researching living practices, practice-based researching, and creative spaces for qualitative research.

RESEARCHING LIVING PRACTICES

The problem with researching human practice is not what to do but how to talk about it (Judt, 2010). How do we articulate and illuminate practice? Traditionally, research has been about the generation and testing of theory (or what we know as opposed to what we do). New theoretical, propositional knowledge has often been seen as the "be all and end all" of any research project. Even applied research is traditionally firmly grounded in theoretical knowledge. In recent years, however, there has been a growing interest in the world of practice, what people do, as opposed to what people know. There is a need to creatively open up intellectual spaces so that we can explore and articulate this world of practice. This is seen in

J. Higgs et al., (eds.), Creative Spaces for
Qualitative Researching: Living Research, 3–12

the work of scholars as varied as Bourdieu (2000), Wenger (1998) and Schatzki (1996).

Bourdieu (2000), for example, argued from a sociology perspective that our practice is not exclusively the result of rational decision making but, in large part, an embodied sense of what is to be done that comes from an implicit understanding of our place in the relationships that make up our social world. Bourdieu exercised his own creativity when he devised new terms to conceptualise the various aspects of these social relationships. He spoke of *habitus, field*, and *capital*. Habitus is the set of dispositions and ways of acting that seem entirely natural to us and that come from the "normal" activities and experiences that are part of our social world. Constellations or microcosms of practices, such as the family, the university or workplaces are fields. Fields are relatively independent and have their own structure and rules. Bourdieu also devised the idea of *symbolic capital*. According to him, the reason that we engage in much of our practice is not just for economic gain but to acquire symbolic capital, which can include such things as social status.

The idea of the "practice turn", generally attributed to Schatzki, shifted the concept of practice firmly into social theory arenas (Schatzki, 1996; Schatzki, Knorr Cetina, & Von Savigny, 2001). The practice turn is an umbrella term for a wide range of approaches to studying and understanding practice. Practice is shaped by meaning, knowledge, power, and social institutions, as well as "timespace" (Schatzki, 2010). Schatzki (2001, p. 2) has described the *field of practices* which is the "total nexus of interconnected human practices". The argument is that a focus on practice can illuminate many phenomena in new ways. For example, Schatzki pointed out that conventional scholarship on language has focused on aspects such as semiotics and abstract discourse, whereas a practice approach looks at language as discursive activity; he cited Foucault's (1976, 1980) work as an example of this.

Wenger (1998) drew our attention to the importance of communities of practice and the ways in which practitioners need to come together and share stories of practice so that they can learn from each other and enrich their practice. Wenger pointed out the importance of the ways in which an individual develops an identity as a practitioner through participating in such communities of practice. A community of practice also needs to develop as a community in which the members are willing and able to support each other in their practice, be they novices or experienced practitioners. The community of practice is a vitally important means of giving meaning to what individuals do as practitioners. Thinking in terms of communities of practice is another way in which we can creatively explore what people do.

It is clear from this body of literature that it is very difficult to make one's practice meaningful all on one's own. As isolated individuals it would be difficult, if not impossible, to learn how to effectively conduct a practice, let alone give it meaning. For example, Wittgenstein (1958) argued that the apparently simple practice of expressing pain to others is something learned and made meaningful through social interaction. The meaning of our practice is as important as the fact that we engage in it. Humans engage in practice for reasons, even though they may be only dimly aware of those reasons and other people (such as researchers) may find a variety of plausible and different reasons to explain particular practices.

This is part of a greater realisation that practice is as important as theory. For too long it has been assumed, for example in professional education, that if we can only get the theory right then the practice will follow. There has been a reaction against this idea, with several scholars proclaiming the "primacy of practice" (e.g. Toulmin, 2002). Toulmin pointed out that ever since the time of Descartes in the seventeenth century there has been a preoccupation with establishing the propositional knowledge (*episteme* in Aristotle's terms) that is assumed to underpin all practice. This preoccupation implies that the job of researchers is to establish what this propositional knowledge is so that it can be applied more effectively. Toulmin argues against this, claiming that what has been forgotten is that practice often depends on a form of practical wisdom (*phronesis*) that is contingent upon the circumstances around a particular practice problem. Such localised and timely practical wisdom may be the best available theory for dealing with a practice problem. There is no need always to subordinate practice to timeless propositional knowledge or any sort of general theory.

It can be argued that theory and practice are interdependent, with each being equally important. Rather than arguing for the primacy of practice, perhaps we should be arguing for the primacy of the theory–practice nexus. You can't have one without the other. There is no cause–effect relationship between theory and practice; rather an intense dialogical relationship, with each dependent on the other and interpenetrating the other. This interdependency is evident in the notion of praxis, which has been defined as morally informed and morally committed action (Carr & Kemmis, 1986). This is practice in which a large part of its meaningfulness is an ethical awareness that shapes it through and through, affecting not only how the practice is acted out but what it means to those involved.

All this raises the question of how we might open up the intellectual spaces where we can articulate the combination of theory and practice. This is where researchers, especially qualitative researchers, need some degree of creativity. Pedestrian, routine research might get away with merely documenting phenomena, but if research is to be truly useful and move our understanding forwards then it also needs to be creative and transformative (see Higgs & Titchen, 2007). The creativity comes from seeing things in new ways that can open up our thinking and our insight. Great artists such as the Impressionists helped us see the world differently by using their creativity to paint pictures that showed it to us in new ways. Their creativity lay both in being able to see the world differently themselves and in being able to express and share this new vision through their artwork. Likewise, qualitative researchers need to be creative, both in seeing the world differently, and in being able to express this new understanding in ways that help the rest of us understand the world in these new ways. It is not easy. As Davey (2006, p. 152), inspired by Gadamer, pointed out, "the sensitive use of words brings to light what is held within intense experience and thereby opens the possibility of extending it."

For the vast majority of qualitative researchers, creativity entails being creative with words, both in the ways in which textual data are read and analysed and the ways in which creative insights are then articulated for the rest of the world to share. Examples include the way in which clinical reasoning can be "revisioned" as a complex linguistic phenomenon rather than a simplistic process of cognitive computation and calculation (Loftus, 2009) or how the critical insights of Habermas can be used to understand and extend physiotherapy as an emancipatory practice so that it becomes much more than "only" a *physical* therapy (Trede, 2008). New ways of articulating a practice can open it up so that we can see what were formerly hidden depths and help us to be sensitive to new and better ways of conducting practice.

For example, the clinical encounter between doctor and patient was traditionally seen as little more than a mechanical exchange of information between doctors and patients in which the patients were assumed to be rational agents simply handing their bodies over for repair. However, Svenaeus (2000) used Gadamer's philosophical hermeneutics to creatively articulate medical practice in a way that offered new and more compassionate insights into what happens in the clinical encounter, so that more attention is focused on the reality that patients are worried, help-seeking people. This new and more creative articulation revealed the weaknesses of the more traditional view of the clinical encounter, and could draw attention to the ways in which practice might not be as morally informed or as morally committed as we believed it to be. Qualitative research needs to focus on creative articulation if it is to be truly interesting and useful.

Novice researchers might worry that creative articulation means moving away from accurately describing practice as it really is. Such a concern shows a misunderstanding of what description involves. It is worth remembering the words of Rorty (1998), who wrote:

> Human beings, like computers, dogs, and works of art, can be described in lots of different ways, depending on what you want to do with them – take them apart for repairs, re-educate them, play with them, admire them, and so on for a long list of alternative purposes. None of these descriptions is closer to what human beings really are than any of the others. Descriptions are tools invented for particular purposes, not attempts to describe things as they are in themselves, apart from any such purposes.

For too long the Western world has simply assumed that the scientific description of something is the most accurate and reliable. Rorty's point is that the best description or portrayal of a phenomenon is the one best suited for the purpose of the description. There is no one best description or interpretation. In qualitative research we need to be quite clear about the purpose of the research and creatively come up with an interpretation that best suits that purpose. This means that the same practice can be portrayed in quite different ways depending on what the research is meant to achieve. A portrayal (articulation) that seeks to emancipate people from an oppressive practice needs to look and sound quite different from one that seeks to come to a deeper understanding of what that practice entails and means for its participants. Each interpretation can be equally valid. The point is not which description or interpretation is true but which is most credible by being true to its purpose and true to the strategy that generated it.

CREATIVE RE-PRESENTATIONS OF LIVING PRACTICES

We can conclude from the section above that living practices are understood to be situated, cultural, moral, dialogic, historical, embodied, relational, technical, creative, propositional, craft, political, personal, strategic, procedural, intuitive, discursive, informal, contextual practices. In short, living practice is conceptualised as something much more complex and ambiguous than technical skill and competence. Researching such practice can benefit from creatively re-presenting research data and findings (Willis, 2000; Galvin & Todres 2007; Todres & Galvin 2008). Researchers have drawn on expressive, aesthetic, arts-based, poetic, and performative approaches to re-present their research findings.

Key purposes and tasks of creatively researching living practices are to richly describe practice phenomena so that we can appreciate and come to know (what are they like? what do they feel like?) and more deeply understand (what are their perceived meanings?) such living practices. Some of the reasons to conduct research into living practices are to evoke an aliveness of practice, to facilitate an experience of emotional homecoming, to empathise with others, to reduce suffering. One of the foundational concepts of qualitative research that underpins these purposes is the notion of multiple interpretations of experiences and the rejection of the notion of one external reality and universal truth. Experiences cannot be accurately and objectively represented. This crisis of representation opens up creative spaces for new approaches (Winter, 2010). Researchers who use creative approaches seek symbolism rather than authenticity in their re-presentation. Symbolism avoids explanatory written words and can potentially unleash the imagination of the reader/consumer of such research, ultimately creating openness and readiness for other possibilities of being, knowing and doing in practice. The task of creative approaches to researching living practices is to reveal and symbolically re-present them. This task is most credibly accomplished through collaborative, participative and co-productive strategies. There is an inevitable reciprocity between researcher and researched. Qualitative research seeks to explore the diversity, uncertainty, ambiguity and complexity in and of practices. The acceptance of multiple perspectives welcomes creative and diverse ways of collecting, re-presenting and interpreting data. Qualitative researchers assert that knowledge generation is a complex process of interwoven and interrelated interpretations. And they seek to establish interdependent connections and relationships between knowing, feeling and doing in practice.

Although written academic texts remain the key mandatory requirements for presenting and publishing research work there is a growing movement that accepts other ways of re-presenting research of living practices (Higgs, Cherry, & Trede, 2009). A creative qualitative paradigm enables researchers to explore other than the dominant ways of knowing, being and becoming in practice and to powerfully reveal and interpret ambiguities, emotions, social justice stances and embodied knowing in practice. Such creative approaches to re-presenting practice can be categorised into three broad modes: creative writing, which includes stories and poems; visual arts, which include painting and sculpture; and performances, which include drama, film and dance (Willis, 2000).

FT has used all these three creative modes to mirror back practice situations in different ways and modes in order to assist patients and their carers as well as clinicians and their managers to rediscover practice and practice experiences, and to appreciate them with different eyes. In a large emergency department of a teaching hospital in Sydney, FT and her research team used patient complaints data and in-depth interview data with emergency staff (including receptionists) to extrapolate eight themes that led to miscommunication and misunderstandings between staff and patients (Trede, Jochelson, & McCarthy, 2005). They then employed a script writer/film director who wrote eight prototypical scenarios based on the eight themes. These scripts were read out to emergency staff members, to check with them that the scripts sounded real and credible and resonated with them. They employed actors and produced eight film vignettes. These vignettes are creative re-presentations of research findings about health communication issues in an emergency department. These films are creative due to their performative nature and symbolic value.

In an acute cardiac ward of a teaching hospital in Sydney, FT and her research team collected stories from staff (about what it is like working with people with acute cardiac conditions) and patients (about what it is like living with a heart condition, and what they learned about their condition on the ward) through dialogical interviews (Trede & Flowers, 2008; Trede, Flowers, & Bergin, 2008). We summarised their stories and gave their stories back to them for editing to ensure that the stories were credible and truthful. We also employed artists who were present at the interviews. Each storyteller was asked to tell us what colours, shapes and symbols they would use if they were to paint their story. The artists used these suggestions to create an oil painting for each story; we called the story and accompanying painting a storyboard. All the storyboards are exhibited in this cardiac ward.

The key focus of these creative research methodologies was to privilege embodied, cultural and relational knowing, and to re-present experiences by including, if not foregrounding, emotions and bodily perceptions. Our purposes were to reveal the diversity of perspectives in practice, to enhance empathy and appreciation of what it is like to practise and to receive such practice, and to open up possibilities for genuine dialogue at a reciprocal compassionate level. Creativity was used as an ontological existentialist stance as well as an epistemological process of coming to understand practices.

The abovementioned projects adopted arts-based approaches because the arts are implicit in character, opening up the imagination and creating possibilities for interpretation. Further, the arts-implied symbolism was a powerful tool to allow co-researchers to re-present themselves in different ways. The aim of these approaches was not to accurately and authentically represent practice; because they worked in a creative, qualitative framework. Symbolic re-presentations in the form of storyboards, vignettes and creative writing are used as a transformative force where the symbolism re-presents reality, triggers reflection, and stimulates debate.

CREATIVE SPACES FOR QUALITATIVE RESEARCH

In the first theme we looked at researching practice; the second theme focused on the multiple dimensions of living practices that researchers seek to illuminate; this third section addresses the implications of these two pursuits. We ask here: what is needed for researchers conducting qualitative research in these areas? Our answers lie in considerations of creating spaces within us, between us and around us.

Creating spaces within us entails first seeking to know ourselves: what are our present understandings and prejudgments, what are our goals, interests and values, what are our preferred or desired ways of being in the research space, where do we want to go in our research journeys, how do we want to be – as self and with others. This reflection can be painful, cathartic, illuminating, bewildering and empowering. From reflection come choices to change or reassert the known or unknown choices we have already made about all these questions. Then we set forth into our next research adventure with our choices made – or at least made enough to get started, with the reminder to review again later. Our space for self as persons doing research then becomes one of seeking authenticity, agency and capability to pursue these choices.

Creating spaces between us first asks the question: Who is us? The answer is likely to be our co-researchers, because that's the rather obvious thing about being in a team. But how often do we identify the need for shaping the living and "to be lived in" space of the research team (e.g. through an exploratory values exercise)? Or do we just concentrate on articulating the task space (e.g. roles, tasks, timelines)? Another answer that is needed relates to the type of space we wish to create both for and with our research participants. Is this space ideally (for *this* project and philosophical frame of reference) one of appreciation for their contribution ("Thanks for your input to my/our project"), one of process collaboration ("How can we all participate in this task?"), one of shared project leadership ("How shall we go about doing this research together?").

Importantly, the spaces we create are evolving, not static phenomena. In research supervision journeys, for instance, we commonly aim for the novices (students) to gain superior knowledge in their specific topic areas, to experience times of high agency where the supervisor takes a back-seat role and times when they need help from their wise mentor. For a research group engaged in an extended term project there are likely to be members coming and going, changes in leadership, tensions that need resolution, times of shared achievement, even exhilaration, and times of redirection and revisioning. Research needs to balance rigour (rather than rigidity) and creative endeavour (rather than disorganised chaos) to achieve credibility and meaningful knowledge of human being and practices.

Creating spaces around us is, in essence, creating spaces in which to be creative. The following poem seeks to reflect such spaces. Consider the value of these ideas for research spaces.

> We met to start our research journey
> We came in all shapes and sizes
> of ideas, lives, experience – multi-hued people.
>
> Creation of ways of being together was a constant happening
> spontaneous and planned – preset and like breathing
> We met sometimes in work places
> for convenience and to bring others in remotely
> Often we met in "our space"
> This was a large sunroom leading out
> into a wide verandah and a leafy garden
> in an old family home – it was Grandma's place
> belonging to one of our group
> There was plenty of space for sitting and coffee
> For eating by grazing or feasting
> For lots of laptops to be plugged in
> And drawing on newsprint on the floor
> The cooking created such aromas
> I will always relate these to creative thinking
> And good times and shared endeavour
> "Our space" was where we debated, argued and disagreed
> where we collaborated, shared insights and made plans
>
> Our space was physical, it was people, it was ideas
> It was word and wordless knowing
> It was being and being there

FROM HERE

One of the exciting things about being involved in qualitative research is that we can give ourselves permission to open up new intellectual spaces and be creative, from the time we start to think through the questions we might ask all the way through to the final articulation/creation of what we have found and what it means. This is probably true of all research and scholarly activity to some degree. There is the well-known story of the famous physicist, Nils Bohr, who once reprimanded a student for being logical all the time and not thinking. To think means to be creative. There is still a need to be rigorous and to keep ourselves firmly grounded in the data that we gather, but beyond this we can (and should) use our creativity to open up our understanding of the many ways in which humans engage in living practices. The rest of this book provides many examples of the diverse ways that people have exercised this creativity in qualitative research. We hope you enjoy it.

REFERENCES

Bourdieu, P. (2000). *Pascalian meditations*. Stanford: Stanford University Press.

Carr, W., & Kemmis, S. (1986). *Becoming critical: Education, knowledge and action research*. Melbourne: Deakin University Press.

Davey, N. (2006). *Unquiet understanding: Gadamer's philosophical hermeneutics*. Albany, NY: State University of New York Press.

Foucault, M. (1976). *The archaeology of knowledge* (trans. A.M. Sheridan Smith). New York: Harper & Row.

Foucault, M. (1980). *Power/knowledge* (Ed. Colin Gordon). New York: Pantheon.

Galvin, K., & Todres, L. (2007). The creativity of "unspecialization": A contemplative direction for integrative scholarly practice. *Phenomenology & Practice, 1*, 31–46.

Higgs, J., & Titchen, A. (2007). Qualitative research: Journeys of meaning making through transformation, illumination, shared action and liberation. In J. Higgs, A. Titchen, D. Horsfall & H. Armstrong (Eds.), *Being critical and creative in qualitative research* (pp. 11–21). Sydney: Hampden Press.

Higgs, J., Cherry, N., & Trede, F. (2009). Rethinking texts in qualitative research. In J. Higgs, D. Horsfall & S. Grace (Eds.), *Writing qualitative research on practice* (pp. 37–47). Rotterdam: Sense.

Judt, T. (2010). *Ill fares the land*. New York: Penguin Press.

Loftus, S. (2009). *Language in clinical reasoning: Towards a new understanding*. Saarbruecken: VDM Verlag.

Loftus, S., & Rothwell, R. (2010). The origins of qualitative research: The importance of philosophy. In J. Higgs, N. Cherry, R. Macklin & R. Ajjawi (Eds.), *Researching practice: A discourse on qualitative methodologies* (pp. 19–29). Rotterdam, The Netherlands: Sense.

Rorty, R. (1998). Against unity. *Wilson Quarterly, 22*(1), 28–39.

Schatzki, T.R. (1996). *Social practices: A Wittgensteinian approach to human activity and the social*. Cambridge: Cambridge University Press.

Schatzki, T.R. (2001). Introduction: Practice theory. In T.R. Schatzki, K. Knorr Cetina & E. von Savigny (Eds.), *The practice turn in contemporary theory* (pp. 1–14). New York: Routledge.

Schatzki, T.R. (2010). *The timespace of human activity: On performance, society, and history as indeterminate teleological events*. Toronto: Rowman & Littlefield.

Schatzki, T.R., Knorr Cetina, K., & von Savigny, E. (Eds.) (2001). *The practice turn in contemporary theory*. New York: Routledge.

Svenaeus, F. (2000). *The hermeneutics of medicine and the phenomenology of health: Steps towards a philosophy of medical practice*. Dordrecht, The Netherlands: Kluwer Academic.

Todres, L., & Galvin, K. (2008). Embodied interpretation: A novel way of evocatively re-presenting meanings in phenomenological research. *Qualitative Research, 8*(5), 568–583.

Toulmin, S. (2002). The primacy of practice: Medicine and postmodernism. *Philosophy of Medicine and Bioethics, 50*(1), 41–53.

Trede, F. (2008). *A critical practice model for physiotherapy practice: Developing practice through critical transformative dialogues*. Saarbrücken: Vdm Verlag Dr. Müller.

Trede, F., & Flowers, R. (2008). *Evaluating a process of storymaking to enhance communicative dialogues*. Paper presented at European Association of Communication in Health Care conference, Oslo.

Trede, F., Flowers, R., & Bergin, P. (2008). *Arts and co-production for diversity health*. Paper presented at Diversity in Health Conference: Strengths and sustainable solutions, Sydney.

Trede, F., Jochelson, T., & McCarthy, S. (2005). *In their shoes*. DVD accompanied by Communication handbook, Department of Health (NSW): South Eastern Suburbs Illawarra Area Health Service.

Wenger, E. (1998). *Communities of practice: Learning meaning and identity*. Cambridge: Cambridge University Press.

Willis, P. (2000). Expressive and arts-based research: Presenting lived experience in qualitative research. In P. Willis, R. Smith & E. Collins (Eds.), *Being, seeking, telling: expressive approaches to qualitative adult education research* (pp. 35–65). Flaxton, QLD: Post Pressed.

Winter, R. (2010). Ein Plädoyer für kritische Perspektiven in der qualitativen Forschung. *Forum Qualitative Sozialforschung / Forum: Qualitative Social Research, 12*(1), Art. 7, available: http://nbn-resolving.de/urn:nbn:de:0114-fqs110171, accessed 23 July 2011.

Wittgenstein, L. (1958). Philosophical investigations (G.E.M. Anscombe, Trans., 3rd ed.). Upper Saddle River, NJ: Prentice Hall. (originally published 1953).

Stephen Loftus PhD
The Education For Practice Institute
Charles Sturt University, Australia

Joy Higgs AM PhD
The Education For Practice Institute
Charles Sturt University, Australia

Franziska Trede PhD MHPEd
The Education For Practice Institute
Charles Sturt University, Australia

NITA CHERRY AND JOY HIGGS

2. RESEARCHING IN WICKED PRACTICE SPACES

Artistry as a Way of Researching the Unknown in Practice

> Practice confronts us with "wicked" problems (Rittel & Webber, 1973) that
> constantly challenge our commitment, courage and expertise, as individuals,
> as organisations and as societies. These problems are messy, circular,
> aggressive and feature ill-defined design and planning problems. Such
> challenges can seem very difficult and personally demanding. Even without
> these stimulating opportunities and wicked problems, our individual and
> collective practice constantly needs to develop to keep pace with the
> perpetual change of our globally connected world. (Higgs & Cherry, 2009, p.
> 4)

We live in interesting times. Global connectivity creates opportunities and
problems that have multiple drivers, many spin-offs, and stakeholders with varying
and often incongruent interests. Building knowledge and expertise that is capable
of engaging helpfully with this complexity sometimes challenges the fundamental
research paradigms and practice disciplines which define and organise what we
think we know and can do. It requires us to bring multidisciplinary perspectives
and creative research strategies to bear on issues and possibilities, and often to
think outside the existing boxes. And it poses some significant challenges for
educators, researchers and practitioners.

But sitting under this are some even more fundamental issues. Creating and
effectively applying knowledge through practice is the work which engages us all,
whether through major innovation or less dramatic day-to-day practice. Even without
the pressures of contemporary innovation and change, the development, or crafting,
of an individual's professional practice is a genuinely complex phenomenon. The
challenges – and opportunities – this presents for researchers who care to investigate
the development and application of professional practice are very interesting.
Something as basic as describing the way an individual's professional practice works
– the countless unconscious and conscious choices that are made about how to
intervene and when – represents a major undertaking for research practice, let alone
more complex tasks such as explaining how this practice developed or why it works.
This chapter explores these issues and suggests some ways in which qualitative
researchers might usefully engage with them.

J. Higgs et al.,(eds.),Creative Spaces for
Qualitative Researching: Living Research, 13–22
© 2011 Sense Publishers. All rights reserved.

WHAT PRACTICE REPRESENTS

By *practice*, we mean that set of behaviours, strategies, frameworks and underlying beliefs and knowledge through which a single human being or group of people consistently tries to engage with the tasks, situations and issues that face them in the context of their life and work. In the context of professional practice, practice comprises a range of complex phenomena, responsibilities and situations which the person is charged to deal with. The development, integration and application of professional knowledge draws on many forms and ways of knowing (Scott, 1990; Eraut, 1994; Higgs & Titchen, 1995; Drury Hudson, 1997). Beyond theoretical or conceptually derived knowledge, practice requires personal knowledge (derived from life experiences and what seems to the individual to be either shared or personal ways of understanding or doing things), practice wisdom (deep practical knowledge born of reflexive experience), procedural knowledge (knowledge of context and local rules) and empirical knowledge (derived from systematic research and theory testing). Professional practice is also profoundly personal. Professional associations try to codify key elements of practice, but it is the individual operating in a particular context who must exercise judgment about what to do and how to do it. Practice also requires that knowledge can be translated into skilled, effective and wise action in particular and specific situations. To be successful in practice over time, practitioners must possess a range, or repertoire, of skilled behaviours; this in turn implies that choices, whether conscious or not, must be made as to what to do at any particular time. Some time ago, Revans (1982, p. 493) made a very cogent observation about the connection between practice and theory:

> The science of praxeology – or the theory of practice – remains among the underdeveloped regions of the academic world. And yet it is, or should be, the queen of all ... successful theory is merely that which enables him who is suitably armed to carry through successful practice. This is the argument of the pragmatists, William James, John Dewey and even Karl Marx: to understand an idea one must be able to apply it in practice, and to understand a situation one must be able to change it. Verbal description is not command enough. It is from consistently replicated and successful practice that is distilled and concentrated the knowledge we describe as successful theory.

However, as Polanyi (1967) has pointed out, many aspects of skilled practice become tacit and we come to know much more than we can say. And the precise ways in which individual and collective practice integrates knowing and doing remain, arguably, among the biggest conundrums of human development. We know that it happens, we see it and experience it every day, but it remains a challenge to effectively, credibly and reliably influence practice, as every parent, every teacher and every leader knows.

PRACTICE AS ARTISTRY

Psychologists and sociologists for decades have produced many theories of how we make sense of things, learn and apply skilled behaviours. However, many of these theories are only capable of exploring individual elements of learning. Capturing the holistic nature of practice has called for metaphor, and it was his recognition of the complexity of practice development that led Donald Schön (1987) to frame practice in terms of artistry. Schön's starting point was the same as that of Polanyi (1967). He was struck by the kinds of competence and knowledge that do not depend on our being able to describe what we know how to do, or even to hold in consciousness the knowledge our actions reveal or imply. We know the "feel of things" – the feel of driving a car or swinging a golf club, and we can readily detect when something is wrong, but it is often easier for us to describe deviations from "normal" performance or experience than it is to describe the norm itself. Schön used the term *knowing-in-action* to describe spontaneous skilful performance which we are unable to make verbally explicit.

Schön suggested that much of the skilled behaviour which we associate both with the arts and with the traditional professions cannot be taught in a literal sense. In this framework, the facilitation of adult learning involves a dialogue between facilitator and learner, in which the learner experiments, takes action, reflects (both alone and dialoguing with the facilitator) and reflects on further experience. The dialogue is not about prescription or rule-giving, but it is about creating or crafting something that emerges gradually, individualistically, and on the basis of extensive disciplined practice. It is not about one person simply handing to another a blue-print or vision of effective performance. He observed that the vision – if it exists – is often difficult to articulate, let alone share or prescribe. And the discipline is that of reflection, close attention to the experience, the doing and the remembering:

> The design studio shares in a general paradox attendant on the teaching and learning of any really new competence or understanding: for the student seeks to learn things whose meaning and importance she cannot grasp ahead of time … [She] knows she needs to look for something but does not know what the something is. She seeks to learn it, moreover, in the sense of coming to know it in action. Yet, at the beginning, she can neither do it nor recognise it when she sees it. Hence, she is caught up in a self-contradiction: "looking for something" implies a capacity to recognise the thing one looks for, but the student lacks at first the capacity to recognise the object of her search. The instructor is caught up in the same paradox: he cannot tell the student what she needs to know, even if he has words for it, because the student would not at that point understand him. (Schön, 1987, pp. 82–84)

The paradox Schön described becomes even more troublesome when practice must engage with situations that are more complex and novel, that require the practitioner to dig more deeply. To help us understand what is going on in these situations – which he referred to as indeterminate zones of practice – Schön used the term *artistry*, which he defined as:

an exercise of intelligence, a kind of knowing, though different in crucial respects from a standard model of professional knowledge. It is not inherently mysterious; it is rigorous in its own terms; and we can learn a great deal about it ... by carefully studying the performance of unusually competent performers. (Schön, 1987, p. 13)

RESEARCHING THE UNKNOWN IN PRACTICE

Schön's articulation of the paradox of practice development, both under normal circumstances and in the indeterminate zones of complex practice, poses particularly interesting questions for both researchers and educators in universities. How is the development and application of practice wisdom described and articulated? How is it explained? How is it turned into theory? How is theory used in practice? How is practice wisdom taught? And in an age of juicy problems and wicked problems, how is the convergence of multidisciplinary constructs and paradigms connected with practice wisdom? How do we engage with the problematic knowledge generated by contemporary innovations such as surveillance technology, the human genome project and access to euthanasia?

Since Schön's elegant articulation of the dilemma, others have taken up the theme. The issue, for some at least, is not only about being able to learn fruitfully despite not "knowing" (where "not knowing" is framed as an obstacle to be overcome), but about deliberately cultivating and sustaining a state of not-knowing as a research and learning strategy. From this perspective the practitioner values tacit knowledge and understands the power of forgetting the name of the thing one sees (Weschler, 1982), making the familiar strange and new again (Emmett, 1998) and re-enchanting everyday life (Moore, 1996). Consider the images and opportunities created for rethinking the familiar in the following figures (2.1, 2.2).

Figure 2.1. Making strange the natural elements

In this "strange" space, nothing is taken for granted, everything can be seen with fresh eyes, some issues and experiences now become problematic, while others can be experienced without the clutter of previous expectations and baggage.

Paradoxically, we may feel both freer and more challenged. In this space, some things that were undiscussable become open to discourse, while the need to justify and explain other things simply falls away. Here we might come to experience both our inner and outer worlds in different ways, and even the distinction between those worlds in different ways. This space can become a container or site for tremendous creative activity for researchers, and the rest of this chapter explores the ways in which research practice might take on artistry.

Figure 2.2. Making human touch abstract

ARTISTRY IN RESEARCH PRACTICE

As a term or idea, artistry is often associated with an aesthetic dimension in seeing and engaging with the world. Certainly that particular notion of artistry in research practice is not new, and aesthetic modes of knowing (Eisner, 1985) have taken their place in qualitative research practice over the last three decades. Many of these offer helpful ways of researching how practitioners develop their practice and how they apply their practice under conditions that challenge it. However, artistry in the sense that Schön suggested implies something different from aesthetic forms of engagement. It is a way of approaching professional practice in almost any professional or disciplinary setting that draws attention to the way knowledge is exercised and the way things are done. Schön's own exposition of artistry as a way of knowing and doing centred on reflection in practice, involving reflection-in-the-midst-of-action (not post-event) and reciprocal dialogue with others during this "reflection-in-action" (Schön, 1987, p. xii). In his own extended exposition of reflective practices, Bleakley suggested that artistry in higher education is an act of what Heidegger (1993) would call "care", "under which each act is an apprehension collapsing history, presence and future implications in the moment, embedded in an informing and intentional object world" (Bleakley, 1999, p. 328).

Over the past decade, The Centre for Creative Leadership in the United States has articulated a suite of six creative competencies that they also associate with what they call crafting or artistry in professional practice (see Palus & Horth, 2002). They suggest that these skills are particularly helpful when professionals engage with issues that are complex, novel and important. Although developed with professional leadership practice in mind, we suggest that their ideas open up some interesting possibilities for researchers trying to get to grips with how they might explore practice from any discipline under conditions of complexity. Three of their original six competencies or skill sets struck us as being of particular potential value to researchers: paying attention, serious play and co-inquiry.

Paying Attention

Paying attention at the outset is the first – and in some sense foundational – competency Palus and Horth (2002) described. Their argument is that practitioners across many disciplines spend as little as ten percent of time in diagnosing or framing situations up front, and respond to a range of pressures to move to action as quickly as possible. When issues are genuinely complex and critical, the trade-off for speed can be oversimplification and serious errors of judgment. Certainly researchers at all stages of their practice frequently find themselves under exactly this sort of pressure: to tightly frame complex research questions to apply for grants; to specify all details of methodology in order to obtain ethics approval; to write definitive literature reviews ahead of creating data.

The advice of Palus and Horth is to use whatever time is available for diagnosis more effectively, engaging with the issues in ways that do justice to their complexity. Paying attention can incorporate the skill of shifting between different modes of attention. What they call "high-gear attention" provides speed when the terrain is smooth, and is the kind of attention associated with experienced performance in familiar terrain. But when we need to dig deep, in the face of the novel and complex, they suggest that we need low-gear attention, where we take the time to look yet again, to suspend assumptions that we know what we see, and to make the familiar strange to us. They also contrast left-mode and right-mode attention: the contrast between word-based deductive logic that is sequential and analytical and non-verbal, intuitive perception, operating in the moment, based on images and patterns, in the moment nonverbal. For the researcher, this might take the form of making a deliberate effort to use contrasting modes during initial engagement with a research project, perhaps using narratives, images and metaphors alongside analytical and logic-based approaches.

A more radical suggestion is that we use kinaesthetic attention based on physical movement and the wisdom of the body. This can range from something as simple as walking and talking about issues rather than opposed to sitting and thinking, to something more sophisticated and time-consuming making things – objects or models, that physically represent the issues. Also we can pay attention to the negative "white" space: the space between issues, like the unoccupied space in a picture or text. While we focus on the objects, the words or the issues, we are attending to the familiar, going straight to what we think we know.

> The activity of drawing is a powerful device for understanding negative space … drawing a picture of a specific tree can be difficult when your preconception of a tree … gets in the way of your ability to see the real, individual tree. But you have no preconceived symbols for the shapes between the branches of a tree. So if you faithfully attend to and draw these negative spaces, the real tree gradually emerges … not your symbol for one;

in addition, the tree will appear woven into its context, not abstracted from that environment (Palus & Horth, 2002, p. 19).

In this way, we focus on the particular, "attending to the question: What is this?" (Palus & Horth, 2002, p. 20). This is a very powerful idea, because it focuses attention on the context which helps to create and define the issue, raising questions like: To whom is this important and why? Why is it important now? How has it been approached in the past? With what result? What was learned? What has been ignored? Qualitative researchers can have a belief that knowledge is contextual but still fail to get to grips with the quite fundamental way in which the context – the negative or white space – shapes the phenomenon with which they are trying to engage. By listening for what is not said, the voices that are absent, we pay more attention to what is excluded from our first framing of the more obvious.

Paying attention also includes asking powerful questions – a skill familiar in the research context, where we understand that framing good questions is fundamental to the journey of generating useful answers. Palus and Horth invoke the metaphor of poking the embers to stir up the flames, creating heat and energy, and suggest that powerful questions have three qualities: they invite exploration, they resist easy answers and they invoke strong passions, pulling attention to the otherwise unnoticed white spaces. This is a very different mode from expecting ourselves as researchers to be always in control, having all the answers and being definitive about what we are doing. Powerful questions can come from the different modes of attention mentioned

already: right-mode questions that ask, What are the patterns? left-mode questions that ask, What is the dominant logic operating here? questions from negative space that ask, What are we neglecting to ask? and questions from other perspectives: the what-if questions that explore unexpected scenarios, and the questions of appreciative inquiry familiar to many researchers: What's right about what we are doing? What's already well built and fit for purpose? What is unappreciated and therefore possibly under-leveraged or taken for granted?

Serious Play

So far, we have considered the application to research of a set of skills that Palus and Horth (2002) associated with what they called paying attention. They offered two other ideas that are worth consideration in the context of researching practice: the skill sets associated with serious play and co-inquiry. They noted that the idea of serious play has some currency in the social sciences, citing Gergen's (1991) perspective that serious play allows people to communicate even in the face of entrenched differences, drawing on a way of communicating that:

explores similarities and differences, not by deconstructing the other's point of view (an all too frequent response) but by playfully exploring new combinations of perspectives for something fresh and useful. Serious play … is matter of learning to hold your deepest beliefs lightly for a moment, rather than squeezing more tightly when they are challenged (Palus & Horth, 2002, p. 107).

Serious play challenges the idea of being in control at all times, creating the possibility for surprise, for the kind of creative disruption (Schumpeter, 1934) that precedes innovation. Even if it doesn't produce radical innovation, serious play might just loosen our tight grip on concepts or methods that restrict our capacity to see, experience and engage with complex issues in ways that do appropriate justice to them. Palus and Horth (2002) had some ideas about serious play that are very relevant to the research enterprise. For example, they suggested that "serious play is matter of building a toy in the best sense of that word – a model or a prototype – and then batting it around with others exuberantly and creatively; often it breaks" (p. 108). Although many academic forums are not the site of serious play in these terms, and indeed can be the scene of just the opposite, there is no reason why a researcher should not invite a group of group of colleagues to experiment with the kind of play that is being suggested.

Radical sabbaticals are another idea: deliberately choosing to spend time with people in contexts, on projects, and working in ways that are very different from our own. And of course this doesn't need to be a sabbatical in the literal sense; it could be a week or a day each month spent in the company of people and ideas that are unfamiliar and deeply enriching. What they call *"the aesthetics of imperfection"* (Palus & Horth, 2002, p. 181) involves capitalising on experiments that have failed, learning deeply from things that have gone wrong. This is a useful idea that emphasises the value (rather than the down-side) of things being not quite right at our first attempt, or even being quite wide of the mark. When we don't have the mastery we would like, we might be forced to think again about our assumptions, our understanding, our technique, even our intentions.

Co-Inquiry

Co-inquiry is the third broad skill set that Palus and Horth (2002) offer us that raises some interesting possibilities for researchers. Of course, co-inquiry is well established as a research method, perhaps most beautifully articulated by Heron's (1988) framing of it as co-operative inquiry. Indeed, we would argue that in a time of converging disciplines and messy problems and opportunities, it is a requisite for being an effective researcher in almost any context. The newer twists raised here include a focus on crossing borders, improvised relationships, inviting others to play, playing kindly, and deliberately seeking feedback. Crossing borders in the academy means not just spending time with researchers from other disciplines but actually inviting them to sit with us and use some of their lenses and methods to see and engage with our issue in different ways: a practical way to make the familiar strange or, indeed, to engage with the unfamiliar.

Improvised relationships are built opportunistically, by taking advantage of unplanned meetings, accidental connections, and casual conversations with people we haven't met before, whose perspectives are unfamiliar but potentially interesting and valuable. Inviting others to play is about being proactive, not simply waiting to be asked, and deliberately crafting rich descriptions and striking frames for the issues of interest – and for the methods of co-inquiry themselves – that are likely to attract the attention of others.

Co-inquiry does not have to entail long-term associations; it can be about time-limited encounters where the value comes from a different kind of conversation. Instead of debate and advocacy, immediate critique and evaluation, this kind of dialogue is intended to cultivate ideas, to allow them to emerge with respect – perhaps a kind of appreciative inquiry. Unlike brainstorming, that encourages many ideas to emerge and then parks them for later consideration, the idea is to deliberately build on an idea, to take it somewhere. This kind of inquiry would certainly profit from the range of ways of paying attention that were described earlier in this chapter. Another suggestion from this skill set that draws on those mentioned previously is the idea of putting something in the middle: an object or a physical prototype, or a symbol, picture or image that somehow represents or invokes the issue in question, that engages both the collective attention of the group and also invites different kinds of attention and diverse perspectives.

RESEARCHING PRACTICE WITH ARTISTRY

In this chapter we have suggested that adopting the stance of artistry can be helpful when researching issues of professional practice that challenge existing practice wisdom. Studying the ways that practitioners themselves engage with these issues is also a fruitful space for researchers, but a challenging one, as practitioners struggle to name what they don't yet know. Researchers share the dilemma of the practitioners in both these situations: having to engage without being able to satisfactorily describe or even name the issues and processes in play. By adopting a stance of artistry that combines reflection-in-action (Schön, 1987) and care (Bleakley, 1999) with the sorts of creative competencies suggested by Palus and Horth (2002), we might enhance the skills that we bring as researchers into the unknown spaces.

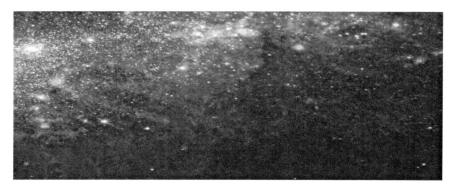

REFERENCES

Bleakley, A. (1999). From reflective practice to holistic reflexivity. *Studies in Higher Education, 24*(3), 315–330.

Drury Hudson, J. (1997). A model of professional knowledge for social work practice. *Australian Social Work, 50*(3), 35–44.

Eisner, E. (1985). Aesthetic modes of knowing. In E. Eisner (Ed.), *Learning and teaching the ways of knowing: Eighty-fourth yearbook of the National Society for the Study of Education* (pp. 23–36), Chicago: University of Chicago Press.

Emmet, P. (1998). *Janet Laurence: Gatherings.* Sydney: Art and Australia Monographs, Craftsman House.

Eraut, M. (1994). *Developing professional knowledge and competence.* London: The Falmer Press.

Gergen, K. (1991). *The saturated self: Dilemmas of identity in contemporary life.* New York: Basic Books.

Heidegger, M. (1993). *Basic writings* (Ed. D. F. Krell). London: Routledge.

Heron, J. (1988). Validity in cooperative inquiry. In P. Reason (Ed.), *Human inquiry in action* (pp. 40–50). Beverley Hills, CA: Sage.

Higgs, J., & Cherry, N. (2009). Doing qualitative research on practice. In J. Higgs, D. Horsfall & S. Grace (Eds.), *Writing qualitative research on practice* (pp. 3–12). Rotterdam, The Netherlands: Sense.

Higgs, J., & Titchen, A. (1995). The nature, generation and verification of knowledge. *Physiotherapy, 81*(9), 521–530.

Moore, T. (1996). *The re-enchantment of everyday life.* Rydalmere, NSW: Hodder and Stoughton.

Palus, C., & Horth, D. (2002). *The leader's edge: Six creative competencies for navigating complex challenges.* San Francisco: Jossey-Bass.

Polanyi, M. (1967). *The tacit dimension.* New York: Doubleday.

Revans, R.W. (1982). *The origins and growth of action learning.* Bromley, UK: Chartwell Bratt.

Rittel, H., & Webber, M. (1973). Dilemmas in a general theory of planning. *Policy Sciences, 4*(2), 155–169.

Schön, D.A. (1987). *Educating the reflective practitioner: Towards a new design for teaching and learning in the professions.* San Francisco: Jossey-Bass.

Schumpeter, J.A. (1934). *The theory of economic development.* Cambridge, MA: Harvard University Press.

Scott, D. (1990). Practice wisdom: The neglected source of practice research. *Social Work, 35*(6), 564–568.

Wechsler, L. (1982). *Seeing is forgetting the name of the thing one sees: A life of contemporary artist Robert Irwin.* Berkeley, CA: University of California Press.

Nita Cherry PhD
The Australian Graduate School for Entrepreneurship
Faculty of Business and Enterprise
Swinburne University of Technology, Australia

Joy Higgs AM PhD
The Research Institute for Professional Practice, Learning & Education
The Education For Practice Institute
Charles Sturt University, Australia

ANNE CROKER AND JULIE-ANNE TOOTH

3. CREATING SPACES TO BRING RESEARCH INTO LIVING PRACTICE

The research space for exploring living practice is replete with latent possibilities for creation and expansion. This is a *potential* space that, when realised, is situated, collaborative and transformative in nature. It is a space formed and forged through researchers' *curiosity*, shaped by their *creativity,* and cultivated through their *care* about people. Throughout its creation, this space is sustained by researchers' *reflexivity* and *responsiveness*, qualities that enable the blurred boundaries between research and practice to be embraced. In this chapter we outline key aspects of the multifaceted nature of this space. We then explore issues related to creating and sustaining research spaces by drawing on literature and research projects, including our own PhD research experiences and the reflected-upon experiences of colleagues, Sam and Jay (pseudonyms). Although these projects are predominantly interpretive, issues related to critical research are also considered.

We understand the term *living practice* to highlight the dynamic nature of practice and the individual differences of the people involved. We view the notions of person-centredness and authenticity as central to this understanding. We focus on (a) *person-centredness* as requiring high regard for each individual's values, perspectives and capabilities, and (b) *authenticity* as the integrity involved in upholding the moral values and ethical concerns of self in relation to others and where self-interest is overridden by concern for others.

MULTIFACETED NATURE OF THE SPACE

Potential Space

Creating spaces to bring research into living practice often involves making a space where there wasn't one initially. This *potential* space transpires from the meaning-making possibilities arising from a synergistic blending of (a) research philosophies and approaches to understanding, and (b) the ambiguities, uncertainty and unpredictability of practice. Qualitative research offers opportunities to understand more deeply the person-centred qualities of practice in all their complexity. Living practice provides numerous possibilities for the propagation of person-centred research questions and a dynamic context in which to research them.

We view the space that brings qualitative research into living practice as an emergent interplay of authentic person-centred research and living practice. In this space, researchers and practitioners engage, dialogue and learn with each other in a

*J. Higgs et al., (eds.), Creative Spaces for
Qualitative Researching: Living Research, 23–32*

mutual manner to produce new knowledge to transform practice. This is depicted in Figure 3.1.

Figure 3.1. Space for bringing research into living practice

Research questions addressing practice issues can arise from practitioners located within the practice context, or from researchers who are external to it. For example, in Scenario A Julie-Anne sought to explore issues related to executive coaching that arose within her work context, whereas as an outsider Anne brought her interest in collaboration into the context of rehabilitation teams.

Scenario A: Research questions in living practice
Julie-Anne – Research question **arising from within** the practice context:

> As a human resources practitioner working in a large company, I wondered what coaching really was, and what it could do. Yet after undertaking a coach development program and becoming a coach practitioner myself, I found I was still wondering. My research questions came from my curiosity and desire to understand this phenomenon more deeply.

Anne – Research question **introduced into** the practice context:

> My fascination with teams had been heightened by my experience in a particular health care team where I experienced an almost exhilarating sense of "so-this-is-collaboration"! I decided to explore the phenomenon of collaboration in the context of rehabilitation teams because teamwork has long been integral to this setting.

The research space has a *potential* that can be initiated and brought into being by appropriate research questions. For researchers exploring others' practice, creating the space for research can involve fostering interest among practitioners to participate in their research. For practitioners bringing research into their practice world, creating the space may require them to acquire and augment their research capabilities or to access the research skills of others.

Situated Space

The research space in living practice is a *situated* space influenced by the characteristics of the practice context. For example, organisational cultures that value research activity are likely to facilitate research, whereas contexts where research participation is viewed as "time away from real work" may be less supportive. Practitioners' perceptions of the value and usefulness of research can also be influenced by colleagues' stories about their research experiences.

Scenario B provides examples where characteristics of the practice context influenced the potential for undertaking research. As a health care practitioner, Sam found that her research was supported by members of her clinical team and the research community associated with her health care facility. She was able to access mentoring by qualitative researchers to understand practice more deeply. Stories shared about other practitioners' research encouraged her positive view of research. Yet such opportunities and support are not readily available to all practitioners, as in Jay's situation. The space created for researching the ambiguities and uncertainty of living practice often needs to be developed alongside or fitted around the structurally embedded focus on measurement that characterises many practice contexts. This can present challenges to researchers.

Scenario B: Opportunities and barriers for creating research spaces

Sam – Research space opportunities:

> It was opportunistic how I came to be researching this. Just as our team wanted to understand more about collaborating with teachers of children with brain injuries, the Research Development Program Scholarship applications were announced. I applied for it as a way of developing my, and my team's, skills within a supportive structure.

Jay – Research space barriers:

> In reality it is difficult to find a voice, a space or a time to research. The guilt associated with doing your own project means that it is usually done in your own time. The exception is around accreditation time when there are more opportunities and support available to explore issues. But the support is usually limited to issues related to measurable processes rather than complexities such as decision making.

A workplace commitment to measurement was evident in barriers encountered by Jay as she struggled to find the conceptual and practical research space in her organisation to explore the transition from clinician to manager. With no pathways or guidance for research she had to create her own research space, often outside work hours. If her research was to progress, her drive to understand living practice needed to be greater than the institutional barriers she encountered.

In health care organisations like Jay's, such contextual reliance on measurement can be attributed to current requirements for financial accountability and regulation, as well to the dominance of biomedicine and its reliance on positivist knowledge. Evidence of ongoing and un-critiqued support for the collection of quantifiable information is plentiful in the literature, with many studies seeking (with limited success) to measure complex human constructs such as innovation, leadership, inter-professional relationships, and communication.

Attitudes towards research are frequently influenced by leaders and managers who manifest the dominant cultural views within the organisation through the emphasis placed (or not placed) on research activities during practitioner goal-setting performance reviews and reward allocations. Beverly Axford (2005) argued that such organisational focus on assessment regimes emphasises performance evaluation in accordance with a predetermined set of skills and competencies, rather than embracing the complexities of living practice. This situation tends to encourage practitioners to "play the game" and do what is required, often at the expense of other activities such as creating spaces for research.

We propose that an unmediated focus on measurement can eclipse interest and inhibit the spaces for understanding the dynamic, unpredictable and uncertain nature of living practice. In such situations a predominant measurement focus may need to be acknowledged and addressed in order that spaces for qualitative and quantitative research can co-exist, or ideally contribute dialectically to understandings of living practice.

Collaborative Space

Researchers and participants *collaborate* within their co-created space. Their communication capabilities are important for engaging with the diversity of practitioners' contexts, experiences, actions and perspectives. In doing so, researchers also need to be aware of their own judgement and beliefs and be able to act reflectively about them (Árnason, 2000).

Reflecting Carl Rogers' (1961) influential work on the nature of human relationships, the researcher's ability to build a relationship with a participant is primarily important for conducting authentic and person-centred research into living practice. In valuing diversity the researcher can be viewed as being "open to the other", and it is only with this openness that a genuine human relationship is formed (Gadamer, 1975). Forming relationships and clarifying understandings can take time. For example, researchers took several months to negotiate a space in a remote Australian school where community members, organisations, students and teachers could explore and negotiate "the world of local cultural knowledge, protocols, relationships" (Yunkaporta & McGinty, 2009, p. 59).

Transformative Space

The space created by bringing research into living practice is a *transformative* space. Increased understandings of the qualities of practice generated through trustworthy, rigorous and credible research can transform people, infrastructure, culture and practices (Higgs & Titchen, 2007). For example, in the collaborative research space described above, the interface between Western school curriculum knowledge and Indigenous knowledge was explored and teaching practices were changed (Yunkaporta & McGinty, 2009, p. 59). Although this *transformative* space for bringing research into living practice relates easily to critical research where change is an integral outcome, interpretive research can also transform practice, as Sam describes in Scenario C.

Scenario C: Transforming one's living practice

Sam

> Now I am involved in researching practice, I find that in clinical contexts I am able to consider more the clients' perspectives, world view and life experiences, and how these contribute to their actions.

In the collaborative research space, reflection can often be *profound*, as it is typically shared aloud by the practitioner in the presence and with the full attention of the researcher (based on Knights, 1985). Such reflection can lead to unexpected outcomes (based on Boud, Keogh, & Walker, 1985). Reflective discoveries were expressed as delight by one practitioner in Julie-Anne's research as described in Scenario D.

Scenario D: Reflections and discoveries

Julie-Anne

> I was surprised during interviews with coach practitioners how frequently they remarked that participating in my research had enabled them to think deeply and reflect on their coaching practice. I guess I had assumed they would be systematically doing this anyway, so the interview process would not have involved anything different. One coach shared her enjoyment arising from her reflective discoveries in the research process: "Yes, interesting, this is really good, and I'm really enjoying this. It's like oooh, oooh, yes, oooh".

CREATING SPACES THROUGH CURIOSITY, CARE AND CREATIVITY

Curiosity as the Impetus for Creating Space for Research

Acknowledging Zora Neale Hurston's (1996, p. 143) oft quoted claim that "research is formalized curiosity" and Mihaly Csikszentmihalyi's (1997, p. 87) proposal that "without a burning curiosity, a lively interest, we are unlikely to persevere long to make to a significant new contribution", we highlight the role of curiosity as an impetus for creating space for qualitative research. Curiosity and its related notion of wonder are well-recognised motivating factors for qualitative research. For example, in his Phenomenology Online website, Max van Manen (1999) proposed that "when we are struck with wonder our minds are suddenly cleared of the clutter of everyday concerns that otherwise constantly occupy us … from this moment of wonder, a question may emerge that addresses us and that is addressed by us". Sam describes in Scenario E how her curiosity led over time to the emergence of a series of research questions focused on collaboration between teachers and rehabilitation coordinators. In contrast to Sam's slowly emerging idea for research, Jay's impetus for exploration of practice was a sudden insight.

Scenario E: Impetus for research questions

Sam

> For a while now I've noticed rehabilitation coordinators often seem to have problems working effectively with teachers to help children with traumatic brain injury learn, get along with their peers and successfully engage with others at school. We always seem to be chasing teachers to communicate and liaise about a child. I'm not sure why this is. Are schools such busy places that there really isn't time? Is what we are trying to offer not seen by teachers as useful? Are we unrealistic in expecting teachers to collaborate; if so, why?

Jay

> My spark, my light bulb moment triggering my research question came at a meeting where bureaucrats were talking about our work in terms of KPI's [key performance indicators] and I realised that their talk was different to that of clinicians at the coal face of practice who interact with people.

Creativity as a Shaper of Space for Research

Creativity, in conjunction with the impetus of curiosity, is a key shaper of the space for researching living practice. As it is a potential space, that can be moulded and perhaps nudged into existence, researchers can craft it to suit the context, question and participants. No research space is the same. Each has its individual challenges and opportunities, and requires creativity fuelled by curiosity to ensure a meaningful fit between research and living practice.

Charles Wright Mills (1959, p. 122) referred to "playfulness of mind" and "a truly fierce drive to make sense of the world" as part of his famous concept of "sociological imagination". Anthony Giddens (1993, p.18) proposed that "the sociological imagination necessitates, above all, being able to think ourselves away from the familiar routines of our daily lives in order to look at them anew". At times help may be accessed to look at issues anew, as described in Scenario G.

We propose that working with others and ensuring that the environment supports innovation are important factors for shaping the space for research into living practice. For example, Julie-Anne and Anne have found their PhD research community of practice invaluable in encouraging creative ways of thinking, such as exploring emerging research insights through group activities including performance and painting. The responsibility for the creation of space for research to occur does not lie with any one person, but rather requires a collaborative effort. According to Mihaly Csikszentmihalyi (1997, p.1), creativity "arises from the synergy of many sources and not only from the mind of a single person. It is easier to enhance creativity by changing conditions in the environment than by trying to make people think more creatively".

Scenario F: Accessing help for looking at things anew

Sam – Help **from within** the research space:

> I found I was able think more deeply and widely about my topic when I was liberated from the need for "getting the structure right". Being part of the research development program has really given me the means to develop a feasible project plan. Creative thinking doesn't necessarily happen early on, because a beginning researcher might be paying attention to the procedural aspects of research; that is, the "rules".

Jay – Help **from outside** the research space

> There is not a lot of innovative stuff happening in my workplace. There is limited time for thinking. Discussions with people outside work fostered enthusiasm and insights for my research.

Care as the Cultivator of Space for Research

The person-centred core of professional practice can be applied also to the research of living practice. Just as practitioners need to care about people as individuals with worth and dignity, so do researchers exploring living practice need to care about the complexities of practice and people involved. Through person-centredness, the space created for research of living practice can be cultivated to be responsive to people's individual perspectives, capabilities, values and contexts. For example, to co-research with their students, teachers in the Aboriginal action research project described by Yunkaporta and McGinty (2009) needed to understand their school's community context (such as the importance of communal knowledge) and address their own entrenched beliefs (such as what constitutes knowledge and who owns it). Through that research the school developed a learning environment in which story-telling and sharing became the cornerstone of successful lessons. Care about people can be motivating for researchers and can help ensure that participants' voices are heard. Sam explained this as follows: "The participants' interest in the research and eagerness to share their stories was motivating. And now that I'm trying to uncover the essence of their experiences, I feel a duty and responsibility to express and encapsulate what they had to say".

Care *about* the researcher and research topic by others may also be integral to cultivating research spaces. As described in Scenario H, Sam appreciated being part of a research development program. Conversely, without care for the researcher (and others involved in the research), the research will not flourish and might even disappear, as explained by Jay in Scenario G.

Scenario G: Caring for the researcher

Sam

> It would have been easy for my project to lose momentum without my research project mentors' constant encouragement and availability. I always feel that my contacts are welcomed and they always get back to me really quickly and positively – even if my processes or thinking are completely on the wrong track.

Jay

> Shared excitement about the research idea and findings legitimises what you do and encourages you further. You want a level of scrutiny to challenge your thinking, rather than passive agreement type of support, but unless there is enthusiasm from "outside" accompanying the scrutiny it is easy to let other things at work take up space. For example, a person in a high position in the organisation was dismissive of my findings. I felt she had her head in the sand and did not want to consider the implications. Where I work it seems that research is more supported if it doesn't cause waves. At the moment I now cannot legitimately continue in work time. If I were to continue I would need mentors, funding and more head space.

SUSTAINING RESEARCH SPACES THROUGH REFLEXIVITY AND RESPONSIVENESS

Through curiosity, creativity and care, the space for bringing research into living practice needs to be sustained by reflexivity and responsiveness to maintain its relevance and meaningfulness. Through reflexivity, people learn from their experiences and monitor their actions in relation to the needs, capabilities and situations of others. They become aware of *self* in relation to other, and of how their actions can influence other people. Being situationally responsive enables people to deal with dynamic contexts and people's different interactive needs, styles and preferences. We propose that just as reflexivity and situational responsiveness are important to living practice, they are similarly important for researchers as they develop their research skills and deal with the changes, unpredictability and uncertainties inherent in these contexts. Being reflexive is also an important quality for transforming practice through research.

Sustaining space for research into living practice can be seen in terms of pragmatic issues. Sustaining the space often requires reflection on research skills. Beginning researchers, particularly those who see themselves primarily as practitioners, might need to participate in a formal research training program. Sam alludes to involvement in such a program in Scenario H. Matters of time and resources must also be considered by researchers in creating space for research to occur. Moreover, when practitioners are integrating a research component into their practice they may need to prioritise research time, as Sam's Scenario H also shows.

Scenario H: Finding time to research

Sam

I have had to restructure a bit of my time outside the development program hours to fit in the reading and thinking. And I still don't think I've found enough! The university department proved to be a really good environment for reading/thinking/writing. Conversely, in my work office there is too much general busy-ness. At the same time, home doesn't work either; there is rarely "alone time". So I have not found a space yet, but I have not given up!

CONCLUSION

In this chapter we explored how multifaceted research spaces can be created and sustained by researchers through qualities of *curiosity, care,* and *creativity,* intertwined with their capabilities of personal *reflexivity* and *responsiveness* to context. In this way, the researcher is an *inquiring self* (Higgs, 2010), a person who is stimulated and motivated to question and explore areas of practice, and also to critically reflect and be challenged both as a person and as a researcher. In the often dehumanised context of organisations, the researcher co-creates a space for research with practitioners by using person-centred qualities of openness, trust, and dialogue to create close connections between them. In these relationships, researchers and practitioners work together to create and sustain spaces in which different insights, perspectives, capabilities and motivations can be synergistically merged. For researchers, the creation of research spaces provides the privilege of deep engagement with the delicious complexities of living practice.

REFERENCES

Árnason, V. (2000). Gadamerian dialogue in the patient-professional interaction. *Medicine, Health Care and Philosophy, 3*(1), 17–23.

Axford, B. (2005). Entering professional practice in the new world order: A study of undergraduate students and their induction to professional work. *The Australian Educational Researcher, 32*(2), 87–104.

Boud, D., Keogh, R., & Walker, D. (Eds.) (1985). *Reflection: Turning experience into learning.* London: Kogan Page.

Csikszentmihalyi, M. (1997). *Flow: The psychology of optimal experience.* New York: Harper Perennial.

Gadamer, H.-G. (1975). *Truth and method* (J. Weinsheimer & D. G. Marshall, Trans., 2nd rev. ed.). London: Continuum.

Giddens, A. (1993). *Sociology* (2nd ed.). Cambridge: Polity Press.

Higgs, J. (2010). Researching practice: Entering the practice discourse. In J. Higgs, N. Cherry, R. Macklin & R. Ajjawi (Eds.), *Researching practice: A discourse on qualitative methodologies* (pp. 1–8). Rotterdam: Sense.

Higgs, J., & Titchen, A. (2007). Becoming critical and creative in qualitative research. In J. Higgs, A. Titchen, D. Horsfall & H. Armstrong (Eds.), *Being critical and creative in qualitative research* (pp. 1–10). Sydney: Hampden Press.

Hurston, Z.N. (1996). *Dust tracks on a road*. New York: HarperCollins (Original work published 1942).

Knights, S. (1985). Reflection and learning: The importance of a listener. In D. Boud, R. Keogh & D. Walker (Eds.), *Reflection: Turning experience into learning* (pp. 85–90). London: Kogan Page.

Mills, C.W. (1959). *Sociological imagination*. New York: Oxford University.

Rogers, C.R. (1961). *On becoming a person: A therapist's view of psychotherapy*. New York: Houghton Mifflin.

van Manen, M. (1999). *Phenomenology online: Phenomenology of practice*. Available: http://www.phenomenologyonline.com, accessed 26 May 2011.

Yunkaporta, T., & McGinty, S. (2009). Reclaiming Aboriginal knowledge at the cultural interface. *The Australian Educational Researcher, 36*(2), 55–72.

Anne Croker PhD Candidate
School of Community Health
Charles Sturt University, Australia

Julie-Anne Tooth PhD Candidate
The Education For Practice Institute
Charles Sturt University, Australia

SECTION 2: DOING CREATIVE RESEARCH

ANGIE TITCHEN AND DEBBIE HORSFALL

4. CREATIVE RESEARCH LANDSCAPES
AND GARDENS

Reviewing Options and Opportunities

What is creative research? Isn't all research creative? Well, yes it is, in the sense that all research is attempting to create new knowledge and understanding, but no, in that it may follow formulaic rather than creative research methodologies and methods. When we research with people and about people interacting in and with their social and life worlds, and when we are also concerned with bringing about change and transformation of self, others, groups, cultures, systems, practices and organisations simultaneously with knowledge creation, then formulaic approaches are unlikely to be sufficient. This is because such approaches may not be able to cope or work with the contextual and human complexities of such work. Working with complexity requires creativity.

Imagine you are in a hot air balloon, floating over a landscape of your choosing. What is the bedrock of your landscape? What colour and texture is the earth? What kind of climate and weather conditions are you experiencing? What is the quality of the light? What kind of vegetation grows in these conditions? What evidence is there of people working creatively with the terrain and conditions? Now your balloon floats on to a completely different landscape and conditions. Are the vegetation and the ways people are working with the land also very different? It is likely that they are. So it is with creative research landscapes and gardens.

The bedrock for creative research that works with complexity is the underpinning philosophical and theoretical assumptions and principles that we choose. That choice is guided not only by the impulse or purpose of the research that drives us but also by our research questions and the research product that we want to create (see Chapter 18 by Titchen & Horsfall). Thus choices must be made consciously, critically and creatively. We have found that the more we are open to different research bedrocks (i.e., world views or paradigms) and to combining assumptions from them carefully, the greater our options and opportunities for creative research become. In our metaphor, research-gardeners work with the

J. Higgs et al.,(eds.), Creative Spaces for
Qualitative Researching: Living Research, 35–44

climatic conditions (i.e., the historical, social, cultural and political contexts). They create a unique garden structure and design (i.e., research methodology, culture and conditions within which people and the research will flourish). They do this by working with the soil (created by the bedrock and climatic conditions), the type of vegetation that thrives in that soil, and the people in touch with the land. In other words, the creative researcher develops a methodology that is congruent with the philosophical and theoretical principles and assumptions, and is responsive to the people with whom, and the contexts in which, the research is carried out. Here we use this metaphor to examine how this can be facilitated and how the options and opportunities of creative research can be broadened by landscape gardeners creating research cultures in research organisations and academic and practice communities. The chapter is necessarily only a starting point and an overview of the journey to creative research. By offering you examples of our own doing and supporting creative research we hope to give you a beginning sense of possibility.

OPTIONS AND OPPORTUNITIES: OPENNESS TO DIFFERENT LANDSCAPES

In qualitative research, there are two macro-landscapes, the interpretive and the critical research paradigms, with many micro-landscapes within each. The interpretive paradigm is concerned with seeking new understanding of practice and innovation, and the critical is about democratising, enabling empowerment, emancipation, and power with rather than power over. The intention of the following discussion is to show you how important it is for creative researchers to be able to consciously choose an appropriate research paradigm or research landscape in which to conduct their studies. This choice is highly significant because the bedrock or philosophical stance of the study will shape everything the researchers do and are: the roles they adopt, what they do, how they relate to participants, how they gather, analyse and interpret data and how they share findings. The types of bedrock relevant to this chapter are the philosophical stances of *idealism, hermeneutics* and *realism*. Are you beginning to see the connection with your imaginary hot air balloon ride and the different landscapes formed by distinct types of bedrock?

The interpretive research paradigm can be underpinned by *idealism, hermeneutics* or a combination of these stances. In *idealism*, there is emphasis on the ideas of actors as the determinants of social reality, so the researcher creates a research methodology around enabling participants to articulate and share their conscious ideas. In contrast, *hermeneutics* emphasises pre-reflective knowing, doing, being and becoming, so it is concerned with embodied, aesthetic, artistic or ancient traditional ways of knowing. A creative inquiry could be located in this stance and the researcher might, for example, attempt to access the unconscious (because they are taken-for-granted) ideas of participants and/or the pre-reflective understanding that is embedded in a work of art/creative expression/story produced by participants or others. Thus, emotional, spiritual, aesthetic knowing and creative imagination are primary points of access to things that show up as mattering or having significance. Finally, the critical paradigm is often in a "yes, and" relationship to these philosophical stances within the interpretive paradigm, the "and" being the philosophical stance of *realism*. So in addition, or sometimes as an alternative, critical research assumes that social structures and cultures shape practice in relation to broader society, which means that structures and cultures are also determinants of reality. The researcher is concerned with exposing the historical, social, cultural and political contexts of structures and cultures that get in the way of people achieving their full potential and human rights, for example.

The central concerns and associated concepts of interest are different with each type of philosophical bedrock. For instance, the central concern of *idealism* is epistemological (concern with knowledge, how it is created and used), whereas in *hermeneutics* it is ontological (concern with being and becoming). So in *idealism*, a concept of interest is rational action, as opposed to the concepts, for example, of being with, wisdom, and professional artistry in *hermeneutics*. Within *realism*, either or both of these concerns may be central, but in addition there is an intention to change the situation being studied and to generate knowledge about that change. The researcher here is concerned with the surfacing of unexamined assumptions and contradictions and overcoming inner and outer challenges to achieving desired change. So within realism, researching, learning about and developing practice are facilitated simultaneously by researchers. Concepts of interest are therefore enlightenment, empowerment, emancipation, communicative action and praxis (mindful doing with a moral intent).

There are also epistemological differences in terms of the kind of knowledge created in the research (i.e., the nature of the research product). For example, in the interpretive paradigm, it is practical knowledge that is revealed. Practical knowledge can be experiential, ethical/moral, personal, intuitive, aesthetic or spiritual. If researchers wish to create practical knowledge that has mental representation, then they are likely to work in the idealist stance, but if they are interested in such knowledge that is embodied (known by the body), then they are likely to choose *hermeneutics*. Again in a "yes, and" relationship, the critical paradigm is also concerned with creating emancipatory or transformative knowledge.

As you begin to read about and discuss these broad (macro-) research landscapes (paradigms) (see Titchen & Higgs, 2007, for more in-depth comparisons), you will discover that there are a huge number of micro-landscapes within each one, such as phenomenological sociology, creative inquiry and feminist research. These micro-landscapes may have been formulated by staying firmly at the core of a particular philosophical position (e.g., phenomenological sociology, which is rigorously located in *idealism*) or they may have been created by a careful laying out and testing of assumptions from different macro-landscapes, showing how these assumptions are congruent and/or work together.

So now we get at the nub. These very fundamental philosophical differences lead to methodological differences. For example, if the determinant of reality is the ideas of actors or their mental representations about the thing being studied, as in *idealism*, then the researcher will attempt to seek understanding through detached contemplation, adopting an uninvolved, detached observer/researcher role, and will be concerned with the rational thinking of the participants and transferability of findings through abstraction/theorisation and/or rich description. But if the determinant of reality is embedded in the body and not the mind, as in *hermeneutics*, then researchers see pragmatic/involved activity as a way of knowing/being and will need to access that knowing through being involved, connected observer/researchers. Rather than rational thinking, these researchers are concerned with the unconscious, unknowing and intuitive judgements of participants. In contrast to aspiring for transferability of findings through abstraction, these researchers are concerned with the particular and with pointing out relevance. They invite readers to seek the particular in their own practice/context. Or, as in creative inquiry in which aesthetics, creative expression and imagination are predominant, the researcher poses a personal test of truthfulness: "Will the study be useful to others and me?" In the critical research paradigm, you will remember the additional bedrock of *realism* within which the determinant of reality is structures and cultures. Here researchers are not only concerned with exposing the limitations that structures and cultures place on people's freedom, self-determination and reaching their full potential, they are also aiming to enable participants to free themselves from these limitations. Therefore, in terms of methodology, researchers in this paradigm are involved, connected and interested in whether their own or others' actions to transform structures, cultures or practices have been achieved. And when they come to the point of demonstrating transferability or usefulness of findings or pointing out the particular (as in the interpretive paradigm), critical researchers may also seek to generate and test potentially transferable principles for action.

And here is the impact of the nub of this argument. The methodological differences in these research landscapes in turn lead to different opportunities for research-gardeners to realise the strategies of observing, questioning, interpreting, critiquing and reporting in very different ways and for different purposes and intents. For example, in studies based in *idealism*, researchers want to access what is in people's minds and create faithful theorised representations of people's ideas and their understandings of, and the meanings they attach to, these ideas. Therefore, they are unlikely to choose observation as a key data gathering method because it cannot reliably access participants' subjective meanings. Rather they would choose interviews to access participants' consciousness and to facilitate their reflection on participants' ways of construing their social contexts, situations, logic, intentions, and judgments. By asking questions, researchers prise open the taken-for-granted by helping participants to doubt it. On the other hand, observation is an essential method in studies based on *hermeneutics.* This is because researchers can observe unreflective activity, embodied wisdom and ways of being in the world physically, emotionally, intuitively, spiritually and imaginatively. In terms of questioning in this tradition, researchers help participants to tell stories about things that matter and have value for them in everyday language rather than reflecting-on-action or theorising about the thing being studied. The researcher may also be able to question those things that participants do not have words for but can express creatively through creative arts media such as painting, picture cards, poetry, body gestures or photography (see Chapter 18 by Titchen & Horsfall). Similarly, researchers in these different landscapes will approach interpretation and critique in very different ways, as shown in the two examples below.

Thus in terms of options and opportunities for creative research, people need to be very clear about the implications of existing philosophical options that they might decide to accept for creating their unique research strategies, roles and relationships, or the implications of combining assumptions from different philosophical stances. Creating new combinations of philosophical assumptions is often necessary due to the contextual and human complexity mentioned earlier. To show you how creative researchers do this, we offer you two examples. The first is Janice Ollerton's (2011) emancipatory action research (located in the critical research paradigm) in which she helped a group of young people labelled as having mild-to-moderate learning difficulties to become her co-researchers (see also Ollerton & Kelshaw, Chapter 26). Her intent was to provide an opportunity for these people to identify for themselves barriers to their self-determination and then to help them understand the barriers so that they could work together to dismantle them. Janice appeared to accept the assumptions of *realism* because she expected that the barriers that disable people labelled with learning difficulties would be caused by the structures and cultures of ableist society. From her experience of working with such people she knew she had to create a research methodology and methods that would be accessible to her co-researchers. Therefore, a methodology based on *idealist* assumptions of a systematic study of the ideas or mental content of the young people's inner worlds would be less likely to succeed with people with "othered" ways of knowing than a methodology based on a blend of *hermeneutic* and *realist* assumptions. Such a blend enabled her co-researchers, who had no or very limited literacy skills, to access their pre-reflective understanding, that is, the understanding embedded in their bodies and everyday interactions with the structures and cultures of ableist society.

Janice chose Photo-Voice as a research method, to enable her co-researchers to gather factual and metaphorical data about the barriers they met in their everyday lives, such as poor signage on public transport, restricted access to their own money, food preparation and, in one case, sexual abuse. The co-researchers were able to analyse their data and create new understandings about disabling structures and cultures because they were working with images rather than text. Through the critical paradigm processes of consciousness-raising and problematisation, Janice helped them learn about their human rights to self-determination, and through dialogic (communicative) spaces they were able to see the contradictions of an ableist society claiming to enable people with learning difficulties to be in control of their own lives, while at the same time disabling them. This emancipatory use of communicative spaces is also located in the critical paradigm, and it enabled the co-researchers to achieve some successful outcomes (see Chapter 26). Finally, the presentation of the research sang up the voices of the co-researchers. Throughout the report, their dialogues and photos as text were presented as they analysed their data (photos), interpreted them and used them to plan their actions. Photographs, a photographic journal and PowerPoint presentations played a prominent role in the telling of the research. Janice's success in creating the conditions that enabled the co-researchers to emancipate themselves and flourish is evident from the group being now entirely self-directed and self-funded.

The second example shows how Brendan McCormack and Angie developed a new option and opportunities for creative research. We (Brendan and Angie) were involved in a co-operative inquiry with a group of nursing practice developers and researchers from the U.K., the Netherlands and Australia. The inquiry aim was the creation of an international theory for practice development which at that time was located in the critical paradigm (with idealist and realist assumptions). With others, Brendan and I had previously experimented in our practice development research with ideas and theories from creative arts therapy, arts facilitation in health care and diverse spiritual traditions. We were concerned with creativity and the use of the body, creative imagination and expression to promote human flourishing. In particular, Brendan and I were beginning to feel that the emancipatory/critical world view did not provide us with sufficient theoretical and methodological support for our emerging transformational practice development research, so we were keen to address this inadequacy within the co-operative inquiry. This led to our development of the assumptions in Box 4.1.

Philosophical assumptions

- There is a creative connection and blending of assumptions, if assumptions across different development and research paradigms are combined within a project
- The use of creative expression to foster synergy between cognitive and artistic critique approaches
- Transformational development and research is person centred
- The three philosophical assumptions above are blended with spiritual intelligence (thought to be closely connected with creativity and working at the boundaries of the known).

Theoretical assumptions

- Conscious to unconscious blending of assumptions
- Connecting world views
- Human flourishing is an intentional means as well as the ultimate end
- Human becoming.

Box 4.1. Assumptions underpinning critical creativity (McCormack & Titchen, 2006)

Thus there was a blending of assumptions about cognitive approaches (i.e., idealist assumptions about consciousness, ideas, rational thinking); artistic approaches (i.e., hermeneutic assumptions of pre-reflective, embodied knowing and interpretation); critique (realist assumptions around creating new knowledge through contestation and debate); and spiritual traditions (searching for meaning and working at the edge of the known (see Titchen & Niessen, Chapter 15). Such blending created a new micro-landscape (paradigm) called critical creativity. Guided by these blended assumptions, Angie and Brendan created theoretical (McCormack & Titchen, 2006) and methodological (Titchen & McCormack, 2010) frameworks for human flourishing within the critical creativity landscape, using creative inquiry methods that enabled the blending of conscious ideas and creative imagination and expression. For example, they used creative arts media, walking and being in nature and framing reflection and reflexivity in the world around, whether physical, metaphorical or metaphysical; dancing – physically, metaphorically and metaphysically; cognitive critique and scholarly inquiry, reiterative and creative writing; and interplaying all the above with critical dialogue to engage in methodological knowledge creation through cognitive and artistic critique.

Through this work, Angie and Brendan were able to articulate clearly for the first time the conditions and principles for action that enabled human flourishing for the practitioner-researchers with whom they work, and for themselves as transformational research facilitators. They help practitioner-researchers to transform themselves (if they so wish) and/or their practices, teams, cultures, systems and organisations, while creating new understanding about how to bring about this transformation. The conditions, pointed out in the examples below, are: *stillness in a landscape:* being still, open and empty in the research place and space; *becoming the rock:* embodying the philosophical stance; *nurturing, flowing, connecting:* the ontology of the transformational, creative researcher.

DEVELOPING RESEARCHERS AND CULTURES FOR CREATIVE RESEARCH

Extending options and opportunities for creative research requires us to pay attention to the conditions that will enable research-gardeners to develop new skills and new ways of knowing and being. We have already established that the bedrock of creative research is determined by the philosophical choices made. This choice has to be supported by paying attention to creating research cultures, not only in funding bodies, universities, practice organisations and communities, but also in the research-gardens themselves (see Figure 4.1) that are shaped and influenced by the nourishing minerals and underground streams in the bedrock, the type and quality of the soil, quality of the light, the climate and weather conditions, and the research-gardener tending the people, land and vegetation.

Figure 4.1. A garden in the Cotswolds, England, supported by yellow limestone bedrock and a temperate climate (left) and a garden in the NSW Tablelands Australia, supported by pink granite bedrock and a temperate but much drier climate (right)

Developing researchers and cultures for creative research means that staff in the above organisations and research-gardeners must have a clear vision and common purpose in terms of the values that underpin their ways of working and providing support for creative research education and conduct. For creative research genuinely to flourish, transformational research cultures and conditions conducive to creativity must be fostered. Openness to all ways of knowing, doing, being and becoming is essential, as we show next.

Supporting Creative Research

If an organisation/community/researcher wishes to extend support of creative research, as with any new endeavour, it is wise to create a vision of what the people in the organisation, community or research project aspire towards. This is essential if the notion of creative research is to be owned by all those involved in or influenced by it (i.e., all stakeholders). Vision statements and the strategies that are created from them are based on the values and beliefs of those involved. Therefore landscape and research gardeners enable others to make their values explicit. Values that are often deeply embedded and embodied can be revealed by using creative imagination and expression (see Chapter 18 by Titchen & Horsfall).

A university school that developed a transformational, creative research culture is the Knowledge Centre for Evidence-Based Practice in the School of Nursing at Fontys University of Applied Sciences in the Netherlands. As a Clinical Chair of the newly established Centre, Angie helped the team to develop a vision, infrastructure and ways of working that embodied the values of creative research. Through her body and ways of being she consciously modelled (Becoming the rock) for the team and research students the epistemology and ontology (Nurturing, flowing, connecting) of working in a critical creativity landscape. For example, she showed how to set up an infrastructure that involved all stakeholders through Image Theatre, and how to design and facilitate regular team meetings, team-building and strategic "away days" that bring both creative expression and imagination into play, as well as critique. The team particularly like re-connecting and evaluating their monthly meetings by choosing picture cards in silence (Stillness in a landscape) and then sharing with each other the meanings of the metaphors and symbols (Artistic and cognitive critique). Simple and quick to use, images open up new perspectives and help them to communicate with each other on a deeper level, to express the unsayable. Strategic away days and meetings with stakeholders, designed by the team, always use creative methods of some kind, such as painting, collage work, drama, body sculpture, games and reflective walks in nature. Working in this way spills over into research supervision. For instance, we would agree at the start of a reflective walk to walk in silence and notice what we noticed. When the student is ready, discussion begins often by framing thoughts and ideas in the landscape and using body senses to frame reflection and capture and retain new insights, understandings and meanings (Titchen & Ajjawi, 2010). Back in the office, new insights are expressed through painting, poetry or clay-modelling. Supervising in such ways has resulted in all the PhD students designing creative research studies (see e.g. Chapters 22 and 27, by van Lieshout & Cardiff and Boomer & Frost respectively). Over time, other academic staff in the school and practitioner-researchers the Centre supports in local health or social care settings also came to use such methods (e.g., Chapter 15 by Titchen & Niessen).

In 2010 Debbie led a research team who sought to harvest in-depth qualitative data about contributions to social capital, social networks and communities of people who are aged, and their carers. Moving from a deficit model, our underlying assumption was that caring can contribute to the development of social networks, bestowing a common and individual benefit. This was a new approach. Indeed, in the literature, all forms of eldercare are usually associated with a reduced ability to engage in the community, for the older people and often also for their carers. Adding to this challenge, community networks and relations are, by definition, nebulous and often invisible phenomena. Ageing is often an emotionally charged experience of complex and competing emotions, as is supporting someone as they age. Reconceptualising ageing and caring for an aged person as processes that potentially increase social networks and contribute to social capital is an unspoken discourse, and talking about this phenomenon was not necessarily going to be easy for participants.

Our task, then, was complex. We needed to persuade a fairly traditional government department firstly that moving from a deficit approach would be useful and secondly that talking with frail aged people and their carers was central to the research design. With few positive examples to draw upon we were laying down the path in a new landscape. We had to design methods which enabled frail older people and their carers to talk to us about social networks and relationships, not about problems or wished-for services. As such the methods we chose were photo elicitation, where the aged people and their carers were given cameras and asked to take photos of significant acts of caring. These photos then served as entry, or trigger points for focus groups/interviews. No-one in the research team had used these methods in research before, and there was some resistance and scepticism about the benefits and do-ability of such an approach. Debbie had to stand with her feet firmly planted in the bedrock of this approach (Becoming the rock, maybe); in this case her belief that people have something to say and that what they have to say is the starting point for our research. If they find it difficult to speak – for whatever reasons – then our job as inclusive researchers is to get creative about finding ways to enable them to speak. This stance had to be revisited and nurtured throughout the project. Standing firm was useful in enabling the team to walk into the unknown (Nurturing, flowing, connecting). In retrospect, Stillness in a landscape was not incorporated into team meetings and this would have been useful. For example, using images as part of the team process would have further enabled acceptance of this way of working. In the stillness and deep reflection involved in writing this example, Debbie now sees that she had not quite become the rock – she was standing on it.

However, this choice of methods was the main reason we received funding. The ideas had grabbed the funding bodies' imaginations, like a breath of fresh air. They were looking forward to a report with photographs in it and they could see how it could be inclusive of people not usually included in the research they commissioned. We ended up having critical conversations with 158 people in under 6 months, and we produced a report and photographic exhibition where participants' voices and pictures were centred.

LET'S REST AWHILE

Opportunities for creative research will grow if we pay attention to creating the conditions for such research to flourish. Transformational research cultures in practice settings, academia, funding bodies, government departments and publishing houses play a significant part here, in terms of promoting an equal valuing of different ways of knowing and different modes of inquiry, and an acknowledgement that these differences can be complementary. Within such cultures, the need for educational support and critical-creative review will be met by providing a variety of facilitation structures and strategies. If there is a lack of experience in using creative imagination and expression in an organisation, there will be opportunities to learn from and work with people experienced in the use of creative arts (see e.g. Coats, 2001), such as artists-in-residence in care and educational organisations. The motto of such a culture might be *Trust the process*!

REFERENCES

Coats, E. (2001). Weaving the body, the creative unconscious, imagination and the arts into practice development. In J. Higgs & A. Titchen (Eds.), *Professional practice in health, education and the creative arts* (pp. 251–263). Oxford: Blackwell Science.

McCormack, B., & Titchen A. (2006). Critical creativity: Melding, exploding, blending. *Educational Action Research: An International Journal, 14*(2), 239–266.

Ollerton, J.M. (2010). Rights, camera, action! A collaborative exploration of social barriers to self-determination with people labelled with learning difficulties. Unpublished PhD thesis, University of Western Sydney.

Titchen, A., & Ajjawi, R. (2010). Writing contemporary ontological and epistemological questions about practice. In J. Higgs, N. Cherry, R. Macklin & R. Ajjawi (Eds.), *Researching practice: A discourse on qualitative methodologies* (pp. 45–55). Rotterdam: Sense.

Titchen, A., & Higgs, J. (2007). Exploring interpretive and critical philosophies. In J. Higgs, A. Titchen, D. Horsfall & H.B. Armstrong (Eds.), *Being critical and creative in qualitative research* (pp. 56–68). Sydney: Hampden Press.

Titchen, A., & McCormack, B. (2010). Dancing with stones: Critical creativity as methodology for human flourishing. *Educational Action Research: An International Journal, 18*(4), 531–554.

Angie Titchen D.Phil, MSc, MCSP
Adjunct Professor
Charles Sturt University, Australia

Debbie Horsfall PhD, MA, B.Ed
Peace and Development Studies, School of Social Sciences
University of Western Sydney, Australia

DEBBIE HORSFALL AND JOY HIGGS

5. BOUNDARY RIDING AND SHAPING RESEARCH SPACES

I remember many years ago talking with Richard Winter in a coffee shop in Oxford. He has used action research for years. I asked him if he ever got fed up with the struggle to justify the type of research methodology he uses. He said no. He felt that if he didn't have to continuously justify, then it would mean that the methodology had become mainstream and was no longer pushing the boundaries of accepted practice or challenging the status quo.

The metaphor of boundary riding captures several essential elements of the professional artistry of expert qualitative researchers: traversing research territories, crossing discipline and personal/professional boundaries, having an ability to imagine transformation in personal and social practices, being curious about the unfamiliar, and being open to exploring new territories and learning along the way. We also find it a liberating metaphor that enables researchers actively to choose which research territories or spaces they will inhabit. This is important. Where researchers actively locate themselves shapes their research practices and influences decisions about how best to conduct research that is imbued with moral agency and concerned with transformative social practices.

When we talk about boundaries in this chapter, we mean rules, conventions or taken-for-granted assumptions about the way "research is done", because historically they have served the purposes of the people conducting the research. In our experience, staying within established boundaries, which are often quite heavily guarded, can seem safer than riding or crossing them. There are many examples in research of staying within the boundaries, re-producing the same methodologies and methods. Sometimes this is the most useful sort of researching to be doing. There are times, however, when it is more useful and creative to cross, blur and even ignore the way things have been done before, especially when concerned with a research agenda that seeks change at personal, organisational or societal levels.

What We Mean by Boundaries

In the writing of this chapter five core meanings of *boundary* became evident to us. First, boundaries are not necessarily fixed and rigid. Writing a bibliography is a good example of how academic boundaries can change: until fairly recently all author entries in bibliographies consisted of family name and initials only; now it

J. Higgs et al.,(eds.) ,Creative Spaces for
Qualitative Researching: Living Research, 45–54
© *2011 Sense Publishers. All rights reserved.*

is often acceptable to also write given names. Likewise, it *always* used to be considered transgressive to use "I", to write up research in anything than a disembodied voice. This is no longer always the case (see e.g. the *Journal of International Qualitative Review* and *Reflective Practice*) although that boundary is still policed quite heavily especially in universities! Second, boundary sites can be fertile places that promise different sorts of relationships. In the natural world, in the places and spaces where boundaries meet there is abundance, diversity, creativity and difference. It is our experience that this can also be true in the qualitative research world. Third, boundaries can serve to illuminate the different characteristics of two (or more) peoples or approaches without forming a harsh barrier between them. Fourth, boundaries can also be divisive, destructive and isolating, sometimes leading to a *them and us* perception of the world. Finally, while the idea of reflexive, transdisciplinary research using multiple research methods may seem familiar to many experienced qualitative researchers, our experience tells us that many people still struggle, in multiple ways, with riding research boundaries.

We would like to snatch this debate out of the abstract realm of *this is how it should be* to the creative and imaginative realm of *this is how it can be*. Indeed, the idea presented in this book of qualitative research as transformative and illuminative demands the traversing of boundaries in our research practices. Our intention here is not to describe the many boundaries encountered in the research journey; boundaries are shifting, nebulous and encountered differently by different people. Rather, our aim is to make visible some of the boundaries qualitative researchers might expect to encounter, by embedding in this discussion some of our own practices and experiences as boundary riders. Although not all our experiences have been easy, we have found that riding and, often, crossing boundaries are both possible and rewarding, and have enabled us and the people we have worked with to be creative and active in designing and inhabiting our research spaces. This creativity is possible through the freedom that comes with embracing the depth and breadth of research opportunities provided by abandoning the traditional constraints of experimental research and the legacy this gave (and can still give) to qualitative research. We support the hope that qualitative researchers can balance the rigour of sound research with creative exploration to seek out the many opportunities that qualitative research provides.

When researchers collide with or seek out these boundaries, they must challenge themselves to ask with fresh, not tired, minds several questions. *Why is this boundary here? What purpose is it serving? Whose interests is it protecting?* This requires a certain amount of audacity as well as insight into research practices and purposes. It also requires knowledge that any boundary, or set of conventions, is a social construct – people make them up.

> One of my students wanted to use qualitative research to investigate experiences of sexuality. The postgraduate committee, in a tradition of quantitative research, finally approved her proposal, provided that she presented the research as an "exploratory study" to generate questions for investigation via experimental research. Their approach failed to

acknowledge the value of her phenomenology-based proposal and the knowledge it would generate. They did not recognise the difference between researching the incidence of sexuality and researching people's lived experience of sexuality. In her final thesis we concentrated on the latter. In moving beyond the traditional boundaries of this research field her research facilitated greater enrichment of knowledge in this field.

Often the boundaries that constrain us, or that threaten to make us ride a different course, are difficult to challenge. They frequently come cloaked in "reason, logic, objectivity, relevance and professionalism" (Susan Thompson, 2001, p. 155). Being strong and clear about what is being researched, and why the research is important can illuminate the *how,* as shown in the two examples above. Susan (pp. 165–166) discussed some strategies she found useful in being a boundary rider/crosser in her own research. They are listed here with comments from us to illustrate experiences of these strategies:

– *See the critics/boundaries as an ally.* When completing my PhD I had a number of struggles with my supervisor. I felt that she wanted me to write up my research in quite a different way. Feeling scared and lonely I then got angry and wrote her a furious letter, full of passion, which explained why I wanted to do it my way. I then re-wrote the letter as the introduction to my thesis. What I realised was that my passionate outpourings were actually a very clear, sound and articulate explanation of my position. I never did send the letter, but the thesis introduction presented a convincing message!

– *Learn to be a rigorous qualitative researcher.* Sloppy research is bad research. In first embracing qualitative research I had the feeling of throwing off the shackles and bureaucratic restrictions I had experienced with quantitative research. I wanted real, not prescribed, rigour, richness not reliability, value not formulated validity. Of these three discarded terms, I, along with many qualitative researchers, have since, with delight, reclaimed rigour: not in the sense of narrowness or persistence with a predetermined protocol, but as a commitment to quality, transparency and systematic, accountable process. This is indeed a goal of all researchers. Let's not earn the negating labels of "soft science" or "thinky–feely" that are directed at qualitative researchers. Rather, we need to be as thorough in our investigations as we are creative and courageous in exploring research possibilities.

– *Seek out support in as many ways as you can.* When writing for publication it is often important for me to list both first and family names of authors in my bibliography. This often is not done. I have to repeatedly argue strongly that not listing first names can keep the gender of the writer invisible. And I want to acknowledge the input and contributions of flesh and blood people, not just their work. The convention of listing only last names encourages writing to be disembodied and detached. I want to unsettle this convention so I actively seek out published work which also uses the convention of listing first and family names. In this book we have encouraged authors to include first names, if they wish, in the text.

– *Believe in yourself and your work and realise that you can never please everyone.* How many times do we see the goalposts changing? The playing field and the expectations are no sooner learned and addressed but they're changed again. There really is something (very much!) to be said for believing in what you're doing and the value it can bring to the field or to society, without adopting a narrow focus on the changing "goals for credit" (e.g. what is the latest ruling on "research credit points" and grant committee preferences?).

– *Get your credentials as a researcher.* It's an amazing thing, this title of researcher. How is it earned? Qualifications help, but are they enough? What else counts in terms of quality and respect? Apart from wanting to recognise the value of teaching and other roles as well as research, we also recognise the importance of the journey towards becoming a *good* researcher in terms of being a critical self-evaluator and being credentialed in the relevant research community.

Creatively Crossing Discipline Boundaries

Often, in social research, a particular discipline boundary is established. For example, researching poverty from within the discipline of history might include an exploration of what poverty has looked like in different times, which groups of society it has affected and how it might have changed across time periods. Researching poverty from the discipline of economics could mean examining the differences in gross domestic product, who owned how much wealth, what the numerical differences were in the relative poverty of people. Using a psychological perspective might mean conducting an in-depth study of the identity and feelings of the person experiencing poverty, and using a sociological approach researchers could explore how this personal impact affected the social grouping of the family. Each of these perspectives has value and has a genre (including writing style, language, and expectations).

Crossing disciplinary boundaries, using a transdisciplinary or multidisciplinary approach, would yield different information and outcomes. A more holistic picture of poverty could be illuminated by exploring the lived experience of people alongside historical, sociological and economic trends, providing a transformative potential for individuals, policy development and service provision. This fuller picture can emerge when doing qualitative research which is transdisciplinary, as it enables researchers to see both the details (of, say, individuals living in poverty) and the bigger (socioeconomic and historical) picture.

A prospective research student came to chat to me one day about her passion for researching chairs. Over the following few years we journeyed together through many millennia and cultures, through science and art and different research strategies. We forged a bridge between the discipline of history, the sciences of ergonomics and biomechanics and the framework of interpretive research. The learning – enormous; the illumination – unique! The transdisciplinary approach added much more to the understanding of the field than many previous within-discipline studies.

Shifting to thinking creatively, to using diversity as a mode of thought and a context of action allows multiple choices, multiple explanations and multiple solutions to emerge. This requires a tenacity of practice and a suppleness of mind (The Dalai Lama & Howard Cutler, 1998) and enables researchers to see the macro-picture(s) and micro-picture(s) at the same time. One way of working with and seeing multiple pictures is to work with both the fluidity of our positions as researchers/people in the world and the seemingly frozen structures (boundaries) in our social contexts and relationships. This could mean that in research, instead of identifying people who are marginalised and working with them to find a voice, the relationship between the margin(alised) and the centre is illuminated. The gaze is not on the marginalised (e.g. Indigenous people) but on the relationships that marginalise (e.g. the non-Indigenous history of dispossession of Indigenous people). This could mean that advantage as well as disadvantage is documented.. Such research efforts can also be used to seek understanding of how some people are advantaged by existing social structures (see for example Mike Donaldson & Scott Poynting, 2007, whose book explores the experiences of ruling class men).

Documenting and making public stories of resilience facilitates a sharing of transformative strategies for success, engendering hope. Qualitative research itself and networks of researchers debating research issues can achieve or foster such transformation.

Transgressing Boundaries

A group of social activists and two university researchers had been meeting for over 5 years. Their reflective, critical research project was called "good news stories of difference and resistance". They met monthly, drinking coffee, eating, laughing and telling stories of their practices. They began a collaborative research inquiry into the concerns of feminism and poststructuralism with everyday local actions and critique of grand narratives, and at the same time tried to bring a critical perspective to reconstructing what social and environmental research could look like in community contexts.

In this example the researchers transgressed many traditional boundaries. Many of the transgressions were not new but they were, and still are, often resisted. The "transgressions" this group engaged in included:

- Writing a book chapter collaboratively and including, as authors, all seven of the people who were part of the research group. (When we received a copy of the book we found to our dismay that the names of all authors except the two academics had been removed by the editors at time of publication, without asking permission. We needed to make sure the intention matched the act.)
- Using "I", "we" and "feeling".
- Including poetry and performance in their writing.
- Challenging adherence to strict political standpoints and suggesting that a more flexible approach could be useful.

– Suggesting that revolution/social transformation could occur as a result of many small local resistances. A central feature of the work was the use of a metaphor for social change. This metaphor clearly suggested that social change could occur from the margins rather than the centre, and it would happen in multiple ways.
– Including themselves, their hopes, fears and desires.
– Naming what was already happening (but never spoken publicly about) in social and community work.
– Theorising from their data. They were not testing any hypothesis, but built the theory from the ground up (see Judy Pinn & Debbie Horsfall, 2000; Debbie Horsfall, 2005, 2008).

Naming, crossing or justifying boundaries is most relevant in academia. This practice can enable researchers to map the field, to know who else has done work in the area, and to receive guidance about what to read, which journals are worth looking at, and who the so-called experts are. Knowing that there are co-travellers potentially makes for a less lonely journey. It is also respectful to acknowledge the community of scholars who have come before. Naming the boundaries also enables researchers to know which bodies of knowledge they are contributing to and in which way. None of the boundaries crossed in the above example was without precedent, and the participants knew that. They were drawing on rich traditions of feminist theory and practice, collaborative research and grounded theory, poststructuralist theory and feminist community work. They knew that not everyone would like what they were saying, and why.

Boundary riders can be aware of multiple boundaries, and know that they merge into and inform each other. This awareness means that researchers know that boundaries are constructed and so can be deconstructed, that they are chosen or at least complied with, and can be chosen afresh, reframed or discarded. Thus researchers have many positions to inhabit. They can sit on the fence, viewing many fields, or jump on and off, looking at different fields, finding things that matter there. This could involve, for instance, experimenting with different research approaches to the same question, trying out a new research approach to discover what types of (new) questions it can answer, and working alongside experienced researchers in other fields to learn more about their areas and modes of study. In pursuing these explorations it is important to leave a visible trail (a transparent reflexive record of your questions, methods, insights, etc.) so that you can reflect on your journey and learning.

Getting to the Heart of the Matter

Boundaries can often stop us getting to the heart of the matter. Many disciplines are happy to explore and research abstract concepts that do not involve messing around in how those concepts are actually experienced, what they might feel like for many people day-to-day, and what meanings people construct from these experiences. Staying within the realm of the abstract can enable researchers to remain cool, detached, objective and unbiased observers of the people with whom they are working.

One of the projects I am currently doing involves researching the community development potential of supporting someone to die at home. The methods include focus groups with carers, family, friends, neighbours, and work colleagues and sometimes the dying person. The groups have been filled with laughter, stories of love and compassion, and often tears. It was impossible not to be profoundly affected by these stories. What was important, though, was establishing a system of support for the researchers. Establishing supportive spaces where we could talk about how the research was affecting us, how we were feeling, enabled the research to get done. Recognising our own humanity and emotions was vital. Over the course of the project we experienced the ups and downs of life, births and deaths. Without critically reflecting on these experiences we ran the risk of silencing stories we found too personally confronting and upsetting. Doing so would have resulted in sloppy, incomplete research.

Researchers often encounter the so-called boundary between subject and object. The notion of subject/object is a dualistic device or convention, found in discourse and language (the grammar of a sentence, for example), which creates and supports separation of the researcher and researched. Within this device researchers are seen as the experts who view the object under research and collect data about how it responds. This way of researching comes from the natural sciences and often supports the interests of the already powerful. The subject/object discussion is an old one and has been thoroughly critiqued by feminist educators (see e.g. bell hooks, 1984; Patti Lather, 1991; Liz Stanley & Sue Wise, 1993) and critical social scientists (see e.g. Peter Reason, 1988; Stephen LittleJohn, 1992). This critique has meant that the idea of the uninvolved, objective researcher in qualitative studies has been rethought, if not completely abandoned.

This seemingly tired old discussion of subject/object has identified the way that qualitative researchers seek to negotiate, form and dissolve research relationships instead of restricting them by the conventions of objectivity, rigour, and university ethics committees, and to re-examine these issues by asking questions about their usefulness and whose interests they serve. In the past, when conducting (quantitative) research, researchers were expected to remain detached and omnipresent. To be valid the research needed to be objective; to be generalisable the variables needed to be controlled and the research experiment needed to be repeatable. A re-framing and expansion of these concepts can provide a more thorough and useful set of guidelines for today's qualitative researcher. However, often the boundaries shift. We have noticed that with the rise of auto-ethnographic research, ethics committees struggle over what can be said, or researched. This is an interesting development, especially as this tradition of research is often informed by feminist theory and practice. It is a research space where the object and subject of the research are one and the same, and it is an institutional space which we watch with interest to see how the issues are negotiated. For example, many qualitative researchers have sought to reclaim and reframe rigour, a word often used by the border guards to send qualitative researchers cowering into a corner. Rigour is often invoked in the suggestion that research that is not objective cannot be rigorous. We have found that "[rigorous] qualitative research negotiates the structures that constrain us from speaking ... Attending to detail, the relationship, the ethics, the conventions and structures are also rigorous" (Debbie Horsfall, Hilary Byrne Armstrong, & Joy Higgs, 2001, p. 12). This might mean, for example, stating from the beginning that you are interested in social change; that you think there are problems with the status quo.

> I remember my first meeting with the Community Health Managers. They had invited me to a meeting as they were interested in my research. I was hoping to form a collaborative inquiry group. But I wanted to be as honest as possible from the beginning. At this meeting to my surprise I found that Sandra, Joan and Dot shared many of my assumptions, dreams and desires; we all had similar critiques of the health system. I worked with these women for five years. The initial honesty, voicing of beliefs, values and biases of researchers can be the basis for good, useful, objective and critical research. It certainly seemed to be the case in this example.

The relationships central to qualitative research are often seen as superfluous to the process of research. Yet quite clearly they are not. *People* do qualitative research; qualitative research usually involves people working with other people. Talking about research relationships, however, is still a marginalised practice and this makes it difficult to do.

> We had been asked to do some research with women who were homeless. The services contracting us wanted a clear and detailed report to help them push for better service provision in the area. They wanted the voices of the women to be central. We knew how to do this sort of research and write that sort of report. Our greatest fears at the beginning were to do with relationships with the homeless women. We feared that we would not be able to talk with them meaningfully; we feared exploiting them for yet another research report; we feared offering a sense of false hope and we feared for our own safety – emotionally and physically. Many of the women were living in very difficult circumstances in very undesirable and unsafe areas. This was not without challenges for two white middle class university academics. Eventually we settled on the sausage sizzle research method. We and some of the service providers arranged to provide free sausage sizzles for women and children. We advertised the fact that we would be there and they could talk to us if they wanted to, or not. We ended up going to meet the women with service providers who knew them, and knew of the areas we went into. In another context, I still remember the advice I was given – in the tones of an order – when I began working with people who have disabilities, "not to become involved". But my experience showed me that only when I became involved did any change take place, both in the person with a disability and in me. It happened only when I or someone else cared enough, when I allowed myself to be compassionate, when I tried to find ways for people to feed themselves, to shut toilet doors, to work out communication systems, to help people walk. This caring enough meant that people's lives

took a different shape. It also meant having to deal with frustration, fear, loneliness, anger and despair, as well as joy when things did work out.

We have found in our research that caring about ourselves, the people we are working with and the issue we are working on yields the most powerful results, personally and professionally. Being in relationships, negotiating these relationships, and acknowledging how we and others are or might be feeling, are essential parts of the research process. Often it is relationships that researchers are seeking to both understand and transform: relationships with each other and the world with/in which we live. Racism, sexism, discrimination and isolation are all forms of domination and oppression that are rooted in relationships. The boundary fences of so-called proper knowledge are well protected but not invincible. There are ways of producing dangerous and improper (or perhaps liberated!) knowledges which quite clearly challenge many taken-for-granted assumptions, ignore many rules and conventions, and are transformative along the way.

> We had been invited to present our collaborative work on good news stories of difference and resistance at a conference. Our work together had been lively and passionate. The work itself in both form and content had challenged many rules about THE way to do research. And we did not want simply to present a paper. So we wrote and performed a play … it was loud, lively, chaotic and fun. It was threaded through with findings which the audience recognised, roaring with laughter. We sang, we clowned, we ate, we rushed around. We handed out chocolates, we did a bicycle ride and we had a great time. The people watching/participating gave great feedback. They were able to reflect upon multiple issues that we had raised in our performance and mostly we felt that the points had been seen, heard and understood. We have repeated this performance many times. We had wanted to explore working with difference and diversity in community; inclusions and exclusions; forming new and unusual alliances; and the value of small, local, creative resistances to the status quo. These issues in themselves are difficult to deal with, and the performance was a challenge for many of us accustomed to giving academic papers. Most of us couldn't wait to do it again and believed it was a successful, fun and extremely transgressive way to discuss such potentially abstract concepts.

The writing of this chapter, in both form and content, is a material, concrete practice that shows another way of riding and crossing boundaries. We have brought ourselves as qualitative researchers into the foreground in the process of discussing boundaries, their purpose, and some ways we can ride and transgress them to enhance our research and more fully address our research questions. This practice of foregrounding our own practice is another boundary crossing, as we make ourselves visible and vulnerable, albeit in a fairly controlled manner. The form of the chapter is such that it is a reflective piece, containing metaphors, stories and multiple voices. It is not necessarily the more traditional form of structured academic writing. This is deliberate, as we wanted our writing practice to be congruent with our content. Our hope is that in so doing we have provided some spaces for you to ride and cross your own boundaries; at the very least to recognise boundaries when you encounter them. If you, like us, are interested in transformative research, research that unsettles, questions and destabilises the status quo in your desire to contribute to a more just world, then action is required, and this action will often involve riding and crossing boundaries.

REFERENCES

The Dalai Lama (his Holiness), & Cutler H.C. (1998). *The art of happiness*. New York: Riverhead.

Donaldson, M., & Poynting, S. (2007). *Ruling class men: Money, sex, power*. Oxford: Peter Lang.

hooks, b. (1984). *Feminist theory: From margin to center*. Boston: South End Press.

Horsfall, D. (2005). Creative practices of hope. In D. Gardiner & K. Scott (Eds.), *Proceedings of international conference on engaging communities*. Brisbane, Qld: Queensland Government. Available: http://www.engagingcommunities2005.org/abstracts/Horsfall-Debbie-final.pdf

Horsfall, D. (2008). Performing communit(y)ies. *Forum Qualitative Sozialforschung / Forum: Qualitative Social Research, 9*(2), Art. 57. Retrieved from http://www.qualitative-research.net/fqs-texte/2-08/08-2-57-e.htm

Horsfall, D., Byrne-Armstrong, H., & Higgs, J. (2001). Researching critical moments. In H. Byrne-Armstrong, J. Higgs & D. Horsfall (Eds.), *Critical moments in qualitative research* (pp. 3–13). Oxford: Butterworth-Heinemann.

Lather, P. (1991). *Getting smart: Feminist research and pedagogy with/in the postmodern*. New York: Routledge.

LittleJohn, S. (1992). *Theories of human communication*. San Francisco: Wadsworth.

Pinn, J., & Horsfall, D. (2000). Doing community differently: Ordinary resistances and new alliances. In J. Collins & S. Poynting (Eds.), *The other Sydney: Communities, identities and inequalities in Western Sydney* (pp. 360–378). Melbourne: Common Ground.

Reason, P. (Ed.) (1988). *Human Inquiry in Action: Developments in new paradigm research*. London: Sage.

Stanley, L., & Wise, S. (1993). *Breaking out again. Feminist ontology and epistemology* (2nd ed.). London: Routledge.

Thompson, S. (2001). Breaking through with subjugated knowledges: Pushing the boundaries of urban planning. In H. Byrne-Armstrong, J. Higgs & D. Horsfall (Eds.), *Critical moments in qualitative research* (pp. 153–168). Oxford: Butterworth-Heinemann.

Debbie Horsfall PhD, MA, B.Ed
Peace and Development Studies
School of Social Sciences
University of Western Sydney, Australia

Joy Higgs AM PhD
The Education For Practice Institute
Charles Sturt University, Australia

JAN FOOK

6. DEVELOPING CRITICAL REFLECTION
AS A RESEARCH METHOD

Critical reflection is normally used in professional learning settings to assist practitioners to improve practice. I have worked for some time using critical reflection in this way with many different types of professionals. Over time, however, I have been impressed by the deeper and more complex understanding of practice experience which the process enables, and which practitioners themselves often cannot initially express. And so I have begun to speculate about the research potential of the critical reflection process, and whether it might be developed as a research method to allow better formulations of practice experience, and therefore, ultimately, better practice.

I am aware, however, that if critical reflection is to be fully accepted and used as a research method, a good deal of work needs to be done to legitimise it in this way. Although there can be much overlap between learning and research activities, the respective fields tend to occupy different social positions and are located in different academic traditions and sets of literature. Moreover, there is a political dimension to the task, as research may often be seen as a more prestigious domain than education or learning, in the same way as the research world relates to the practice world. I am interested in developing a critical reflection research method which makes that leap between the two worlds, by legitimising its usage within existing research traditions. This will involve some extensive development of the rationales, theoretical frameworks and specific practices involved.

In this chapter I aim to begin this task by outlining the preliminary case for developing critical reflection as a research method. I begin by outlining my approach to critical reflection and the process involved. I then reflect on my experience of undertaking critical reflection with many different professionals, and draw out what has brought me to the point of wanting to develop the process as a research method. This leads to a firmer intellectual case for the potential benefits of using such a process to research experience. I finish by pinpointing some of the intellectual and political tasks that must be undertaken to develop critical reflection further as a legitimate research method.

Critical reflection, although widely used and endorsed in professional learning, encompasses many different understandings and many different theoretical approaches. There are also associated terms and concepts like reflexivity (Taylor & White, 2000) and reflective practice (Schön, 1983) which make the concept quite complex. In this chapter I acknowledge this multiplicity of uses, but I am *not* making the claim that all methods of critical reflection may be used as research

J. Higgs et al., (eds.), Creative Spaces for
Qualitative Researching: Living Research, 55–64

methodology. Neither am I addressing the issue of how critical reflection or reflexivity may be incorporated into research design in many different ways (such as in contributing to different levels of analysis) (Steier, 1991). Nor am I considering the broader issue of reflexivity in research (Alvesson & Skoldberg, 2000). My specific concern here is to explore how the method I use might be adapted as a way of actually collecting and creating understandings of the experiences of practising professionals.

A BRIEF OUTLINE OF THE CRITICAL REFLECTION PROCESS

My particular approach to critical reflection involves an overall process of learning from experience, with the express aim of improving professional practice. I define critical reflection as a way of learning from and reworking experience. Participants begin by presenting a story of their experience which they believe is crucial to their learning about their professional practice. They reflect on this experience with the help of colleagues in small groups. The process is divided into two stages. It begins with unearthing fundamental assumptions (primarily those that are to do with power and connections between the individual and the social context) that are implicit in the participant's story. Examining these assumptions allows for better scrutiny of blind spots or discrepancies. This initial process usually enables participants to recognise values or beliefs that are fundamentally important to them (stage one), and this allows them to remake their understanding of their experience in a way that fits better with these fundamental ideas (stage two).

This new awareness can be used, in stage two, to devise new (and better) approaches to practice, which may be more in line with the person's fundamental value system and more responsive to the social environment of practice. Thus participants are encouraged to envision how this new understanding of their experience might change their practice. Once they can articulate ideas they are invited to reformulate their "theory of practice" (so called because it names and links both their basic theoretical principles with possible actions) so that they have a new framework from which to further develop their practice. It is important that this "theory of practice" uses language that is meaningful to the participants, and also manages to capture what they see as the essence of their experience and fundamental beliefs.

In the overall process people often incorporate other crucial experiences and rework their understanding of them in order to arrive at a perspective that allows integration of these other experiences with their world view, fundamental values or sense of themselves. They often include strong emotions as an important aspect of experience, which can indicate significant values or beliefs. They may unearth many different types of assumptions and at different levels, but are usually able to find a fundamental level that helps to integrate the other levels.

A brief example will illustrate further. Wanda, a social worker, raised an incident in which she had become angry with, and had sworn at, a student she was supervising on placement. She was very distressed by her behaviour. Critical reflection (in stage one) revealed that she believed herself to be a bad professional, in this instance, and that her behaviour contradicted her own strong beliefs about good social work. She felt that the incident happened because she believed the student did not conform to good social work values, but she felt very conflicted about having expressed herself to him in this way. Further reflection led her to question her beliefs about good professional social work, in part because they did not allow for the place of strong (especially negative) emotion. Yet her experience showed her that negative emotions might in fact indicate good beliefs. She therefore (in stage two) decided to remake her idea of being a good professional to include emotional reactions, especially if they indicated a strong and good set of beliefs. Her new theory of practice became "the passionate professional", and she decided to devise ways in which she could use her emotions to good effect in her professional practice.

A combination of different theoretical frameworks and concepts of reflection is used in this approach to critical reflection (see Fook & Gardner, 2007, for detail), including the idea of reflective practice (Schön, 1983), learning from experience (Dewey, 1933), reflexivity, deconstruction (Fook, 2002) and critical reflection (Brookfield, 2009). The process is basically a socially interactive one, even though participants begin with an example of their own practice experience. Through dialogue with colleagues and the various frameworks and perspectives and interpretations, they are helped to reflect further and connect personal experience with social and cultural beliefs and practices.

It is essential that the process is facilitated by an appropriate climate for open learning and risk-taking to support trying on new, multiple or even opposing ideas. Participants are therefore asked to maintain an environment of trust, respect and acceptance, to create a safe climate.

MY REFLECTIONS ON CRITICAL REFLECTION

Although this might seem like a relatively straightforward process, one of the things that stands out for me is the initial difficulty many people have in articulating their experience in a way which feels satisfactory to them. Often they present stories of incidents that happened many years previously, which still puzzle, bewilder or distress them. (For example, experienced practitioners might relate incidents in which they were required to remove a child from parents.) Sometimes they are stuck in making what they regard as constructive meaning of the experience because there are too many conflicting strands or perspectives, and they cannot sort through them or work out which is more important. (They are aware that they had "done the right thing" in taking a child away but are acutely aware of the rights of parents, the situation which might have led to this, the distress of the child, and also their own feelings of sadness or distress.) Sometimes they bend over backwards to incorporate the perspectives of others in order to be "fair" or "professional" in their outlook, so much so that they no longer recognise what is important to them. Often they feel that their experience does not tally with what they think they should have felt or thought, or they cannot find adequate frameworks from their knowledge to make sense of what happened. Sometimes, of course, they feel that they cannot reconcile their own value system with the outcomes delivered within their organisations.

This "stuckness" concerns me, as it appears to indicate that perhaps current theories for approaching practice are ineffective in providing frameworks for disparate practice experiences. Or are we letting down our fellow professionals by not providing effective support? Alternatively there might be something about professional cultures, and unspoken expectations, which construct impossible scenarios in which practitioners are caught. Can current understandings of practice capture the diversity and complexity of experiences, and provide requisite frameworks so that practitioners are able to use these experiences to develop? If they cannot, why not? What role has research to play in addressing this gap?

A second observation I have made, given the "stuckness" above, is that it is extraordinarily interesting to see how people's stories of their experiences can change over the course of undertaking critical reflection. The changes that occur are usually completely unpredicted and also unpredictable. What starts as a reasonably straightforward process to "unearth assumptions" often ends up as "making new meaning of the experience", and it is this new meaning which often cannot be predicted, but which nevertheless seems to function as an effective compass in redirecting thinking and actions. People not only find successive layers of assumptions which are important but also can reformulate more generic principles that function both as a guide for professional practice and often also as general principles for living. They are developing a form of agency, a sense of personal power to act within and to influence their environments (Heaney & Horton, 1991; Fook & Askeland, 2006)

My third observation therefore concerns what it is about the process which might enable such transformative experiences that often occur very quickly. Although it is helpful for a person simply to tell a descriptive story about an experience, it is not enough. Also needed is a choice of theoretical frameworks to help the person interpret and see the experience in a variety of ways; some dialogue to help craft alternative views; and an enabling environment to try out radically different ideas. Usually people will continue the process on their own, and after reflecting further (only overnight in some cases), may return to a second session, having completely reworked their idea of what their fundamental assumptions were. I have begun to think that the critical reflection process provides a type of concentrated microcosm of the process people might (hopefully) normally go through in attempting to learn from experience. Thus it is an intense process, one which provides the wherewithal to learn from experience using the means most of us would normally use.

In summary then, the process perhaps works because it is both personal and social; it is structured, yet fluid and flexible; it is intentional, being based on clear theoretical frameworks for interpreting experience; and it is enabling because it is built on ethical and mutually beneficial principles which balance safety and risk.

THE CASE FOR USING CRITICAL REFLECTION AS A RESEARCH METHOD

If the critical reflection process can enable such a radical reworking of experience to fit better with a person's sense of self and personal history, I began to wonder what the implications might be for researching experience. Could the outcome of this process elucidate experience in ways that were not formerly achieved through research? This process might lead us to new ways of understanding and communicating about experience that might be more "valid" from the perspective of the person and the way that person makes meaning of experience in the social context, as it mirrors the "normal" way this might happen. I found this approach particularly attractive, as it seemed to incorporate both personal and social elements of experience, and to mimic the primarily interactive process involved in making meaning of experience.

I began to speculate about whether critical reflection for individuals could be turned into a more collective way of researching experience, so that the learning could become more transferable to other professionals. If there was a more systematic way to conduct critical reflection (in order to reach more systematically identifiable outcomes), then the collective learning derived might be used to develop professional knowledge, and might also develop the distinctive contributions to knowledge made through professional practice experience itself.

One of the key problems in qualitative research into professional practice is to represent practice experience in a way that captures its complex, often dynamic, holistic and contextual nature. This issue has been acknowledged by Denzin and Lincoln (1994, p. 2) in reference to the need for multi-methods and perspectives to "attempt to secure an in-depth understanding of the phenomenon in question", realising that "objective reality can never be captured". Practice experience changes its shape and texture depending on the various perspectives of those involved, the time and location in which it is examined and experienced, and many other factors. Most research can therefore at best only deliver a partial explication of practice experience, as what is elicited will depend on the particular frameworks of interpretation and methods for eliciting the experience.

There are at least three main areas in which particular research approaches or methods might be limited in researching experience. Most of these issues have been raised in some form or other by qualitative researchers, but here I attempt to summarise the main areas of concern. First, there can be a dominance of one perspective. It is difficult to conduct research which incorporates many perspectives in dynamic interplay. Most approaches to research foreground either the researcher's or the participant's perspective. For example, methods like deconstruction or discourse analysis ultimately use the framework of the researcher to analyse, interpret (and sometimes implicitly judge) participants' experiences. On the other hand, methods like narrative analysis or grounded theory run some risks inherent in "standpointism", namely over-privileging the participants' perspective (Brown, 1995). For instance, there might be discrepancies between what people say about a situation and what they actually did in it, or between what they say about it and what they are aware of. They may not be able to access hidden or tacit knowledge which can be revealed to have a major influence on their actions and experience. Moreover, many conventional research methods often assume that people can articulate or be aware of all influences on their experience (so that all that has to be done is to ask them about it), and that this does not necessarily change according to context. Many methods also assume that a pre-existing (and jointly understood) language that will accurately represent their experience. Given that many research methods rely on a relatively static "give and take" of information, the opportunity to discuss meanings, language, and to probe for other perspectives is not available, and therefore the resulting "findings" might represent a relatively simplistic, one-sided or even inaccurate view of a whole situation.

Second, serious validity issues can be raised by the use of pre-existing theoretical frameworks, both in the frameworks used to understand the problem being researched and in the designing of tools to undertake the research. This is a problem in both positivist and post-positivist inclined research. Both approaches normally require (a) a framework for selection and analysis of data (however weak or open-ended), which inevitably restricts the capacity to represent experiences that might be new or not previously articulated; and (b) a relatively specific (often narrow) focus on some aspect of practice experience taken out of context (e.g. outcomes, beliefs, actions, decision-making, emotions). The complexity and contextual meaning of experience is ignored; yet it may be this very context, and the actual interplay of different aspects, which constitute the complexity that is the key to understanding the experience itself.

Third, there can be major issues to do with relevance. This refers to the capacity for the research to be translated into meaningful change and action by practitioners/users, in specific and concrete situations. Relevance problems arise for a number of reasons: practitioners' and users' interests might not be represented in the research (for example, the research problem has not come from them) so they feel little responsibility for acting on it; practitioners' experiences or perspectives are not represented (the research and findings might be framed in a way that practitioners or users do not find meaningful, so they are unable to act on it); the research might also have been conceptualised and designed based on assumptions that (a) the worlds of practice and research are separate, (b) the worlds of the "personal" and the "social" are separate, and (c) the worlds of professionals and users are separate. Thus it may be difficult for practitioners or users to actually translate the research between the different worlds and to act upon it within the practice world.

How then might critical reflection be used as a research method to address these issues? The process I have outlined above addresses these limitations in three main ways through its dialogic, integrative and transformative nature. First, it is *dialogic*, in that it creates a *shared* representation of experience through a *dynamic interaction* between participant and researcher. Participants provide the initial data (i.e. their own experience) which they craft jointly with the researcher, using different frameworks to forge a new meaning of the experience. This effectively means that both "personal" and "social" views are represented in an interactive process. The result of this dialogue is that participants can speak about their experience in a language which, although devised through interaction, still represents their own view. In this process it is probably best to speak of the participant and the researcher as "co-researchers".

Second, the critical reflection process is *integrative*, in that it provides a framework and process for integrating all aspects of complex experience (emotions, beliefs, values, actions) by articulating its meaning *in context* and representing it by creating relevant language. This means that the "uniqueness" of the experience is preserved. Furthermore, by creating a relevant language for the experience, it can be communicated, discussed, modified and so on with others.

Lastly, such a method is *transformative*, in that it can lead to fundamental and empowering changes at both personal and social levels. In particular, it can instil a sense of agency and can provide a framework for action. By linking personal learning, research and change possibilities, people are better able to see how research and learning can translate directly into actions, and can also envision how this process might transfer to different settings. Through linking an understanding of personal experience in social context, people are often able to gain a better idea of how to act in a way that will influence their social context. This increases their sense of agency. Overall, the process reaffirms the value of practice experience and also creates a legitimate role for the practitioner as researcher.

Through its dialogic, integrative and transformative characteristics, then, critical reflection used as a method to research experience can address some of the major limitations inherent in many mainstream methods. It may allow us to represent the complex, contextual, fluid yet integrated nature of practice experience in a way that also enables transformative action to occur.

WHAT ARE THE ISSUES INVOLVED IN USING AND LEGITIMISING CRITICAL REFLECTION AS A RESEARCH METHOD?

Clearly, there are more methodological questions that need to be addressed in thinking through the practicalities of how this critical reflection process might be used to understand professional practice experience. These are the questions facing all researchers, which become more difficult to answer the more complex the phenomena under study. For instance, what is the actual aim of the research, the research problem being addressed, and the research question which emanates from it? And what then is the focus of our research (i.e. how do we define and identify what professional practice experience is?). What actual "data" are being collected or created and how will data recorded, captured, and written up?

Some of the answers to these questions regarding the aims, the research problem, question and focus of research lie in how critical reflection is conceptualised. For instance, if it is seen as a way of evoking the complexity of practice experience from the perspective of the experience in social context, then the aim will be to elicit that complexity from that perspective. The research problem will be conceptualised as the difficulty of eliciting such experience, and the question will revolve around the characteristics of such experience. The focus will be on how such complex experience is expressed. Alternatively, if critical reflection is conceptualised primarily as a method for surfacing the tacit dimension of practice experience, then that will be the focus of study. In a similar way, the process might be seen as a way of connecting emotions with practice experience; a making meaning of experience; excavating the fundamental values in practice; and so on. Each of these conceptualisations suggests a slightly different focus and set of aims.

The major concepts involved in researching practice experience are, however, not uncontested. They are subject to different perspectives, and are undergoing constant development. The concepts of "practice", "experience", "practice experience", and what it means to "research" need to be thoroughly understood if we are to be clear about how critical reflection claims to research them. There is quite an intellectual endeavour here, as there is a wealth of developing thinking about the concepts of both practice (Green, 2009) and experience, which is theorised in many different disciplines, including philosophy (Dilthey, 1961), psychology (Bradley, 2005), anthropology (Turner & Bruner, 1986), and education (Dewey, 1933). Moreover, the notion of experience is theorised from different perspectives, such as constructivist, pragmatist or symbolic interactionist perspectives. Of course, it may be said that the problem of experience is in a sense the problem that qualitative research grapples with – how do we express and access it? We also see continuing development of ideas around how we research experience, from whose perspective, what are the best methods, and so on (Stephenson & Papadopoulos, 2006).

These intellectual aspects of developing critical reflection research methodology are also accompanied by political dimensions. I have identified three fronts on which changes need to be made in order to legitimise such a method.

– Raising the research profile of critical reflection through creating research-related discourse about it. For example, it is important to identify aspects of critical reflection that require further research, such as the outcomes and benefits of critical reflection (Fook & Gardner, 2007); and to undertake comprehensive literature reviews and undertake and publish research (e.g. Fook & Askeland, 2006). It is also important to submit grant applications to prestigious funding bodies, so that traditional bodies become more aware of the research potential in the less traditional arena of critical reflection.
– Locating critical reflection within a context of similar research methodologies. In establishing the theoretical basis for a critical reflection method, it is politically and intellectually important to show how it is aligned (or not) with such methodologies. Elsewhere I have developed critical reflection as a deconstructive and reconstructive method, using these concepts as the major theoretical underpinning for critical reflection (Fook, 2002). There are also aspects of action research (Reason & Bradbury, 2001) which include reflective cycles in the design, but are dissimilar in that the reflection is not the sole method for the collection of information about experience. There are other methods such as auto/biographical (e.g. Merrill & West, 2009) which incorporate the participant's life story, and narrative methods (Elliot, 2005), which use the person's story as a source of data for analysis. Autoethnography may also be seen as a reflexive research method (White, 2001). Memory work (Haug, 1987) shares much in the way of the politics and conceptualisations of

the research problem, as well as the process of dialogue in researching past experience.
- Developing appropriate epistemologies (and practices), and being aware of and resisting incongruent epistemologies (and practices). Current mainstream research culture tends to be based on positivistic assumptions, whether or not they are openly espoused or acknowledged. This means that there is almost a natural resistance to qualitative ways of thinking. This is even more of a problem when seeking to research practice, as the concerns of the practice world are often marginal in academic contexts. Many accepted and taken-for-granted research practices may therefore inhibit the study of complex and fluid experience using critical reflection. With this in mind I would suggest that the following ways of working with research require further development to devise platforms for more effective researching of experience through critical reflection.

  - Defining the topic. Research topics are often deliberately defined relatively narrowly, in the belief that this will make the researcher's task more doable. Yet if we are to understand experience in a more "valid" way, then we may actually need to define the topic more broadly, in keeping with the potential that a critical reflection method promises.
  - Working with critical reflection suggests a need to work across different disciplinary silos in appreciating the complexity of human experience.
  - Choosing a perspective. Many researchers feel they must choose a particular theoretical perspective or framework on which to base their research. That, however, can limit understandings in the same way that staying within disciplinary silos may do. We need a more integrated way of understanding phenomena which is cognisant of different theoretical approaches and can integrate them in some way.
  - Who are legitimate researchers? There needs to be recognition for people to be legitimate researchers of their own experience, along with others who participate in and contribute to the process. In this sense, there may be many different kinds of co-researchers involved in research.

CONCLUSION

I have made a case for developing a critical reflection process as a method for researching experience, in particular, professional practice experience, arguing that the process can elicit deeper and more complex understandings and can allow the fluidity and integrated nature of experience to emerge. I showed, in a preliminary way, how this might happen, first by describing the process, and then by illustrating with a brief example of how practitioners often radically change their understanding of crucial experiences, and the way they make meaning of and express them. I then drew out three key ways in which such a process might address some of the known limitations (problems of perspective, validity and relevance) of existing methods. I argued that it might do this as an essentially dialogic, integrated and transformative process. I finished by pointing up the main intellectual and political tasks yet to be undertaken to legitimise such a method in academic social research circles. These tasks involve raising the research profile of critical reflection, developing congruent cultures in research practices, and locating the potential contribution of critical reflection in the context of current debates and developments in research methodology.

What I have discussed here is indeed an ambitious task. Yet I am convinced that it is crucial to develop the intellectual and academic credibility of the critical reflection process for understanding professional practice experience. Its capacity to illuminate the way we engage with our work in complex, integrated and fluid ways may yield new and invaluable insights about professional practice and about ourselves as human beings within it.

REFERENCES

Alvesson, M., & Skoldberg, K. (2000). *Reflexive methodology.* London: Sage.

Bradley, B. (2005). *Psychology and experience.* Cambridge: Cambridge University Press.

Brookfield, S. (2009). The concept of critical reflection: Promises and contradictions. *European Journal of Social Work, 12*(3), 293–304.

Brown, W. (1995). *States of injury.* Princeton: Princeton University Press.

Denzin, N., & Lincoln, Y. (Eds.) (1994). *Handbook of qualitative research.* London: Sage.

Dewey, J. (1933). *How we think: A restatement of the relation of reflective thinking to the educative process.* New York: D. C. Heath & Co.

Dilthey, W. (1961). *Pattern and meaning in history.* New York: Harper Torchbooks.

Elliot, J. (2005). *Using narrative in social research.* London: Sage.

Fook, J. (2002). *Social work: Critical theory and practice.* London: Sage.

Fook, J., & Askeland, G.A. (2006). The "critical" in critical reflection. In S. White, J. Fook & F. Gardner (Eds.), *Critical reflection in health and social care* (pp. 40–53). Maidenhead: Open University Press.

Fook, J., & Gardner, F. (2007). *Practising critical reflection.* Maidenhead: Open University Press.

Green, B. (Ed.) (2009). *Understanding and researching professional practice.* Rotterdam: Sense.

Haug, F. (1987). *Female sexualisation: A collective work of memory.* London: Verso.

Heaney, T.W., & Horton, A.I. (1991). Reflective engagement for social change. In J. Mezirow (Ed.), *Fostering critical reflection in adulthood* (pp. 74–98). San Francisco: Jossey-Bass.

Merrill, B., & West, L. (2009). *Using biographical methods in social research.* London: Sage.

Reason, P., & Bradbury, H. (Eds.) (2001). *Handbook of action research: Participative inquiry and practice.* London: Sage.

Schön, D.A. (1983). *The reflective practitioner: How professionals think in action.* New York: Basic Books.

Steier, F. (Ed.) (1991). *Research and reflexivity.* London: Sage.

Stephenson, N., & Papadopoulos, D. (2006). *Analysing everyday experience.* Basingstoke: Palgrave Macmillan.

Taylor, C., & White, S. (2000). *Practising reflexivity in health and welfare.* Maidenhead: Open University Press.

Turner, V.W., & Bruner, E.M. (1986). *The anthropology of experience.* Chicago: Uni. of Illinois Press.

White, S. (2001). Autoethnography as reflexive inquiry: The research act as self-surveillance. In I. Shaw & N. Gould (Eds.), *Qualitative research in social work* (pp. 100–115). London: Sage.

Jan Fook PhD
Interprofessional Institute
South West London Academic Network, UK

JAN DEWING

7. BRINGING MERLEAU PONTY'S INSPIRATIONS TO THE DOING OF RESEARCH

New Ways

Here new ways go.
Quietly let us fare.
Come, let us seek
a new flower, and fair.

Throw away what we possess!
Everything attained, complete
lifelessly oppresses us,
not worthy of dream, song and deed.

Life is that which awaits,
what one cannot know of, or speak...
Come, let us forget!
New things and fair let us seek!

(Karin Boye, 1924)

For my PhD I undertook in-depth research with older persons living with dementia and who resided in a nursing home. My topic was wandering. I was exploring what wandering was and what meaning it had for the older person who "did it". I was doing this as no one had previously done any similar research on wandering with, rather than on, persons with dementia. I was driven by the fact that wandering had previously been researched from a behavioural and generally a reductionist perspective.

This appreciation pushed me further than I would originally have gone to find a philosophy that could avoid reductionism and account for embodiment and diminishing cognition; by no means a straightforward quest. In this chapter I describe how I went about bringing a few of Merleau-Ponty's philosophical tenets to life in my research on wandering.

The research took me on a personal quest to discover, or rediscover, the original experience and essence of the phenomenon under investigation (see van Manen, 1984). This chapter should offer readers insights into a small part of Merleau-Ponty's philosophy and help stimulate ideas for how these can be realised in actual research.

J. Higgs et al., (eds.), Creative Spaces for
Qualitative Researching: Living Research, 65–76

Human Experience

Traditional scientific explanations of particular forms of human action in the form of behaviour are derived from a mind-body dualism where human behaviour is reduced to the same level as that of simple organisms. Within Merleau-Ponty's thesis, however, human action and behaviour such as wandering cannot be understood as a simple mechanistic response to defined stimuli but is instead best understood as active embodied perception, problem-solving and meaning making.

Merleau-Ponty (1965) suggested that the actions of human beings can be symbolic and individualised, in that meanings relate to individual conceptions of need rather than generalised needs of the species. To understand what the body-subjects are doing requires more than observation of bodily movements and their neurological or other causes; it is most important to know the description under which the body-subject is acting, the desires and reasons for performing an action under that description (Matthews, 2002). Reductionist observation of wandering provides only a partial picture of the lived experience of wandering. Human beings as body-subjects respond as a whole (holistically) to their surrounding world in an attempt to solve problems and create meaning.

Several approaches or methodologies could have suited the research topic and my questions. Yet I am not so sure how many other philosophies would have worked as well. I chose to go on the phenomenological path. Wandering down that path I soon discovered that it was too easy to stop at the first philosophy that superficially appeared to fit my purpose. My review of many of the popular nursing phenomenology research papers offered a limited perspective on phenomenology or what is termed "new" or nursing phenomenology (Dowling, 2005).

Probably originating from a critique by Crotty (1996), there has been some debate about the way in which nursing phenomenological research has "watered down" the original purpose of phenomenology. This new or nursing phenomenology needs to be valued within the evolution of phenomenology and within the nursing and health professions as it develops greater understandings about lived experiences (ontology), although it does not necessarily add to our understanding of phenomena in themselves (epistemology).

I felt concern that new phenomenology in my research would lead me to lose sight of the philosophical origins of phenomenology and just what was possible to achieve with it. This could mean I that would be focusing on just the lived experience of wandering, which seemed to me to be only half the reason for undertaking the research. I also wanted to learn more about wandering as a phenomenon. From this I concluded that I must search within the philosophy of phenomenology for my own way ahead, an endeavour that felt complex and uncomfortable at times.

Admittedly, it was appealing to look at taking the easier path and just focusing on the ontological aspect, something I discussed several times in my reflective diary. I was oscillating between taking the easier route and stretching myself; between theory that was already known and certain and something that was still unknown and uncertain; between using the philosophy and being creative with the philosophy. I made the choice to follow the unknown uncertain path.

Even at that early stage, doing my research involved a series of decisions about what was the best course of action, rather than the easiest. Much of the early research activity was about reading and thinking, slow work and so time-consuming that it was tempting always to opt for the easiest option. I was not comfortable exploring primary phenomenological texts in depth. It felt like a millstone slowing me down when I wanted to get on to what I felt were the exciting parts of the research.

Put simply, I had an internal barrier about the real value or contribution philosophy could make to my research. Everything, it seemed, needed to flow from the philosophy but when the philosophy didn't flow within or from me it seemed impossible to move on. My desire was to create a framework that I could believe in, that could embody the research principles, and where older people's lived experience of wandering could be theorised in positive or person-centred ways.

In retrospect I realise that inspiration and creativity are interrelated and both need to come from a strong desire to achieve something that matters and has personal meaning and thus significance. It probably took me a year of mostly solitary activity of reading and reflection. I did have some dialogues with my research supervisor.

By the end of that time I had accumulated a hunch that Merleau-Ponty's phenomenology would be useful. I was hesitant about this as I had not identified other published work in dementia care drawing on Merleau-Ponty at the time. I also had what I believed were five necessary values-based conditions for my philosophical framework:

– sentience or feeling, necessary for moral consideration as a person and also related to having the power of sense-perception or consciousness
– relationality or being-in-relation, necessary for being a person in the world
– "doing" derived from non-cognitive knowledge
– space and place
– temporality, which I conceived of as the temporal dimensions of past, present, and future or the horizons of temporal landscape.

The first two conditions were central elements of my values and beliefs about personhood; the next three were, I felt, necessary and potentially transformational when theorising about the lived experience of wandering, in the context of dementia.

At this point I felt no real sense of achievement and was almost embarrassed at how little I had to show for my efforts. Also around that time I started to play more creatively with my five values or conditions. I imagined I had five colours that intermingled – simply a sea of colour. Drawing on creative imagination, I painted the conditions. This helped me to see that I had core conditions or criteria for the theoretical framework, but they were still essentially a splurge of colour with a dispersed unrecognised pattern, as seen in Figure 7.1.

Figure 7.1. The early conditions

In retrospect, this "splurge" was symbolic of my lack of conceptual clarity at the time, and the murkiness probably reflected my feelings about where I was at. Around this time I started testing out a phenomenological stance in the world; my own and that of people living with dementia. For example, I would look at objects and ask myself: If I didn't know this was a … what could it be? What does it look like? what does it feel like?

I would go for walks and, using the landscape around me, would try to see it differently. I imagined myself as a young child exploring things and what it might be like to explore without things being already named and given to the child with certain properties. I drew on the creative ways in which many older people with dementia can perceive things and places differently and noticed how, using the same cues, the perceptions they arrived at were so different from my cognitively weighed ones. Stripped bare, phenomenology gives a direct description of our experience as it is, without taking account of its psychological origin and the causal explanations which science, history and sociology may be able to provide.

On one of my reflective walks by the sea I came across a length of old rope with four strands, and this prop enabled me to represent the next phase of creating my mental picture or image of a coherent and workable framework for the research. The painting took the shape of two transverse waves (relations and the body) twisting around each other to form a pattern both from the outside and from within. The other two waves (of space and time) were present but not as obvious (see Figure 7.2).

Figure 7.2. Waves of space and time

Then began a bit of a struggle, although this time with a determined effort, to make sense of the relationship between Merleau-Ponty's ideas and my research. The personal commitment and my visual representation helped me stay focused on my search. As I became clearer about relations and the body I could see I had duplicated one of the tenets, so I refined my tenets from five to four and I could align these with the four existentials of Merleau-Ponty's philosophy. There are four fundamental life-world themes (or existentials) that constitute lived experience: lived body (corporeality), lived human relation (relationality), lived space (spatiality), and lived time (temporality).

Thus in research terms, the existentials provide helpful heuristic or discovery guides for reflecting on human experiences. In retrospect, I had connected with values and principles that would heighten my curiosity and serve me far more widely than the research for which they were intended. The challenge, I felt, was to make the existentials real, present and vivid, within the doing of the research; the data collection, analysis and written word. At last I really sensed I was on to something; that I had discovered what I needed. Again, much of this was solitary activity and it took more time that I would have thought necessary. Already one year had passed and more months were piling onto that. I had thought maybe 3 to 6 months would be sufficient to pull together a few principles. The principles underpinning the Merleau-Ponty thesis were so radically different that grasping their significance needed more time than I could have imagined or had been prepared to allow into my very organised plan.

I went on to create a mandala. A generic construct found in many cultures, a mandala is a circular drawing that essentially depicts how a scheme, a plan or pattern is sensed symbolically. Mandalas can facilitate internal meaning-making as processes move up through the layers of consciousness for articulation (see Figure

7.3). Releasing and drawing on creative imagination helped me to have a picture of the overall research framework. In retrospect, I also believe it eventually enabled the ownership of the philosophical tenets to be more deeply embedded in me as a person and not just exist as something lodged in my brain.

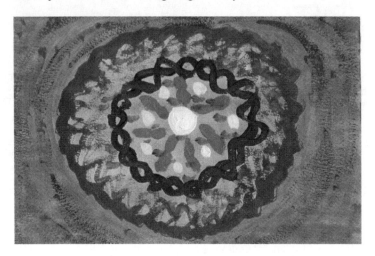

Figure 7.3. My mandala: The sensed conceptual framework

**Unconcealling the essence
(the whiteness) of wandering**

Blue circling sea of values
and beliefs.

Woven red rings
of philosophical ideas,

meshed into waves
of methodological principles.

Footprints of method intermingling,

With discoveries on lived experience.

Finding My Way with Merleau-Ponty

For the philosopher, the many continuities and discontinuities among the various phenomenological schools or movements are a source of primary, lifelong scholarly activity. For researchers such as me, apparent discontinuities can make getting a grasp and establishing a thread of continuity in this challenging field of knowledge messy and uncertain.

Further, for me as a researcher primarily interested in applying a small part of a philosophy into research in the context of my professional practice and my life world, a practical approach was needed. So I set out to find a companion – someone who I could see was already modelling the way in terms of making the philosophy present and vivid in research. This came through the work of Max van Manen (1997, pp. 11–12; p. 16), who conceived of phenomenology as a human science and a profoundly reflective inquiry into human meaning. Van Manen presented a phenomenology of practice, where the phenomenological approach is applied in professional contexts such as nursing, clinical psychology, medicine, education or counselling, and the phenomenological method is used in contexts of the practical concerns of everyday living. Going back and forth between the philosophy texts and the methodological texts of van Manen helped enormously. Again, I underestimated just how long I would need to work on this method. The time needed to learn about a new subject and to be able to adopt a critical stance was extensive. I did learn that another critical activity in making philosophy vibrant in research is to match it with the best suited methodology.

Deepening the Understanding of the Four Tenets

Merleau-Ponty grounded his many ideas in a phenomenology based on perception. Perception is Merleau-Ponty's term for the pre-reflective experience of being-in-the-world. Perception, therefore, is an active process of the body-subject (the person) projecting itself upon its surrounding space and the objects in it. Thus a philosophical analysis of pre-reflective human experience is different from an empirical scientific analysis. The world of perception is not only about searching for meaning but also about ambiguity. That is because the world, already present, is possessed with significance (Matthews, 2002). "The world is not what I think, but what I live through. I am open to the world, I have no doubt that I am in communication with it, but I do not possess it" (Merleau-Ponty, 1989, p. xvii).

Getting anywhere close to "doing this" as a researcher requires constant effort and a high level of commitment to reflection. Our primary relationship with the world as an experiencing body-subject is not a cognitive relationship to a purely objective reality; it is not detached, like the relationship between objects in the world. Because it is not detached we overlay pre-reflective perception with cognition.

Merleau-Ponty (1989, p. 12) summarised it thus: "our relation to the world is not that of a thinker to an object of thought". Thus, for Merleau-Ponty (1962; 1989) the empirical approach means that perception is viewed from the objective standpoint of science, where it is seen as the effect of causal activity of external stimuli on the sense organs, brain and nervous system. The subjective experience of being-perceivers is an embodied active experience. The challenges I encountered were:

– learning how to embody the tenets of the philosophy
– learning how to become aware of the mind-body dualism which I as a Westernised person have culturally and uncritically absorbed
– learning to put to one side sources of evidence, along with all the cognitive overlayers other than the actual experience.

According to Merleau-Ponty, perception starts through awareness and description of phenomena as we actually experience them, before any theorising through rational thought begins:

> I cannot put perception into the same category as the synthesis represented by judgements, acts or predications. We must not, therefore, wonder whether we really perceive a world, we must instead say: the world is what we perceive...
> To seek the essence of perception is to declare that perception is, not presumed true, but defined as access to truth. (Merleau-Ponty, 1962, p. xi)

Thus, when describing wandering I had to aim to describe it as the older persons showed me, not as I have "taught" myself or been taught by others through science and intellectualism. It is precisely this level of subjectivity, rather than objectivity, that makes human experience meaningful. Body-subjects are committed to make meaning, but for others to try and understand their world, to make rational sense of it and to make connections – this can never be fully achieved because of changing perspectives in the four existentials: lived space (spatiality), lived body (corporeality), lived time (temporality), and lived human relations (relationality).

One example of this was to suspend my assumptions that wandering was a behaviour and a meaningless one at that. By doing this I could see how older people with dementia who were wandering were doing it to make sense of their world, which was ever-changing and never fixed. For people with dementia, place and time are very different entities which move and change their form in ways those of us with intact cognition find hard to appreciate.

The bringing to life of this research also involved much descriptive writing and learning to write well-crafted descriptions of experiences. This was essential, as getting close to perception provides access to the truth. At the same time, perception is also complex and multidimensional. Since within any given context or whole there can be uncertainty about parts, human perception is both fluid and ambiguous. When investigating a topic within this approach, researchers need to decide how they will know they know enough for the time being. Accepting that the fundamentals of perception are complex and multi-dimensional opened up many possibilities for non-reductive analysis in research. At another level, it added to my questioning of how I experience the world and had a considerably destabilising effect on my understanding of several things about my experience that I had not previously questioned.

Thus, bringing this philosophy to life was not a depersonalised activity; instead it was to become life-transforming. Working in a deeply connected way with philosophy can bring inspiration to the research and it can bring challenges, even chaos, to the researcher as a person. I had not expected this as an outcome and, looking back, I am not sure I could have been prepared for it. To Merleau-Ponty, the person/body-subject is a creature of significance, constituted by relationships, meanings and memberships (Edwards, 2001). Being-in-the-world and embodiment are fundamentally interdependent, as only a subject that is embodied (i.e. inseparable) can have a place in the world, in space and time. Being-in-the-world is about our whole involvement, sensory, emotional, practical and intellectual.

Again, this reinforces the subjective nature of the research. I resisted the pull to show how I had managed to disconnect in order to achieve some distance or objectivity from my research subject. To keep the rigour of the research I used the concept of radical reflection. This mode of reflection reacts against the notion of putting things to one side, on the grounds that it is not possible to any significant degree. I also argue that the psychological dissociation I see often advocated in phenomenology is not healthy process. Instead, radical reflection supports in-depth reflection. I chose to do this cognitively and with other ways of knowing, including aesthetics, so that a deeper awareness came into existence for me. This enables greater mindfulness to be achieved in the research as senses are highlighted and insightful awareness is enhanced. I also argue that it is this process that is core to the active embodying of knowing, something I now discuss further.

Being Active

From my research I propose that the inspiration in Merleau-Ponty's ideas came about through being active and creative. Our sensory perception is interwoven with praxis and bodily action. Bodily existence is organic, in that it is both actional and oriented (Merleau-Ponty, 1962) and there are intentional threads that run from the body to objects (p. 136). The body-subject is a form-giver, and form comes out of movement and action in the world. Body-subjects are active – they do. Practical knowledge (i.e. how-to-do knowledge) is possessed by the body not just the mind, as the Platonic view holds (Merleau-Ponty, 1962), so that body and mind are one in the generation of meaning and action (Palermo, 1978). Edwards (2001), for example, argues that the performance of complex motor tasks can be seen as an exemplification of bodily knowledge stemming from bodily intentionality (Merleau-Ponty, 1962; Hammond, Howarth, & Keat, 1991).

In regard to my research, once I had grasped the foundations or the form, I committed to carry out different activities that facilitated praxis and bodily action: walking, especially before supervision; taking photographs; going to art exhibitions and galleries; being creative, making things such as sculptures and painting and writing. Thinking alone was not enough. All these bodily activities supported bringing the philosophy of Merleau-Ponty alive and making it meaningful for me. It started to become an extension of me rather than an externally situated check-list to work from. In other words it became embodied. Reflecting back, I could perhaps have taken a greater leap of faith and been less cognitively bound at the beginning, but at that time I hadn't yet appreciated what my scheme of things was.

All body-subjects have a "scheme of things" in the way that the range of choices are realised. Choices are not conscious ones, although they do emerge from pre-reflective intentionality. Merleau-Ponty suggested that there are multiple possibilities that involve an "organic" or dialectical interplay (not merely a coming together) between physiological and psychological factors, either within the body or to others in the world or to the world in general. Raising of individual conceptions to full consciousness and recognising them as "my own" is a result of sustained reflection. If reflection does not raise conceptions, then our perception of the world remains "an intention of our whole being of a pre-objective view which is what we call being-in-the-world" (Merleau-Ponty, 1989, p. 76).

In what I have already written here it should be clear that the four existentials also pervade the notion of perception. For Merleau-Ponty these four existentials belong to the life-world and are thus a fundamental part of all human experience. We are bodily in the world and relate to everything through our bodies and embodied perception. As we are in the world as active perceiving body-subjects we are relating with the world and others and things in it. Lived space and lived time are part of our perception and our experiences in the life-world. I understand that these four existentials can be differentiated to a degree, yet they cannot be separated as ultimately they are one. That they can be differentiated means they can be used to investigate lived experience. In this instance, I made use of the four existentials to investigate the lived experience of wandering.

Thus, I believe I created a fourfold and yet unified perspective on lived experience that also enabled me to present persons with dementia as active creative body-subjects in the world. As these four existentials are fundamentally part of the life-world it made sense to me that they should play a key role in helping me to get as close as I could to the experience of wandering as it is lived rather than as I conceived of it. I was also able to use these existentials to organise and shape the way I presented my data on the essence of wandering as a phenomenon. Through the ancient form of haiku prose, I was able to present data on each of the existentials in relation to the lived experience of wandering.

The overarching challenge for me, of using a theoretical framework embedded in tenets of Merleau-Ponty's phenomenology, was to find a way of grasping the phenomenon of wandering in the context of persons with dementia being-in-the-world as active body-subjects. Applying the four tenets holistically, it follows that persons [with dementia] are embodied body-subjects in the world who are actively involved in creating meaning primarily because they are in the world and through pre-reflective perception. As with all humans, the body, relationality, space and time are all essential to lived experience, describing and interpreting it. As descriptions of phenomena form the building blocks for human science and the basis for all knowledge development, they must themselves be explored and investigated in rigorous ways.

From this, therefore, phenomenology was a helpful and revealing tradition in which to locate my research. It required me as the third person, with an external point of view embedded in causal scientific thinking, to abandon scientific notions as far as possible, and to commit to understanding wandering from the inside, as the body-subjects see it and as an expression of their being-in-the-world (Merleau-Ponty, 1989). This does not dismiss the contribution of explanatory science, but was for me to embody the research process, acknowledging that genuine description precedes explanation. It began with my belief that describing wandering as experienced by older persons with dementia was possible. However, being able to grasp and thus embody the method to achieve an expanded understanding of wandering from the person with dementia's perspective was a significant challenge.

Concluding Remarks

> There is absolute certainty of the world in general, but not of any one thing in particular. (Merleau-Ponty, 1962, p. 42)

In this chapter I have set out part of my journey in relation to building and embodying a philosophical framework – which required a leap of faith. Although evolving such a structural framework was core to the research, more fundamental was the process of re-learning to look at the world and breaking free or un-learning the tendency to view everything objectivity through science. Merleau-Ponty (1989) suggested that philosophy is about the perpetual beginner relearning to look at the world. I emerged with a "new way'" for me to investigate wandering, based on four philosophical tenets: the primacy of perception, being-in-the-world, embodiment, and four existentials. More vitally, this new way was to provide a way of picturing and accounting for wandering that felt real and offered a positive and hopeful perspective of being a person or body-subject with dementia in the world.

Accounts of being a body-subject in the world are attempts to make sense of experience from one point of view, and to give rise to truthful descriptions about body-subjects' experience, but are at the same time set against a reality where truth is not fixed, is inexhaustible and never to be fully comprehended. From my explorations it is clear to me that reading about phenomenology and doing phenomenological research, although related, are very different activities. It also strikes me that one can draw on and use Merleau-Ponty's and probably other philosophical tenets as tools, or one can go further and embody them in some way. It is through this latter experience that philosophy can become inspirational in both practical and existential ways.

REFERENCES

Boye, K. (1924). New ways. In *Karin Boye: Complete Poems* (Trans. D. McDuff, 2005). Available: http://www.karinboye.se/verk/dikter/dikter-en-mcduff-hiddenlands.shtml, accessed 13 June 2011.

Crotty, M. (1996). *Phenomenology and nursing research*. Edinburgh: Churchill Livingstone.

Dowling, M. (2005). From Husserl to van Manen. A review of different phenomenological approaches. *International Journal of Nursing Studies, 44*, 131–142.

Edwards, S.D. (2001). *Philosophy of nursing: An introduction*. Basingstoke: Palgrave.

Hammond, M., Howarth, J., & Keat, R. (1991). *Understanding phenomenology*. Oxford: Blackwell.

Matthews, E.H. (2002). *The philosophy of Merleau-Ponty*. Chesham: Acumen.

Merleau-Ponty, M. (1962). *The phenomenology of perception* (C. Smith, Trans.). London: Routledge and Kegan Paul.

Merleau-Ponty, M. (1965). *The structure of behaviour* (A.L. Fisher, Trans.). London: Methuen.

Merleau-Ponty, M. (1989). *Phenomenology of perception* (Trans. C. Smith, rev. F. Williams & D. Gurriere). London: Routledge.

Palermo, J. (1978). Merleau-Ponty and Dewey on the 'Mind-Body' Question. *Philosophy of Education*: Proceedings 34: 462–69.

van Manen, M. (1984). *Doing phenomenological research and writing; An introduction*. Monograph no 7, University of Alberta, Available: http://www.uofaweb.ualberta.ca/secondaryed/pdfs/Monograph%20No.%207-van%20Manen.pdf accessed 13 June 2011.

van Manen, M. (1997). *Researching lived experience: Human science for an action sensitive pedagogy* (2nd ed.). London, ONT: Althouse Press.

Jan Dewing PhD, MN, BSc, RN, RNT, Dip Nurs Ed, Dip Nurs
Professor of Person-Centred Research and Practice Development
Nursing and Applied Clinical Sciences
East Sussex Healthcare NHS Trust
Canterbury Christ Church University, Kent, England

ANNA PARK LALA AND ELIZABETH ANNE KINSELLA

8. EMBODIMENT IN RESEARCH PRACTICES

The Body in Qualitative Research

The purpose of this chapter is to inquire into how attention to embodiment can enhance qualitative research practices. The chapter begins with an overview of the notion of embodiment from a phenomenological perspective. This is followed by an examination of three dimensions of embodiment – the body as a path to access the world, the body's skilled intelligence, and the body's intercorporeality – and a consideration of the implications for research practices. The chapter draws on examples from the literature, and from Anna's doctoral research, "the End-of-Life study" (Park Lala & Kinsella, in press a,b), a phenomenological study that investigates what people do (occupations) at end-of-life. The chapter concludes by proposing that attention to embodiment in research practices encourages new perspectives that illuminate the role of the body as a medium for lived meanings, and through which we may begin to better understand the phenomenon at hand.

EMBODIMENT IN RESEARCH PRACTICES

The notion of embodiment has largely been neglected in scholarly investigations until recently (Johnson, 1999). Embodiment draws attention to the body as a means of "perceptual experience and mode of presence and engagement in the world" (Csordas, 1994, p. 12). Ellingson (2006) has argued that the absence of the body as a means of perceiving the world in qualitative social science research "obscures the complexities of knowledge production and yields deceptively tidy accounts of research" (p. 299). Similarly, Benner (2000) points out that neglecting our bodies as vehicles for lived and worldly meanings results in research that is "silent" about human experience. In the last decade, attention to embodiment has received increased attention in philosophy (Campbell, Meynell, & Sherwin, 2009), science (Gallagher, 2005) and social science (Johnson, 1999). Research that focuses on embodiment has also garnered growing attention in qualitative research practice; indeed, some scholars have suggested the need to re-embody qualitative inquiry (Sandelowski, 2002; Sharma, Reimer-Kirkham, & Cochrane, 2009).

A Phenomenological, Embodied Perspective

Phenomenology is the art and science of examining phenomena from the perspective of people's firsthand accounts (van Manen, 1997). Taking a phenomenological perspective involves setting aside culturally ascribed

J. Higgs et al., (eds.), Creative Spaces for
Qualitative Researching: Living Research, 77–86

assumptions and examining phenomena as lived and directly experienced (Husserl, 1907/1990; Heidegger, 1927/2008). In the phenomenological tradition, the lived body is considered a fundamental and grounding dimension of human existence, what some phenomenologists refer to as a "lived existential" (other existentials include lived time, lived space and lived relations) (van Manen, 1997). French philosopher and phenomenologist Merleau-Ponty (1945/2006) has been particularly influential in illuminating the primacy of the body in human perception. Merleau-Ponty contends that day-to-day experiences cannot be fully encompassed through a conception of human beings as "thinking things". Rather he argues that the body is the absolute source; we do not *have* bodies, we *are* our bodies. From this perspective, human beings are not spectators, but are rather involved, interwoven, and *living* in the world as embodied beings. In other words, the lived body is viewed as a means through which the world and our lived experiences come to be (Carman, 2008).

The Lived Body as a Path of Access to the World

An embodied perspective begins with the assumption that our bodies are mediums through which we experience the world. Leder (1990) described the lived body as "first and foremost not a located thing but a path of access, a being-in-the-world" (p. 21). Rather than conceiving of the body as a static and lifeless entity, this perspective recognises the body as always present in a state of bodily being-in-the-world, as a means of perception itself (Merleau-Ponty, 1945/2006).

Viewing the body as a path of access to the world, as a mode of being-in-the-world, brings new conceptual lenses to research practices. Such a perspective challenges the assumptions of a separate body ruled by the mind (inherent in Descartes' (1641/1996) famous dictum "I think therefore I am"). Some argue that Cartesian perspectives view the body as a passive, machine-like appendage, directed by consciousness and the mind (Ryle, 1949), rather than as an entity richly implicated in perception itself (Merleau-Ponty, 1945/2006). Merleau-Ponty (1945/2006, p. 445) points out that our active engagement in the world, our *performance* as opposed to only our *thoughts*, is what brings existence to light:

> Hence it is not because I think I am that I am certain of my existence: on the contrary the certainty I enjoy concerning my thoughts stems from their genuine existence. My love, hatred and will are not certain as mere thoughts about living, hating and willing: on the contrary the whole certainty of these thoughts is owed to that of the acts of love, hatred or will of which I am quite sure because I perform them.

Our bodies, in this view, are not structures of "I think" but rather structures of "I can" (Merleau-Ponty 1945/2006). The lived body as a path of access to inquiries about the world can readily be overlooked because the everyday body is typically recessive and invisible (Leder, 1990). Attention to embodiment reveals that while the primacy of the body is evident upon examination, its presence in day-to-day life is frequently concealed. Van Manen (1998, p. 11) described the body's mode of being as "near self-forgetfulness"; we tend not to notice our bodies in our everyday affairs, such as when we drive, wash the dishes, or go for a run. In fact, he wrote, a healthy body "thrives on the smoothness of forgetfulness" (p. 13).

In the End-of-Life study, an embodied perspective was brought to the design of research questions and to the research lens. This contributed to data being collected that would probably not otherwise have come to light. For example, one participant in the research, PJ, described an awareness of his body's centrality to his existence through a coughing episode that could potentially end his life:

> You're focused very, very much on that [life-threatening coughing] happening and your whole body is a part of it. And I know the end result will be that somehow I'll collapse and I'll be gone. And I trust I'll be gone with the Lord. 'Cuz Paul said, "To be absent from the body is to be present with the Lord" ... And yet there's a real desperation, a quiet desperation to do what you have to do to get things going again ... And then it comes back slowly, the breathing possibility. It's something, when you're plugged here in the earth.

PJ's words speak of a world that appears to be unknowable and unliveable without the body; it is through the body that we are "plugged in to the earth", to be separate from the body is to be gone from the world. The body and its capacities render lived possibilities, and attention to the body reveals the impossibility of conceiving of existence without a bodily channel. Moreover, these findings highlight how the lived body as a path of access to perception of the world may become increasingly visible when the smoothness of our bodily access to the world is disrupted.

This example demonstrates how attending to embodiment in our research designs can illuminate embodied dimensions in the participants' responses and can offer a more in-depth perspective on their lived experiences. In the End of Life study, the significance of the body as a path of access to the world appeared to be amplified when taken-for-granted bodily access to the world was challenged, suggesting that the body's role in perception (as distinct from simply the mind) is often revealed in times when its path of access to the world is disrupted.

One important implication regarding the body as a path of access to perception in research is the situation where participants express feelings of separation from the body. According to Leder (1990), becoming conscious of the body and, at times, feeling disembodied is an important dimension of embodiment. He pointed out that even the mind as a "thinking thing" that is associated with the brain is not how consciousness is actually experienced. Instead, we do not feel or see our consciousness originating or emanating from our brains, rather "human mentality can ... seem immaterial, disembodied ... this disappearance arises precisely from the embodied nature of mind. The body's own structure leads to its self-concealment" (p. 115). Although there are experiences that can elicit feelings of separation from our bodies, or where we may seek to dissociate from our bodies, we are fundamentally embodied beings (Leder, 1990). Taking seriously the notion that the body is a path of access to the world, a mode of perception, can contribute to increasingly rich understandings of human perception, and can have important implications for research design and practice.

Bodily Intelligence

Attending to embodiment in the research process also draws attention to the body's skilled intelligence in the world. According to Merleau-Ponty (1945/2006), intelligence is not limited solely to the mind but is also tied to the body: "our body is not an object for an "I think", it is a grouping of lived-through meanings which moves towards its equilibrium" (p. 177). Three interrelated concepts from Merleau-Ponty contribute to understanding the body's skilled intelligence in the world. *Bodily schema* refers to the body's skilled intelligence, its dynamic ability to know and engage the world, and to retain and develop skills over time: "my body is the fabric into which all objects are woven, and it is, at least in relation to the perceived world, the general instrument of my 'comprehension'" (Merleau-Ponty, 1945/2006, p. 273). *Meilleure prise*, translated as maximal or best grip on the world, refers to the body's preference to be in an optimal bodily state; for example, "for each object, as for each picture in an art gallery, there is an optimum distance from which it requires to be seen ... we therefore tend towards the maximum of visibility, and seek a better focus as with a microscope" (p. 352). *Motor intentionality* involves the body tacitly adjusting to maintain a best grip on the world (Merleau-Ponty, 1945/2006). This involves attending to a felt sense of rightness and wrongness through tacit, directed and self-adjusting skill to seek a state of bodily equilibrium (Carman, 2008). These three phenomenological concepts help us to better understand how we live through skilful and knowing bodies without actively *thinking* about how we do it.

The body's skilful intelligence may be overlooked in research because of the way the body reveals perceptual experience. Our bodily-being-in-the-world provides a unified experience; in other words, "we do not perceive the world in pieces or meaningless sensations but as a whole pregiven, prereflexive world" (Benner, 2000, p. 6). The body tacitly and selectively chooses what perceptual material is important to bring to attention, which allows us to go about our daily affairs without noticing or attending to our bodies. Bodily intelligence may also be overlooked because many bodily skills can be difficult to identify as they are hidden beneath our everyday activities and intentions.

An example of the body's skilful intelligence is portrayed in the findings of an ethnographic study of miners (Somerville, 2006). The findings describe the body's skilful intelligence in the context of safety while working in a mine:

> Miners initially learned safety from experienced workers in the mine, but over time they learnt from their own experience. They described the most important aspect of their embodied learning of safety as "pit sense," learned by the experiencing body in interaction with the physical and social environments of the mining work/place. In pit sense all the senses are employed in a complex interconnected way to provide information about whether the body-in-place is safe. This includes sound, smell, touch, and kinaesthetic sense as well as other senses that have no name such as a sense of the heaviness of the air, the particular feeling of the air on the hairs of the

legs or the backs of the ears, as well as an uncanny sense of just being uncomfortable. (p. 43)

Here, Somerville's participants described their bodily intelligence, ways of knowing that were felt and experienced through the body. Using Merleau-Ponty's concepts, bodily intelligence can be seen through the bodily skills in the workplace that the workers developed over time (bodily schema), how they learned to "know" and attentively engage in safe mining practices (*meilleure prise*), and how they skilfully attended and adjusted to their bodily cues of right and wrongness (motor intentionality). It is interesting to note that many bodily cues seem to have no name (i.e. the heaviness of the air).

According to Todres (2007), knowledge, felt in the body, is "the primary source of knowing" (p. 33) that exists before symbolisation and language. Todres (2008) proposed attention in research practices to "embodied interpretation" as a means to examine bodily ways of knowing. Embodied interpretation attempts to focus on what words cannot say, and on the junction and meanings that emerge between words and bodily felt sense. For example, the words of a participant can elicit cognitive understandings, but also an embodied, felt response that reveals a "lived sense" of the informant's account (Todres, 2007).

Researchers' bodily intelligence – embodied responses that contribute to deeper interpretations of phenomena – may also contribute to research practices. They might not be considered or shared in textual research findings, although such responses can harbour important information about the findings themselves. As Sandelowski (2002) suggested, one concern about qualitative research is that interviews and textual accounts are hailed as the gold standard. What is said by participants is often taken at face value, yet, she cautions, "people use interviews strategically to present, account for, and even justify themselves and their actions" (p. 106).

As an example of the significance of the researcher's embodied intelligence, a situation arose in the End of Life study when the account of a participant was incongruent with what the researcher observed and "felt" in an embodied way. One participant shared multiple anecdotes throughout the interview process about engaging in "hug therapy" with many women in his community. He said:

The nurses, they have a blood pressure clinic every Tuesday. They come up and the lady there she says, 'You know … I thought you were spoiled before, but now I know it." She said, "This is the first time, at any clinic that I've been at, [where] as the patient comes in the nurses line up to hug him."

This anecdote led to a "face value" interpretation of his relationship with these health care workers in his community as friendly and mutually shared. Later, the first author was present at a blood pressure clinic when the participant reached out to hug a nurse; she nearly pushed him away, firmly stating "No, no". Although the nurse explained that due to the flu epidemic scare and the spread of germs, she was unable to hug or shake hands with her patients, this incident was unexpected and elicited surprise on the part of the researcher. Upon reflection, it was not simply the rejected hug, but the lack of warmth in the nurse's demeanour and the distance she projected towards the participant (which did not reflect the friendly and loving relationships he had described) that elicited an embodied response:

> I perceived something beyond words by being present to my experiencing body within the physical and social research environment, and by attending to the tension between what my body was telling me and the verbal account rendered by the participant. It would be difficult to depict the tension in the room if one simply read an encounter transcript. (Anna's reflective notes)

While there is little doubt as to the sincerity of the participant and this account, this example reveals how what is being said can never reflect the entirety of a phenomenon; our bodies also act as witness. Attention to the bodily intelligence of participants and of researchers potentially contributes to deeper embodied interpretations of what is occurring in the research context.

Intercorporeality

Another dimension with relevance to embodiment in research is intercorporeality. Weiss (1998) stated that "to describe embodiment as intercorporeality is to emphasize that the experience of being embodied is never a private affair, but is always already mediated by our continual interactions with other human and nonhuman beings" (p. 5). Our interactions with others, our lived relations, are an important dimension of how we experience our everyday lives (van Manen, 1997). From a phenomenological perspective, intercorporeality highlights the space between individuals, but also the *experience* of being with the "other". In other words, being with an "other" may be seen as an immediate, fully engaging, and unreflected experience (Pollio, Henley, & Thompson, 1997). Csordas (2008) drew on Ricœur (1991) to show how intercorporeality influences embodied perception "I understand myself on the basis of thoughts, feelings, and actions deciphered directly in the experience of others" (Csordas, p. 112). In terms of research, intercorporeality can be considered by examining the embodied response in the space between the researcher and the participant.

The way we are with the "other" is a bodily affair, which becomes manifest in our everyday, intentional ways of being, such as through the stern look a parent gives a child or an intimate kiss between lovers. Van Manen (1997) wrote that we form expectations about who people are based on our embodied responses (e.g. a voice on the phone) even before meeting (consider the disappointment felt when the character in a novel-based film is not as you had imagined). The mutuality of our embodied subjectivity does not turn off in a research context (Burns, 2003).

Drawing on examples from the End of Life study, intercorporeality is examined from the perspectives of the researcher's body in relation to participants. The impact of inter-subjective, embodied interactions became evident in Anna's reflexive writings. First, the researcher's body in interaction with the bodies of participants can contribute to research processes and accounts:

> Participants often asked about my situation and placed assumptions about the kind of person I was based on, for example, my age (28) and ethnicity

(Korean). My age impacted my relationship with my participants (all older than 60 years). Some participants alluded to my age in subtle and implicit ways. For instance, Cali shared an anecdote where she struggled to remember an actress she had seen perform in the 1950s. "You've probably never even heard of her," she pointedly said to me. Cali later became emotional about the loss she was experiencing as friends from her generation were predeceasing her ... I noticed that her account stirred feelings of inadequacy and sadness in myself. The corporeality of my young age meant that I could never connect with Cali in the way that she longed for. (Anna's reflective notes)

From a research perspective, this same corporeality contributed to the quality and depth of what could be understood about Cali's experience at end-of-life. For instance, the loss of friendships that can occur as friends predecease a person and the emotions of sadness and loneliness that can ensue were enhanced by the intercorporeality (the age difference) fostered within this exchange.

Ethnic background can also be part of the intercorporeality of the research process. Anna noticed that her ethnicity could not be silenced in her interviews. In one instance (see below), the researcher's ethnic background led the participant to speak with caution, whereas for another participant, ethnicity was tied to his interpretation of the motivations of the researcher in undertaking research with people at end-of-life. These accounts suggest that the embodied presence of the researcher can influence what stories participants share and their way of engaging with the researcher. They also reveal how some participants might have pre-conceived notions about who the researcher is in light of his or her corporeal (embodied) presence, including characteristics such as ethnic background. Assumptions can be formed implicitly from the researcher's corporeal presence, before words are spoken.

In one instance, the participant appeared to be concerned not to offend me when she drew on my ethnicity as a starting point for an anecdote. The participant asked me if I was Chinese. I said no, that I was Korean and she said, "Oh okay, then this story won't offend you." Then she conveyed a story about her son and his friend, Charles, who was Chinese. It wasn't an offensive story so I was kind of surprised. I was expecting something that she might have interpreted as offensive. (Anna's reflective notes)

Intercorporeality can also be considered by examining the embodied response to the presence of the researcher in participants' homes:

Something that surprised me was the participants' openness about their involvement in the study. While I had indicated that their involvement in this study would be confidential on my part, several participants openly introduced me to neighbours and health care practitioners who unexpectedly stopped by. For one participant, it appeared that her friends even knew me by name. When I came in for the interview, she [Julia] was on the phone and before she got off, she said, "I have to go because Anna's here." So she's obviously told people about being involved in my study enough that she can refer to me in first person. ... It became evident to me that I became somebody in her life ... I also became an embodied being to people in her life, and I wondered how they pictured me, and how I had been described. (Anna's reflective notes)

Finally, through interactions with participants, researchers can gain a sense of bodily awareness as they became attentive to the changes in personal, embodied responses to different participants:

I find it interesting thinking about how I am, how I react to her versus [another male participant]. When I'm with him, I find that I have to force myself to laugh a lot and to nod a lot and to joke around a bit because I feel that's what he wants ... so I feel like I have to give him that. Whereas with her, you know I just sit and nod and I'm quite quiet ... I'm noticing quite a difference between how I am, and that's a bit of a surprise to me ... I find myself acting, kind of responding and orienting myself differently given the participant. They all just come from completely different worlds. (Anna's reflective notes)

These reflections highlight the intercorporeal nature of the research process, and offer insights into the difficulties researchers may face when actively trying to adopt the stance of a disembodied, neutral researcher. Furthermore, they suggest that perhaps researchers need to reflexively acknowledge the intercorporeality of the research process, and the implications of their embodied presence in the research sites and the relationships they inhabit. There are elements of who the researcher is that cannot be silenced (age, race, gender), and one may question whether it is ever possible to replicate a fixed version of who one is with each participant. Indeed, would the attempt to do so spoil the process of connecting with each participant and gaining rapport? As Burns (2003) contended, researchers are truly participants in the research, an "other" entering the participants' lives and shaping what emerges as the research unfolds. The intercorporeal dimension of embodiment is revealed within the researcher and within the participant, within the space between them, and through the interactions between their lived bodies.

CONCLUSION

In this chapter we have proposed three dimensions of embodiment from a phenomenological perspective and considered the implications for embodied research practices. First, we argued that an embodied perspective can be seen as recognising the body as a path of access, a medium through which the world comes to be (Merleau-Ponty, 1945/2006). From such a perspective, our experience of the world cannot be imagined without a body (Leder, 1990). Second, we highlighted how the body may be seen as entailing a skilful, embodied intelligence that is often overlooked in research practices. Our bodily intelligence contributes to a "felt" knowledge that exists even before symbolisation and language (van Manen, 1997; Todres, 2007). Lastly, we proposed that embodied research recognises that embodiment does not occur in a vacuum but rather through intercorporeality, that is, our embodied, relational interactions (Weiss, 1998; Csordas, 2008). The intercorporeality of the researcher's body can elicit pre-formed understandings, assumptions and responses from participants. The researcher's body may adopt an embodied presence in the research context, and reveal its own embodied responses.

This chapter illustrates that there is more to our bodily way of being than we can often articulate, and that this has important implications for research practices. The body is not a passive, machine-like appendage, but rather the "nexus of lived meanings" (Merleau-Ponty, 1945/2006, p. 175). As Frank (2002) eloquently explained, "what happens to my body happens to my life" (p. 13).

Attention to embodiment in research practices encourages new perspectives that honour findings beyond the text. We are not suggesting that textual accounts are not of merit, but that a large part of lived experience is overlooked when understandings and interpretations are drawn from textual accounts alone. By witnessing our participants' and our own embodied engagement and responses in research we may begin to better understand the phenomenon at hand and how our bodies serve as a means of perception itself. When entering a research setting, we and our participants cannot rid or shed what we bring: our bodily-being-in-the-world. In closing, we echo Todres (2008) who suggested that through embodied research practices, we may begin to elicit understandings that ring true in both the head and the heart.

REFERENCES

Benner, P. (2000). The roles of embodiment, emotion and lifeworld for rationality and agency in nursing practice. *Nursing Philosophy, 1*, 5–19.

Burns, M. (2003). Interviewing: Embodied communication. *Feminism & Psychology, 13*(2), 229–236.

Campbell, S., Meynell, L., & Sherwin, S. (Eds.) (2009). *Embodiment and agency*. University Park, PA: The Pennsylvania State University Press.

Carman, T. (2008). *Merleau-Ponty*. New York: Routledge.

Csordas, T.J. (2008). Intersubjectivity and intercorporeality. *Subjectivity, 22*, 110–121.

Csordas, T.J. (Ed.) (1994). *Embodiment and experience: The existential ground of culture and self*. Cambridge, UK: Cambridge University Press.

Descartes, R. (1996). *Meditations on first philosophy* (J. Cottingham, Trans.). New York: Cambridge University Press. (Original work published 1641).

Ellingson, L.L. (2006). Embodied knowledge: Writing researchers' bodies into qualitative health research. *Qualitative Health Research, 16*(2), 298–310.

Frank, A. (2002). *At the will of the body: Reflections on illness*. New York: Mariner Books.

Gallagher, S. (2005). *How the body shapes the mind*. Oxford: Clarendon Press.

Heidegger, M. (2008). *Being and time*. New York: Harper & Row. (Original work published 1927).

Husserl, E. (1990). *The idea of phenomenology* (W.P. Alston & G. Nakhnikian, Trans.). Norwell, MA: Kluwer Academic. (Original lectures presented 1907).

Johnson, M. (1999). Embodied reason. In G. Weiss & H.F. Haber (Eds.), *Perspectives on embodiment: The intersections of nature and culture* (pp. 81–102). New York: Routledge.

Leder, D. (1990). *The absent body*. Chicago: University of Chicago Press.

Merleau-Ponty, M. (2006). *Phenomenology of perception*. New York: Routledge. (Original work published 1945).

Park Lala, A. & Kinsella, E.A. (in press a). The embodied nature of occupation at end-of-life. *Canadian Journal of Occupational Therapy, 78*(4).

Park Lala, A. & Kinsella, E.A. (in press b). Phenomenology and the study of human occupation. *Journal of Occupational Science, 18.*

Pollio, H.R., Henley, T., & Thompson, C.B. (1997). *The phenomenology of everyday life.* Cambridge: Cambridge University Press.

Ricœur, P. (1991). *From text to action: Essays in hermeneutics II.* (K. Blamey & J.B. Thompson, Trans.). Evanston, IL: Northwestern University Press.

Ryle, G. (1949). *The concept of mind.* Chicago: University of Chicago Press.

Sandelowski, M. (2002). Reembodying qualitative inquiry. *Qualitative Health Research, 12*(1), 104–115.

Sharma, S., Reimer-Kirkham, S., & Cochrane, M. (2009). Practicing the awareness of embodiment in qualitative health research: Methodological reflections. *Qualitative Health Research, 19*(11), 1642–1650.

Somerville, M. (2006). Subjected bodies, or embodied subjects: Subjectivity and learning safety at work. In S. Billett, T. Fenwick & M. Somerville (Eds.), *Work, subjectivity and learning: Understanding learning through working life* (pp. 37–52). Dordrecht, The Netherlands: Springer.

Todres, L. (2007). *Embodied enquiry: Phenomenological touchstones for research, psychotherapy and spirituality.* New York: Palgrave Macmillan.

Todres, L. (2008). Being with that: The relevance of embodied understanding for practice. *Qualitative Health Research, 18*(11), 1566–1573.

van Manen, M. (1997). *Researching lived experience: Human science for an action sensitive pedagogy.* London, ON: Althouse Press.

van Manen, M. (1998). Modalities of body experience in illness and health. *Qualitative Health Research, 18*(1), 7–24.

Weiss, G. (1998). *Body images: Embodiment as intercorporeality.* New York: Routledge.

Anna Park Lala MSc(OT), PhD Candidate
Occupational Science Field
Health & Rehabilitation Sciences
University of Western Ontario, Canada

Elizabeth Anne Kinsella PhD
School of Occupational Therapy & Occupational Science Field
Faculty of Health Sciences
University of Western Ontario, Canada

PAUL MCINTOSH

9. CREATIVE AND VISUAL METHODS TO FACILITATE REFLECTION AND LEARNING THROUGH RESEARCH

This chapter explores the experiences both of developing methods for creative research and of the process of doing the research itself – in particular its direct impact on me as a person. In educational life, research approaches such as ethnography or symbolic interactionist studies might uncover some unseen or unconsidered aspects of education, but as Bogdan and Biklen (2009) explained, they might not be perceived as contributing to the "science" of teaching, and are of limited use. When we come to use the creative arts for educational use and inquiry we are immediately confronted by the issues of interpretation and individual perception. It is essential that any inquiry that uses these approaches is grounded in methodologies that can produce a reliable and valid outcome to its undertaking. In this chapter I hope to contribute to ways in which methods can be developed in this field that are both creatively rich and theoretically grounded.

SOME INITIAL MUSINGS

When invited to contribute this chapter I was forced to think about how I might present it. Though it is essentially about doing research, it is also about the experience of doing that research and my own philosophical and conceptual stance on its doing. The aim of all of my work so far has been for professionals to become reflexive through creative processes that facilitate reflection and learning. How I present what I have experienced in a creative and reflexive way is a crucial question. As a backdrop to this, you need to know that my reading and learning have crossed a number of theoretical, conceptual, and disciplinary boundaries; and central to all of this has been the application of the creative arts and humanities as a tool for critical engagement in both external and internal worlds.

Doing the Research

My research didn't start at the beginning of a project, a doctorate, or a piece of teaching: it started many years before that, because I have come to think of it as part of a life trajectory. I went to Art School to pursue a career as a fine artist. Later I realised that this was not the life for me, so I trained as a nurse, and later

J. Higgs et al., (eds.), Creative Spaces for
Qualitative Researching: Living Research, 87-96

still I became a university lecturer. My feeling for the arts did not ever leave me, and by my own admission I was no clinician. Technical nursing skills left me cold.

In 2003 I was asked to develop a module on reflection for a postgraduate program for lecturers and practice educators in the health professions. When asked about this I had some pretty firm ideas about what I didn't want it to be, i.e., trotting out the same old jaded work on reflective models, but very few about what I did. Then I spent a week on the Isle of Mull of the Scottish West Coast. It was while sitting on a rock on the beach at the Iona ferry that I began to imagine reflective practice as a landscape; something that could be presented through imagery, sculpture, literature, and any other form of media. The module "Reflexivity in Professional Practice" came out of these deliberations: a module that focused on the development of awareness of skills for reflection through the use of creative arts and humanities. In essence the work for the module is accomplished by the development of a "creative portfolio" as a formative assignment, and it is summatively assessed through a critical discussion on the experience of reflecting through its creation. Initially I could not see beyond its potential uses for teaching and learning in the classroom. The application of this method as a teaching technology was blocking my vision of it as potential for an approach to action research and as an approach to support the concept of being a "practitioner researcher" (Fish, 1998).

Reality and Culture Shock

Spaces of professionalism, social structures, ways of learning and appreciating and individual perception are some of the conditions in which learning occurs. Bourdieu and Wacquant (1992) wrote of the concept of *habitus* as being the negotiable connection between social structures which are objective and the acts of individuals as a result of certain dispositions. Painter (2004), drawing on Bourdieu's ideas, suggested that these dispositions are acquired through a certain set of social conditions and are unavoidable. These unique dispositions are then played out within social structures and can be loosely described as the similarities and differences between others. Indeed, Painter (2004, p. 243) wrote:

> Structured dispositions are also durable: they are ingrained in the body in such a way that they endure through the life-history of the individual, operating in a way that is pre-conscious and hence not readily amenable to conscious reflection and modification.

Bourdieu and Wacquant (1992) suggested that because of such embodiments it is possible for distortions and prejudices to be apparent in any form of inquiry. When healthcare practitioners, in this case skilled and senior professionals in the role of learners, are confronted with forms of learning outside their own forms of professional and personal habitus, they can enter a new and uncomfortable place: the thinking space has changed form. It is no longer in this case about the application of theory or science in the helping professions, it is about how they uncover their personal habitus. Using the creative arts pushes this discomfort further, for how can drawing a picture or listening to a poem further professional knowing? Tuan (2003) noted that at first, spaces are uncomfortable but over time form a kind of neighbourhood, a place, as they acquire definition and meaning. Spaces, he suggested, are more divisional – think of architectural spaces which serve to carve up areas of physical space – but can also be divided intimately through experiences relating to our innermost being. It is our ability to make these intimate spaces accessible that interests Tuan, and the partitions that are created as part of this process. In relation to the work described above, it is perhaps useful to describe the learner's initial feelings towards the module through Tuan's words (2003, p. 36):

> The human being, by his mere presence, imposes a schema on space. Most of the time he is not aware of it. He notes its absence when he is lost.

When the rug is pulled from you, in this case in relation to all that you understand professionally and all that you have experienced educationally, then you are lost. Whereas some participants have embraced this new and different place, others have experienced profound discomfort and disorientation. In retrospect, this has produced many forms of symbolic space, some of which are illustrated later. It is also fair to say that my own experience was similar, for I had mapped out a path with certain expectations and visions. When the learning experiences of the participants deviated from my path I too was lost for a while before regaining a sense of direction. Referring once again to Tuan (2003, p. 36):

> The flickering light has established a goal. As I move towards that goal, front and back, right and left, have resumed their meaning.

What helped me to see this direction was a realisation of this process of learning as a form of action research methodology. The beauty of action research as an approach to human inquiry lies in its diversity of methodological possibilities while it maintains at its core the ethic of reflection (Reason & Bradbury, 2008).

Being Creative with Action Research

I now provide in a "live" example of how this process has worked in practice. Taken from my own work (McIntosh, 2010) it provides an apt illustration of the kind of transformation that is possible:

> This module is so stupid. I feel so bloody cross that I have got to do this.

> I just don't think I can – I don't understand it and I know that I can't write poetry or draw. I am the most uncreative person in the world – I can't do that stuff – draw, sing, play music, knit, sew, cook, anything like that.

> Even other people tell me I'm uncreative – in fact my uncreativity is a renowned joke. What is making me mad is creative people telling me that I am creative – like it's an untapped talent and they know me better than I know myself. I have collected pictures and words expressing how stupid this assignment is. I don't want to do it and I don't think I can do it.

My Working Day

The colours reflect my day:
First thing in the morning there is peace and calm (white)
As the morning progresses, the nausea
intensifies as my son becomes more anxious (green)
The blackness starts as we leave home &
the anxiety takes hold.
The black continues during the working
day, with a few bright spots as the day draws to a close.
The yellow is blissful, reunited.
The pink is fun & laughter.
Then the black starts again at bedtime as he fears he
won't live to see the morning.

Figure 9.1. Expressing resistance through paradox

Figure 9.2. A landscape of my working day

A more in-depth analysis is available in McIntosh (2010, pp. 132–133), but for the moment I wish to explore this from the perspective of a collision of habitus and learning with an uncovering of latent and unknown consciousness through the use of creativity as an approach to action research. Figures 9.1 and 9.2 are produced by the same author. They are texts that are rich in their various ways, but underpinning both is the realisation of transformation. It is for me a symbol of a defining moment as an educator and an action researcher. It may not be a work of "quality", but it is certainly a work that articulates qualities and that is its purpose. In relation to this point, Eisner (2008, p. 24) discussed the difference between arts-based research which is "original", "creative", and "novel". For Eisner, both the approach and the outcome must have utility, for there is little use if they are only aesthetic. Aesthetics is important, but must not be the only consideration, because the danger is that the work becomes "novel" yet insubstantial. The distinction that Eisner (2008) has suggested is concerned with the notion of novelty value, and work which provides only this will quickly lead to a loss of interest and regard among colleagues – the gatekeepers as to what is considered valid and creative (Czikszenkmihalyi, 1997).

From my experience of analysing such texts as above and my exposure to Eisner's thinking, I believe that we should be aiming for a balance between aesthetics and substance, whether researching or teaching. In the two figures above we see the emergence of qualities of which the participant was unaware or which the participant was unwilling to accept as observations from others. The second example (Figure 9.3) provides us with a different form of habitus. This image comes from a series, each accompanied by a narrative which was then developed as part of the summative critical commentary:

When anger or despair dominates reason, the Child is in control, at this time my internal reactions to an external event were making it impossible to make any rational plan to resolve the issue. I remained within this frame for over 10 years. ... I realised that my Child and Parent Ego state continued to greatly affect my ability to explore beyond familiar social and working class boundaries. I retained beliefs that my position in society was one of subservience. (McIntosh, 2010, pp. 126–127)

Figure 9.3. The opening frame

In using the creative process and by applying what is experienced to a field of theory, in this case transactional analysis, the participant was able to consider new insights into her own status and sense of self. There is a realisation of dispositions acquired through cultural exposure and upbringing, at both personal and professional levels. For many years she had been struggling to raise an important issue regarding a fundamental skill and equipment deficit at her place of work. With a change of line-management, and invested with responsibilities to audit this issue, she became liberated professionally and personally to make change occur. As a result she is more able to achieve that which was previously a source of frustration. At a personal level, her experiences and words had resonance with my own life experiences and subsequent dispositions; those of coming from a working-class background, which create a feeling of status and place, accompanied by self-boundarying as a form of action.

Reaching a Crossroad

Entering such a process of reflection creates at least two pathways that can be taken. The first is that of the practitioner-researcher, whereby such uses of creativity can be developed to support personal reflection and learning. When one engages in an act of writing, drawing, or sculpting as examples, the act itself allows space for a critical dialogue with self. It opens up fields of cognition, emotion, certainty and uncertainty, and realisation, which in turn lead us to a greater appreciation of ourselves as practitioners (see e.g. Johns, 2004; Somekh, 2006). As McNiff wrote, "*I have become certain of the need for uncertainty*" (2003, p. 5). This uncertainty reduces the possibility of over-confidence in our work, and in so doing increases our safety in practice, though we must also guard against becoming under-confident. It is human nature to focus on negative events, and there is a danger that critical reflection is weighted too heavily on negative forms of criticality. Reflection of any sort needs to be thought of as *an ethic of practice,* constructed *ethically* for human flourishing.

One pathway to be taken is therefore that of personal knowing and observation for personal and professional development; an informal yet disciplined form of action research. The second pathway is more formal and involves being more rigorous in gathering and interpreting data for more structured inquiries into human being and behaviour. Developing ways in which creativity can be applied within parameters of interpretation is a means to open up philosophical approaches to human inquiry which, while still leaving room for personal engagement, offer a structure to knowledge generation (see Higgs, Titchen, Horsfall, & Armstrong, 2007; McIntosh, 2010). This guards against what Eisner (2008, p. 24) called the novelty value of research – that which may be entertaining but ultimately of no empirical use. In my own work I started by taking the first pathway towards reflection for professional development, but over time, at another crossroad, I took the second pathway towards a more structured approach to establishing means by which I could construct ways of knowing professional practice through the arts.

Construction, Interpretation and Analysis

Many introductory textbooks to research methodology describe the construction, analysis, and interpretation of research as linear; that it is ordered and that *a* must be done before *b* and so on. Even in many forms of qualitative research this appears the dominant doctrine, with discrete models of data collection and analytical methods drawn from the various theorists and literature, such as ways of interviewing or thematically analysing data. In my view this is a superficial and mechanistic approach to any intellectual inquiry. Real intellectual inquiry recognises the synergy between the theories and principles that underpin the collection of data and those that facilitate its analysis and interpretation. In its most simple state I can describe the development of my methodology thus: The development of *images* (both textual and visual) creates forms and symbols. These symbols are metaphorical and they lead into dialogues with self and with others. Using the concept of *imagery* as central to the data-collection process, participants are freely able to be symbolic in their production, which in turn yields artefacts for metaphorical and dialogical interpretation (see below). The metaphors open up possibilities for dialogue (and therefore new ways of knowing), rather than closing them down as some methodologies do.

Validity is found in three ways here: firstly through the voices that are heard in the data, as Elliott (2007) discussed in his work concerning educational action research; secondly through the rigour in which newly constructed methodologies and data analysis methods are formed and tested in practice; and thirdly through ensuring that there is transparency in how the methodological processes have been arrived at. However, this is not unproblematic from the interpretive and critical researchers' view, for this transparency creates questions and challenges, leaving them exposed to criticism as to their approach. I see the science of research as a broad canvas. Just as interpretivist/critical research can be viewed as one version of a truth, so can reductive research: As my friend Jack Sanger once noted, "*a quantitative researcher is like a magician. He puts numbers in a hat and pulls out a table*" (McIntosh, 2010, p. 178). What this refers to is that depending on the way in which figures are jumbled, different results will occur and the audience can be deceived into thinking one way or another. If we accept that research can be viewed as one version of a truth and that the attempts to make it valid are transparent, then it should stand as having integrity for knowledge generation.

In my case, the data collection process was arrived at accidentally because it began life as a teaching and learning methodology. More specifically, the data were in fact material submitted for both formative and summative assessment for a reflective practice module. The conceptual framework for this is arguably tied up in the rationale for the module itself, which was to increase understanding of reflection through creative approaches and to critically appraise the experience of reflecting in this way. Once I realised the extent of the diversity and quality of the submissions for assessment, the question of how this could be applied to a form of action research became a matter for development: In what ways could this work be considered data, and how could it be subject to any form of rigorous analysis? In the end, this came down to three conceptual ideas: (i) theories of metaphor (Black, 1998; Lakoff & Johnson, 2003; Ricoeur, 2003), (ii) theories of dialogics[1] (specifically the work of Bakhtin, 1984) and (iii) theories of symbolism and psychoanalytics, particularly the work of Jung (Read, Fordham, & Adler, 1953–78). By melding together these three different and at times polarised concepts (e.g. dialogics and metaphor, for Bakhtin's form of dialogic was grounded in a precise form of sociolinguistics which left no room for the non-literal language of metaphor) I felt that an analysis tool could be developed that made sense of data, not as truth but as one way of examining it. The extensive work in developing this tool led to the creation of a simple table through which data could be interpreted and analysed (see Table 9.1).

Table 9.1. Coding the unconscious through metaphor

A Coding Through the Unconscious	A Coding Through Metaphor
− The conceptual functions of language to communicate tone, ideas and their relationships − The visibility of authors in their work and their connection to the reader − Ego, persona, and the uncovering of self identification − Production of the unconscious and the decoding and redefining of self	− Extensions of the used part of the metaphor, the use of the novel metaphor and the deepening of metaphorical image constructs through the experience of the speaker and hearer − Emphasis, resonance, and the interplay of text − Spatial understanding and the context of human beings, and constructs of internal and external landscapes
Awareness of barriers to self-knowing The shadow and its impact upon psychological growth	
The Realisation of Transformation	
− The shifting in self-realisation and the development of individuation	− The post-confrontation of self-crisis

In terms of the table above, the constructs of psychoanalysis and metaphor are the primary conceptual forms. Bakhtin's (1984) theory of dialogics was applied later, because I felt that moving from establishing results through the table above progressed the discussion into one of "voices" in the data and the ways it could be presented in sociolinguistic terms. In the process of reflecting in the ways described above, a threshold is encountered. In earlier work I found Bakhtin's (1984) notion of this relevant:

> Not that which takes place within, but that which takes place on the boundary between one's own and someone else's consciousness, on the threshold. And everything internal gravitates not toward self but is turned to the outside and dialogised, every internal experience ends up on the boundary, encounters other, and this tension filled encounter lies in its essence. (p. 287, cited in McIntosh, 2009, p. 9)

If we apply the interpretive/analytical framework above (Table 9.1) to Figures 9.1 and 9.2, we can begin to see how the forms of metaphor and symbolism can be "voiced" as a dialogic. As well as being interpretive, the table facilitates reciprocal discussion between the images and ourselves − a critical dialogue. Further, it acts a conceptual map that helps us find a way through uncharted territory. Upon immersion in this type of data, two types of threshold exist. The first emerges through the construction of the visual and literary data, and the second when we act as the viewer to such data from the perspective of the "other". I describe this as an "impassioned play of voices" because there is a plurality in what is voiced and what is heard. It is an opportunity to appreciate different experiences, perceptions, and ethical commitments without needing to generalise or place constraints on them through structure. Further to this, the threshold also facilitates a reflective stance on the experience of reflecting to occur for the "other" because, as Sartre (1996) suggested, it is possible to stand away from our thinking and act as an observer on it. When we begin then to engage with the data supplied above (Figures 9.1–9.3) these are the ways in which we can approach it: as metaphor, as symbol, as dialogic or threshold. The reflection and learning that occur through the process can be either individual or collective. For the purposes of teaching and learning I chose to insert "creative portfolio" workshops into the Reflexivity module. Learners had the chance to share their work and thinking with their peers, with the outcome that the work in progress generated ideas and discussion leading to the participants' further refinement of their creative artefact. This could be utilised as a strategy in research data collection too, acting as a form of collaborative inquiry during the process.

CONCLUSION

Horkheimer and Adorno (1972) suggested that in order to find oneself, one must first become lost. In the course of development of this work for a while I became lost. The learners I worked with also became lost: we were all in uncharted territory. But ultimately we were able to find ourselves once more, with greater understanding and appreciation of our selves. For myself, I emerged into a new landscape of thinking about research and knowledge production.

The process of learning through any form of practitioner research involving reflection is neither easy nor comfortable. When it is attempted through the use of media alien to all experiences of professional and educational learning then the difficulties are amplified and can be met with resistance, an understandable and natural reaction. However, once the learners with whom I have been fortunate enough to work challenged their reservations, they produced powerful reflections that opened up much space for dialogue with themselves and with the viewers and readers of their work. The contributions in Figures 9.1–9.3 were chosen simply because of their ease of use for this chapter, but are by no means representative of the media produced, which have included drawing, sculpture, anthologies of poetry, photographs, digital video and music, quilting, and even a plate of baked confectioneries! These media have uncovered hidden talents, revisited lost skills, or simply provided ways of illustrating feelings impossible to represent through words alone. Various writers, practitioners and researchers from a range of disciplines are engaged in this work; see Eisner's (2008) use of arts-based educational research, descriptions by Higgs et al. (2007) of developments in the visual and performing arts for professional practice development, and Forceville's (1998) theoretical work on pictorial metaphor. The Collaborative Action Research Network is also establishing creativity as a major strand of its future co-inquiry.

NOTES

¹ Dialogics is not the same as dialogue. It is more than a conversation with something, rather it is a construction of voices that come to mean something very specific.

REFERENCES

Bakhtin, M. (1984). *The problem of Dostoevsky's poetics*. Minneapolis: University of Minnesota Press.

Black, M. (1998). More about metaphor. In A. Ortonay (Ed.), *Metaphor and thought* (2nd ed., pp. 19–42). Cambridge: Cambridge University Press.

Bogdan, R.C., & Biklen, K. (2009). Foundations of qualitative research in education. In W. Luttrell (Ed.), *Qualitative educational research: Readings in reflexive methodology and transformative practice* (pp. 21–44). London: Routledge.

Bourdieu, P., & Wacquant, L. (1992). *An invitation to reflexive sociology*. Cambridge: Polity Press.

Czikszenkmihalyi, M. (1997). *Creativity, flow, and the psychology of discovery and invention*. New York: Harper Collins.

Eisner, E. (2008). Persistent tensions in arts based research. In M. Cahnmann-Taylor & R. Siegesmund (Eds.), *Arts-based research in education: Foundations for practice* (pp. 16–28). London: Routledge.

Elliott, J. (2007). Classroom research: Science or commonsense. In *Reflecting where the action is: The selected works of John Elliott* (pp. 91–98). London: Routledge.

Fish, D. (1998). *Appreciating practice in the caring professions: Refocusing practitioner development and practitioner research*. Oxford: Butterworth Heinemann.

Forceville, C. (1998). *Pictorial metaphor in advertising*. London: Routledge.

Higgs, J., Titchen, A.., Horsfall, D., & Armstrong, H. (2007). *Being critical and creative in qualitative research*. Sydney: Hampden Press.

Horkheimer, M., & Adorno, T. (1972). *Dialectic of enlightenment*. New York: Continuum.

Johns, C. (2004). *Becoming a reflective practitioner*. Oxford: Blackwell.

Lakoff, G., & Johnson, M. (2003). *Metaphors we live by*. Chicago: University of Chicago Press.

McIntosh, P. (2009). The puzzle of metaphor and voice in arts-based social research. *International Journal of Social Research Methodology*. Published on iFirst; URL http://dx.doi.org/10.1080/13645570902969357.

McIntosh, P. (2010). *Action research and reflective practice: Creative and visual methods to facilitate reflection and learning*. London: Routledge.

McNiff, J. (2003). *Action research: Principles and practice*. London: RoutledgeFalmer.

Painter, J. (2004). Pierre Bourdieu. In M. Crang & N. Thrift (Eds.), *Thinking space* (pp. 239–259). London: Routledge.

Read, H., Fordham, M., & Adler, G. (Eds.) (1953–78). *The collected works of C.G. Jung*. London: Routledge.

Reason, P., & Bradbury, H. (Eds.) (2008). *The Sage handbook of action research: Participative inquiry and practice*. (2nd ed.). London: Sage.

Ricoeur, P. (2003). *The rule of metaphor: The creation of meaning in language*. London: Routledge.

Sartre, J.P. (1996). *Being and nothingness*. London: Routledge.

Somekh, B. (2006). *Action research: A methodology for change and development*. Maidenhead: Open University Press.

Tuan, Y.F. (2003). *Space and place: The perspective of experience*. Minneapolis: University of Minnesota Press.

Paul McIntosh PhD, MSc, PGCE, BSc(Hons), RNMH
Institute for Health Sciences Education
Barts and The London School of Medicine and Dentistry
Queen Mary University London, UK

DEBBIE HORSFALL AND JOY HIGGS

10. CREATIVE RESEARCH RE-PRESENTATIONS

In the quiet closed places
Of expected form
Silenced voices scream through tightened lips
And I who would know
And release their angst and their song
Search the outer reaches
Of my imagined other selves
To bring their stories (or is it my story?)
Into voice and shape and feel
To shatter the stability

ACT 1: OPENING THE CONVERSATION SPACE

Joy sits at her office desk surrounded by books and papers. Debbie phones.

Debbie:	Joy, Hi. Glad I got you. I've been thinking about that chapter we have to write for the *Creative Spaces in Qualitative Researching* book. I'm thinking we could build on our writings around *The Dinner Party* by Judy Chicago (1996). Judy's aim was to foreground women who had been inspirational for her, but were not hugely well known. It was an instalment piece of art.
Joy:	Great. Last time we invited people we knew who had used paintings, poetry, performance and singing as part of their research activities, and we included some honoured invited guests. They all contributed to the conversation in our imagination.
Debbie:	Yes, I think we should do the same again. The argument is still relevant and we can show our ideas in the practice of our writing. And I would still like to invite the people who inspired us, and gave us permission to do things differently, all those years ago.
Joy:	Let's invite some different guests this time – there are new people in the field and some more recent work we could talk about.

ACT 2: DINNER TIME

Everyone has arrived and we're sitting at a table overflowing with food, flowers, pieces of paper, laptops, books, articles, diaries, wine. It is a warm spring evening. The table has been set outside. Frogs and crickets compete with the conversation.

*J. Higgs et al., (eds.), Creative Spaces for
Qualitative Researching: Living Research, 97–104*

Scene 1: Stories From the Field

Joy: Well, we thought we could start off by talking about some of our lived experiences of presenting research results differently – in papers, theses and research reports and at conferences.

Virginia: OK, my turn ... The first time I tried using theatre, over 20 years ago now, three of us presented our research findings of women TAFE managers. We decided on non-scripted performance to try and capture the variety of values and views that emerged, at the same time protecting identities. Worked well.

Judy: In the late 80s three of us were presenting research findings at a conference. We did a non-scripted performance too, in the middle of a conventional paper. We wanted it to arise seamlessly so it would take people by surprise – a kind of popular theatre approach. (Peter Martin, Judy Pinn, & Jim Woodhill, 1989)

Debbie: What was it that inspired you to do a performance?

[Food continues to be passed around, glasses get refilled]

Judy: Our research had identified contradictory ideas. We wanted to present the different ideas simultaneously. We wanted to explore presenting our findings just like we had been experimenting with our large-scale participatory action research project.

Norman: Interesting ... "Becker, McCall and Morris introduced in 1989 the concept of performance, a play on performance art" (in Denzin, 1997, p. 194).

Debbie: They wrote about it first. I'm not sure they actually introduced it!

Norman: OK, good point. They wrote about their experiences. "This format allowed them to present their work as a collaborative project, without privileging the single authorial voice. The script format permitted the presentation of emotion and mood. Through the use of intonation and pacing they could alter the meaning of their text, thereby openly acknowledging the constructed nature of their social science data" (Becker et al., 1989, pp. 94–95). "Performances made the research process more visible and alive to outsiders, voices became real people" (Norman Denzin, 1997, p. 194).

Judy: We found that too. The moment we began the performance, we could visibly see the audience wake up and attend to us!

Joy: It seems that creatively formatted or structured texts can facilitate inclusivity, especially in collaborative research, and make participants' voices more real and prominent in research reports.

Judy: Yes, and the structure enables a plurality of research themes to come out, as well as an internal but visible critique, and enables differences to be spoken without needing to resolve them into a seamless unmessy text. All those years ago what we were doing had no name. Now performance ethnography seems to be catching on.

Debbie: Yes, there was a special edition of an on-line research journal recently focusing on performative social sciences. It included many different examples of performance research texts (see Forum: Qualitative Social Research, 2008).

Catherine: Mmm. When I first showed my paintings in a "paper" session at an international conference I was terrified! I've never given a paper as such! My work just can't fit into that form alone.

Charlie: We used a chat room approach to achieve a similar goal of opening up the research conversation and having many ideas heard. A couple of us took on two personas (self and devil's advocate) to spice up the debate when it all got too harmonious.

Judy: These ways of presenting research illuminate the cracks and fissures in theory and in practice, which are often smoothed over, or out, in research discussions and reporting. They enable people to enter the text in some way.

Joy: Debbie, remember our research and writing retreat when we used art and dance to explore wordless ideas of practice, to open our minds and eventually find words to write about our collaboration. We used our paintings as chapter logos and book covers.

Debbie: Yes, I was thrilled when my painting became a cover for our book.

[Judy begins to clear plates and food off the table.]

Debbie: Patti, you use creative re-presentations of research as a way of moving from an argumentative structure of reporting research.

Patti: Yes, the traditional focus is on "hostile interrogation" and the "concept" is exhausted. It's about time the "analytical, argumentative, dialectical reasoning invented by Plato" was displaced and we embraced ways of knowing and logic "that are more about the economy of the unconscious, juxtaposition, paradox, montage, palimpsest, the structure of emotions, the logic of sense" (Patti Lather, 1997, p. 237).

Debbie: I loved your article about AIDS and Angels (Patti Lather, 1997). I've always seen you as such a straight theorist. It grabbed my attention – the title pulled me in. It's a serious report of research – you used paradox and juxtaposition and got me engaging on an emotional level.

Scene 2: Pleasurable Processes, Difficult Subjects

Debbie: Most of us have worked in difficult areas, haven't we? Homelessness, illness, AIDS, disability, suppression of minority voices, sustainability. Making the research process engaging can enable people to continue working in such emotionally fraught and academically contested areas.

Virginia: Absolutely. I work with all sorts of different, amazing people – poets, dancers, actors, singers – all these other ways of being in and interpreting the world. It opens up alternative change possibilities.

[Judy walks back outside bringing fruit and cake]

Judy: I love performing! I don't enjoy doing conference papers where you stand behind the lectern and put on the traditional academic voice.

Debbie: I don't enjoy writing disembodied research reports either.

Judy: I have an embodied response to this sort of stuff. It makes me feel sick. It has something to do with having to always locate myself in that argument tradition, negating the emotions and the body. It's not very inclusive, is it?

Debbie   That's why I love coming across material practices which show another way.

Joy: Remember that one you sent me, about how the textual practices in hospital when … someone is dying actually shape the dying process. The whole thing was written as a poem (Boris Brummans, 2007).

Kerrie: It seems so much easier to connect with the research and researcher when you read stuff like that. You can feel part of an intellectual community. It reminds me of that performance poem we wrote, Debbie. The one you did at the conference, about gate keeping and dying at home called "can we send a letter?" (Debbie Horsfall & Kerrie Noonan, 2010).

Debbie: Oh yes. People had said amazing things about why we shouldn't be doing the research, or why carers wouldn't want to talk to us. Privacy seemed to be their biggest concern; that we were expecting people to be public about what they saw as a private matter. They also thought the research may be a burden to already stressed people.

Judy: How was it received at the conference?

Debbie: You could have heard a pin drop to start with. Then people would not stop talking – to me, to each other. It really engaged them. And it was less confronting doing it this way, than telling all these service providers that they had been obstructive basically. I have a copy here if you'd like to see it.

[Debbie passes copies round the table and people skim read]

Judy: I can see why it got people talking. It's an interesting way to present data, different to the snippets we usually use. I like the last verse [reads]

We wondered who got the letters.

Who got to choose?

To consider

To say yes, or

Drop it in the recycling bin.

Debbie: I have to say it takes longer. Why not settle for the easy life?

Joy: What about the argument that there are times that we need to understand the rules and boundaries in order to get past the gate-keepers (like journal reviewers) to publish or present the papers we really want to give?

Catherine: I find these barriers so hard to accept. Whose boundaries? Who decides? And who gives the power to decide? Debbie, remember what we talked about writing up my re-search?

Debbie: I know it made a difference in both our understandings. We were at the café – food again! [laughs]

Catherine: Yes! I included that conversation in my text "I decide[d] to stay true in my writing to the messiness of this lived experience of growing up in madness while knowing how ingrained and well socialised is my need to neaten" (Catherine Camden Pratt, 2002, p. 25).

Scene 3: Socially Constructed Research Texts

Debbie: Yvonna, you write eloquently about the postmodern idea of partiality, that all texts are historically, culturally situated and always highly gendered. I love how you said that any text which claims to re-present the totality of any experiences, events or understandings is "a realist pretence" (Yvonna Lincoln, 1997, p. 38). No one text can tell the whole story, but we can try to re-present a bigger partial picture.

Judy: And to make it more complex, of course our multiple selves or subjectivities feed into the text, whatever its structure. Co-author, researcher, activist, storyteller, friend, colleague, supervisor, co-researcher, participant …

Debbie: You're so right. These are our multiple selves wanting to be realised and liberated, but there's also our choices. So many times it depends on our audience and whether we want to creep in under their expectations, or unequivocally shake them up.

Virginia: [bringing out more wine] Going back to the politics of partiality, it doesn't mean "anything goes!" That's relativism gone nuts! When blurring the boundaries between social science and art, literature and scientific reports, do we still need criteria or guidelines?

Carolyn: Before we can merge these worlds, we need to appreciate the differences between making something and making it up. I want to retain a distinction between saying our work is selective, partial and contestable and saying that the impossibility of telling the whole truth means you can lie (Carolyn Ellis, in Bochner & Ellis, 1996).

Kerrie: So do you mean that it's not just about knowledge for knowledge's sake? It moves from the realm of the abstract to that of the material. From the whys to the hows?

Charlie: Yes, but not just how to do, but also how it is to be, how we know and come to know, and how we feel.

Scene 4: Collaborative and Accessible Texts

Debbie: So, what does using more creative processes do?

Judy: For me it's mostly about a commitment to collaboration. To jointly constructing knowledge(s), to working with people as subjects rather than objects, and also doing what we enjoy, doing something that is both useful and makes us feel good?

Virginia: And there is usually food and lots of laughter. So the process is more fun, more holistic, more ecological than what we imagine producing more traditional forms of research is?

Judy: Come on, Virginia, it's not in our imaginations. We have all done those (traditional) sorts of reports we haven't completely avoided them.

Virginia: OK, it's certainly part of our experiences. But our experiences are not everybody's. Using creative ways of working isn't necessarily better for everyone and everything – for all researchers.

Charlie: And could this laughing be labelled as trivial? People might question what there is to laugh about if you're working with homeless people.

Debbie: I can see that, but while we're all deadly serious about the issues we are dealing with, we're not going to be deadly boring in the way we work.

Joy: It's also about communication with many people. Moving beyond what Yvonna said earlier about writing for ourselves or others like us.

Janice: The use of visual texts can include people with so-called "othered" ways of learning. I've just finished a project with people who have an intellectual disability. They were co-researchers and we used photo voice. The photos enabled us to find a common language to talk about abstract ideas – social barriers to inclusion. We also used poetry, images, patchwork quilts, metaphors and we talked about huge ideas and concepts in practical ways. It's more like the way people actually communicate, so it's got the potential to be more accessible to more people. Here are some of the photos the co-researchers took.

Debbie: They are beautiful and certainly show a different way of knowing.

Janice: And our analysis of them led to concrete changes, both in the transport system and residential housing.

Judy: Part of this imperative is an expression of subjectivity, a practice of the self that is not written into logocentric writing or what usually passes for knowledge and ways of being a researcher in the academy – the centrality of an objective, disembodied logic and rationality.

[Silence as people look at the photos]

Scene 6: Doing Justice

Patti: What we're saying is kind of old fashioned, "that it is possible to present the voices of others in a more or less unmediated way" via evocative portraits, a type of data reporting that "emphasizes direct exposure to other 'voices' … unassimilated to given concepts, theories, and analytic frames" (George Marcus, 1993, pp. 13–15). "Such words help me locate myself both within and against conventional notions of social science research, but I remain haunted by the task of doing justice to the women's words" (Patti Lather, 1997, p. 253).

Debbie: Most of us here have felt this, whatever form of research we're doing. My hope is that reporting methods that encourage readers' emotive and visceral responses allow some sort of justice to be done.

Catherine: Sometimes it's not always about what we think of as justice either. What about embodied justice? "As a researcher I could not deny my body as a re-search instrument … I was unprepared for and initially surprised by the intensity of my somatic narrative – of what my body has to say … My paintings became a way of letting my body's knowing tell aspects of my story" (Catherine Camden Pratt, 2003). And as I worked with my paintings I came to know myself at a visual and visceral depth that I had not been able to articulate fully prior to these series of paintings.

Debbie: Yes, if we present a clean, safe text allowing the reader to not feel any-thing this doesn't fit with researching such difficult areas. We need to enable people to "learn otherwise", to not keep on producing research which furiously documents what we already know. Remember that the way we work as researchers impacts our bodies, the bodies of those we are researching with and the bodies of the readers/ audiences. All research has an impact. Perhaps all we are doing is making the impact visible, acknowledging it.

Scene 7: Othered Knowledges Counting for Something

Judy: It's also about pushing boundaries of knowledge. Who gets to say what counts as knowledge and what counts as real presentation of knowledge? Janice's photos, Catherine's paintings and Debbie and Kerrie's poem are wonderful examples of different knowledges.

Debbie: Hey Judy, say more about that.

Judy: OK [clambers up on her chair and puts on a posh voice]. Artful representations bring forward new and different forms of knowing. This is because writing or performance or visual art taps into the visceral, emotional and visual terrain that is often written out or silenced in orthodox academic writing. This writing can transgress dualities such as mind/body and truth/fiction and enable layers of meaning to be represented. For a reader connecting with the writing there is more room to interact. It is not so much about holding tightly to truth. It is about applying multiple perspectives and understandings. Poetry, performance, visual arts all belong to academic disciplines. Yet the debate seems to be about these being out of place when applied to research. Who says? [Takes a bow and sits down to much applause.]

Joy: There's a pragmatic way to engaging creativity in writing/performing research texts. The world is full of information overload. Even the best written scholarly paper can disappear into the white noise of academic research-speak. Writing differently can make our words, the voices of our participants heard by people other than us.

Judy: I agree. When I was doing some work for the department of housing, I presented some of my findings back as a performance. They were not expecting that. They get far too much to read. Something different yet rigorous, can leave a lasting impression. Working this way can enable a different sort of relationship to happen between the text and the reader, based upon both empirical analysis and visceral responses, evoking a more holistic relationship and a richer response from readers. I think this can lead to people feeling moved to take action.

Kerrie: And I think that they find it easier to read than regular old academic writing. I mean – there's a lot of discussion about the gap between research and practice. Maybe if our research reports were more engaging, accessible and inviting, more practitioners and policy- makers would read them, or listen to them, or watch them?

Judy: As researchers, surely our role is to represent the phenomenon, as well as interpret the data. The purpose of research stories is dual: to evoke and provide the basis for the interpretation. Stories and images can allow the reader to experience the phenomenon vicariously and have the basis for judging the credibility of the interpretations.

Scene 8: Legitimating Creative Re-presentations

Debbie: You know, we've been doing this for years yet it still feels new.

Virginia: We have to work hard to legitimise such approaches in the academy and the wider world of publishing and getting grants. Debbie, didn't you just get a big research grant for a project using photography?

Debbie: Yes, and they said it's one of the main reasons we got the money – they liked the creative approach!

Joy: It's important to remember that we are members of a community of scholars, researchers and writers who have been working this way.

Debbie: And it can be useful for us to name academic traditions such as auto-ethnography and critical auto-biography and narrative inquiry.

Judy: Feminisms and the post-structural turn have been hugely freeing in the way we both do and represent research.

Catherine: And art as social practice and the action of imagination.

Judy: And storytelling, cultural action, and different ways of knowing and Indigenous epistemologies (see Aileen Moreton-Robinson, 2004).

[Time passes. Night draws in. Everyone helps to clear the table.]

Debbie: [to Judy as they walk into the kitchen] I wonder about ensuring quality of the art-based offerings. How do we face the demands of critics with amateur ability as poets, writers and artists?

Judy: What worries me is the time spent arguing the value of this work, whereas those involved in logocentric writing don't have to argue their case – it's taken-for-granted. It's important to assume that creative approaches to inquiry exist and are valid, and to not always have to spend huge amounts of time and energy arguing for our bibliographic pedigree!

Debbie: It is a struggle because at the same time I don't think that is the important thing. These forms can be learned and practised in the same way that conventional academic writing is learned. What a great place to start our next dinner party!

REFERENCES

Becker, H.S., McCall, M.M., & Morris, L.X. (1989). Theatres and communities: Three scenes. *Social Problems, 36*, 93–116.

Bochner, A.P., & Ellis, C. (1996). Talking over ethnography. In C. Ellis & A.P. Bochner (Eds.), *Composing ethnography: Alternative forms of qualitative writing* (pp. 13–48). London: Alta Mira.

Brummans, B.H.J.M. (2007). Death by document: Tracing the agency of a text. *Qualitative Inquiry*, *13*(5), 711–727.

Camden-Pratt, C. (2002). *Daughters of Persephone: Legacies of maternal "madness".* Unpublished PhD thesis, University of Western Sydney, Australia.

Camden-Pratt, C.E. (2003). *Waiting to be re-membered.* Paper accompanying exhibition at the Women's Health Centre, Katoomba, NSW, August 30.

Chicago, J. (1996). *The dinner party.* London: Penguin.

Denzin, N.K. (1997). Performance texts. In W.G. Tierney &Y.S. Lincoln (Eds.), *Representation and the text: Re-framing the narrative voice* (pp. 179–218). Albany, NY: State University of New York Press.

Forum Qualitative Sozialforschung / Forum: Qualitative Social Research. Available: http://www.qualitative-research.net/index.php/fqs, accessed 4 November 2010.

Horsfall, D., & Noonan, K. (2010). Bringing our dying home: Creating community at end of life? Paper presented at Association of Death Education and Counselling Annual International Conference, Kansas, Missouri, April 7–10.

Lather, P. (1997). Creating a multilayered text: Women, aids and angels. In W.G. Tierney & Y.S. Lincoln (Eds.), *Representation and the text: Re-framing the narrative voice* (pp. 233–258). Albany, NY: State University of New York Press.

Lincoln, Y.S. (1997). Self, subject, audience, text: Living at the edge, writing in the margins. In W.G. Tierney & Y.S. Lincoln (Eds.), *Representation and the text: Re-framing the narrative voice* (pp. 37–56). Albany, NY: State University of New York Press.

Marcus, G. (1993). Interview, in Inside Publishing. *Lingua Franca*, July/August, 13–15.

Martin, P., Pinn, J., & Woodhill, J. (1989). Total catchment management – Towards 2000: Perspectives and approaches for community participation. Paper presented at the Total Catchment Management Conference, Wollongong University, NSW, Australia, July 2–5.

Moreton-Robinson, A. (2004). *Whiteness, epistemology and Indigenous representation.* In A. Moreton-Robinson (Ed.), *Whitening race: Essays in social and cultural criticism* (pp. 75–88). Canberra, ACT: Australian Studies Press.

Debbie Horsfall PhD, MA, B.Ed
Peace and Development Studies
School of Social Sciences
University of Western Sydney, Australia

Joy Higgs AM PhD
The Education For Practice Institute
Charles Sturt University, Australia

SALLY DENSHIRE

11. RE-INSCRIBING GENDER INTO THE HERITAGE OF OT IN AUSTRALIA

"The Sock Knitter"

AUTO-ETHNOGRAPHIC INQUIRY INTO PROFESSIONAL PRACTICE

An auto-ethnography describes one life to illustrate a way of life, by connecting personal and cultural worlds (Ellis & Bochner, 2000). The larger auto-ethnographic inquiry into everyday professional practice that I conducted for my PhD (Denshire, 2009)[1] was about re-reading and re-writing practice in order to re-inscribe the things that are "written out" of public accounts of practice, especially when a profession becomes a scholarly discipline. The challenge then was to foreground, not just the inconsequential ordinary, but the "writing out" that happens when you move from practice itself to representation of that practice within disciplinary, and especially scientific regimes.

Auto-ethnographic methodologies can hold rich potential for doing identity work in the context of professional socialisation, as shown by a new approach used with student occupational therapists at the University of Oklahoma:

> Inward-outward backward-forward story-telling, demanded by auto-ethnography, helps students understand their personal stories are, in fact, tiles in a larger mosaic that is the culture of becoming an occupational therapist. (Hoppes, Hamilton, & Robinson, 2007, pp. 139–140)

As I show in this chapter, I chose auto-ethnography to locate the particular and the personal within an historical and cultural context. Auto-ethnography is about everyday experience, enabling us to name what hasn't been written before. Writing an auto-ethnographic account can bring out unarticulated dilemmas occurring in an occupational therapist's practice as it is lived. Portraying emotions, bodies, sexualities and heritages existing outside the dominant discourses may contribute to the re-shaping of a profession that, at first glance, seemed to be uniformly homogeneous and conservative. Any tellings of this re-shaping have gone largely unwritten to date; the "tension between the values of a *profession* and the practitioner's *lifeworld* is a largely ignored and unarticulated dimension of professional life" (Kinsella, 2006, p. 39).

As professional practitioners we may think back on, and perhaps talk about, ordinary everyday moments of practice, but rarely write them publicly. I wondered what happened to all the lost stories, the forbidden stories, to the stories of the

J. Higgs et al., (eds.), Creative Spaces for
Qualitative Researching: Living Research, 105–114

other. What happened to the undocumented moments of everyday practice? Questions flowed about troublings, ambivalences, losses and struggles. These "lost property" questions led me to the two research questions that underpin this chapter:

– How can auto-ethnography contribute to an understanding of occupational therapy practice?
– More particularly, how can a painting be used as a stimulus to auto-ethnographic writing about the heritage of this profession?

So this chapter is about a particular approach to auto-ethnography that is inspired by a visual image[2] for the purpose of examining the problematic of researching selves and drawing findings that have a wider professional relevance. First, I show the "everydayness" of practice in occupational therapy and the emergence of a critical literature that led to the research questions. Then the use of a visual image as the stimulus to my auto-ethnographic writing is introduced. I draw on the painting by Australian artist Grace Cossington Smith, titled *The sock knitter* (see Fig. 11.1) to tell/show cultural positionings, embodiments and experiences of middle class, feminine, feminist Whiteness.

The sock knitter seems to embody the wartime origins of occupational therapy and the inflections of gender and class that coloured and shaped its first steps. Through my writing in and around the emblem of *The sock knitter* I represent some of the collective history of the profession, at the same time noting intersections between my biography and the history of occupational therapy in Australia. In closing, I speculate on stories not yet told and offer suggestions to those wondering about embarking on auto-ethnographic journeys of their own.

The "Everydayness" of Professional Practice in Occupational Therapy

Every profession has rich oral and practice traditions that are located in the everyday. Occupational therapists have a "double dose", because the work we do explicitly concerns the everyday activities of others. Participation in all the ordinary things that people need and want to do every day is that part of human experience that "does not speak" (Hasselkus, 2006, p. 630).

Occupational therapists can be found working in many different roles in a wide range of clinical, rehabilitative and community contexts. Frequently they have adapted to their surrounding habitat by "filling gaps" (Fortune, 2000, p. 225) according to the situation and human environment they are presented with. Typically, these chameleon qualities often mean that the varied contributions of occupational therapy may be highly regarded within the immediate environment but still little understood by the general public. Inevitably, much occupational therapy practice remains subjective, culturally bound and hard to describe.

The personal, ordinary tasks that people do every day are the legitimate concerns of occupational therapy practice. Typically, occupational therapists find themselves using common sense to adapt equipment and do ordinary things in new ways, using creative problem-solving and clinical reasoning in "the uncommon world of the clinic" (Fleming, 1994, p. 108). Thus they are members of a translational profession, bridging in both directions the everyday lived world and the medical world (Polatjako et al., 2007).

Figure 11.1. Grace Cossington Smith, "The sock knitter" (1915)
oil on canvas, 61.6 50.7 cm, purchased 1960.
Collection: Art Gallery of New South Wales,
© Estate of Grace Cossington Smith,
Photograph: Jenni Carter

Occupational therapists endeavour to work collaboratively with people whose lives have been disrupted through illness, injury, dislocation or transition. Within political, governmental and resource constraints they facilitate engagement in meaningful everyday occupations to improve the health and wellbeing of individuals and groups. Concepts such as "occupation" (in the sense of everyday activity) are based on Western world views and social norms (Iwama, 2006;

Hammell, 2009). As most occupational therapists are White, Western, middle class women, our theories and ourselves are unavoidably part of "invisible" White cultural privilege, which inevitably impacts on transactions with people from all cultural groups (Iwama, 2006).

Emergence of a Critical Literature in Occupational Therapy

The complex plurality of evidences for practice is being recognised (Blair & Robertson, 2005). But there are still tacit agreements among clients and therapists to tell narratives solely in medical terms, and practitioners need to break this trend if we are to generate communities of practice through stories (Frank, 1995). I argue that the representation of occupational therapy practice constitutes a major problematic for the field whenever scholarly writing, including my own, succumbs to the pressures of "authoritative discourse" (Bakhtin, 1981).

Since the 1980s, Australian occupational therapists such as Lindsey Howie (1984) and Janet Bell (Anderson & Bell, 1988) have touched on gender issues. However, expressions of gendered accounts have been sporadic and unsustained within the Australian literature. Generally, there has been strong reliance on outside authorities at all levels of the profession. The discourses dominant in the profession inevitably marginalise others, both service users and co-workers. In part, this is because the discourse community of occupational therapy has yet to establish a shared vocabulary that goes unambiguously beyond disembodied abstractions of practice drawn from a range of disciplines.

The hybrid field of occupational therapy in Australia is ambivalently represented in the early 21st century. Since its beginnings, occupational therapy has been theorised with varying degrees of success. It has been conceptualised as "paramedical" in relation to medicine, and similarly compared to physiotherapy, a profession that is closely allied to medicine in ways that, since the invention of an "occupational science" in the late 1980s, occupational therapy is not. A phenomenon of borrowing knowledge from everywhere has meant that notions of disciplinarity continue to remain unsettled for occupational therapists.

Critical literature, including auto-ethnographic accounts that transgress and challenge dominant discourses within/against occupational therapy, is emerging in the field. And, as already mentioned, conversations are beginning about cultural privilege. The new critical directions that are emerging within occupational therapy are starting to re-inscribe relations between self and other, opening spaces to re-define more complex, reflexive and ethical occupational therapy identities in our relationships (Mackey, 2007). However, it is still uncommon to read alternative accounts that contest and dismiss the dominant power relations in circulation (Wall, 1995). Indeed, the feminisms and gender literature and the extensive literature of disability studies have been largely ignored by health professionals (Hammell, 2006).

The political potential of occupational therapy is starting to emerge, particularly with communities in the developing world. For example, in 2010, occupational therapists from Latin America assembled to host the World Congress in Chile. And in the context of a recent democracy, South African occupational therapists have identified four levels of service – therapy, community development, transformation through occupation and re-distributive justice (Watson, 2006).

THE PAINTING AS A STIMULUS TO AUTO-ETHNOGRAPHY

A range of images inspired my auto-ethnographic writing. A visual image – painting, photo, video, cartoon – can do more than affirm the text. Rather, such an image, in portraying places of difficulty (Richardson & St Pierre, 2005) may reveal untold stories, communicating the otherwise unsayable. Like fiction, visual images can make the familiar strange (Davidson, 2004). The image can help us recognise the symbolic and nonverbal content in the social world, as a locus of discovery by itself and in combination with other forms of data (Davidson, 2004).

Ekphrasis, or evocative writing that is inspired by visual arts forms (Holman-Jones, 2005), is the Greek word for the meditations on paintings. My use of a pictorial device is influenced by Catherine Brighton's (1985) *The picture*. This is an illustrated children's story of illness experience written in poetic language that evokes telling images with very scant lines. Working with images conjures associations and productive tensions for an ensuing tale, "writing in" what is not written about in occupational therapy generally. This "writing-in"/re-inscribing was the thesis method. *The sock knitter* painting served as an emblem of occupational therapy heritage in my research.

Auto-Ethnographic Reflections on "The Sock Knitter"

The striking image of *The sock knitter*, painted by Australian artist Grace Cossington Smith in 1915 (Gray, 2005) at the beginning of World War I, encapsulates, for me, both the wartime beginnings and the ethos of occupational therapy. The practice of occupational therapy originated to assist returned soldiers in World War I in the United States, and during World War II in Australia (Anderson & Bell, 1988). Around the same time as Cossington Smith was painting *The sock knitter*, an American architect, recovering from illness and injury, set up Consolation House with like-minded colleagues as a centre for occupational re-training in Clifton Springs, New York (Schwartz, 2003).

The subject of the painting, Madge, the artist's sister, has an air of both resolve and compliance as she sits in a domestic interior in everyday clothes doing "busy work". A portrait of a middle class woman at home in wartime doing volunteer work for the feet of men in active war service, *The sock knitter* features the always useful and often restorative craft of knitting. Knitting socks to send to soldiers in the trenches, her "active hands are the focus of the picture" as Anne Gray (2005) comments. She continues, "both her eyes and hands create a mood of intense concentration on the task at hand" (p. 121). Hands have long been an unquestioned motif of occupational therapy, which some now begin to question. For someone without hands or someone unable to use them, hands may be little more than the symbol than an able body is the norm (Hammell, 2009).

Continuing this questioning note, there is something about *The sock knitter*, something about her pose and demeanour, that resonates with the gendered, sexed, racialised and classed heritage of occupational therapy that I wished to make visible in my auto-ethnography. Perhaps *The sock knitter,* in portraying the ordinary-everyday domesticity of a middle class woman's contribution to the war effort in Australia, is depicting something of what women of her class were expected to do within the prevailing "gender order" (Matthews, 1984).

The term "gender order" was first used by feminist historian Jill Matthews (1984) in her doctoral study of asylums in South Australia entitled *Good and mad women: The historical construction of femininity in twentieth century Australia.* A gender order is the way in which societies turn barely undifferentiated babies into social women and men and order the patterns of relationships among and between them (Matthews, 1984). Just as an economy could be feudal, communist or capitalist, so a gender order could be matriarchal, patriarchal or egalitarian (Matthews, 1984).

With some important exceptions (Howie, 1984; Anderson & Bell, 1988; Nelson, Allison, & Copley, 2007) the gendered, racialised, classed intricacies of everyday domestic practices seem largely absent from the professional record in Australia, maintaining a traditional gender order within the literature and the official culture. Even though nearly all occupational therapists are women, dominant discourses in occupational therapy still do not appear to question the exclusion of gender that has been built into the concept of profession (Witz, 1992), by default, accepting the masculine as universal (Butler, 2006). The concept of gender remains tacit in a brand new study (Liedberg, Bjork, & Hensing, 2010) of Swedish occupational therapists who did not seem aware of "the possibility that they were 'doing gender' in their encounters with clients" (p. 337).

What I have almost neglected to say is that *The sock knitter* is only one part of the story of gender and participation in war. Clearly, there is a class dimension as to whether women during the war got to stay at home while the men were away or, in between caring for their families, went off to work in shipyards, steel mills or munitions factories. The propaganda figure, Rosie the Riveter (Honey, 1984), for example, advertised a very different picture of war work for working class women. My partner tells me that his grandmother, Grace Purvis, worked as a welder and her photo was used on recruitment posters put up around the inner west of Sydney during World War II.

There is more to be said about *The sock knitter* and more to be said about the class heritage of occupational therapy. In fact, we will re-visit her in order to witness my Sydney North Shore class beginnings insofar as they connect with the culture of occupational therapy and to stories that are still to be told.

Intersections between my Auto-Biography and a History of the Profession

I first graduated in 1977 and my personal history (as practitioner and author of a body of work) sits inside the history of occupational therapy. The first generation, from 1937 to 1976, is the period of early history of occupational therapy in Australia, and the second generation, from 1977 to 2008, could be regarded as a period of coming-of-age for the profession. My auto-ethnographic project connects personal experience with professional culture. I am part of the stories that are to be told and so I will match my own biography with the history of the profession and examine points of intersection. As the profession went through its particular phases and interests in terms of its origins, values and work patterns, so did I. On reflection, though, perhaps I departed from the script once I became an academic and moved to inland Australia.

The overwhelming majority of Australian occupational therapists are women (93%), mostly Anglo-Australian and young, and 59% work part-time (OT Australia, 2005). Occupational therapists are under-represented between the ages of 30 and 40 years compared to other professions, presumably due to family responsibilities, although this is not recorded. 55% of therapists are under 35 years of age and an additional 25% are under 45 years. Typically, occupational therapists with young children work part-time and certainly that is what I did.

Many occupational therapists live in urban middle class localities such as the reputedly middle class North Shore of Sydney (or the capital city equivalent in the other states). Cultural diversity is slow to be reflected in the growth and development of occupational therapy and there appear to be few bilingual therapists outside metropolitan centres. As I grew up in several suburbs of Sydney and now live in a regional city, aspects of my Anglo-Australian existence could be construed as middle class.

With the nationwide transition from college to university education in the late 1980s, the face of the profession in Australia has continued to change. In 2006, 12 Australian universities (in Queensland, NSW, Victoria, South Australia and Western Australia) offered occupational therapy at undergraduate and postgraduate levels, with a trend toward Masters level entry courses (OT Australia, 2007). When occupational therapy courses across the country entered the universities in the late 1980s I followed, becoming an academic at Charles Sturt University in 1995.

My partner, an experienced welder and now a welding teacher, grew up in Erskineville at the time when it was still a working class Sydney neighbourhood where neglected children sometimes risked being taken away by "the Welfare". Often as not, the partners of my occupational therapy colleagues have worked as artisans in the trades. Not surprisingly, there is an ongoing conversation around the respective values of both practical work and university qualifications at our dinner table.

THOSE STORIES NOT YET TOLD

The sock knitter lingers as an auto-ethnographic image for me as an occupational therapy academic with Sydney roots, now living and working in inland Australia. The young woman sitting knitting can also represent aspects of my former self as well as the feminine/ feminist/ middle class Whiteness of the occupational therapy profession. The painting has associations of Sydney North Shore-ness for me, of geographic, cultural and class memories of the quiet life, worn sandstone steps, gardens planted with Australian native plants, the back verandah bright with parrots, bats silhouetted at dusk, grevillea and jacaranda overlooking bushy gullies. Inside a Californian style bungalow are well stocked bookshelves and tapestry-covered window seats, a polished piano upright in a corner, the decorative woodwork of the Arts and Crafts movement...

The artist Grace Cossington Smith spent her life living in what is now considered an affluent suburb on Sydney's North Shore. For me as a woman who grew up on the North Shore, in some ways the painting calls up my class beginnings as somewhat typical of many White, middle class women who became occupational therapists. The early occupational therapy premises, although modest, were in affluent parts of inner-city Sydney and nearby suburbs. The painting signifies both my personal and professional middle class heritage.

My interest in group work and sense of community seems to have come more from my mother, and my love of language and humour from my father. Mum would drive off to mental health meetings after dinner – once we kids were put to bed – in her bright yellow '60s winter overcoat. I can also remember my father's professed lack of interest, his refrain of "all that mental health tripe". I became an occupational therapist out of this history.

My interest in how people used to live is longstanding. As a teenage girl, one of too many books I borrowed from local library to take on holidays, to the Trades and Labour Council holiday cabins nestled in a secluded waterside location in a national park, was *Manners and morals in the ancient world.* As the keeper of the robes at the Victoria and Albert Museum, the author, James Laver, wrote histories of costume and everyday objects that I loved to read. When I look to my own becoming literate, and to the parts my parents and the library played, I find that this interest in cultural history, in museums and cultural artefacts, led me to occupational therapy. So I have come from a broad interest in cultural institutions – museums, zoos, universities and libraries. A constant is my enduring interest in the writing of lives.

Auto-ethnography has the political potential to tell middle class, feminine, feminist Whiteness and how the cultural backgrounds and the bodies of professionals can be represented. There are many more stories to be told: stories about gender and class, stories in response to contemporary post-colonial questions about race and Whiteness, stories about occupational therapists of different generations, stories of war and patronage, of rurality and urbanity. Speaking of the painting conjures up Whiteness, "do gooder-ness" and activism, and the class beginnings of occupational therapists. Other re-readings of *The sock knitter* could involve telling the handcrafts of knitting and basket-weaving, telling unpaid work and volunteering pre-capitalism. The untold stories of practitioners working in the caring professions will say the unsaid things that are too hard and too uncomfortable for the majority of the profession to put into words. These are just some of the stories not yet told, because stories take shape out of what happened, out of what it was possible and what it was not possible to tell at the time.

As You Set Out on Your Journey...

Beginning to write an auto-ethnographic account may feel somewhat daunting at the start. Reading the work of other auto-ethnographers in related fields will enable you to digest the extent of writings in this genre. Given the possibility that "abandonment is… a common practice of the would-be auto-ethnographer" (Bruni, 2002, p. 32), acquaint yourself with both the risks and pleasures in using the self as the only source of data and also with the "resilience and conviction" (p. 19) vital to sustaining writing in this genre (Holt, 2003). Any gender story resisting the dominant discourse will involve the discomfort of transgressing "the proper" in order to create new knowledge and contribute to the collective biography of the profession. To work productively with the visual within the word-based research culture, you need determination.

Bonne chance!

NOTES

[1] I would like to acknowledge Professor Alison Lee, Director of the Centre for Research in Learning and Change at the University of Technology Sydney, for doctoral supervision.
[2] I would like to acknowledge Teena Clerke, doctoral colleague and design academic, for her perspectives on working with the visual as a stimulus to writing.

REFERENCES

Anderson, B., & Bell, J. (1988). *Occupational therapy: Its place in Australia's history*. Sydney: NSW Association of Occupational Therapists.

Bakhtin, M. (1981). *The dialogic imagination*. Austin, TX: University of Texas Press.

Blair, S.E.E., & Robertson, L.J. (2005). Hard complexities – soft complexities: An exploration of philosophical positions related to evidence in occupational therapy. *British Journal of Occupational Therapy, 68*(6), 269–276.

Brighton, C. (1985). *The picture*. London: Faber & Faber.

Bruni, N. (2002). The crisis of visibility: Ethical dilemmas in autoethnographic research. *Journal of Contemporary Ethnography, 35*(4), 410–418.

Butler, J. (2006). *Gender trouble*. New York: Routledge Classics.

Davidson, J. (2004). 'I am fieldnote': Researching and teaching with visual data. *Qualitative Research Journal, 4*(2), 48–75.

Denshire, S. (2009). *Writing the ordinary: Auto-ethnographic tales of an occupational therapist*. Unpublished PhD thesis, The University of Technology, Sydney.

Ellis, C., & Bochner, A.P. (2000). Autoethnography, personal narrative, reflexivity: Researcher as subject. In N.K. Denzin & Y.S. Lincoln (Eds.), *Handbook of qualitative research* (2nd ed., pp. 733–768). London: Sage.

Fleming, M.H. (1994). A commonsense practice in an uncommon world. In C. Mattingly & M.H. Fleming (Eds.), *Clinical reasoning: Forms of inquiry in a therapeutic practice* (pp. 94–115). Philadelphia: F.A. Davis.

Fortune, T. (2000). Occupational therapists: Is our therapy truly occupational or are we merely filling gaps? *British Journal of Occupational Therapy, 63*(5), 225–230.

Frank, A. (1995). *The wounded storyteller: Body, illness and ethics*. Chicago, IL: University of Chicago Press.

Gray, A. (2005). The sock knitter. In D. Hart (Ed.), *Grace Cossington Smith* (pp. 119–121). Canberra: The National Gallery of Australia.

Hammell, K.W. (2006). *Perspectives on disability and rehabilitation: Contesting assumptions; challenging practice*. Edinburgh: Elsevier Churchill Livingstone.

Hammell, K.W. (2009). Sacred texts: A skeptical exploration of the assumptions underpinning theories of occupation. *Canadian Journal of Occupational Therapy, 76*(1), 6–13.

Hasselkus, B.R. (2006). The world of everyday occupation: Real people real lives. *American Journal of Occupational Therapy, 60*(6), 627–641.

Holman-Jones, S. (2005). Auto-ethnography: Making the personal political. In N.K. Denzin & Y.S. Lincoln (Eds.), *The Sage handbook of qualitative research* (3rd ed., pp. 763–790). Thousand Oaks, CA: Sage.

Holt, N.L. (2003). Representation, legitimation, and autoethnography: An auto-ethnographic writing story. *International Journal of Qualitative Methods, 2*(1), 1–22.

Honey, M. (1984). *Creating Rosie the Riveter: Class, gender and propaganda during World War II.* Amherst: University of Massachusetts Press.

Hoppes, S., Hamilton, T.B., & Robinson, C. (2007). A course in autoethnography: Fostering reflective practitioners in occupational therapy. *Occupational Therapy in Health Care, 21*(1/2), 133–143.

Howie, L. (1984). *Occupational therapy and feminism: A reluctant sisterhood.* Paper presented at the 13th Federal Conference of the Australian Association of Occupational Therapists, Perth.

Iwama, M. (2006). *The Kawa Model: Culturally relevant occupational therapy.* Toronto: Elsevier.

Kinsella, E.A. (2006). Poetic resistance: Juxtaposing personal and professional discursive constructions in a practice setting. *Journal of the Canadian Association for Curriculum Studies, 4*(1), 35–49.

Liedberg, G.M., Bjork, M., & Hensing, G. (2010). Occupational therapists' perceptions of gender – A focus group study. *Australian Occupational Therapy Journal, 57,* 331–338.

Mackey, H. (2007). 'Do not ask me to remain the same': Foucault and the professional identities of occupational therapists. *Australian Occupational Therapy Journal, 54*(2), 95–102.

Matthews, J. (1984). *Good and mad women: The historical construction of femininity in twentieth century Australia.* Sydney: Allen & Unwin.

Nelson, A., Allison, H., & Copley, J. (2007). Understanding where we come from: Occupational therapy with urban Indigenous Australians. *Australian Occupational Therapy Journal, 54,* 203–214.

OT Australia. (2005). *Issues paper to the Productivity Commission Health Workforce Study.* Melbourne: Prepared by OT Australia (Australian Association of Occupational Therapists).

OT Australia. (2007). *Occupational Therapy (OT) Australia website.* Available: http//www. ausot.com.au, accessed 13 March 2007.

Polatajko, H., Davis, J., Stewart, D., Cantin, N., Amoroso, B., Purdie, L., et al. (2007). Specifying the domain of concern: Occupation as core. In E.P. Townsend & H. Polatajko (Eds.), *Enabling occupation II: Advancing an occupational therapy vision for health, well-being, and justice through occupation* (pp. 9–36). Ottawa, Ontario: CAOT Publications ACE.

Richardson, L., & St Pierre, E. (2005). Writing: A method of inquiry. In N.K. Denzin & Y.S. Lincoln (Eds.), *The Sage Handbook of Qualitative Research* (3rd ed.). Thousand Oaks, CA: Sage.

Schwartz, K.B. (2003). The history of occupational therapy. In E.B. Crepeau, E.S. Cohn & B.A.B. Schell (Eds.), *Willard and Spackman's occupational therapy* (10th ed., pp. 5–13). Philadelphia: Lippincott, Williams & Wilkins.

Wall, A. (1995). Levels of discourse and levels of dialogue. In C. Thompson & H. Raj Dua (Eds.), *Dialogism and cultural criticism* (pp. 65–82). London, ON: Mestengo Press.

Watson, R. (2006). Being before doing: The cultural identity (essence) of occupational therapy. *Australian Occupational Therapy Journal, 53*(3), 151–158.

Witz, A. (1992). *Professions and patriarchy.* London: Routledge.

Sally Denshire PhD
Faculty of Science
Charles Sturt University, Australia

NARELLE PATTON, JOY HIGGS AND MEGAN SMITH

12. ENVISIONING VISUAL RESEARCH STRATEGIES

And what is word knowledge but a shadow of wordless knowledge?
Khalil Gibran (1926)

Visual research gives primacy to the visual, and through incorporation of images aims to develop deeper understanding of the lived experiences of research participants through critical exploration of often taken-for-granted experiences. Visual research strategies are increasingly being employed to explore and develop deeper understandings of human worlds, such as the worlds of children, adolescents, individuals with mental health problems and patients within hospitals (Radley & Taylor, 2003; Mizen, 2005; Prosser, 2007; Thompson & Ninci, 2008). This chapter briefly overviews the historical development of visual research from its origin in anthropology to its current and more widespread use. Contemporary use of visual strategies is illustrated with examples from Narelle's doctoral research exploring the influence of context on physiotherapy students' clinical learning. In Narelle's research, physiotherapy students undertaking clinical placement were invited to take photographs of places, spaces and objects they considered influenced their clinical learning. Meanings of participants' lived experiences were then collaboratively constructed between Narelle and participants in photo-elicitation interviews. The use of photo-elicitation techniques in this research provided an enjoyable, empowering and meaningful experience for participants, eliciting multiple meanings and interpretations, bringing a richness and depth to the research, and proving to be broader and more nuanced than Narelle had considered at the outset.

VISUAL RESEARCH APPROACHES

Visual research is primarily concerned with the production, organisation and interpretation of images, which may be pre-existing or produced by researchers or research participants. Visual research strategies provide immediate, tangible and intimate ways of understanding participants' experiences. A defining characteristic of visual research is that it gives primacy to what is visually perceived rather than to what is said, written or statistically measured (Prosser, 2007). Visual research encompasses a wide range of visual techniques including observation, art, drawing, artefacts, video-recording, film and television. Visual imagery is not restricted to two-dimensional representations; museum ethnographers, for example, may well

J. Higgs et al., (eds.), Creative Spaces for
Qualitative Researching: Living Research, 115–124
© *2011 Sense Publishers. All rights reserved.*

employ objects rather than images to interpret and/or elicit responses from participants (Banks, 2007). Researchers may use images collected as data per se and through analysis and interpretation of the images gain deeper understandings of the worlds they are exploring. Alternatively, images may be used to co-construct meanings and understandings between researchers and participants, with photo-elicitation interviews being one such example. Banks (2007) described visual research as having two major strands. The first revolves around images created by social researchers (typically photographs, film and videotape, but also drawings and diagrams), and the second revolves around the collection and study of images produced or consumed by research participants (typically television, magazines, advertisements, drawings, paintings, photographs and videotape). Regardless of the method of production or the visual medium employed, a strength of visual research lies in the capacity of images to tap into wordless or tacit knowledge, the ambiguity between what we see and what we describe (Rhodes & Fitzgerald, 2006).

EVOLUTION OF VISUAL RESEARCH STRATEGIES

Visual research strategies are not new; they have a long history of both practice and debate in anthropology and sociology (Harper, 2002; Pink, 2007). It could be argued that field studies involving participant observation heralded the beginning of visual research. Observation has long been a central technique in ethnography (Russell, 1999), with the purpose of seeing another way of life as the members of the community themselves view it, capturing phenomena in and on their own terms, and grasping a culture in its natural environment (Lincoln & Guba, 1985). When undertaking participant observation the researcher acts largely as a camera, taking note of environment (space, colour, sound and smell), people and behaviour, becoming explicitly aware of things usually blocked out through selective inattention (Spradley, 1980; Grbich, 1999).

Image-based research is well developed within social anthropology and social ethnography (Mason, 2005). Social anthropology is underpinned by at least a century and a half of history and development, with photography used to investigate and document social welfare dating back to the 1930s (Banks, 2007). As early as 1860 Huxley photographed colonial subjects to facilitate morphological comparisons, which allowed identification of differences between the "races" of mankind (Banks, 2007). In another example of early image-based research, Collier first described photo-elicitation (the simple act of inserting a photograph into an interview) in 1959 while exploring mental health issues in Canada (Harper, 2002).

The last two decades have witnessed exponential growth in the use of visual research strategies, contributing to improvements in the robustness and complexity of visual research studies (Prosser & Loxley, 2007). Sociological and anthropological research based on visual data is being published more frequently, and there several established journals such as *Visual Anthropology* and *Visual Studies* publish articles on visual representation. although visual research is claimed to have come to play an increasingly meaningful role in education, health and social research (Radley & Taylor, 2003; Prosser, 2007) visual methods are not yet considered part of the mainstream repertoire of approaches available to most researchers. According to

Grady (2008), visual research is currently at a crossroads in that it can remain in a niche position or move into the mainstream. Visual strategies have the potential to enrich qualitative research, and their movement into the mainstream should be encouraged, but visual strategies should be employed only when it is appropriate and enlightening to do so and when development of a deeper and richer understanding of the phenomenon under investigation is facilitated.

ALIGNING VISUAL STRATEGIES WITH PHILOSOPHICAL UNDERPINNINGS

Visual research strategies can indeed provide a powerful medium through which to engage participants in collaborative, empowering and enjoyable research, but it can be tempting to embrace visual research without due consideration of the appropriateness of the method to the research question or reporting context. The uniqueness of each qualitative research project requires researchers to tailor selected strategies to their individual project so as to facilitate ethical production of credible and trustworthy data. In the pursuit of quality and rigour, the selection of visual strategies should be underpinned by a clear understanding of the philosophical principles informing qualitative research, a clear vision of the phenomenon under investigation and the ability to creatively imagine and credibly enact ethical and trustworthy research.

In the investigation of human phenomena a qualitative paradigm provides a congruent framework to develop a deeper understanding of the worlds and lived experiences under investigation. Having established an appropriate paradigm to frame the research, researchers should question how what exists can be known and which strategies can be used to explore what can be known (Higgs & Trede, 2010). To undertake credible and rigorous research using visual research strategies such strategies must be congruent with the research project's aims, questions and philosophical underpinnings. As an example, photovoice, a participatory-action research method in which participants use photos to document their own worlds and then critically discuss the images produced with policymakers (Wang et al., 2004), is congruent with research projects aiming to achieve social change.

WHY INCORPORATE VISUAL RESEARCH STRATEGIES?

Increase richness of the research. Visual research is frequently used in conjunction with other research strategies, such as observation and interviewing, to add richness to the research findings (Banks, 2007; Hurdley, 2007; Pink, 2007). Visual data can provide a wellspring for the development of new understandings about the phenomenon being investigated (Davidson, 2004) through the incorporation of data not accessible by other means (Pink, 2004; Banks, 2007). Participants' viewing and reflecting on images can facilitate the development of a new understanding of their views, which often represents taken-for-granted experiences. We agree with Davidson's (2004) view that there is often a cloak of invisibility over activities, places and people with whom we interact daily, and visual data has the ability to reflect back these sights and sounds, making the familiar strange and allowing examination of the familiar with a more critical eye.

Photo-elicitation techniques, with photos incorporated into interviews, engender collaboration between researchers and participants as they together construct the meaning of photographs (Harper, 2002). Photographs also sharpen participants' memory and give interviews an immediate character of authenticity and realistic reconstruction. This quote from a participant in Narelle's visual research project exploring contextual influences on physiotherapy students' clinical learning illustrates the ability of images not only to sharpen participants' memories but also to provide a bridge to those memories.

They do just trigger everything and if you hadn't done that I don't think I would have remembered as much. It's not so much remembering, it's resurfacing those memories.

Photographs can challenge participants more than verbal interviewing or artwork because the literal character of the image intercepts the participant's memory and returns attention to a familiar image of reality (Collier, 1986). Photographs may be charged with unexpected emotional images that trigger intense feelings and stimulate deep and meaningful dialogue between researchers and participants. Emotions spontaneously evoked by photographs may illuminate new ideas and ways of thinking not previously considered by researchers. Figure 12.1 stimulated rich dialogue and enabled new understandings to emerge between Narelle and the participant. This was illuminating and led to the unexpected generation of new knowledge.

Figure 12.1. Photograph of a dining room table

Expand data collection. Visual strategies have the potential to greatly expand both the quantity and quality of data that can be collected within a given time frame. As researchers are not required to be physically present to collect data at all points throughout the research, visual methods are relatively unobtrusive, inexpensive strategies that are not labour-intensive (Frith & Harcourt, 2007). For many qualitative researchers, practical constraints such as finite funding and time limitations constrain the amount of time they can spend observing participants, ultimately providing them with a snapshot of participants' experiences. Similarly, interviews are often constrained by time and perhaps also by participants' memories of their experiences. Inclusion of visual strategies such as artwork, photography and drawing allows participants to paint a more complete picture of their lived experiences, overcoming potential limitations of data collection strategies dependent on the researcher's continued presence.

In Narelle's research the use of photography provided participants with the freedom to represent factors beyond the immediate workplace that they perceived were influencing their clinical learning. Figure 12.2, a photograph of a pier (as a space for learning) represents an example of how photo-elicitation strategies provided participants freedom from temporal and physical restraints to represent and discuss matters meaningful to them. The use of visual strategies in Narelle's research enabled participants to represent spaces and places where it might have been inappropriate for Narelle to be present. For example, ethical protocols would deem it inappropriate for Narelle to enter students' accommodation and homes. Visual methods allowed students to display meaningful images of these spaces, further expanding and enriching the interpretation of their experiences.

Figure 12.2. Photograph of a pier

Address researcher-participant power imbalances. Research is an interactive process with power relations embedded in its every aspect, including choice of phenomenon to be explored, framing of research questions, participants to be included, histories of researchers, values of funding bodies, and choice of methodology. Explicit examination of the potential influence of power relations on research outcomes is warranted in any research project. The use of visual data collection strategies, such as providing participants with a camera and inviting them to take photographs that represent their feelings or thoughts, shifts the research power balance towards participants. This technique allows participants a measure of control in data collection and gives them the power to raise topics of importance to them in subsequent interviews. During photo-elicitation interviews, researcher and participant examine photographs together, relieving participants of the stress of being the subject of an interrogation (Collier, 1986).

Visual research strategies are increasingly being used to develop deeper understandings of marginalised groups in society such as children, adolescents, individuals with mental health problems and patients in hospitals (Radley & Taylor, 2003; Mizen, 2005; Prosser, 2007; Thompson & Ninci, 2008). We agree with the view of view Kaplin and Howes (2004) that students represent a group whose perspectives are often marginalised, if not ignored completely. In the context of Narelle's research we felt that it would be particularly difficult for physiotherapy students to provide their views on clinical learning environments due to temporal challenges such as limited time spent at clinical sites and perceived power relationships between students and clinical supervisors and students and academics. Therefore Narelle used photography to engage participants in a more empowering research process, to alter the dynamics between the researcher and participants and to ensure that the experience was enjoyable and meaningful to participants (see Close, 2007). Figure 12.3, a photograph taken to represent a regular morning meeting, provides an example of how participants were freed to talk about issues that were important to them. In this case the participant felt comfortable enough to discuss not only superficial aspects of the meeting but also potentially sensitive areas such as power imbalances among the team and the effect of that hierarchy on her learning.

Figure 12.3. Photograph of a morning meeting

Facilitate researcher reflexivity. Qualitative researchers need to reflexively identify their current horizon of understanding regarding the phenomenon they are exploring, and to remain aware of how their presence and views influence the research process. Spradley (1980) cautioned that heightened awareness does not come easily particularly for researchers investigating their own cultures, and emphasised the importance of "making the familiar strange" (see Gadamer, 1989) during research by explicitly taking a wide-angled approach. Images are tools with the potential to facilitate researcher reflexivity through their capacity to resurface memories. Images can provide a trigger for researchers to reflect upon their current horizon and to come to a deeper understanding of factors that underpin it and the ways in which those factors might influence the research process.

WHEN NOT TO USE VISUAL RESEARCH STRATEGIES

It is important to remember that although images are ubiquitous in our society and can be powerful and seductive, the use of images in visual research should be considered critically (Rose, 2007). Visual data will not solve all problems or answer all questions and there may be times when use of photographs would be inappropriate, intrusive and unethical (Davidson, 2004). The method may lean toward the unethical obtaining of images. For example, cameras in mobile phones can allow photographs to be readily and surreptitiously taken without the consent of the subject of the image. Researchers contemplating the use of visual strategies should clearly identify the way in which such use will be ethical as well as how the strategies strengthen research outcomes. Researchers planning to undertake visual strategies must ensure that these strategies are culturally appropriate, will encourage and empower participants and will illuminate the phenomenon.

ENACTING VISUAL RESEARCH STRATEGIES

The decision to include visual strategies in research studies opens multiple meaning-making possibilities, requiring researchers to make many considered decisions, often best addressed at the planning stage of the research.

Ethical Conduct of Visual Research Strategies

Ethical considerations should be paramount in the conduct of all research, but visual research strategies present unique ethical challenges. Such strategies raise particular concerns surrounding issues of informed consent, anonymity, permission and copyright (Flick, 2007). Consent is a complex issue in visual research (Close, 2007); anonymity cannot always be assured, particularly when people are captured in images. Careful consideration must be given to what will happen to images once they are produced. When images are publicly disseminated control over them is lost; therefore publication intentions must be clearly articulated to participants at the outset of the research.

Image ownership may raise ethical concerns regarding analysis, publishing and copyright when employing visual research strategies. Generally, image ownership resides with the person who takes the photograph (Rose, 2007). Ethically, visual researchers need to find a balance between the benefits gained from the research and the risk and potential burden to participants. Careful planning, anticipation of potential problems and clear articulation of research strategies to participants can reduce both the potential burden on participants and the risk to credibility and trustworthiness of data generated.

Practicalities of Visual Research

When planning a visual research study due consideration must be given to practical aspects of the research as well as to philosophical and ethical aspects. Budgetary considerations such as cost of equipment (digital cameras, video cameras, and so on) and consumables (paper, paints, batteries, data cards and so on) and costs of distribution and representation of the final outcome may guide researcher choice of technologies employed. Research budgets may place constraints on hardware choice when purchasing equipment, but researchers should remain aware of technological developments and consider the research context and the quality of final results required for the project (Pink, 2007). Further, when choosing hardware for visual research strategies, researchers should ensure that the equipment is appropriate for participants' use. Consideration should be given to participants' expertise and experience with drawing or photography and with selected equipment, as well as the quality of the final image required to facilitate data interpretation.

Data Interpretation

Qualitative interpretation draws on both critical and creative thinking. The interpretation of qualitative data involves creativity, intellectual discipline, analytical rigour and a great deal of hard work (Patton, 2002). Qualitative interpretation must be systematic and rigorous, bringing together all extracts of data that are pertinent to a particular theme, topic or research question. Interpretation within visual research methodology should address the varied and dynamic interrelationships between images, interview transcripts and theoretical interpretations, through which meaning is constructed rather than simply found (Felstead, Jewson, & Walters, 2004).

Data interpretation in visual research may focus on the meanings ascribed to the images by the individuals who generated the images, the researchers and readers of the research; this includes consideration of the context of the images and the relationship between visual and other (including verbal) meanings (Pink, 2007). When photo-elicitation research strategies are employed, participant-generated photographs are not analysed, as the purpose of the photographs is to facilitate access to deep and rich data through discussions with participants. In this way photographs' meanings are co-constructed through dialogue between participants and researchers. As an example, a photograph of a tearoom produced by a participant in Narelle's research stimulated rich discussion of social influences, particularly influences of physiotherapy staff and other students on students' clinical learning. Aspects such as being welcomed and feeling part of the physiotherapy community of practice were highlighted as particularly significant to students' learning.

IMAGINING FUTURE POSSIBILITIES

Visual research strategies will continue to evolve rapidly, with technological advancements placing digital technology within reach of the general population. Accessibility of digital image-making equipment, with the declining cost of digital cameras and most mobile phones today incorporating cameras capable of capturing both still and moving images, opens a world of possibility for visual researchers. Web-based technologies also provide rich possibilities for visual research, with virtual worlds or Web-based, simulated multi-media environments designed so that users can "inhabit" and interact via their own graphical self-representations known as avatars (Boulos, Hetherington, & Wheeler, 2007). Three-dimensional virtual worlds can be considered as social networks, where people can collaboratively create and edit objects in virtual worlds besides meeting with each other and interacting with existing objects. The potential of virtual worlds to provide rich and meaningful research data has yet to be fully explored.

CONCLUSION

In this chapter we proposed that the critical use of visual research strategies has the potential to enhance qualitative research projects and to develop deeper and richer understandings of phenomena being explored. Visual research is an exciting and rapidly evolving field, providing researchers with opportunities to creatively imagine new and powerful strategies to develop deep and meaningful understandings of human worlds. Credible and ethical employment of visual research strategies can broaden and deepen research findings through the illumination of unanticipated meanings, as well as providing an enjoyable and rewarding experience for research participants.

ACKNOWLEDGEMENT

We acknowledge with thanks the student participants in Narelle's doctoral research whose photographs are reproduced in this chapter.

REFERENCES

Banks, M. (2007). *Using visual data in qualitative research* (Vol. 5). Los Angeles: Sage.

Boulos, M., Hetherington, L., & Wheeler, S. (2007). Second Life: An overview of the potential of 3-D worlds in medical and health education. *Health Information and Libraries Journal, 24*(4), 233–245.

Close, H. (2007). The use of photography as a qualitative research tool. *Nurse Researcher, 15,* 127–136.

Collier, J. & Collier, M. (1986). *Visual anthropology: Photography as a research method.* Albuquerque: University of New Mexico Press.

Davidson, J. (2004). "I am fieldnote": Researching and teaching with visual data. *Qualitative Research Journal, 4*(2), 48–75.

Felstead, A., Jewson, N., & Walters, S. (2004). Images, interviews and interpretations: Making connections in visual research. *Studies in Qualitative Methodology, 7,* 105–121.

Flick, U. (2007). *Designing qualitative research* (Vol. 1). Los Angeles: Sage.

Frith, H., & Harcourt, D. (2007). Using photographs to capture women's experiences of chemotherapy: Reflecting on the method. *Qualitative Health Research, 17*(10), 1340–1350.

Gadamer, H.-G. (1989). *Truth and method* (J. Weinsheimer & D. Marshall, Trans., 2nd ed.). Gloucester: Sheed & Ward.

Gibran, K. (1994). *The prophet.* London: Bracken Books.

Grady, J. (2008). Visual research at the crossroads. *Forum: Qualitative Social Research, 9*(3), 1–34.

Grbich, C. (1999). *Qualitative research in health: An introduction.* St Leonards, NSW: Allen & Unwin.

Harper, D. (2002). Talking about pictures: A case for photo elicitation. *Visual Studies, 17*(1), 13–26.

Higgs, J., & Trede, F. (2010). Philosophical frameworks and research communities. In J. Higgs, N. Cherry, R. Macklin & R. Ajjawi (Eds.), *Researching practice: A discourse on qualitative methodologies* (pp. 31–36). Rotterdam, The Netherlands: Sense.

Hurdley, R. (2007). Focal points: Framing material culture and visual data. *Qualitative Research, 7*(3), 355–374.

Kaplin, I., & Howes, A. (2004). "Seeing through different eyes": Exploring the value of participative research using images in schools. *Cambridge Journal of Education, 34*(2), 143–155.

Lincoln, Y.S., & Guba, E.G. (1985). *Naturalistic Inquiry.* Newbury Park, CA: Sage

Mason, P. (2005). Visual data in applied qualitative research: Lessons from experience. *Qualitative Research, 5*(3), 325–346.

Mizen, P. (2005). A little "light work"? Children's images of their labour. *Visual Studies, 20*(2), 124–139.

Patton, M.Q. (2002). *Qualitative research and evaluation methods* (3rd ed.). Thousand Oaks, CA: Sage.

Pink, S. (2004). Visual methods. In C. Seale, G. Gobo, J.F. Gubrium, & D. Silverman (Eds.), *Qualitative Research Practice* (pp. 361–376). London: Sage.

Pink, S. (2007). *Doing visual ethnography* (2nd ed.). London: Sage.

Prosser, J. (2007). Visual methods and the visual culture of schools. *Visual Studies, 22*(1), 13–30.

Prosser, J., & Loxley, A. (2007). Enhancing the contribution of visual methods to inclusive education. *Journal of Research in Special Educational Needs, 7*(1), 55–68.

Radley, A., & Taylor, D. (2003). Images of recovery: A photo-elicitation study on the hospital ward. *Qualitative Health Research, 13*(1), 77–99.

Rhodes, T., & Fitzgerald, J. (2006). Visual data in addictions research: Seeing comes before words? *Addiction Research and Theory, 14*(4), 349–363.

Rose, G. (2007). *Visual methodologies: An introduction to the interpretation of visual materials* (2nd ed.). London: Sage.

Russell, C. (1999). Collecting and evaluating evidence: Participant observation. In V. Minichiello, G. Sullivan, K. Greenwood & R. Axford (Eds.), *Handbook for research methods in health sciences* (pp. 431–448). Sydney: Addison-Wesley.

Spradley, J. (1980). *Participant observation.* New York: Holt, Rinehart and Winston.

Thompson, N., & Ninci, L. (2008). The experience of living with chronic mental illness: A photovoice study. *Perspectives in Psychiatric Care, 44*(1), 14–24.

Wang, C., Morrel-Samuels, S., Hutchison, P., Bell, L., & Pestronk, R. (2004). Flint Photovoice: Community building among youths, adults and policymakers. *American Journal of Public Health, 94*(6), 911–913.

Narelle Patton BAppSc(Phty), MHSc, PhD Candidate
School of Community Health, Charles Sturt University Australia

Joy Higgs AM PhD
The Education For Practice Institute, Charles Sturt University, Australia

Megan Smith PhD
School of Community Health, Charles Sturt University, Australia

SHANON PHELAN AND ELIZABETH ANNE KINSELLA

13. PHOTOELICITATION INTERVIEW METHODS AND RESEARCH WITH CHILDREN

Possibilities, Pitfalls and Ethical Considerations

In this chapter we consider the rationale and practical issues in using photoelicitation interviews (PEIs) in the conduct of research with children. We begin with an overview of photoelicitation and its promise as a method when conducting research with children. We then discuss pitfalls and considerations in using photoelicitation methods; conflations between photoelicitation and photovoice; practical examples of current research using PEIs; ethical considerations; and practical considerations when conducting visual research with children. Our concluding perspective is that photoelicitation is a promising method as a means to elicit children's voices in research, and that it is best used within a broader methodological framework.

It is interesting to note, as Prosser and Burke (2008, p. 407) have done, that "words are the domain of adult researchers and therefore can be disempowering to the young. Images and their mode of production, on the other hand, are central to children's culture from a very early age and therefore empowering". Given this insight, the potential of visual methods when conducting research with children takes on a practical significance (i.e., gathering meaningful data) as well as a potentially moral one (i.e., overcoming disempowerment).

WHAT IS PHOTOELICITATION?

Photoelicitation is a method of visual data collection used in combination with an interview process. Images or photographs created by participants, researchers, or drawn from the media are used within interviews to draw out viewers' responses (Harper, 2002; Prosser & Burke, 2008). PEIs draw attention to the subjective meaning of images for participants, and provide an entry point for understanding participants' social worlds (Clark-Ibanez, 2004). Participants are often asked to take a sequence of photographs which tell a story about their understanding of social phenomena and draw attention to contextual issues (Harper, 2000). Frohmann (2005) and Harper (2002) have pointed out that photographs taken by participants can also be seen as a window to the self, connecting the self to society, culture and history. Meanings are elicited and constructed through the use of photographs and through dialogue between researcher and researched. Thus the

J. Higgs et al., (eds.), Creative Spaces for
Qualitative Researching: Living Research, 125–134

PEI is a means of collaborative interpretation about the social phenomena being studied (Evans, 1999).

Photoelicitation has been employed in anthropology, but is now becoming more common in visual anthropology and visual sociology research (Harper, 2002; Frohmann, 2005; Epstein, Stevens, McKeever, & Baruchel, 2006). It is important to distinguish that photoelicitation is a method rather than a methodology. A research method is a concrete technique or procedure used to gather data, whereas a methodology is philosophically and theoretically informed, and represents the process of design underpinning the research (Crotty, 2003). Although predominantly used as a method within ethnographic methodologies, PEIs are also used in action research, narrative inquiry, phenomenology, case study, grounded theory and other methodological approaches.

Using PEI without a methodological framework may be likened to setting sail without a map; methodology links the choice and use of PEI methods to the broader epistemological, philosophical and theoretical assumptions of the research design (Crotty, 2003). The use of PEI methods alone creates the danger of a purely utilitarian and technical focus, whereas the methodology informs in-depth and high-quality research engagement (Jaye, 2002).

PHOTOELICITATION INTERVIEWS IN RESEARCH WITH CHILDREN

Using photography in research with children can allow researchers to learn more about complex social issues influencing children's lives. Children can find it difficult to express their experiences with abstract social issues verbally. For example, it might be difficult to talk about dimensions of identity such as appearance, style, culture, and gender (Hethorn & Kaiser, 1999; Croghan, Griffin, Hunter, & Phoenix, 2008). The use of photographs allows children to approach the social and cultural dimensions of their experience in different ways, potentially generating rich discussions. Croghan et al. (2008) point out that the PEI is useful for studying identity as it "offers participants an opportunity to "show" rather than "tell" aspects of their identity that may have otherwise remained hidden" (p. 1).

Taking a sequence of photographs to represent a visual narrative can also tell a story about a person or phenomenon. Therefore, giving cameras to children can prove empowering to the extent that it offers them the opportunity to create their own narratives and to consider their personal expressions with respect to the phenomenon under investigation (Prosser & Burke, 2008).

PEIs not only allow a unique representation of narratives, but also give participants a chance to become active in the research process, an issue of particular importance in research with children. The assumption of the PEI is that it has the potential to break down power imbalances between the researcher (adult) and the researched (child). Power can be shared with the child through participant-generated photographs, making it possible for the child to have some control over the research process (Dell Clark, 1999; Frohmann, 2005; Epstein et al., 2006). PEI methods can potentially overcome the limitations of language and memory by offering visual cues within the interview. This is particularly important when undertaking research with children, as limitations in these domains can present significant challenges depending on the child's developmental stage (Dell Clark, 1999; Cappello, 2005; Epstein et al., 2006).

Photoelicitation has been successfully used with children to tap into their unique perspectives (Burke, 2005; Cappello, 2005; Epstein et al., 2006). Darbyshire, Macdougal and Schiller (2005) used focus groups, visual maps, and photographs to examine children's perceptions and experiences of place, space, and physical activity. They found that without maps and photographs important aspects of children's activities would not have been revealed (i.e., the role that pets play with respect to participation in physical activities). They contended that flexibility and creativity in data collection methods are essential when undertaking research with children. These researchers stressed the importance of engaging in discussions about visual data with children to gain an understanding of the cultural, social, and geographic contexts. Such dialogue can help researchers reveal the child's voice.

PITFALLS AND CONSIDERATIONS OF USING PEI IN
RESEARCH WITH CHILDREN

Despite the potential advantages of using PEIs with children, it is also important to acknowledge that the approach is subject to unique limitations. For instance, at times the method can be influenced by parents or caregivers (for a variety of reasons), reducing the child's control in the research (Barker & Weller, 2003; Clark-Ibanez, 2004). Moreover, the researcher's decision as to who will take the photographs also influences the power balance. For example, Clark-Ibanez (2004) suggested that although researcher-produced photographs or images can be useful when conducting theory-driven research, they also reduce the child's influence. On the other hand, in more inductive research, participants can be asked to take their own pictures, for photoelicitation "autodriven" interviews (Dell Clark, 1999). Ideally this technique enables children to "drive" the interview process so that the phenomena discussed are relevant to them and they maintain a sense of control. So who is taking the pictures, and explication of the rationale for anyone other than the child taking pictures (if the study design calls for the child's perspective) become significant considerations in photoelicitation research (Dell Clark, 1999; Clark-Ibanez, 2004; Burke, 2005). Such issues have implications for whether or to what extent the "voice" of the child is present in the work.

The researcher must also be sensitive to children falling into a role where they feel they must be on their best behaviour and provide information that they think the "teacher" wants to hear (Burke, 2005; Cappello, 2005). It is important, therefore, to establish a relationship distinct from the teacher-student relationship, and to find ways to elicit responses from children that represent their perspectives. For instance, in our current study using PEIs with children with disabilities, we have found that the children automatically regarded the researchers as a "helper" (support staff) who would be visiting them on a regular basis, just like their care workers who came for respite or range of motion therapy interventions. This situated the researcher in a particular role with a certain amount of authoritative power from the child's point of view. It also implied that the researcher was there to help the child, which might not necessarily be the case. Thus it is important to establish and clarify one's role as a researcher to ensure that children know how the researcher's presence in their life is distinct from that of others. Children should understand that the relationship is a voluntary one, that they can choose to participate or withdraw at any time, and that the researcher will be involved in their lives for only a short period of time. This is also where rapport building becomes a key component to the research process, a topic discussed later.

Another potential challenge is that using PEIs relies heavily on what can be captured on film. In the context of studying something like identity, for example, this raises questions such as "what parts of identity are not visible" (Harper, 2002, p. 18). Because photographs represent only one moment in time, what is excluded from the pictures and why are important questions to explore with participants.

A final possible limitation is that what children do is often seasonal in nature; therefore, depictions of the phenomena under investigation might not be truly representative, and seasonal variations will likely influence the data collected. This is an important consideration in the design of the study, and can call for interviews that elicit stories beyond what is seen in the pictures, and building questions about seasonal events into the interview guide.

CONFLATIONS: PEI AND PHOTOVOICE

Gaining increasing use in qualitative research is another visual approach, photovoice. It is sometimes conflated with PEI, yet there are significant differences between them. As discussed above, PEI is a research method that can be used within a variety of methodologies. Photovoice, on the other hand, is not a method, but is usually depicted as a methodological approach within the school of community-based participatory action research (Wang & Burris, 1994, 1997; Catalani & Minkler, 2010). According to Wang and Burris (1997, p. 370) the three main goals of photovoice are to use photographs (a) to enable people to record and reflect their community's strengths and concerns, (b) to promote critical dialogue and knowledge about important community issues through large and small group discussion, and (c) to reach policymakers. In photovoice research, participants always take their own pictures, and these pictures are used as a starting point in the interview or focus group, and to initiate ideas to enact change (Wang & Burris, 1994, 1997).

Like PEI methods, photovoice has evolved since its original emergence as a methodology, and is not a unified field or a definitive concept; what it entails can be contentious or interpreted differently by different people (Prosser & Burke, 2008; Catalani & Minkler, 2010). In a systematic review of photovoice literature, Catalani and Minkler found that a large majority of researchers using photovoice drew upon the seminal work of Caroline Wang and her colleagues. Some photovoice projects modify traditional approaches to fit specific research questions and populations; this has resulted in various levels of participatory involvement (Frohmann, 2005; Oliffe & Bottorff, 2007; Catalani & Minkler, 2010). In most photovoice research projects, people are asked to take photographs and discuss them within large or small groups as a means to enact social action and policy change (Wang & Burris, 1994, 1997; Catalani & Minkler, 2010). Some photovoice research projects, with less of a participatory action focus, have used one-to-one interviews as a method, specifically employing photoelicitation techniques (Baker & Wang, 2006; Catalani & Minkler, 2010). Only the more participatory projects encompass all three of the goals of photovoice research originally outlined by Wang and Burris (1997). This can create tensions regarding whether a study design is truly representative of photovoice methodology or is moving more toward the use of photoelicitation method. So, although depictions of these two approaches are sometimes conflated and contested in the literature, we view photoelicitation as a method that can be used in combination with many methodological approaches and photovoice as a methodology for community-based action research.

PHOTOELICITATION INTERVIEWS: EXAMPLES OF RESEARCH WITH CHILDREN

We are currently working on a case study research project, using photoelicitation interviews as a method to examine identity with children with physical disabilities. We have asked children to take pictures of activities they participate in, and are conducting interviews using the children's pictures to elicit discussion about what they do and to consider the implications for how identities are shaped. As well, a comic software program, *Comic Life* (Version 1.5.4), is being used to create portraits containing 10 of each child's pictures. Using the *Comic Life* program, children can add titles, speech bubbles and thought bubbles to their pictures. The combination of the pictures and the child's words is powerful and offers representations of the child's perceptions. In the current study, an interview using the photographs taken by an 11-year-old girl with cerebral palsy created an opportunity for her to share what was important to her in the moment, as well as at the time the photographs were taken. Moreover, discussion of her photographs allowed her to exert some control over the direction of the interview. For example, when asked what she wanted to put in one of the bubbles, she replied "I don't know what to say ... whenever I say it, it sounds stupid". When offered the opportunity to type her comment without saying it out loud, she could articulate her thoughts. She was then able to share her thoughts about her disability through discussion about the picture and text rather than talking directly, which, like many children, she found difficult. The photograph and her words, provided a rich starting point to develop insights into disability and self-image, social perceptions of disability and the child's own perceptions of her disability which might not otherwise have been discerned.

A unique advantage of using photographs in interviews is that you can learn something new about the phenomenon, which might not come up in general conversation. The pictures themselves and the questions prompted by the pictures can reveal unique aspects relevant to a child's life. For example, in our study we received several pictures pertaining to Halloween, a North American holiday that falls each year on October 31st. In one picture, an 11-year-old child with cerebral palsy is with her carved pumpkin. What is not seen in the picture is the person who helped her carve the pumpkin, or how this might make this activity more meaningful to the child. The picture inspired a valuable interview question which revealed a relational dimension to this activity: when asked who helped her carve the pumpkin, she excitedly replied "my Dad did!" Until that point, the child had not mentioned her father, perhaps because her he is often at work in the evenings and weekends, and it appears that her mother is usually home and helps her with a majority of her activities.

Photographs can be used together to tell a story – to depict a participant's narrative. For children this can serve as a window into more discussion about the phenomenon of interest. In our study, children are creating comic strips using their photos and developing a narrative of the everyday activities that are of particular importance to them. Interestingly, not only are the comics full of activities that children like, but they often include activities they do not particularly like, such as homework. This observation might not have arisen through conversation alone. In one particular comic, the homework picture was included in the top ten pictures (out of 15) that the child deemed important to tell a story about who she is. In this particular narrative, most of the pictures take place at home or at the place where she rides horses. Yet there are many other contexts that she inhabits and many interesting reasons why they do not appear in the pictures. This too is valuable data, in that what is invisible may be just as important, or perhaps even more revealing, than what is. Questions that probe the "absences" in photographs taken by children offer potentially important insights.

ETHICAL CONSIDERATIONS IN CONDUCTING VISUAL RESEARCH WITH CHILDREN

There are several ethical considerations to bear in mind when conducting research using PEIs with children. Some of these are important with respect to research with children generally (see Mishna, Antle, & Regehr, 2004), and others arise more particularly when using PEIs. Our attention here is with the latter, with the issues of disclosure and representation in PEI research.

PEIs can be problematic in connection with anticipating potential risks associated with disclosure, pertaining to both the photographs and the actual interview. Mishna et al. (2004) have asserted that these risks may be more pertinent in research with children. Considering that children might lack the capacity to anticipate the information they may be asked to disclose, they might not understand the potential risks and benefits. It is important, therefore, that the researcher anticipates and explains potential risks and benefits in a way that is meaningful to the child. Creating an environment that is too comfortable might lead to the unintentional disclosure of information (Mishna et al., 2004).

The issue of representation in photovoice ethics was discussed by Wang and Redwood-Jones (2001). They were concerned that researchers could place participants "in a false light by images and by words" (p. 566). Researchers must be sensitive to how participants are being represented and the potential implications. It is important to acknowledge that researchers play a role in interpreting and representing the research findings, and that they, therefore, depict their interpretations as only one of many possible representations. Depending on the context, measures might be taken to conceal the child's identity, such as blurring the face or blacking over the eyes, or a decision might be made not to use the photographs but to draw on other forms of data in representing the findings.

REFLECTIONS ON ENGAGING CHILDREN IN THE PEI METHOD

In this section we reflect on practical considerations for engagement in the PEI method, including flexibility, sensitivity to time demands, attention to developing rapport with the children, and the use of digital versus disposable cameras.

Flexibility

We have noted that using the PEI method with children requires considerable researcher flexibility, both in the design of the study and within each individual session. It is helpful to design semi-structured interviews to guide sessions, but to know that the interview will likely take on a life of its own, guided by the child's uses of and responses to the photographs. We have found that the best interviews allow children to shape significantly the interview process and the direction of discussion. We often ask questions in a roundabout or creative manner.

Building follow-up interviews into the research design is helpful, as what is planned in one session may have to happen in another, depending on the child's mood, interest, and the directions in which stories unfold in response to the photographs. This also allows children to decide whether and when they want to talk about a certain topic, and can prevent unintentional disclosure.

Another reason why flexibility is essential is that asking children to do something they do not want to do can adversely shape the data. In the moment, a researcher might decide to stick to the original plan to keep things running smoothly, but that may not be beneficial in representing the overall picture. For example, Shanon began to ask a child the first question on the interview guide, "Tell me about yourself and the things you like to do". The child responded, "This is stupid". Instead of persisting with the question Shanon skipped the first few questions and immediately began introducing the pictures. The child was waiting to see her pictures, and this completely changed the tone of the interview to more of a positive and fun atmosphere. Shanon was then able to ask some questions while looking at the pictures, saving other questions for the following session.

Time

The PEI method can be time-consuming to do properly, and it is important to consider not only the researcher's time within the study but also the significant time commitment for children and families involved. It is not always easy for parents to create time for children to take pictures, and they might forget or encourage children to take all their pictures at the beginning or end of the time period (Dell Clark, 1999). Dell Clark suggested that researchers acknowledge the time commitment involved and be aware (and accepting) that dynamics within the home, time of year and other family commitments can mean that they cannot always obtain as many pictures as they might wish. The possibility of time constraints affecting the quality and quantity of visual data is worth considering, and provides an additional reason why it is crucial to ask about the pictures that are missing or the pictures that children might wish to have taken. All this provides valuable data.

Rapport Building

Building rapport is particularly important in undertaking the PEI method; spending time to get to know the children is central. Knowing and asking them about their interests goes a long way. We have found that children love to talk about what is meaningful to them when they feel comfortable with the person they are talking to. It is also advantageous for researchers to be familiar with popular media so that they can relate to children's likes and dislikes. Knowing about the latest popular movie or pop-star opens up avenues for conversations and helps to build credibility from the child's perspective. Building rapport requires flexibility, in the sense that researchers might have to leave behind some of their affinities for structure and order. For example, Shanon was asked to hold a family guinea pig in the middle of her interview session, whether she was comfortable with it or not. Clearly that was important to the child at that moment, and so she did hold it! Shanon discovered that instead of becoming anxious about the session not going as planned, she could embrace the guinea pig, have fun with it and take it as an opportunity to develop rapport and thus see into the child's world.

How researchers present themselves can help minimise power imbalances. For example, the language they use, the clothes they wear, their body language and the nature of their interaction with the child are significant. The context of the interview also can set the tone (Burke, 2005; Epstein et al., 2006). Often data gathering is conducted in the most comfortable and natural environment for participants, namely their homes, but it is also important to consider where in the home the interview should take place. Interviews that take place at the kitchen table might seem to be more formal than those that take place on the playroom floor. The nature of the interview can change dramatically depending on the day of the week, time of day, or what has happened during the day prior to the interview session. For example, an interview on Saturday afternoon might be more engaging than one that takes place Friday evening after a week of school. Nonetheless, some of these considerations are not easily negotiable, especially with busy families.

Digital Versus Disposable Cameras

In the design of a research study, decisions must be made about the type of camera (digital versus disposable cameras) and the features of the camera to be used.

Considerations include whether the camera is user-friendly for participants and whether the functions meet the research needs (durability, quality, versatility). We have found multiple advantages of digital cameras over disposable cameras, especially for children with physical disabilities. With a digital camera an almost unlimited number of pictures can be taken. Participants have immediate feedback about the quality of their pictures and can delete those that do not turn out, or that do not adequately represent the image they intended. In contrast, with a disposable camera participants do not receive immediate feedback and could easily click a whole roll of pictures without realising it. Another advantage of the digital camera is the facility for participants to confirm the picture using the camera's LCD if they want to be in it (which they often do) or if they are unable to take the picture for accessibility reasons. Digital cameras are more expensive, which may create a challenge depending on the availability of funding for the research. When considering less expensive cameras it is important to think about the quality of the images and how the photographs will be used. For example, if prints are to be used in publications or art shows then cameras that produce good quality prints will be necessary. Although the start-up costs are higher, digital cameras are reusable and make a good investment for researchers interested in undertaking ongoing research projects using visual methods. The fact that most children are familiar with digital cameras may also be an advantage. Furthermore, children can easily load a copy of their pictures onto their home computer. Many fun software programs for kids exist that use digital pictures, one example being the *Comic Life* program mentioned earlier.

CONCLUSION

In this chapter we have examined the possibilities, pitfalls, ethical considerations and applications of PEIs in the context of working with children. Given Prosser and Burke's (2008) insight that images and their mode of production are empowering to children, the possibilities of PEIs to encourage children's "voices" demands attention. Nonetheless, researchers must be cautious about the potential for power imbalances, unintentional disclosure, and issues of representation, with the children involved. We contend that, in the interests of quality research, use of the PEI method on its own is insufficient. Rather this method is most fruitfully used within a well-articulated methodological framework.

REFERENCES

Baker, T.A., & Wang, C.C. (2006). Photovoice: Use of a participatory action research method to explore the chronic pain experience in older adults. *Qualitative Health Research, 16*(10), 1405–1413.

Barker, J., & Weller, S. (2003). Never work with children?: The geography of methodological issues in research with children. *Qualitative Research, 3*, 207–227.

Burke, C. (2005). "Play in focus": Children researching their own spaces and places for play. *Children, Youth and Environments, 15*, 27–53.

Cappello, M. (2005). Photo interviews: Eliciting data through conversations with children. *Field Methods, 17*, 170–182.

Catalani, C., & Minkler, M. (2010). Photovoice: A review of the literature in health and public health. *Health Education & Behavior, 37*, 424–451.

Clark-Ibanez, M. (2004). Framing the social world with photo-elicitation interviews. *American Behavioral Scientists, 47*, 1507–1527.

Comic Life (Version 1.5.4) [Computer software]. Mt. Pleasant, SC: plasq. Available: https://store2.esellerate.net/store/checkout/CustomLayout.aspx?s=STR2824316198&pc=&page=MultiCatalog.htm, accessed 17 March 2011.

Croghan, R., Griffin, C., Hunter, J., & Phoenix A. (2008). Young people's constructions of self: Notes on the use and analysis of the photo-elicitation methods. *International Journal of Social Research Methodology, 11*, 1–12.

Crotty, M. (2003). *The foundations of social research. Meaning and perspective in the research process.* Thousand Oaks, CA: Sage.

Darbyshire, P., Macdougal, C., & Schiller, W. (2005). Multiple methods in qualitative research with children: More insight or just more? *Qualitative Research, 5*, 417–436.

Dell Clark, C. (1999). The autodriven interview. A photographic viewfinder into children's experience. *Visual Sociology, 14*, 39–50.

Epstein, I., Stevens, B., McKeever, P., & Baruchel, S. (2006). Photo elicitation interview (PEI): Using photos to elicit children's perspectives. *International Journal of Qualitative Methods, 5*(3), 1–9.

Evans, J. (1999). Regulating photographic meanings. Introduction. In J. Evans & S. Hall (Eds.), *Visual culture: The reader* (pp. 11–21). London: Sage.

Frohmann, L. (2005). The framing safety project. Photographs and narratives by battered women. *Violence Against Women, 11*, 1396–1419.

Harper, D. (2000). Reimagining visual methods. In N.K. Denzin & Y.S. Lincoln (Eds.), *Handbook of qualitative research* (2nd ed.) (pp. 717–732). Thousand Oaks, CA: Sage.

Harper, D. (2002). Talking about pictures: A case for photo elicitation. *Visual Studies, 17*, 13–26.

Hethorn, J., & Kaiser, S. (1999). Youth style articulating cultural anxiety. *Visual Sociology, 14*, 109–125.

Jaye, C. (2002). Doing qualitative research in general practice: Methodological utility and engagement. *Family Practice, 19*, 557–562.

Mishna, F., Antle, B.J., & Regehr, C. (2004). Tapping the perspectives of children: Emerging ethical issues in qualitative research. *Qualitative Social Work, 3*, 449–468.

Oliffe, J.L., & Bottorff, J.L. (2007). Further than the eye can see? Photo elicitation and research with men. *Qualitative Health Research, 17*(6), 850–858.

Prosser, J., & Burke, C. (2008). Imaged-based educational research: Childlike perspectives. In J.G. Knowles & A.L. Cole (Eds.), *Handbook of the arts in qualitative research* (pp. 407–419). Thousand Oaks, CA: Sage.

Wang, C.C., & Burris, M. (1994). Empowerment through photo novella: Portraits of participation. *Health Education Quarterly, 21*, 171–186.

Wang, C., & Burris, M.A. (1997). Photovoice: Concept, methodology, and use for participatory needs assessment. *Health Education & Behavior, 24*, 369–387.

Wang, C.C., & Redwood-Jones, Y.A. (2001). Photovoice ethics: Perspectives from Flint photovoice. *Health Education & Behavior, 28*(5), 560–572.

Shanon Phelan MSc(OT), PhD Candidate
Health & Rehabilitation Sciences, Occupational Science Field
University of Western Ontario, Canada

Elizabeth Anne Kinsella PhD
School of Occupational Therapy & Occupational Science Field
Faculty of Health Sciences
University of Western Ontario, Canada

DONNA BRIDGES AND DEBBIE HORSFALL

14. THE GENDERED BATTLEFIELD

Creating Feminist Spaces in Military Places

We are both what could loosely be described as pacifist women. We belong to peaceful activist organisations; we have taught subjects at university that focus on peace studies. We have joined marches for peace in Australia and overseas, signed petitions, refused to smack our children, and helped write policies against bullying. We have tended to hang out with other like-minded women and we have held the belief that patriarchy, by definition, is violent: that the way the patriarchal system maintains its global dominance is primarily through aggression and/or the threat of aggression. We have known each other now for 15 years, but in the context of this chapter we came together as PhD candidate (Donna) and supervisor[1] (Debbie). The research Donna undertook as part of her PhD (Bridges, 2005), a qualitative study using feminist methodology about the experience of women with the masculine culture of the Australian Defence Force (ADF), forms the bedrock of this chapter. The chapter is about the benefits and challenges involved in a working relationship created by us as university academics and the organisation of the ADF.

This research emerged from our collective histories and asked the seemingly simple question, "why do women join the military?" In researching this question Donna uncovered and explored historical, sociological, political and contemporary roles of women in the ADF. In the first few months of research we established that this initial question was quite easily answered. We found that women join the military for the same reasons that men do: educational opportunities, security in employment, travel and adventure, family tradition, a desire to serve their country and an opportunity to do something meaningful with their lives.

Having "the answer" was somewhat disconcerting, although not really so surprising, for both of us. The answer certainly did not constitute a PhD and it meant that we needed to re-focus and work out what it was that Donna really wanted to know; what were the questions beneath the question; what could be really useful knowledge in this context? Through policy, literature and media reviews we developed a preliminary sense of issues affecting military women. We established that the core considerations were those that concerned the process of "full gender integration" in the ADF. The term refers to the process of women's increasing participation into a previously all-male realm, into *all* military positions, including combat employments.

The timing for this research was interesting, as a number of significant events relating to women's integration into the ADF had taken place during the 1990s.

J. Higgs et al., (eds.), Creative Spaces for
Qualitative Researching: Living Research, 135–144

The ADF began the decade with the 1990 governmental recommendation, on the advice of the Chief of Staff's Committee, that women be integrated into combat-*related* roles (Shephard, 1999). Two years later, another governmental decision allowed women to serve in all areas of Defence other than *direct* combat roles. Prior to this women were excluded from any duties that would require them to "work in support of, and in close proximity to, a person performing combat duties ...in which the person performing the work may be killed or injured by an act of violence committed by an adversary" (Australian Government, 1994).

The new legislation opened many new roles to women but still restricted them from combat roles. A combat role is one that requires a person to "commit, or participate directly in the commission of, an act of violence against an armed adversary..." (Department of Defence, 1994, p. 1). The undertakings described above were to initiate a process of increased gender integration and would bring to the fore underlying issues concerning women's roles in the ADF. They also sparked an array of gender-related problems in the ADF that drew the attention of the media and the civilian population. An example is the 1992 "HMAS Swan incident" that concerned the Royal Australian Navy's (RAN) mishandling of sexual harassment. The treatment of women on board the HMAS Swan and the RAN's inability to deal with the situation appropriately drew considerable media attention and resulted in, among other outcomes, a Senate Inquiry into sexual harassment in the ADF. The Defence Organisation countered the scandals regarding women's integration with initiatives designed to overcome them. In 1996 the Burton Report was released (Burton, 1996), documenting an inquiry into women's integration into the ADF. One of the recommendations Clare Burton made in this report was the formation of the Defence Equity Organisation, which was established in 1997. In the same year the Department of Defence released Kathryn Quinn's *Sexual harassment in the Australian Defence Force* (Quinn, 1996). And in 1998 a report of the review into policies and practices to deal with sexual harassment and sexual offences at the Australian Defence Force Academy (Grey, 1998) was released. The findings documented a high level of unacceptable sexual behaviour at the Academy along with organisational tolerance of such behaviour.

For the ADF, the eventful decade of the 1990s was also marked by the Gulf War, where women served on RAN ships and in Iraq. Peacekeeping in the 1990s was significant for the ADF, and women served in operations in the Western Sahara, Cambodia, Somalia, Bougainville, Rwanda and East Timor and on all missions. Some newspaper coverage in the late 1990s showed the successes of women in the Navy, Army and Air Force. The coverage featured trailblazers who were excelling in what were considered to be traditionally male occupations, such as the training and employment of three Air Force female pilots in combat-related roles in 1990 and the training of women sailors in Collins class submarines in 1998. Naturally, there were opposing viewpoints that counteracted these "girls can do anything" reports. The role of gender in relation to military service was just as often discussed in terms of moral imperatives, especially those that sought to protect women from the grisly realities of the battlefield. All in all, for curious feminists at the beginning of the 2000s, the ADF looked like a gendered battlefield.

How we understood gender was enhanced and challenged by Donna's exploration of women's military experiences, and we were to come to see how "uniformed occupations offer fertile territory for the understanding of gender" (Spurling & Greenhalgh, 2000, p. xiii). Women in the military, especially those in employments traditionally staffed by men, seemed to be unwittingly disrupting the very notion of how gender was understood in society. During wartime, traditional gender divisions of labour may be interrupted, but only for as long as the war context demands. When women join volunteer forces *and* serve in roles traditionally assigned to men they confront a great deal of hostility from male colleagues. Problematic gender relations in the work sphere in Australia have been one factor in women's unequal access to employment, opportunities, and equality (Saunders & Evans, 1992). We began to see that the Australian military was no exception to this. In the ADF there were few women in the senior ranks and women rarely served in employments considered to be prestigious, despite policy and initiatives designed to integrate more women throughout the ADF. We began to see that the main issue for gender integration in the ADF was male attitudes toward women. The masculine culture of the military rejects all but hyper-masculine values (Agostino, 2000). Negative assumptions about women's abilities and pervasive myths that women do not have a natural aptitude for military roles are perhaps why progressive ADF policy and initiatives, set up to increase gender integration, did not work effectively. Through early reviews of the literature and research studies we found that harassment was a significant problem in all ranks, that women were discriminated against on the basis of notions about the inferiority of the female body and their potential to disrupt male cohesion.

A new research direction emerged from our fresh understandings of the masculine culture of the military and the challenges and barriers women in the ADF faced. Our new aims for the research were to explore the culture of the ADF and to illustrate the underlying causes of barriers to full integration. The new aims were to understand whence unequal treatment arose, how inequity manifested, and how this impacted on women. The purpose of the research became to determine whether constructions of gender devalued, excluded and therefore oppressed women in the ADF and to determine whether constructions of gender legitimised the subordinate position of women within the ADF.

SHARING THE EXPERIENCE: DONNA'S JOURNEY WITH THE ADF

Extensive reviews of literature, policy, military reports and media documents were rich and illuminating but they took understanding women's roles and experience only so far. I became impatient to hear from women in the ADF and was curious about women's stories. Information about women integrating into militaries was coming from commentators on both sides of the debate (many of them men), from policy, and from reports written about women, but very little was available as first-hand accounts from the women themselves. I decided that it was vital to uncover the voices of women in the ADF and to hear first-hand about their military roles, their experiences, beliefs and understandings. Feminist methodology provided an appropriate framework for the research. We understood the study to be feminist research because it incorporated feminist insights (DeVault, 1996) and the underlying ethics and principles of the study were grounded in feminist methodology; that is, theory about our research practice emerged from feminist critique (Reinharz, 1992). The central goal of feminist methodology is to focus primarily on the experience of women and to make the experience, understandings and knowledge of women visible. Feminist methodology supported us to conduct research that was deeply ethical, inclusive of research participants and collaborative (Reinharz, 1992).

This is how the research journey came to be shared, in part, with the ADF. I had written to the Chief of the Defence Force, after considering sampling and recruitment issues and prior to commencing data collection, to advise that fieldwork for the research would soon begin. I had sought advice from academics from the University of New South Wales who were involved in scholarship about women in the military and asked them about protocols regarding proceeding with the research. They advised that although this courtesy would be appreciated, it was in fact ADF protocol to abstain from contact with outside researchers. It was therefore surprising that, soon afterwards, members of the Directorate of Strategic Planning Personnel and Research (DSPPR) contacted my supervisors and asked for a meeting about the research. Thus Moira Carmody and I attended a meeting with the DSPPR in November 2001. At this meeting we agreed to submit a research proposal to the DSPPR so that we could gain ADF clearance and endorsement for the research, the right to use ADF resources, and support for the recruitment and sampling phases of the research. In return for this support the ADF asked for 6-monthly progress reports and copies of the thesis at its completion. The affiliation agreed between the DSPPR, my supervisors, and me facilitated and enhanced the research, but the experience of working with the ADF would prove to be a complex one. On the one hand the affiliation was collegial and facilitated the research but on the other hand it manifested as a clash of cultures. The academic culture from which we came in some ways mirrored that of the researchers at the DSPPR, yet that was sharply contrasted by the distinct and clearly defined military culture that surrounded it. The DSPPR was to support us in our goal to interview female military personnel currently serving with the ADF, and they did this in constructive ways that enriched the research. However, the bureaucratic nature of the ADF was sometimes a stumbling block that was difficult to work with.

CREATING SPACES

The approach I took to working with the DSPPR was to present them with my ideas and plans through the research proposal and then to gain feedback from them on matters such as sampling and data collection. The DSPPR provided invaluable advice on how to work effectively within the culture of the organisation. For example, in my original research design I had planned to interview 20–30 women who had served for a year or more. I expected to advertise in local newspapers in areas where the ADF bases existed. And I proposed that focus groups would be an interactive way to obtain data that would inspire discussion about issues between colleagues. My DSPPR liaison officer advised that interviewing women who had served only 1 year in the ADF would not produce the depth of understanding that we were seeking. The first year of a defence force career is spent, in large part, in training and in settling into a military lifestyle. It was recommended that I extend the base level of time spent in service to 2 years. I was also advised to consider having half the sample comprised of women who had served since before the 1990 opening of combat-related positions to women. This advice was particularly useful because women who had served both before and after that change were in the exceptional position of being able to reflect on the changes that occurred when the ban was lifted, as well as on the ADF's response to the subsequent integration. One woman, a high-ranking training instructor, described as dramatic the changes for women over the more than 20 years that she had served. When she enlisted she was issued with a regulation handbag and stockings. She stated: *"I've gone through a whole range of changes since I joined the ADF: from makeup classes to 'Annie get your gun' to doing peacekeeping!"*

My decision to have focus groups was positively challenged also. My liaison officer advised that focus groups would be problematic due to the hierarchical nature of the defence force system. This would be further exacerbated by the strong branch system (Navy, Army, Air Force) which did not ordinarily enable collaboration across branches. For focus groups to work they would need to consist of one branch and one rank. I was made aware that the different branches of the ADF did not relate or speak freely together and that mixing ranks would make it difficult for anyone of a lower rank to speak without constraint. Conducting focus groups with mixed branches and mixed ranks would create a degree of awkwardness between personnel that might detrimentally affect the proceedings of the group and therefore the data obtained. On this advice I conducted one-to-one interviews only. This approach was successful and women appreciated the exclusive and confidential nature of the interviews.

The DSPPR raised concerns about my recruitment techniques. I was about to begin advertising in local newspapers, magazines, and community centres near ADF bases to recruit participants. The concern about this approach was the potential for recruiting a sample with a "biased leaning". Recruiting in this way meant, according to the ADF, that respondents were likely to be past-serving members, leading to an skewed sample of disaffected women. The DSPPR was keen to provide the means for recruiting a sample of women who were actively choosing and pursuing careers in the ADF. It was argued that given the nature of the research aims, which included providing a platform for female serving members to relate their experiences and opinions in relation to current debates and to conduct research that could potentially benefit women serving in militaries, it would be more appropriate to interview a sample comprised mainly of women choosing long-term careers in the ADF. Although I saw the value of this reasoning, I was aware that the research would be richer if a proportion of the women interviewed were leaving or had left the Defence Force. Consequently, I interviewed two women who had left the ADF and two who were proposing to resign within the coming months.

Due to the affiliation that we had agreed upon with the ADF I was able to interview women who had or were currently choosing careers in the ADF in authentic settings. Acculturating into the military environment while simultaneously doing interviews was challenging but ultimately very rewarding. I conducted the interviews in environments where women worked, with new recruits marching in formation around us or fast jets screaming overhead. I visited bases, ADF offices and defence housing. By travelling to military establishments I experienced the environment in which women worked. I learned first-hand about work environments, living arrangements and general military infrastructure. The research came alive when I began to have contact with women who served with the ADF. Their active and current involvement, their direct immersion in the reality of gender integration meant that they became the memory of the research, its living parts, its voice and its potential. Issues that had been theoretical prior to the interviews now became personalised in relation to how they were being lived every day by these women.

CLASHING CULTURES/RESISTANCE

Although working with the DSPPR liaison officer was rewarding and beneficial, the experience of working within the bureaucracy of the ADF was not always smooth. The slow working of the bureaucracy proved problematic. For example, I originally contacted the ADF to advise them of the research in June 2001 but the meeting with the DSPPR did not occur until November 2001, and although the research proposal I submitted was accepted by the ADF at the beginning of 2002, it was not until June 2002 that advertising I had worked on with a member of the DSPPR was circulated. The culture of academia to which I was accustomed did not move quite so slowly, and it was frustrating to wait 3 months for a 1-page document to be approved and distributed.

Once the invitation to all women in the ADF to participate in the research had been advertised I received replies within hours, and in total answered 200 emails enquiring about the research. After a period of time sorting through expressions of interest and replying to them I began communications via email and telephone with a group of women who were to be my research sample. During the time that I was compiling information and getting to know the participants I received word from the DSPPR that the Australian Defence Human Research Ethics Committee (ADHREC) required me to submit an application to them before commencing interviews. I had earlier been advised that ADHREC would accept my endorsement from the University of Western Sydney Ethics Committee (UWSHREC) as ethical approval. My application for ethical approval to ADHREC was problematic. The research was given "pending" status for 7 months. During this time I could not have contact with research participants, but I did retain all but 12 of the original group. ADHREC resistance to the study was based on methodological issues. Firstly, the committee was concerned about the qualitative nature of the research and questioned the merits of qualitative methodology. Secondly, the small sample size (25–30 participants) was questioned regarding the benefits of so low a number. Thirdly, the voluntary nature of the study was also problematised and the use of random sampling as a viable alternative was raised. I had to justify my use of a qualitative design for the study, the small sample size, and the use of a self-selection sampling technique. My response to ADHREC was based on the following general points about qualitative research. I show how these general points were used in our study.

The Merits of Qualitative Research

The value and benefits of qualitative feminist methodology in this research were multi-layered. Justifying the use of qualitative methods fell into the realms of aims. Thus the aim of the study was not to collect or compile statistics; rather we aimed to understand *what* was happening but primarily *why* things were happening and *how* they happened. My aim was to explore the sociocultural and political context of the research, such as the radical altering of work and society through women's integration into the work sphere, and how the full impact of this change had affected the masculine culture of the military (Bomford, 2001). As shown in the literature, the increasing roles of women in the ADF had required that organisational changes be made in the military, including policy development, and in day-to-day practice. We wanted to understand how significant change such as this had created cultural and political shifts in the ADF. Alongside the procedural processes of gender integration were negative assumptions about women's abilities and pervasive myths that women had no natural aptitude for military roles. These needed to be explored to see whether and how they accounted for the disparity between policy initiatives and women's progress. Societal changes regarding women's increasing roles in the public sphere and the resistance that accompanied them required interpretation and analysis from the perspective of women directly involved.

Qualitative research goes beyond the collection of statistics and the noting of trends. Research such as this study honours the stories and experiences of the women the research is about. Moreover, such an approach gives women the opportunity to speak their own truths about their own lives. Within qualitative research emphasis is placed upon in-depth investigation and careful scrutiny of social processes (Bryman & Burgess, 1994). Qualitative design is also consistent with interview research, where the focus is upon discussion and free interaction between the researcher and the interviewee/s. This allows "respondents a degree of latitude in describing and interpreting circumstances and events, since the attitudes and the logic underlying them are important factors to be taken into account" (Burton, 1996, p. xxv).

Purposive Sampling

The qualitative nature of the research meant that it contained a necessarily small sample of women. The number of participants in the study (n = 30) represented a small percentage of the 7,400 women in the Permanent Defence Force in the early part of the 2000s. The number of women represented, however, allowed for more in-depth study of each participant. A larger sample would have required the application of quantitative methods. Quantitative techniques (for example, using a survey) would have portrayed the thinking of more women, but on a more superficial level. It is acknowledged that quantitative research has been and is beneficial in this context when providing a broad sweep of the issues, but they would not have provided a detailed examination of the group studied. A smaller representation of female personnel was expected to make the findings richer, deeper, and more significant. They would provide in-depth insight into many of the issues, challenges, and accomplishments experienced by women in the ADF. As Burton (1996, p. xxvi) wrote of qualitative methods in her report *Women in the Australian Defence Force*, "The end result, though a selective slice of 'reality', is also a multifaceted and comprehensively accurate account of gender dynamics within the ADF". To complement my qualitative data, however, I utilised statistics from research conducted in-house by the ADF and research conducted by overseas militaries.

Random Sampling

Random sampling can be identified as the most representative method of sampling. This technique would have ensured that all female personnel within the ADF had an equal chance of being selected for the study. It must be acknowledged, however, that random sampling would not guarantee that a group *representative* of the study would be chosen. I argued that a purposive sample was a strategy designed to develop a sample specific to the needs of the research (and it must be noted that all women in the ADF had a similar opportunity to volunteer for the study, as the invitation to participate was sent to all units in the ADF). The sampling method chosen was "theoretical", "theory-based" or "operational construct" sampling (Bryman & Burgess, 1994) and was appropriate to a qualitative and small inquiry. The initial sample came from an unknown group drawn from *all* female service personnel in the ADF. Next, a possible sample was identified from incoming requests to participate by a group unknown in size, diversity and experience. In this way a sample was chosen by viewing those requests on the basis of individuals' representation of the sample needs and the theoretical constructs of the study. Sampling is done with particular thought to the aims of the study and one uses theoretical principles to guide sampling choices. The researcher assesses what information is required by the study and chooses, from the sample population, who would best add to the developing theory in a manner that would support or contradict that developing theory. The theory can thus be further validated by looking for counter-evidence as well as supportive evidence (Bryman & Burgess, 1994). The researcher then identifies gaps that exist in the research data already obtained and seeks to fill those gaps with "a theoretical construct of interest so as to elaborate and examine the construct" (Patton, 1990, p. 183). For example, I sought a balance between women serving in areas associated with feminine roles such as nursing and clerical with those serving in roles associated with masculinity such as engineering and aviation. I also aimed that half of the sample would be comprised of women who had served in peacekeeping.

A random sampling technique would have required women to participate in the study without their expressed agreement. They would have been chosen rather than volunteering for the study. I needed participation in the study to be entirely voluntary because of my own ethical position, feminist methodology principles and ethics committee stipulations. I wanted to attract women to the research who were particularly interested in informing the debates about women in the military.

The ADHREC application was not the first time that I had argued for self-selection during my time researching with the ADF. The DSPPR had previously advised me that if the proposal were to be accepted I would be issued with a letter that declassified and endorsed the research as having full ADF support. This letter would have permitted me to interview participants chosen from a data base, after I had received permission from their Commanding Officer. In the ethical guidelines I had previously set out in my application to UWSHREC I had explicitly stated that I wanted all participation in the research to be voluntary. Due to the ethical implications, and the significance of gaining full consent to participate, I declined the offer of endorsement and declassification and relied on invitation to recruit participants.

CONCLUDING THOUGHTS: CREATIVE SHARED SPACES

Finding a place for this research that was creative, critical and ethical, within the fortifications of the ADF, took time. Initially we did this through honouring the ethic of the original research design, by not compromising on the processes and methods that were intended to be respectful of the women participating and by upholding our feminist principles. We felt that a qualitative feminist design was imperative for researching women's increasing integration in the ADF and that compromising the use of qualitative methodology would have made it impossible to pursue the research. We also felt that maintaining the use of a purposive volunteer sample was intrinsic to the research. When ADHREC questioned the qualitative design we were concerned that we might have to compromise our feminist ethics to allow the research to move forward. However, the ADF personnel with whom we communicated were always ready to negotiate. Occasionally it was necessary to make minimal compromises. When writing the research proposal, for example, Donna was advised to remove the words "woman" and "women" from the text and to replace them with "female" and "females", a concession we made easily. Regardless of the clashing cultures and the differences we encountered during the research, this groundbreaking qualitative study, replete with the voices of women themselves, with a feminist methodology, was completed without losing any of its integrity.

NOTES

[1]   We wish to acknowledge the valuable contribution of Associate Professor Moira Carmody who was also Donna's supervisor during her candidature.

REFERENCES

Agostino, K. (2000). Women's strategies in the Royal Australian Navy. In E. Davis & V. Pratt (Eds.), *Making the link: Affirmative action and industrial relations* (pp. 59–69). Sydney: CCH Australia.

Australian Government. (1994). *Sex discrimination regulations – REG 3, Combat duties and combat-related duties.* Available: http://www.comlaw.gov.au/Details/C2004H03165, accessed 26 June 2011.

Bomford, J. (2001). *Soldiers of the Queen: Women in the Australian Army.* Melbourne: Oxford.

Bridges, D.V. (2005). *The gendered battlefield: Women in the Australian Defence Force.* PhD Thesis, University of Western Sydney, NSW.

Bryman, A., & Burgess, R.G. (Eds.) (1994). *Analysing qualitative data.* New York: Routledge.

Burton, C. (1996). *Women in the Australian Defence Force. Two studies: The cultural, social and institutional barriers impeding the merit-based progression of women and the reasons why more women are not making the Australian Defence Force a long-term career.* Canberra: Defence Centre.

Department of Defence. (1994). *Defence instruction (general) PERS 32–1- Employment of women in the Australian Defence Force.* Canberra. Australian Defence Department.

DeVault, M.L. (1996). Talking back to sociology: Distinctive contributions of feminist methodology. *Annual Review of Sociology, 22,* 29–50.

Grey, B.D. (1998). *Australian Defence Force: Report of the review into the policies and practices to deal with sexual harassment and sexual offences.* Canberra: Director Publishing and Visual Communications.

Patton, M. (2002). Two decades of developments in qualitative inquiry: A personal, experiential perspective. *Qualitative Social Work, 1,* 261–283.

Quinn, K. (1996). Sexual harassment in the Australian Defence Force. Canberra: Department of Defence.

Reinharz, S. (1992). *Feminist methods in social research.* New York: Oxford University Press.

Saunders, K., & Evans, R. (Eds.) (1992). *Gender relations in Australia: Domination and negotiation.* Sydney: Harcourt Brace Jovanovich.

Shephard, A. (1999). *Trends in Australian Defence: A resources survey.* Canberra: Australian Defence Studies Centre.

Spurling, K., & Greenhalgh, E. (Eds.) (2000). *Women in uniform: Perceptions and pathways.* Canberra: School of History, Australian Defence Force Academy.

Donna Bridges PhD
The Education For Practice Institute
Charles Sturt University, Australia

Debbie Horsfall PhD, MA, B.Ed
Peace and Development Studies
School of Social Sciences
The University of Western Sydney, Australia

SECTION 3: BEING A CREATIVE RESEARCHER

ANGIE TITCHEN AND THEO NIESSEN

15. LIVING RESEARCH PRACTICES

Being in Creative Spaces

This chapter is an exemplar of how we, together and with others, engage in cognitive and artistic critique and create a blend of scholarly and artistic spaces within which to live our research practices. The context of the exemplar is our critical companionship (Titchen, 2004) which we set up as a reciprocal learning journey. Angie now locates critical companionship within a paradigmatic synthesis called critical creativity (Brendan McCormack & Angie Titchen, 2006; Titchen, Higgs, & Horsfall, 2007; Titchen & McCormack, 2008, 2010; Titchen, McCormack, Wilson, & Solman, 2011). In this synthesis, the assumptions of the critical paradigm are blended, balanced with, and attuned to creative and ancient traditions and to the natural environment, for the ultimate purpose of human flourishing.

It is a world view (or landscape as symbolised in Chapter 4) concerned with creating transformational knowledge at the same time as bringing about transformational change, not only through research but also through education, practice development and everyday work practices. Our inquiry work together began when Angie was Clinical Chair in the Knowledge Centre for Evidence-based Practice in the School of Nursing at Fontys University of Applied Sciences in the Netherlands. Theo, now Associate Clinical Chair in the Knowledge Centre, was a senior lecturer in the School at that time. We come out of the university and walk down the busy main road towards the lake.

Angie:	Shall we walk in silence and notice what we notice until we feel ready to talk?
Theo:	Yes, let's do that. Eventually, as we approach the lake, our eyes meet in silence and we nod our readiness.
Theo:	What I noticed was the feeling of "Ah!" (long audible breath out, body relaxes and is still). This was the way my body responded to your invitation. The pace of work in Fontys is so fast that my mind is nearly always racing. Then when we entered the park, I used one of my meditative practices to come fully into this moment with you. This links with what I have been reading and thinking about – Otto Scharmer's (2009) Theory U. This fascinating theory is about leading from the future as it emerges. I would like to spend time now exploring it with you.
Angie:	Oh yes, I would be very interested in doing that too. I have read about it in "Presence" by Senge, Scharmer, Jaworski and Flowers (2005), in which they explore profound change in people, organisations and society. I feel that there are some similarities with critical creativity, but also some important differences. I

J. Higgs et al., (eds.), Creative Spaces for
Qualitative Researching: Living Research, 147–158

would love to explore them with you. Would you be interested in doing that through a cognitive and artistic critique?

Theo says yes! We set off around the lake on our initial exploration of Theory U ... At the end of our walk, we decide that we will submit an experiential workshop abstract to an international conference to stimulate creative responses and dialogue with others about the emerging critique. We will then continue to dialogue using imagery/text by email and Skype to prepare a book chapter (this one!).

LIVING THEORY U: THEO'S STORY

Angie, what I (Theo) have experienced in relation to Theory U is that a research journey informed by this theory becomes more than just an investigation. It is the expression of who I am as a teacher/researcher and who I am becoming in continuing to construe, live and be part of the U's that are mine and the people I work with. Theory U has become a living heuristic for me; a way of living small and large U's through sensing, presencing and realising for each issue. Theory U is, first, a structure describing these cyclical change processes. Second, it is a heuristic for effecting change on an individual personal plane but also on a collective level. Third, it is a way of describing phenomena in our world – as they occur naturally.

Most frequently (and most certainly in Otto Scharmer's book, 2009), Theory U is used as a change process of three phases (see Figure 15.1): sensing, presencing and realising. The *sensing* phase starts by focusing on clear sight, that is, seeing what is present and then, only thereafter, sensing into what is observed. This is meant quite literally. We need to suspend our judgments in a phenomenological sense by bracketing our thoughts and ideas, and dive into the issue at hand; familiarising ourselves to it using our body and all our senses. An open, friendly, and keen attention for detail and context is what is needed in this first phase.

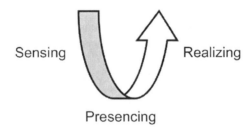

Sensing   Realizing

Presencing

Figure 15.1

Presencing is the ability to listen into the space that is created individually and/or collectively with others by first being thoroughly immersed in the issue and then sinking into the act of letting go. This letting go is the ability to *not-think* about what is encountered in the sensing phase. Rather it is about living within it on a subluminal level. In this manner the "smart unconscious" (Dijksterhuis &

Meurs, 2006) is able to make sense of what needs to be known, that is, what the most pressing issue at stake is. When practising this phase on a collective level Rupert Sheldrake (1988) called for an attunement which he referred to as collective morphogenetic fields. These fields may be seen as invisible organising structures that contain the possible future form of what is emerging collectively. Thus these fields contain a collective and cumulative memory of what is possible. Accessing these fields needs the act of letting go.

Realising is the phase in which one manifests through powerful, quick and wise action. It is the right side of the U; transforming one's lived, embodied and cognitive insights and vision into concrete ideas and/or prototypes. A prototype is a mock-up, either literal or symbolic, of the something new. It brings our vision down to earth with all accompanying practicalities, demands and obstacles. Being aware of the gap between what we sense is possible and the current reality can be discouraging and frustrating. It requires courage and faith. Varela, Thompson and Rosch (1997) symbolised this phase as laying down a path while walking it. When on this path one is only sure that one should take a step. The direction and where to put the next foot down only become clear while engaging the U process.

For me (Theo), working as a facilitator with colleagues within Theory U provides me with intriguing challenges. They are always quite personal, since the quality of the intervention of the facilitator is dependent on the internal quality of the facilitator. Within the book, *Theory U* (Scharmer, 2009), one of the most powerful statements is made at the beginning. Based on Bill O'Brian's observation in his study of learning trajectories, Otto writes, "success of the intervention depends on the interior condition of the intervener" (p. 7). Although this statement makes clear that the context of the book itself is situated within the realm of organisational change and learning, it typifies the more general idea that one's interior stance has a constitutive relationship, not only to the quality of the intervention, but also to its outcome. As a successful facilitator, I should be able to see, instantly and on the spot, straight through or past my own shadow into a focused (or mindful) view that is not hampered by narcissistic or egotistical ideas. Through this channelled or focused view, that is grounded in a vast and open space, I should be able to tap into the greater potential. In the instances where I was able to act from this open space, I "simply just knew" what to do or what was needed to guide a group to a next level.

Being able to characterise and talk about the nature of this facilitating process quite naturally now is the result of many instances when I was not able to tap in to this zone and help the group to a next level. Regardless of the specifics of the situation, the reasons that hampered me were always related to my inability to stay focused and/or inability to act in line with the greater goal. Also my tendency to please people, appropriate in the short term, is not always so good for enhancing people's growth processes (including mine) in the long term. I think that reflecting honestly on these instances was a vital first step for me to act and to grow.

For me, meditation provides the means to cultivate a focused attention that enables me to tap into this greater potential and the experiential nuances that occur when working with the U process. Although to some readers this may seem to be a bit "out there", I find that meditation (mindfulness) cultivates the mental space that is needed to deal with personal discomfort and/or negative thoughts that would otherwise constrain or disempower me in my facilitation. Scharmer (2009) also seems to suggest this mindfulness when he says that the challenge is not so much to understand the abstract concepts of Theory U (such as presencing), but rather to live the subtleties of a concept in the act of experiencing it.

I find now that the instances where I was unsuccessful in my facilitation processes are a positive reminder that everything I do and encounter provides a possibility to fine-tune and improve the quality of my interior stance, in a way that is truly enhancing of my own and others' growth processes. Thus it makes no difference from which position I act, be it lecturer, researcher, colleague or friend. It is the acts of getting to know one's own stream of thought in an observant manner, then leaving it behind and just attending to the other radically and empirically: "On the contrary our empiricism is the radical sort long since commended by phenomenologists: a pristine acquaintance with phenomena unadulterated by preconceptions" (Heron & Reason, 1997, p. 275).

LIVING CRITICAL CREATIVITY: ANGIE'S STORY/CONVERSATION

As a paradigmatic framework for transformational practice, critical creativity can support researchers, practice developers, practitioner researchers, leaders and practitioners and stakeholders (in these or facilitation roles). Through its theoretical framework, a facilitator enables people to become critical. The facilitator helps them to de-construct their context, situation, contradiction or dilemma, politically, socially, historically and culturally, and then to re-construct it in order to develop new understanding for transformation and, simultaneously, generation of new knowledge. This occurs through reflexivity, challenging assumptions, critical dialogue and debate; in other words, cognitive critique. This critique is complemented by using creative imagination and expression.

So the facilitator helps people to grasp the essence and meaning of the whole and to bring embodied, imaginative and symbolic meaning into their cognitive critique of a context, situation or event. Thus a blending and weaving of art forms and reflexivity (critical consciousness) occurs through professional artistry. This blending enables us to bring the meaning that we know in our bodies and imaginations into our cognitive critique. But this is just part of it. The crux is the act of transformation, informed by this critique. As Theo points out, it is living the abstract concept or theory that is the challenge. And this is where the methodological framework comes in. Facilitators are guided by the framework as they create the conditions for people to flourish as they move through the turbulence and pain of transformation of self, teams, practices, workplace cultures, leadership or organisations.

Angie (by Skype): Theo, this morning on my cold winter walk, I was trying to get at the essence of living critical creativity for writing our chapter. I found a hazel tree with catkins in tight primordial bud, not fully formed but full of potential and something to come (holds up catkins to laptop camera). They reminded me of a little Zen Chinese ink painting that I did when Brendan and I were developing the methodological framework, Dancing with Stones. (Holds up painting below). Although I didn't intend it when I painted it (my only intention was to focus deeply on the stones), my interpretation now is that critical creativity is about working in different ways. The first is critical consciousness – see the darker foreground – working critically with that which is right in front of you and in your mind. The second is working at the edge of this consciousness where things are not fully clear in the mind, but the body senses that you are onto something exciting, even though you don't know yet what it is. That's the lighter middle distance and the light radiating from it which symbolises that which is about to become clear. Together they represent creativity which will often have a spiritual dimension.

This working at the edge of consciousness requires being in touch with the wisdom of the body. This is because the body has the capacity to attune to a situation and pick up significance, way before critical consciousness has seen the significance (c.f. Gendlin, 1993). Trusting this wisdom, without having any rationale, paying attention to it and going with it are central to critical creativity. The third way of working is pre-cognitive. That's the knowing that has no mental representation. It's shown by the air at the top of the painting. This is the knowing that is so hidden in our bodies, practices and cultures that it is invisible. We are completely unaware of it, just like the transparent air we breathe as we go about our daily lives. But when we are in touch with nature and use creative approaches, like the painting here and other media, such as writing poetry, drama, music, movement, clay modelling and collage (see Chapter 18), we can surface it to our consciousness. Using such approaches in nature is even more powerful because it can help us (with or without combining it with meditative practices) to connect with our greater potential. So this is similar to what you are saying, Theo, about cultivating your greater potential.

These three ways of working are underpinned by the philosophical and theoretical assumptions presented in Chapter 4 (Figure 4.1) of this book. I would be interested, Theo, in what my painting *evokes* in you, that is, what you see, feel or imagine.

Theo: I see a connection between the hazel catkins metaphor and the painting. First, your story and metaphor of the hazel tree with catkins really resonates with the background ideas of Theory U. The backdrop against which Theory U is drawn is that of systems theory. Perhaps you recall the metaphor of Indra's web we talked earlier about. This is also a metaphor that illustrates the interdependent nature of phenomena. The image of Indra's web was developed within Buddhist philosophy. The web has a multifaceted jewel at each knot and each jewel is reflected in all the other jewels.

http://www.fws.gov/digitalmedia
http://www.fws.gov/faq/imagefaq.html

"Imagine a multidimensional spider's web in the early morning covered with dew drops. And every dew drop contains the reflection of all the other dew drops. And, in each reflected dew drop, the reflections of all the other dew drops in that reflection. And so on ad infinitum. That is the Buddhist conception of the universe in an image." Alan Watts (2011)

Although an interdependent world view can be imagined cognitively it is another thing to realise this profound insight in one's own life holistically (experientially, symbolically, cognitively and practically) (Heron & Reason, 1997). I think this is what Otto Scharmer is ultimately pointing at in his book *Theory U*. To realise this inner stance of connectedness each moment one is living. It is this I call enlightenment. A realisation that is in principle infinite (not bound), but for pragmatic purposes temporarily focused to the boundaries of the issues that needs resolving.

For me your painting embeds this radiant nature (or perhaps Buddha nature) that is already in place in each of us tentatively waiting to be awakened. The beams radiating the upper part of the painting signify this availability that is not yet fully developed or aware, since the source of it is still hidden behind veils of attachment (reified ideas, idiosyncratic norms).

I agree in line with you and Gendlin (1993) that the body is a viable path to get in touch with the wisdom you point at. I think we must realise, however, that the direction or *felt sense* to which Gendlin refers is a transitional stage to an even deeper-seated awareness that points at the collective interconnectedness (and thus emptiness).

Angie: Yes. And when it happens, the experience can be dazzling. One of these moments for me was with Brendan on the volcanic stones of the Giant's Causeway in Northern Ireland. We danced with stones and the methodological framework for critical creativity (see Figure 15.2) exploded into being.

"I sit alone in silence. Attuning myself. In the evening light the stones look like reptile-snake skin. I feel the shedding of my skin, as a transformation, to go into the new with Brendan. I become conscious that I am framing my current experience in this awe-inspiring, mythical landscape. Then, marvelling ... I no longer feel alone. I am connecting, existentially, with Brendan through the space we are creating together, without words; by being fully there with all my body senses" (Titchen & McCormack, 2010, p. 534).

"After moving, we express our experience and learning by painting together. We were dancing on individual rocks and tiny pools in crevices. A natural canvas, ready to hand. In silence, we paint on wet, tessellated stones ... The painting transforms itself, by our brush strokes and by itself. Blue paint flows into a crack in the rock and becomes a blue river. We begin to express contemplatively and poetically the wisdom of the body, without knowing logically where this dialogue is going. By following the lead of the body in our authentic movement and painting, we know that our bodily sense of the situation implies the new, the something more that will unfold at the edge of our thinking (c.f. Gendlin, 1993)" (Titchen & McCormack, 2010, p. 536).

It seems that through this interconnectivity with place, space and each other, we came to understand inductively what we have been doing over time. That is, we could symbolise the conditions we have created and the principles we have embodied to help people to flourish through the turbulence and pain of transformation. Shall I look now, really broad-brush, at the methodological framework?

The Methodological Framework

The framework (Figure 15.2) centres on the basic concept of *praxis* enabled by *professional artistry*. Praxis, symbolised by the dynamic spiral that has no beginning and no end, is mindful doing with the moral intent of human flourishing for all. It includes action that is informed by multiple kinds of knowledge, ways of knowing and intelligences, creative imagination, bodily sense, body wisdom and spirituality. Professional artistry blends these dimensions in unique ways to suit each action and context. At the centre of the spiral is a circle that represents *human flourishing* (HF, maximising individuals' achievement of their growth/ development potential as they change the circumstances and relations of their lives). Flourishing is supported through facilitation strategies that connect with beauty and nature, ancient, indigenous and spiritual traditions and Jan Dewing's (2008) active learning.

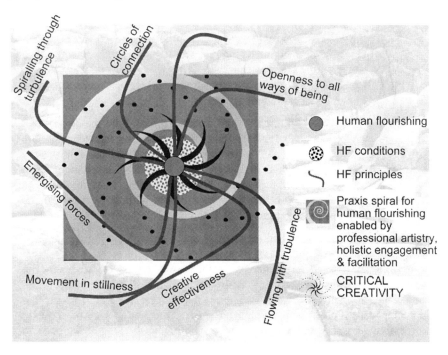

Figure 15.2: Critical creativity: Methodological framework for facilitating human flourishing (Titchen & McCormack (2010) Dancing with stones: Critical creativity as methodology for human flourishing, Educational Action Research) © Educational Action Research reprinted by permission of (Taylor & Francis Ltd, http://www.tandfonline.com) on behalf of Educational Action Research)

Eight principles are shown in the figure as the streamers flying in the wind, anchored by the spotted circle symbolising the conditions (*Stillness in a landscape, Becoming the rock* and *Nurturing, flowing, connecting* (the ontology or way of being and becoming of the facilitator)). The conditions are illustrated in Chapter 4 in the context of creating a research culture in our Knowledge Centre. In the critique process with Theo, I intentionally became the rock by modelling and articulating my embodied knowing of *Stillness in a landscape*, or how to create stillness for reflection within the inner and outer chaos of working in the frantic pace of contemporary workplaces. On the walk round the lake, Theo described my ontology (i.e., being nurturing, flowing, connecting) as coming from my being completely authentic as a facilitator. He linked this with the interior condition of the intervener in Theory U (above) being central to the success of the intervention. I agree with this and with what Theo is hinting at, which is that it takes a lot of deep work to grow and develop this kind of practice ontology as a facilitator of transformation.

Our critique process also used the principles for human flourishing. For example, the principle of *Creative effectiveness* became real for Theo when, back from our walk, we sat down and designed the abstract for the international conference. When we had finished, he said, "I love working with you, Angie, it is so quick and effortless!" The principle, *Movement in stillness*, is the crux of creativity. It is about letting go of or suspending the old, for instance, old patterns, assumptions, ways of seeing, thoughts and images, in order to allow the new to emerge. In our walk and meetings, we did this by stilling our minds through contemplative or meditative practices. We observed our thoughts and then let them float away, allowing stillness and nothing happening. We stayed with it and movement occurred; for example, we came to see how we could connect inner growth with preparing this chapter.

ARTISTIC, COGNITIVE CRITIQUE OF CRITICAL CREATIVITY AND THEORY U

Theo: Angie, to sum up what has been said and expressed artistically so far, both critical creativity and Theory U are concerned with bringing about profound transformational change in self and organisations. We can also freely state that both theories are inductively-derived through research; within Theory U created through interviewing highly effective leaders in organisations and within critical creativity through introspective creative inquiry of self as transformational researcher or practice developer in combination with collaborative creative inquiry with others.

Angie: Yes. There appear to be some similarities, but also key differences. They share the same philosophical background of hermeneutic phenomenology and Heidegger's (1960) notion of the clearing. That links with *sensing* and *presencing* in Theory U and hermeneutic praxis in critical creativity (McCormack & Titchen, 2006), but the extent of that similarity needs much more thought. What really stands out for me is that both are working with ancient practices, for example enlightenment through Buddhist meditative practices, contemplation and artistic and embodied ways of knowing. They are also working with opposites that are needed to define each other, as in the Taoist tradition. Just as you said, earlier, about seeing the opposites in my painting with the dark fore-ground and light background. There is the use of all the senses and then letting go or losing ourselves into stillness. So both the conscious and unconscious are needed for creating the flow required for effective action. Also movement in stillness, that act of letting go amidst hot action is a paradox that Senge et al. (2005) also hint at.

Theo: Yes, this means suspending our habitual ways of seeing; letting go and opening up to sense and observe what is happening from within ourselves, rather from the outside. This is what Langer (1989, 1997) referred to as mindfulness. We could go on and on finding similarities!

Angie: The significant difference, at this point of our critique, seems to be that critical creativity has self-consciously emerged from critical social science and Theory U from systems theory influences. However, there is a parallel process in how Scharmer blends his modernist influences with the ancient wisdom of interconnectivity that we have talked about. In critical creativity we have also blended traditions; for example, the emancipatory praxis of critical social science (i.e., taking mindful action that liberates us of inner and outer challenges to transformation, and human flourishing) with hermeneutic praxis (i.e., reflexivity and transformation of understanding and thus transformation of self, teams, organisations and communities). And this blending has been blended again with ancient traditions, especially, Celtic, Native American and Australian Aborginal traditions, in addition to the Buddhist and Taoist thinking we already talked about. Critical creativity also puts more emphasis than Theory U on working in natural surroundings (where possible) which enables circles of connection – ecological, symbolic and physical-metaphysical circles – and on using creative arts media ourselves to access the artist within us, rather than working with other people's "Art with a capital A" to connect with our tacit knowing. And perhaps, another difference is that critical creativity seems to have paid more attention, in its methodological framework, to *facilitating* informed, transforming and transformative action. What do you think, Theo?

Theo: I am not sure about that. Scharmer provided ample additional work forms that can be applied within each of the three phases, making Theory U practically viable to both skilled and proficient facilitators.

Angie: I would like to look at these work forms, because it seems to me that they might be different, at the very least in intent, given the different philosophical traditions of the two.

Theo: Even though critical creativity and Theory U spring from different traditions, I think they are complementary, not only on a philosophical level but also on a pragmatic one. I also think that Theory U, rather than focusing on being critical and/or creative, is more concerned with *seeing* via the true interdependent and thus empty nature of reality. *Realising* this nature and handling it from this viewpoint, within the context of learning organisations, is paramount within Theory U. Moreover, the notion of Varela et al. (1997) of *enactivism* seems to be one of the default theories in which Theory U is implicitly grounded. Enactivism is a lingering world view drawing on complexity theory, phenomenology and biology. But enough for today. We can explore that on our next walk, if you would like to!

Angie: Yes, I would. I have learned a lot about Theory U from our dialogue. It is an interesting theory. But I think we must be very cautious about making any claims about resonance between critical creativity and Theory U at this stage. So much more work on refining critical creativity needs to be done first.

Closing Space

In this chapter we have been walking two paths simultaneously. The first path showed you how we create artistic and intellectual spaces in which to live our research practices. We uncovered something of our practice ontology and epistemology, the latter in terms of how we create new understanding through artistic and cognitive critique. The second path offered you a critique of Theory U and critical creativity in which we started to look at the similarities, differences and complementarities. We have only taken the first step …

ACKNOWLEDGEMENTS

Angie's contribution to the critique of the two frameworks in this chapter is entirely hers and not that of her colleagues within the critical creativity inquiry.

REFERENCES

Dewing J. (2008). Becoming and being active learners and creating active learning workplaces. In K. Manley, B. McCormack & V. Wilson (Eds.), *International practice development in nursing and healthcare* (pp. 273–294). Oxford: Blackwell.

Dijksterhuis, A., & Meurs, T. (2006). Where creativity resides: The generative power of unconscious thought. *Consciousness and Cognition, 15,* 135–146.

Heron, J., & Reason, P. (1997). A participatory inquiry paradigm. *Qualitative Inquiry, 3*(3), 274–294.

Gendlin, E.T. (1993). Three assertions about the body. *The Folio, 12*(1), 21–33. Available: http://www.focusing.org/gendlin/docs/gol_2064.html, accessed 31 March 2009.

Langer, E.J. (1989). *Mindfulness.* New York: Addison Wesley.

Langer, E.J. (1997). *The power of mindful learning.* Reading, MA: A Merloyd Lawrence Book–Perseus Books.

McCormack B., & Titchen A. (2006). Critical creativity: Melding, exploding, blending. *Educational Action Research: An International Journal, 14*(2), 239–266.

Senge P., Scharmer C. O., Jaworski J., & Flowers, B. (2005). *Presence: Exploring profound change in people, organisations and society.* London: Nicholas Brealey.

Scharmer, C.O. (2009). *Theory U: Leading from the future as it emerges.* San Francisco: Berrett-Koehler.

Sheldrake, R. (1988). *The presence of the past: Morphic resonance and the habits of nature.* New York: Times Books.

Solman, A. (2008). Enhancing practice through strategic planning: Creating Indra's net. Keynote, 8th International Practice Development Collaborative Conference, Veldhoven, The Netherlands.

Titchen, A. (2004). Helping relationships for practice development: Critical companionship. In B. McCormack, K. Manley & R. Garbett (Eds.), *Practice development in nursing* (pp.148–174). Oxford: Blackwell.

Titchen, A., Higgs, J., & Horsfall, D. (2007) Research artistry: Dancing the praxis spiral in critical-creative qualitative research. In J. Higgs, A. Titchen, D. Horsfall & H.B. Armstrong (Eds.), *Being critical and creative in qualitative research* (pp. 282–297). Sydney: Hampden Press.

Titchen, A., & McCormack, B. (2008). A methodological walk in the forest: Critical creativity and human flourishing. In K. Manley, B. McCormack & V. Wilson (Eds), *International practice development in nursing and healthcare* (pp. 59–83). Oxford: Blackwell.

Titchen, A., & McCormack, B. (2010). Dancing with stones: Critical creativity as methodology for human flourishing. *Educational Action Research: An International Journal, 18*(4), 531–554.

Titchen A., McCormack B., Wilson V. & Solman, A. (2011). Human flourishing through body, creative imagination and reflection. *International Practice Development Journal, 1*(1), Article 1. Available: http://www.fons.org/library/journal.aspx, accessed 20 July 2011.

Varela, F.J., Thompson, E., & Rosch, E. (1997). The embodied mind: Cognitive science and human *experience* (6th ed.). Cambridge, MA: MIT Press.

Watts, A. (2011). *Following the middle way.* Podcast, available: http://www.alanwattspodcast.com/index.php?post_id=373289, accessed 17 June 2011.

Angie Titchen D.Phil (Oxon), MSc, MCSP
Visiting Professor, University of Ulster, Northern Ireland

Theo Niessen PhD, MSc, RN
Associate Clinical Chair, Fontys University of Applied Science, The Netherlands

NICOLE MOCKLER

16. BEING ME

In Search of Authenticity

"Being me" as a qualitative researcher can be harder than it looks or sounds. In this chapter I tell the methodological story of a 3-year life history study that aimed to explore the development of teacher professional identity. Through the telling of the story, I argue that critical to the achievement of authenticity in qualitative research is the achievement of a level of congruence between three key dimensions: design, process and reporting.

In the course of the study, I engaged eight secondary school teachers in a "prolonged interview" (Denzin, 1970) over the course of 18 months. In the interviews, participants were asked to discuss the history, key influences and orientations of their careers. Participants were purposively sampled so that they came from a range of contexts and were at various points in their careers – neophyte teachers, mid-career teachers, "middle managers" and principals. My aim, as with most qualitative research, was to take a forensic approach to the collection and analysis of evidence (wherein evidence might be used to "prove" the viability of a particular phenomenon or social practice), as opposed to an adversarial approach (wherein evidence is used for the purpose of developing understanding of a particular phenomenon) (Groundwater-Smith & Mockler, 2007), and to shine a light on the experience of teachers in terms of the changing nature of their professional identity.

The theoretical framework and findings of the study itself have been written about elsewhere (Mockler, 2011a, 2011b), as has a reflection on the experience of conducting this research project as professional learning and development (Groundwater-Smith & Mockler, 2009). In this chapter, I use the methodological story of the study as a touchstone for arguing that authenticity in qualitative research requires an authenticity of design, process and analysis in the enactment of the research enterprise.

AUTHENTICITY OF DESIGN

Authenticity of design lies in a congruence between the researcher's own way of seeing and being in the world and the enactment of the research.

Elliott Eisner (1998, p. 32ff) and Sharon Merriam (1998, pp. 6-8, 2009, pp. 14-18) have both offered a range of characteristics and dimensions of qualitative research that together highlight the importance of researchers' self-awareness

J. Higgs et al., (eds.), Creative Spaces for
Qualitative Researching: Living Research, 159–168

within the research field – the criticality of understanding both self as research "tool" or instrument, and the location and fit of the self within the field. A key part of understanding self as a research tool lies in recognising the links between one's ontological and epistemological positioning and the methods one chooses to employ in the collection of data.

For any project, the selection of methodologies and research methods does not occur in a vacuum, and neither is the process of selection entirely dictated by the subject matter or phenomenon under investigation. Rather, it is linked fundamentally to the way in which the researcher approaches central questions of ontology and epistemology and the adoption of related research paradigms. Figure 16.1 broadly represents the dependent relationship between these elements in the establishment and execution of a research project and the corresponding critical questions that, for this researcher at least, are associated with each of the parameters ontology, epistemology, research paradigm, methodology and method.

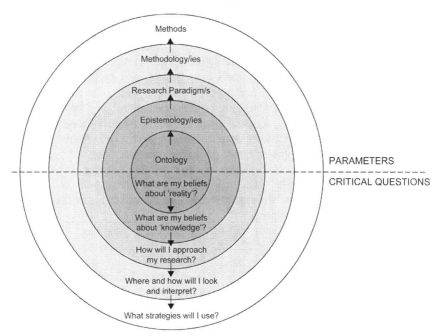

Figure 16.1. Research parameters and corresponding critical questions

It could be argued that with ontology placed at the centre of the circle, the diagram represents the research parameters back-to-front, but a case for particular methodologies and research methods can only be made once one has "pushed through" each of the other layers of meaning by addressing the relevant critical questions. One's epistemology is necessarily formed by the answers to questions relating to ontology and the nature of reality, and the research paradigm within which researchers operates is largely a consequence of their epistemological beliefs, and so on. Furthermore, answers to critical questions relating to ontology and epistemology may give rise to the use of more than one epistemology, research paradigm or methodology within a single study.

This relationship between ontology, epistemology and methodology is explored in much of the literature relating to qualitative approaches to research. Guba and Lincoln (2008), for example, discussed the "competing research paradigms" of positivism, post-positivism, critical theory, constructivism and participatory research and their respective ontologies, epistemologies, axiologies and methodologies. Their thesis was that ontology and epistemology had very practical implications for researchers, and they argued the need for the researchers to reflect, articulate and act upon the values, axiology and beliefs which informed their research at the outset.

Similarly, Patti Lather (2006) represented the likely implications both "backward" (to ontology and epistemology) and "forward" (to methodology and research methods) of what she identified as the key research paradigms currently in operation in social research – the positivist, interpretivist, critical theory and deconstructivist approaches.

The point here is not to impose a simple classification, but rather to map epistemological and ontological multiplicities and "help us recognize both our longing for and a wariness of an ontological and epistemological home" (Lather, 2006, p. 36). Further, if we accept the importance of ontology and epistemology to the choice of particular research paradigms, methodologies and methods, part of the task of the researcher at the outset then must be to contextualise the methodology and methods employed in the current study with an explication of them, and in doing so, respond to Nancy Hartsock's challenge to "'read out' the epistemologies in our various practices" (1987, p. 206), further defined by Lather as "learn[ing] to attend to the politics of what we do and do not do at a practical level" (1991, p. 13).

What, then, might be regarded as the ontological and epistemological home of this researcher? Given my background in history and gender studies, this study drew on my interest in postmodern approaches to history and historical research and the work of feminist scholars and critical theorists in terms of their ontological and epistemological base. Postmodern classicist Nicole Loraux wrote, by way of rationale for her radical reinterpretation of the "Golden Age" of Athens, "When confronted with democracy, with the word as well as the thing, and when confronted with antiquity too, I feel that I am in a strange world and thus entitled to attempt a new reading" (2006, p. 34).

Loraux's new reading of old "text" stemmed from ongoing grappling with an ontology and epistemology not her own, but imposed on her from within the dominant discourse of her field. Her body of work aimed to subvert this dominant discourse, and in doing so established her new reading of old text as an alternative interpretation of history. This notion was similarly advanced by feminist theorist Adrienne Rich (1972, p. 18) in her development of the notion "re-vision" for the purpose of arguing for the equality-within-difference of women. She wrote, "Re-vision – the act of looking back, of seeing with fresh eyes, of entering an old text from a new critical direction – is for women more than a chapter in cultural history: it is an act of survival".

It is from this "strange world" view, then, that I came to this study. The assumptions that underpin my particular ontological and epistemological "home" can be summarised as follows:

– That "reality" is shaped by historical, social, political and social pressures
– That "reality" is constructed and experienced in different ways by different individuals and communities
– That knowledge is necessarily contextual
– That knowledge can be emancipatory.

My decision to employ a life history approach was thus a consequence not only of the topic I chose to study – there are many ways that teachers' professional identity could be studied – but also of a desire to establish a congruence between my own ontological and epistemological home and the methods I chose to employ.

Life history research dates to the early 20th century, when it was used primarily as a tool by anthropologists studying the indigenous peoples of North America (Goodson & Sikes, 2001, p. 6). Adopted by sociologists in the 1920s and 1930s, this approach to research then lay largely dormant in the growth of positivistic approaches to social research, resurfacing in the 1970s and 1980s in response to the "postmodern turn" and the associated rethinking of "evidence" and methodology in sociological as well as historical research (Goodson, 2001).

Life history is about lived experience. In the context of educational research, it presupposes that the connections between work life and personal life are complex and not open to separation. In the words of Goodson and Sikes, "Life history does not ask for such separation: indeed it demands holism" (2001, p. 10). In the investigation of teacher professional identity, then, life history was seen to be a highly appropriate methodology to adopt, because an understanding of teacher identity, of what it is to become and be a teacher, is inextricably linked to the personal and life circumstances of teachers themselves.

While authenticity of design, achieved largely by understanding and "reading out" our ontological and epistemological orientations and establishing congruence between them and the methods we employ in our research, goes some way toward ensuring authenticity in research, much hinges on the subsequent processes of data collection and analysis.

AUTHENTICITY OF PROCESS

Authenticity of process is linked closely to ethical concerns and considerations, most particularly in the context of an extended qualitative study such as this, as they relate to the nature and quality of the relationships between the researcher and the research participants.

A number of ethical considerations are specific to life history research while others are drawn from more general concerns relating to critical research. Conceptualised as in itself an enactment of ethics, critical research has as its primary concern the socially just and democratic production of knowledge and ideas. As such, this study was in some ways "all about ethics". Accordingly, embedded in the methods of data collection and analysis utilised in the study was a concern for the personhood and wellbeing of participants, a determination on my part to minimise the power structure inherent in the participant-researcher relationship, and the hope (although not a demand) that participants would engage with me in constructing their biographical narrative as drawn from the data collected. Framing these guiding philosophies and strategies, however, were the principles of informed consent and confidentiality.

In an attempt to offset the power differential between researcher and participant, interviews were held at a time and place nominated by the participant. I felt strongly that the issue of space was important and that an ideal space for one participant might be a less than desirable one for another. Participants were thus asked at the outset of the study to choose a place for interviews where they would feel comfortable and relaxed, and which also had conditions conducive to reflection and conversation.

In some cases, interviews were held within the grounds of the participant's school, in some cases at the participant's home, and in other cases at another location of the participant's choosing, such as the university campus or a quiet café. I also felt that as far as possible participants should not be inconvenienced by their involvement in the study, and thus participants also nominated the location for interviews; in most cases this meant that I travelled to meet them, but for one participant each interview was treated as a special "escape" and most interviews were held in a location near neither his work nor his home.

In its very nature life history research is personal and close work. The quality of data gained in life history research to some extent relies upon the relationship between the researcher and the research participant, and a range of questions exist about the "relationship bargain" (Measor & Sikes, 1992) struck and the corresponding ethical issues. As Goodson and Sikes (2001, p. 93) suggested, "it would be entirely possible (although certainly unethical) to undertake life history research in a covert manner, under the guise of friendship", engaging in what Lather termed "rape research" (1986, p. 263). Such a practice would surely be abhorrent to any researcher committed to ethical processes, but the very notion raises interesting questions about whose interests get served in the course of research, who gets something out of it and who does not. As Measor and Sikes (1992) pointed out, although the reason for researcher entering into the relationship with participants is usually quite clear – they wish to hear the story of the participant and gather data for their study – the reason behind the respondent's participation is generally less clear.

In early (pre-interview) conversations with participants I purposefully asked each why they had chosen to participate in the study, in an attempt to allow (as far as one can) maximum agency for each within the study. Two indicated that they saw it as a professional development opportunity, a time for reflection and time out from the busyness of school life. A general sense came from all participants that for them it was not really about what they would get out of it, but rather taking pity on a researcher whom they perceived to be doing meaningful work which was aimed at improving life for teachers and, ultimately, students.

The issue of "reciprocity" (Oakley, 1981), as a technique for building relationship and avoiding exploitation of research participants, is also particularly salient in a discussion of ethics in life history research. Reciprocity was initially construed as a means by which feminist researchers could overturn the patriarchal paradigm embedded in more traditional approaches to interviewing, but the potential for manipulation of participants is significant, for as Pat Sikes (1997, p. 21) wrote, "sharing information in order to be, or to appear to be, less exploitative can be seen to be instrumental and manipulative rather than socially supportive". Aside from the ethical issues associated with possible manipulation of participants through reciprocity, I was highly uncomfortable with the assumption of similarities between researcher and participants which is at the heart of this approach.

To approach participants assuming that they shared aspects of my life experience and world view simply because of what I assumed to be their class/race/gender/context seemed to me to undermine the integrity of the project in two ways. First, in a study designed to investigate aspects of identity formation for participants, to make assumptions at the outset about their very "being" seemed counter-productive. Second, as a historian I tried as much as possible to limit at the outset my preconceived ideas about the experiences of participants or the contexts and events that may have led to key decisions in their lives to those factors which contributed to their inclusion in the study (i.e. stage of career and current school context). I admit that I probably achieved this with varying levels of success throughout the process, yet this kind of detachment would have been not at all possible had I been intent on creating a cosy environment based on our similarities.

Instead, I worked hard to be open with participants about the process, to use humour where it was appropriate as a tool to ease discomfort or awkwardness on their part, and to share aspects of my own experience when they inquired or, in very few circumstances, when it seemed appropriate for other reasons. These instances generally came about as a result of a participant asking me a direct question about my experience, rather than at my instigation. My personal style is such that I would have felt uncomfortable engaging in what Stephen Ball called "a reciprocal process of personal 'social striptease'" (1983, p. 95); also I was wary of taking a "mutual storytelling" (Munro, 1998) approach, not wanting to be seen to be self-indulgent or wasteful of participants' precious time.

Shared perceptions and experiences certainly emerged during the course of the prolonged interviews, but they emerged not because I was conscious of emphasising similarities between us but because as educators we found common ground as the relationship between us evolved over time. This may seem like something of a semantic difference, but the key point of differentiation for me lies in the intent. In this case, the common ground evolved organically, out of the discussions that took place over time, and as a result can be seen more as a by-product of the process than a research strategy. Furthermore, these conversations often took place after the conclusion of the interview as such, when a number of times in the packing-up and farewelling process, in the general social or work-related chit-chat that often ensued, participants asked questions of me in passing which had been triggered in some way by our earlier conversation.

AUTHENTICITY OF ANALYSIS AND REPORTING

Finally, "being me" hinges on authenticity in terms of analysing data and reporting the findings of research. Heron (1981, p. 126) argued that participants "have a moral right to participate in decisions that claim to generate information about them", suggesting that participation and collaboration need to happen "not only in the application of research but also in the generation of knowledge". I was wary of expecting participants to engage enthusiastically at every step in the process of analysis, given their already generous commitment of time to the project in interviews. Two strategies were thus used to provide opportunities for participation in analysis and reporting processes, with an invitation issued to all participants to be involved in other ways should they wish. In the first place, each interview opened with a reflection on the transcript of the last, asking participants whether there was anything they wished to change or clarify, if there was anything that surprised them in hindsight, and so on. Second, a biographical narrative, drawn from all six interviews but which I had constructed as a narrative, was returned to participants with an invitation for one final meeting to reflect on the life history

Although it can never be claimed that the power relationship in the context of a research project can be "flattened" any more than it can in the context of a classroom, the orientation of this study was such that it aimed to do so as far as possible. It cannot be denied that the "colonial relationship" (Munro, 1998, p. 12) present in all social research still existed, along with the possible pitfalls and vulnerabilities associated with telling one's story, but my hope was that in being aware and sensitive to these I was best placed to work actively against them throughout the course of the study.

Interviews were digitally audio-recorded and transcribed, with transcripts returned to participants for checking prior to the following interview. This process, usually referred to as respondent validation (e.g. Goodson & Sikes, 2001, p. 36), was a step toward "dialogical data generation" (Carspecken, 1996), where ideally participants and researchers interact dialogically in the collection and interpretation of data, in an attempt to "democratise the research process" (p. 155). In this phase, however, this notion of dialogical or collaborative analysis of data fell somewhat short of my ideal. Participants were very happy to review transcripts and in some way use them as a launching pad for the next interview, yet it became clear that the their prevailing attitude in this process was that they were checking for inaccuracies or for parts of the transcript that they would prefer not to have made public, rather than reflecting upon or clarifying their comments in order to expand upon them. Only one participant who spent a great deal of time reflecting upon her transcripts and notating them for further discussion.

At a subsequent stage, when participants were returned an account of their biographical narrative (which I had constructed) and invited to meet to discuss it, the study came closer to the collaborative ideal promoted by critical research, named elsewhere as "jointly authored statements" (Bonser & Grundy, 1988, p. 6ff). Four of the eight participants took up the invitation to discuss their narrative at length, either by telephone or in person, and two participants entered into the "joint construction" process completely, reworking the narrative to our mutual satisfaction. Interestingly, the focus in this process for both participants was on "tidying" the extracts from the transcripts such that their contribution met what they perceived to be appropriate standards for inclusion in a thesis rather than, as I had expected, on debating and reworking the meaning I had attached to their life experiences as represented in the data.

This unwillingness of participants to engage at a deeper level with the data generated had, I believe, a number of underlying causes. In the first place, the hectic nature of teachers' lives meant that they rarely had time to review transcripts between interviews. In fact, in the initial stages of the study some participants had suggested that rather than sending them transcripts between interviews, they would prefer to schedule extra time at the beginning of each interview to read and digest the transcript. While this seemed to me to be a good option (and preferable to participants arriving at interviews having had time just to briefly skim transcripts), in reality it meant that the transcripts were often subject to only a brief review which had the "check" described above as its aim.

Second, I believe that for some participants a sense of "researcher knows best" prevailed. That is, as the trust evolved within the relationship between us, participants came to understand me as a person who could be relied upon to not misrepresent them and to provide accurate accounts of our conversations. Moreover, it became clear to me during the process that for a number of participants, the process of reading the transcripts, with all of the "ums" and "ers" and half-sentences they contained, was in itself an awkward or embarrassing experience, and one they wished to dispense with as quickly as possible. Finally, it occurred to me that perhaps the participants did not find the data quite as captivating and fascinating as I did, and that this perhaps contributed to their unwillingness to ponder it and "unpick" it as I had hoped they would, seeing the process of analysis as my job rather than theirs.

The multi-layered process of writing, analysing, discussing, constructing, de-constructing and re-constructing accounts over the course of interviews and subsequently in the preparation of the final biographical narratives, however, regardless of its pitfalls, left me satisfied in the end that a level of authenticity had been achieved in analysis and reporting. All eight participants were content and comfortable with their representation as an accurate and authentic portrait of them at that specific point in their lives and careers.

CONCLUSION

The search for authenticity in qualitative research demands a congruence between design, process and reporting. In terms of life history research, authenticity is inescapable as a measure of quality: seeking to constitute and tell participants' life stories in ways that ring true with the participants but are also methodologically rigorous is a complex and multi-layered process. It relies on a level of self-awareness on the part of the researcher that allows fundamental beliefs about knowledge creation and "reality" to be connected to the research enterprise; on the quality of the relationship that emerges between researcher and research participants; and on a commitment to faithful and reflexive analysis and reporting that integrates participants' voices in ways that are respectful and reflective of their desires regarding their involvement. While we may succeed to different extents at different times, the search for authenticity is always a worthy aspiration.

REFERENCES

Ball, S. (1983). Case study research in education: Some notes and problems. In M. Hammersley (Ed.), *The ethnography of schooling: Methodological issues* (pp. 93-95). Driffield: Nafferton.

Bonser, S., & Grundy, S. (1988). Reflective deliberation in the formation of a school curriculum policy. *Journal of Curriculum Studies, 20*(1), 35-45.

Carspecken, P. F. (1996). *Critical ethnography in educational research.* New York: Routledge.

Denzin, N. (1970). *The research act in sociology: A theoretical introduction to sociological methods.* Chicago: Aldine.

Eisner, E. (1998). *The enlightened eye: Qualitative inquiry and the enhancement of educational practice.* Upper Saddle River, NJ: Prentice-Hall.

Goodson, I. (2001). The story of life history: Origins of the life history method in sociology. *Identity: An International Journal of Theory and Research, 1*(2), 129-142.

Goodson, I., & Sikes, P. (2001). *Life history research in educational settings: Learning from lives.* Buckingham: Open University Press.

Groundwater-Smith, S. (2007). Student voice: Essential testimony for intelligent schools. In A. Campbell & S. Groundwater-Smith (Eds.), *An ethical approach to practitioner research* (pp. 113-128). Abingdon: Routledge.

Groundwater-Smith, S., & Mockler, N. (2007). Ethics in practitioner research: An issue of quality. *Research Papers in Education, 22*(2), 199-211.

Groundwater-Smith, S., & Mockler, N. (2009). *Teacher professional learning in an age of compliance: Mind the gap.* Dordrecht: Springer.

Guba, E., & Lincoln, Y. (2008). Paradigmatic controversies, contradictions and emerging confluences. In N. Denzin & Y. Lincoln (Eds.), *The landscape of qualitative research: Theories and issues* (3rd ed., pp. 191-215). Thousand Oaks, CA: Sage.

Hartsock, N. (1987). Rethinking modernism: Minority vs. majority theories. *Cultural Critique, 7,* 187–206.

Heron, J. (1981). Experimental research methods. In P. Reason & J. Rowan (Eds.), *Human enquiry* (pp. 34-35). New York: Wiley.

Lather, P. (1986). Research as praxis. *Harvard Educational Review, 56*(3), 257-277.

Lather, P. (1991). *Getting smart: Feminist research and pedagogy with/in the postmodern.* New York: Routledge.

Lather, P. (2006). This is your father's paradigm: Government intrusion and the case of qualitative research in education. In N. Denzin & M. Giardina (Eds.), *Qualitative inquiry and the conservative challenge* (pp. 31-55). Walnut Creek, CA: Left Coast Press.

Loraux, N. (2006). *The invention of Athens: The funeral oration in the classical city* (2nd ed., Trans A. Sheridan). Cambridge, MA: Harvard University Press.

Measor, L., & Sikes, P. (1992). Visiting lives: Ethics and methodology in life history. In I. Goodson (Ed.), *Studying teachers' lives* (pp. 209-233). London: Routledge.

Merriam, S. (1998). *Qualitative research and case study applications in education.* San Francisco: Jossey Bass.

Merriam, S. (2009). *Qualitative research: A guide to design and implementation.* San Francisco: Jossey-Bass.

Mockler, N. (2011a). Becoming and 'being' a teacher: Undersanding teacher professional identity. In N. Mockler & J. Sachs (Eds.), *Rethinking Educational Practice Through Reflexive Inquiry: Essays in Honour of Susan Groundwater-Smith*. Dordrecht: Springer.

Mockler, N. (2011b). Beyond 'What Works': Understanding Teacher Professional Identity as a Practical and Political Tool. *Teachers and Teaching: Theory and Practice* 17(5), 517-528.

Munro, P. (1998). *Subject to fiction: Women teachers' life history and the cultural politics of resistance*. Buckingham: Open University Press.

Oakley, A. (1981). Interviewing women: A contradiction in terms. In H. Roberts (Ed.), *Doing feminist research* (pp. 30-61). London: Routledge & Keegan Paul.

Rich, A. (1972). When we dead awaken: Writing as revision. *College English, 34*(1), 18-30.

Sikes, P. (1997). *Parents who teach: Stories from home and school*. London: Cassell.

Nicole Mockler PhD
School of Education
University of Newcastle, Australia

JULIA COYLE AND MARISSA OLSEN

17. LEARNING TO BE A RESEARCHER

Bridging the Gap between Research and Creativity

On the surface it would seem that being a researcher and being creative are at opposite ends of a spectrum. However, closer scrutiny of these words and their associated practises/processes lends a different perspective. Research can be defined as *the systematic investigation into and study of materials and sources in order to establish facts and reach new conclusions* (n.d). This presupposes that the researcher has systems in place to address all features of the research necessary in order to reach valid and credible conclusions and establish theory that resonates with the reader. Being creative, on the other hand, has been defined as *relating to or involving the use of the imagination or original ideas to create something* (n.d.). Thus although creativity, like research, has the outcome of adding something new, being creative seems to require less structure and constraint. In this respect there appears to be a disconnect between the systematic and rigorous approaches needed for research and the fluidity associated with creating something original.

However, as we discuss in this chapter, effective research can arise from establishing a symbiotic relationship between the two. Standard approaches recommend being systematic, but we believe that this is only one part of the equation for being an effective researcher. The key to unlocking full research potential is through also being creative in your approach.

This chapter explores these two seemingly opposed concepts. In section one we consider the meaning and value of *being systematic in research*. In section two there is an exploration of what being *creative and remaining open and fluid* brings to the research process. Finally, the merging of these two concepts to enhance research is explored in section three, *bringing it all together through being a creative researcher*. The aim of this chapter is to leave the reader with strategies for marrying the two concepts to enrich both the process and the outcomes of research.

Researching and Being Systematic

The word *research* derives from the middle French word *recerche,* meaning the act of searching closely, from old French word *recercher*, meaning to seek out (n.d.). In the 1630s the word research was used for the first time in processes associated with scientific research (Online Etymology Dictionary, 2010), although such processes had been in existence since the early 11th century with Ibn al-Haytham's scientific method (Steffens, 2006). Perhaps as a result of these origins three words are consistently used in current definitions of the word research: *systematic,*

J. Higgs et al., (eds.), Creative Spaces for
Qualitative Researching: Living Research, 169–178
© 2011 Sense Publishers. All rights reserved.

careful and *diligent* (research, n.d.; Macquarie online, 2010). That is, the original stance of those using the word research has left a mark that is reflected in our current understanding of research and research processes.

Although research is understood to involve the adoption of systematic, or careful and diligent processes, differing perspectives influence our understanding of the use of such practices across the range of research approaches. Perhaps because the word research found its origins in scientific method, a strong link has been forged between being systematic and using approaches associated with scientific method. This perception may persist even in the absence of systematic processes in a research project.

Moreover, the link between being systematic and using approaches linked to scientific method might have triggered the notion that any research that doesn't follow scientific method is not systematic. It may also be that this association has been perpetuated by the interpretive or critical research approaches that explore the complex, messy and unpredictable richness of social interactions. Whatever the cause, it is clear from the literature that the consensus is that systematic processes are necessary for effective research in all approaches. With this in mind, what does being systematic entail, and how does it help when learning to be a researcher?

To be systematic has been defined as something that has been "*done or acting according to a fixed plan or system; methodical*" (systematic, n.d.). Thus being systematic requires researchers to take a stepwise, planned approach throughout each phase of the research. Taking this approach can be beneficial for researchers, as it not only helps researchers to develop a meta-view of their research but also can assist them in choosing a unique path that meets the needs of their particular research question. This may help researchers ensure that the boundaries and potential roadblocks of their path are clearly elucidated and planned for. The result is that researchers are left to experience a smooth research process that supports deepened understanding and the production of useful and relevant knowledge.

A Sense of the Big Picture

Undertaking research for the first time can be likened to taking a maiden journey to a foreign country. Guidance from those who have gone before is invaluable and can be helpful in finding one's way around unfamiliar territory. Introductory research textbooks similarly aim to arm neophyte researchers with a general guide to the research process. For example, in their text *Introduction to Research in the Health Sciences,* Polgar and Thomas (2008, p. 3) described health research as a "systematic and principled way of obtaining evidence (data, information) for solving health care problems and investigating health issues". They then introduced and inculcated within their readers an understanding of the key phases, principles and rules of the research method. For new researchers, taking such a systematic approach to understanding research itself can be an important step in starting to explore the research landscape.

Choosing One's Own Path

A typical meta-view of the research process involves broad phases: first exploring the literature to identify research gaps, then the design and implementation of the research, and finally documentation and communication of results (as presented, for example, by Polgar and Thomas, 2008). If one considers the previously proposed definition of being systematic, taking a systematic approach to research implies that these phases would be conducted in a certain order and in a certain way. This does not mean, however, that all research will be identical.

Research is informed by a range of different philosophical perspectives which can be based on quite divergent views of reality and of the appropriate way to access knowledge (Rothwell, 1998). It follows that research informed by different perspectives will be conducted in different manners. There may also be a more iterative dimension to research rather than straightforward motion, such as in hermeneutic approaches (Rothwell, 1998). Appreciation of the philosophical can thus assist new researchers in both choosing their research path and also determining what being systematic will mean according to their chosen research perspective.

Setting the Boundaries

One of the first steps in determining the research path is an exploration of theoretical and philosophical perspectives relevant to the research topic of interest. Higgs and Trede (2010b) have argued that an in-depth grasp of the theoretical (or content) literature allows researchers not only to identify research gaps but also to delineate boundaries of the research, justify its conduct, and develop insight into the types of perspective that might inform the way the phenomenon of interest is viewed.

Moreover, by exploring different philosophical perspectives (about research approaches), new researchers are better placed to choose and credibly argue for an appropriate research paradigm and approach to inform the research process (Higgs & Trede, 2010a). A research paradigm has been defined by Guba and Lincoln (1994, p. 105) as "*the basic belief system or worldview that guides the investigator, not only in choices of method but in ontologically and epistemologically fundamental ways*". Thus research paradigms provide a structure within which researchers can start to systematically construct a solid methodological foundation for the conduct of their research.

Planning Ahead and Forecasting Roadblocks

Once a research question has been determined and research paradigm selected, decisions can be made about the practicalities of research, such as methods for data collection and analysis and methods for ensuring quality and ethical conduct. Mays and Pope (2000) argued that taking a systematic stance is important in all stages in qualitative research, including the planning phase, as it helps to establish rigorous and high quality research processes. Similar views have been expressed about quantitative research processes (Polgar & Thomas, 2008). An important element in being systematic, therefore, is being organised before commencing research. That is, there is a need to plan ahead and visualise the process in an attempt to forecast potential roadblocks or problems that might arise.

The theoretical and philosophical literature that informs a research project helps us to do this, as can discussions with other more experienced researchers. Although it is not possible to control fully how research will unfold, systematic design helps to ensure that research methods are consistent and remain congruent with the chosen paradigm. Thinking ahead also enables researchers to establish contingency plans that can minimise the effects of problematic events.

Deepening Understanding

Before research can commence, researchers may need to meet certain formal requirements such as obtaining ethical approval and/or approval of a research protocol.

Approval processes such as these can be designed to facilitate a systematic approach, with researchers being required to clearly and succinctly communicate their research plans to people who come from a different research perspective or who may not be researchers at all. Participating in such a process can help deepen understanding about the practicalities of research. It also highlights the importance of addressing different views and perspectives if we are to conduct research safely and ethically. Similarly, taking a systematic approach may help deepen understanding during the implementation of research. For example, Crist and Tanner (2003, p. 202) argued that taking a systematic approach to qualitative research "streamlines and clarifies interpretations". Thus by engaging in a systematic approach to research, researchers may be helped to more deeply understand and engage with their research approach, methodology and findings.

Demonstrating Quality

Various criteria are available to evaluate the quality of research. Which criteria are most appropriate to use depends on the paradigm within which the research has been conducted (Leininger, 1994). That said, there are many perspectives about which quality criteria are important in qualitative research as well as many strategies that can be used to ensure these quality criteria are met. Some of these criteria and strategies are systematic by their very nature. For example, a commonly used criterion for determining the quality of qualitative research is whether the research has been conducted rigorously. Guba and Lincoln (2005) argued that there are two forms of rigour, one relating to the application of the research method and one relating to the interpretation.

Strategies suggested to address the first question of rigour often include systematically documenting research decisions; some examples described in the literature include the construction of decision trails (e.g., Koch, 1994) or reflective journals (e.g., Bulman, 2004) to document research decisions. Methods suggested to address issues around rigour of interpretation include reflexivity, whereby researchers engage in a self-critique of sorts which aims to make explicit the their own frame of reference and how it might have influenced interpretation (Grbich, 2010). Thus a systematic approach to research can mean that strategies to ensure quality criteria are planned for and embedded into the research process well in advance of the research project commencing, and furthermore, that researchers can also take a systematic approach to using individual strategies for ensuring quality.

Individual research journeys can resemble a rollercoaster ride, with peaks of engagement and excitement and troughs when one wishes to disengage with feelings of anxiety. At times there are significant periods of clarity and ambiguity, almost as if the rollercoaster is moving in and out of the clouds. Being systematic helps to smooth out the ride and allow proactive approaches to key elements. However, although being systematic can have many benefits for research, we believe that a systematic approach on its own gives a limited or incomplete view of research. Creativity could be the "yin" to systematic's "yang". Our contention is that an exploration of the concepts and role of creativity is developing research skills and expertise.

Being Creative and Research

Earlier we introduced a definition of being creative as *"relating to or involving the use of the imagination or original ideas to create something"* (*Oxford dictionary online*, 2010b). It is important to understand that this definition serves only as a starting point in understanding creativity and its role in research. Indeed, *exploring the concepts and role of creativity* would seem to be important to developing research skills and expertise.

Although exploring creativity in relation to its importance to research appears to be sound, this task is made difficult by the lack of consensus about creativity and its sources. It is evident that creativity is complex and multi-faceted and that there are no concrete rules about its sources (Ackermann, Gauntlett, & Weckstrom, 2009). In this section we draw on the works of scholars in this field to discuss the role of creativity in research in order to illuminate strategies that might guide the way in learning to be a researcher.

Debate about what constitutes creativity has identified that originality is a key element (Bohm, 1998; Negus & Pickering, 2004), associated with

> always [being] open to learning what is new, to perceiving new differences and new similarities, leading to new orders and structures, rather than tending to impose familiar orders and structures in the field of what is seen (Bohm, 1998, p. 17).

It is evident that this has great relevance to research as people strive to remain open to new possibilities and identify new ways of thinking, and new ways of viewing the familiar. However, as originality is coupled with an element of risk, it has been argued that creativity includes the capacity and the willingness to risk failure (Martin, 2010). This poses a problem for those newly engaged in the rollercoaster of research in learning, to balance the benefits that arise from being open to new ideas and the risks associated with failing to achieve new understanding.

The frameworks from which various protagonists write can make identifying specific types of creativity difficult (Eisner, 1962; Banaji & Burn, 2006). In his seminal work on creativity in education Eisner (1962) identified four different types of creative behaviour: boundary pushing, inventing, boundary breaking, and aesthetic organising. These four types of behaviour can be seen as distinct entities, with one or other being prevalent at any given time. Considering them in relation to research enables us to see the role that creativity might play in developing new understandings and perspectives.

In *boundary pushing* the creative researcher extends the limits around specific items in order to shift understanding of them from that which has become accepted. This act enables researchers to merge seemingly opposing concepts and identify new ways of thinking or find innovative solutions to a problem. A key outcome is the capacity to adopt new ways of practice or a new understanding that blends the ideas, needs and interests of different groups. *Inventing* is where researchers bring known elements together to create something new, for example allowing stakeholders with differing or parallel views to join forces. This requires researchers to cope with a degree of uncertainty and confusion in order to arrive at a new perspective. In *boundary breaking* researchers identify and reject incorrect assumptions and generate solutions by thinking laterally.

An example of this type of behaviour is evident in Copernicus' adoption of the heliocentric model of the universe in an era when the widely held belief was that the earth was at the centre of the universe. This is a clear example of the relationship between risk taking and creative thinking based upon sound reasoning through systematic data gathering. The fourth and final behaviour, *aesthetic organising*, is seen when people seek to find order out of chaos, creating something new out of confusion.

Creativity arises from the merger of three components, knowledge, motivation and creative thinking (Amabile, 1998). Thinking about creativity in this way strengthens its importance in research. A good breadth of knowledge, together with a specific knowledge focus, is an important aspect of being creative (Policastro & Gardner, 1999). It would seem, therefore, that by undertaking research in which we have a specific focus on one aspect within our area of our expertise, we can support our ability to be creative. However, motivation, especially when it is intrinsic (driven by ourselves) rather than extrinsic (externally imposed), has been found to be the vital element in creativity (Amabile, 1998). This helps explain the research experience, and particularly those times when our creative juices appear to run dry and we struggle to feel motivated. Using strategies that regain our intrinsic motivation for the task might be the key to reaching new levels of insight.

Of importance to researchers is that the final element, creative thinking, has been found to involve (a) the capacity to disagree and strike a path that differs from the status quo, (b) the ability to combine knowledge from differing perspectives, (c) perseverance, and (d) the insight to know when to leave an item and return later with a new perspective. All four of these aspects would seem to be invaluable to the capacity to progress in a research project.

It is clear that being creative is as vital to research as being systematic. When creativity is evident in each phase of the research process it helps researchers to think outside the box. Being creative is often associated with something new or novel, such as doing something ordinary in an unusual way, or discovering a new outcome through innovatively designed research. Yet to achieve such creativity the researcher needs to understand the current context fully. This understanding is necessary as it provides a framework from which to break out, or break free. As de Bono (1992, p. 169) wrote, *"There is no doubt that creativity is the most important human resource of all. Without creativity, there would be no progress, and we would be forever repeating the same patterns."*

Bringing it all Together as a Creative Researcher – Strategies Learned

At first glance, being a systematic researcher and being creative seemed to be at opposite ends of a spectrum. Furthermore, debate around methodological issues highlighted the pitfalls associated with creativity and research. For instance, Sanger (1994) raised the widely held belief that the greater the use of strict research process rules with explicit criteria, the more valid the research findings. However, although that view might be of relevance in empirico-analytical research, such regimentation comes at a cost in human research as it can lead to stilted and lifeless interpretations that have little resonance. For this reason, Sanger argued that with less constrained research processes, through a more interpretive stance, a more realistic understanding could be reached. This highlights the real and important congruence between being systematic and being creative.

It is accepted that research should add to the body of knowledge, with researchers actively participating in the process of creating knowledge. In much the same way, creativity is about making new meanings in a transformative process to make new knowledge (Jarvis, 1992). Loehle (1990) argued that success in any research approach requires the combination of four elements: technical skill, knowledge, sound communication and creativity (Loehle, 1990). This grouping gives the sense that creativity is inextricably linked and acts in tandem with other elements required for research (including being systematic). We argue that being a researcher with the systematic approaches involved, and being creative with the need for free-form thinking, should form a symbiotic partnership to drive us to reach new heights and innovative outcomes in our research. Key strategies can be learned from establishing such a partnership, and once learned they will enhance the research process and the experience for researchers involved.

There are many tools available to help people access and enhance their creative research capacity. Some tools, such as drawing, word association and debate, have been used over centuries. Other tools link new technologies with old concepts. For instance a visual thesaurus, available on the Web, provides a novel way to show potential links and commonalities through playing with words (e.g., Snappy Words, 2010). In some respects the visual thesaurus resembles a mind map, and is an example of the creative evolution of an existing tool. When used iteratively throughout the research process it can provide insights that help us to access hidden meaning when we are developing concepts and understandings.

We now provide some other tools and strategies that can help unlock research creativity:

– Rather than choose between different stances, explore what happens when you bring the two together.
– Test your assumptions – be inventive about the ways in which you view things.
– Try not to be constrained by specific beliefs and stances – feel free to explore and extend beyond the boundaries.
– Take time to organise your thoughts – this can happen anywhere, so keep a notebook handy to jot down seemingly random thoughts, relax your mind and let thoughts come – try daydreaming or meditation.
– Use a range of tools that help you make sense of your data – talk with others, try using creative rather than "formal" writing techniques, go back to nature, express yourself "away from the page".
– Read (and listen) widely and consider the ways in which seemingly unlinked material might connect or open your mind to new perspectives.
– Know when to step away and take time out – a break can help you to return with a new understanding (that is, don't force it).
– Persevere – break seemingly insurmountable tasks into manageable chunks and chip away at a task.
– Don't be afraid of failure.
– If you aren't keen to make bold steps, take calculated risks – talk over your new ideas with others.
– Become accustomed to uncertainty and confusion – accept these as part of the process, but make sure you have a means to pull yourself out.

CONCLUSION

The overall aim with any research project is to add to a field of knowledge. The value of this new knowledge can be diminished if research approaches lack rigour and quality. Therefore, being systematic in ways that enhance the quality of what we do is fundamental to our being able to achieve our aim. However, as we have argued, the key to unlocking full research potential is through combining creativity with being systematic in our approach. Opening oneself to identifying and exploring effective strategies to balance and intertwine creativity in combination with being systematic is a highly personal, but ultimately rewarding aspect of the experience of learning to become a researcher.

REFERENCES

Ackermann, E., Gauntlett, D., & Weckstrom, C. (2009). *Defining systematic creativity: Explaining the nature of creativity and how the LEGO® System of Play relates to it.* LEGO® Learning Institute.

Available: http://learninginstitute.lego.com/en-us/Research/Systematic%2BCreativity.aspx, accessed 31 August 2010.

Amabile, T.M. (1998). How to kill creativity. *Harvard Business Review, 76*(5): 76-87.

Banaji, S., & Burn, A., with Buckingham, D. (2006). *The rhetorics of creativity: A review of the literature.* London: Institute of Education, University of London and the Arts Council England.

Bohm, D. (1998). *On creativity.* London: Routledge.

Bulman, C. (2004). An introduction to reflection. In C. Bulman & S. Schutz (Eds.), *Reflective practice in nursing* (pp. 1-24). Oxford: Blackwell.

Creative. (n.d.). In *Online Oxford dictionaries.* Available: http://oxforddictionaries.com/view/entry/m_en_gb0189370#m_en_gb0189370, accessed 31 August 2010.

Crist, J.D., & Tanner, C.A. (2003). Interpretation/analysis methods in Hermeneutic interpretive phenomenology. *Nursing Research, 52*(3), 202-205.

de Bono, E. (1992). *Sur/petition: Creating value monopolies when everyone else is merely competing.* Toronto: Harper Collins.

Eisner, E.W. (1962). A typology of creative behavior in the visual arts. In E.W. Eisner & D.W. Ecker (Eds.), *Readings in art education* (pp. 323-335). Waltham, MA: Blaisdell Publishing.

Grbich, C. (2010). Interpreting quality in qualitative research. In J. Higgs, N. Cherry, R. Macklin & R. Ajjawi (Eds.), *Researching practice. A discourse on qualitative methodologies* (pp. 153-164). Rotterdam: Sense.

Guba, E.G., & Lincoln, Y.S. (1994). Competing paradigms in qualitative research. In N.K. Denzin & Y.S. Lincoln (Eds.), *Handbook of qualitative research* (pp. 105-117). Thousand Oaks, CA: Sage.

Guba, E.G., & Lincoln, Y.S. (2005). Paradigmatic controversies, contradictions and emerging confluences. In N.K. Denzin & Y.S. Lincoln (Eds.), *The Sage handbook of qualitative research* (3rd ed., pp. 191-216). Thousand Oaks, CA: Sage.

Higgs, J., & Trede, F. (2010a). Philosophical frameworks and research communities. In J. Higgs, N. Cherry, R. Macklin & R. Ajjawi (Eds.), *Researching practice: A discourse on qualitative methodologies* (pp. 31-36). Rotterdam, The Netherlands: Sense.

Higgs, J., & Trede, F. (2010b). Theoretical frameworks and literature: Framing and supporting qualitative research. In J. Higgs, N. Cherry, R. Macklin & R. Ajjawi (Eds.), *Researching practice: A discourse on qualitative methodologies* (pp. 57-64). Rotterdam: Sense.

Jarvis. P. (1992). *Paradoxes of learning: On becoming an individual in society.* San Francisco: Jossey-Bass.

Koch, T. (1994). Establishing rigour in qualitative research: The decision trail. *Journal of Advanced Nursing, 19*(5), 976-986.

Leininger, M. (1994). Evaluation criteria and critique of qualitative research studies. In J.M. Morse (Ed.), *Critical issues in qualitative research methods* (pp. 95-115). Thousand Oaks, CA: Sage.

Loehle, C. (1990). A guide to increased creativity in research: Inspiration or perspiration? *BioScience, 40*, 123-129.

Macquarie Online. (n.d.). Available: http://www.macquarieonline.com.au/, accessed 4 December 2010.

Martin, P. (2010). *Making space for creativity.* Creativity Centre, University of Brighton.

Mays, N., & Pope, C. (2000). Qualitative research in health care: Assessing quality in qualitative research. *British Medical Journal, 320*, 50-52.

Negus, K., & Pickering, M. (2004). *Creativity, communication and cultural value.* London: Sage.

Online etymology dictionary. (n.d.). Available: http://www.etymonline.com/, accessed 21 January 2011.

Polgar, S., & Thomas, S.A. (2008). *Introduction to research in the health sciences.* Edinburgh: Churchill Livingstone.

Policastro, E., & Gardner, H. (1999). From case studies to robust generalizations: An approach to the study of creativity. In R.J. Sternberg (Ed.), *Handbook of creativity* (pp. 213-25). Cambridge: Cambridge University Press.

Research (n.d). In *Online etymology dictionary.* Available: http://www.etymonline.com/, accessed 21 January 2011.

Rothwell, R. (1998). Philosophical paradigms and qualitative research. In J. Higgs (Ed.), *Writing qualitative research* (pp. 21-28). Sydney: Hampden Press.

Sanger, J. (1994). Seven types of creativity: Looking for insights in data analysis. *British Educational Research Journal, 20*(2), 175.

Snappy Words. (n.d.). Available: http://www.snappywords.com/, accessed 31 August 2010.

Steffens, B. (2006). *Ibn al-Haytham: First scientist.* Greensboro, NC: Morgan Reynolds.

Systematic. (n.d.). In *Online Oxford Dictionaries.* Available: http://oxforddictionaries.com/view/entry/m_en_gb0839200#m_en_gb0839200, accessed 31 August 2010.

Julia Coyle PhD
School of Community Health
Charles Sturt University, Australia

Marissa Olsen MSc (Nutr/Diet), APD
School of Dentistry and Health Sciences
Charles Sturt University, Australia

ANGIE TITCHEN AND DEBBIE HORSFALL

18. EMBODYING CREATIVE IMAGINATION AND EXPRESSION IN QUALITATIVE RESEARCH

*Figure 18.1. Example of using creative arts in a collaborative inquiry
(Seizing the Fire, 2002)*

Pushing back tables and chairs, Katherine creates a space in the room. In the centre, on the floor, she places a huge jug containing autumn leaves, greenery and a few red and yellow flowers that release earthy fragrance. The arrangement is surrounded by coloured pencils, crayons, oil pastels, children's paint boxes and brushes, plastic cups full of water, a lump of clay in a washing-up bowl and a pad of flip-chart paper. Apart from one flickering candle beside the arrangement, the room is lit only by natural light.

Some gentle music is playing. The space is ready for a visioning exercise in which a group of health and social care professionals, people who use their services, and community workers are about to engage in a collaborative inquiry to explore, through the senses, creative imagination and artistic expression, ways of developing their new roles within a cross-boundary service development.

Their aim is to create a service across acute and community health and social care settings that is experienced as seamless by those who use it. At the same time, they plan to generate theory about the nature and experience of such an innovative service and about the development journey towards it. The group members are co-researchers in a national action research project. Katherine is a member of the research team and has

*J. Higgs et al., (eds.), Creative Spaces for
Qualitative Researching: Living Research, 179-190*

agreed to facilitate the visioning exercise. A babble of voices at the door, group members enter.

Sharp intakes of breath, "Oh no! I can't paint (dance, sing, make music)", "I was allowed not to take art at school, I was that bad", "I am not an artist", "This smacks of regression", "I can't bear this kind of stuff". A few voices murmur, "Oh great, how exciting, it takes me back to the magic and playfulness of my childhood",

"I'm really looking forward to being creative again after so many years". Katherine sees looks of apprehension and even terror on some faces. She invites people to sit in a circle around the candle-lit arrangement, either on a chair or on the floor, wherever they feel comfortable. All but two sit on the floor and one nurse kicks off her shoes. Following nervous laughter, a few others do the same. Katherine knows from previous experience that to help people to get the most out of such a session, time must be spent acknowledging their feelings and helping them to let go of their fears, so that they can step into new (old) territory.

Increasingly, creative imagination and intuition are openly acknowledged to have a place in the epistemology and ontology of qualitative research, and the use of creative arts media as research means (i.e., data-gathering, analytic and interpretive methods) and ends (i.e., research products) is growing (see e.g. Figure 18.1; Sharon Deacon, 2000; Jenny Elliott, 2008; Judy Heitzman, 2002; Joy Higgs et al., 2007).

However, the use of creative arts in other aspects of research, such as involving participants as co-researchers, team-building, generating research questions and distributing findings is less prevalent or understood, although significant work in this area is progressing (e.g., Belinda Dewar, 2005; Janice Ollerton, 2010; Famke van Lieshout & Shaun Cardiff – see Chapter 22).

In this chapter, we offer ideas emerging from our studies of using creative arts within a number of creative and collaborative inquiries, (e.g., Susan Ambler et al., 2002; Debbie Horsfall, 2005; Brendan McCormack & Angie Titchen, 2006; Titchen & McCormack, 2010). We illustrate how you can tap your creative imagination, intuition and embodied knowing, through the facilitation of artistic expression, to generate artistic, holistic research methodologies, methods and research products.

DEFINITIONS

Art: (1) human skill as opposed to nature; (ability in) skilful execution as an object in itself; imitative or imaginative skill applied to design, as in paintings, architecture; (2) thing in which skill may be exercised; (3) practical application of any science, craft; (4) stratagem; (5) established form of composition; medium of artistic expression (*The concise Oxford dictionary*, 1982).

Creative: Creating; able to create; inventive, imaginative; showing imagination as well as routine skill (*The concise Oxford dictionary*, 1982).

Creative arts can be thought of as (1) the media of artistic and imaginative expression, such as paintings, clay models, poems, creative writing, story-telling, dance, body sculptures, dramatic representations, music-making, singing, landscape art, and as (2) the human skills and creative imagination processes involved in expressing an image in any one of these media.

The creative arts can be distinguished from the performing arts in that the focus in the former is on expression of one's vision, understanding, interpretation and so on, rather than on performance for others. Fine arts, in comparison to creative arts, refers to advanced skill, often theory-based, where skill is primarily acquired through learning in addition to experience. The embodiment of creative imagination and expression in research requires internalising the use of creative imagination and expression in both the ends and means of qualitative research.

WELL-SPRINGS

Although a philosophical interest in qualitative research as an artistic endeavour seems to have been first mooted by Elliott Eisner (1981), the philosophical and theoretical basis and use of creative arts in other aspects of research are still undeveloped. In particular, the embodied use of creative arts in the exploration and facilitation of creativity and professional artistry in research is virtually unexamined, at least in the public domain, although such work is now emerging (see Boomer & Frost – Chapter 27). In this chapter, we explore these less developed areas by drawing on our research and facilitation experiences, but first we set out our embodied well-spring of creativity.

We believe that the intuition, images and processes of creative imagination are one step ahead of and integral to the reflective process, so that (as McNiff, 1988, suggests) if we stay close to the images and processes of creative imagination, they will suggest new frontiers of understanding. We also believe that creative imagination and the facilitation of artistic expression through the use of creative arts in qualitative research can promote accessibility, expression and engagement, knowledge development and integration, transformation, person-centredness, facilitation, collaboration and creativity (see Titchen & Horsfall, 2007).

CREATIVE ARTS IN RESEARCH AS MEANS AND ENDS

Qualitative research can be imagined as two parallel spirals (see Figure 18.2), the black spiral representing the epistemological relationships between the research questions, philosophical starting points, the methodology, methods, reporting and the research product; and the white one representing the importance of paying attention to epistemological and ontological authenticity and critical creativity throughout the whole research process. We now unravel these spirals to show how the creative arts can be used to illuminate and transform within the interpretive and critical research paradigms.

Impulses

The creative arts can be used to access the motivations driving researchers to investigate a particular area and tap into the sources of energy and passion (of the researchers and the participants). The internal impulses can be the beliefs and values of the researchers and what they already know in relation to the area.

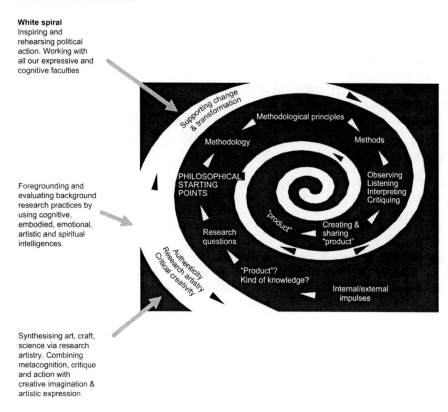

Figure 18.2. The use of creative arts in research as means and ends (after Titchen & Higgs, 2007; McCormack & Titchen, 2006)

These beliefs and values can be accessed through creative visualisation and creative expression, in similar ways to those illustrated in our opening story of the cross-boundary service development and in Figure 18.3.

Another simple way of exploring self is the use of picture cards. The cards are spread out face down and participants are invited to choose the card they are especially drawn to. After looking at their chosen card, they are then invited (in the context of the research or workshop context) to share something of themselves and their values, using the card as a trigger if they want to. The cards are effective in creating a space in which people feel able to express their values and tap into their creativity. The revelation of values through creative expression provides an opportunity for researchers to develop an agreed vision and common purpose for the research. Creative expression also provides a vehicle to expose differences in values or emphasis that can provide an impetus for acknowledging diversity, dialoguing with difference, team building and stakeholder involvement. Creative arts media, such as a group body sculpture (Figure 18.3), image theatre (Boal, 1982) and music-making, also offer excellent opportunities for researchers to become more attuned and sensitive to each other.

Product/Kind of Knowledge

Having an idea at the beginning of the research about the kind of research product desired will help to identify appropriate philosophical starting points to underpin the methodological development. Visioning and creative expression can be used to create a sense of possible products.

For instance, members of a collaborative inquiry imagined the form of a book that was to be the product of our inquiry into professional practice in health, education and the creative arts through their experience of painting, poetry writing and listening to music (Higgs & Titchen, 2001). Through these experiences and the emerging critical dialogues, the group determined that the kind of knowledge to be created in the inquiry would be personal, professional craft and propositional knowledge, and that it would be blended and conveyed through symbolism, metaphor and image as well as through analysis, critique and discourse.

Figure 18.3. Expressing values through body sculpture

In terms of accessing the knowledge people bring to the research, the work of Simons and McCormack (2007) provides an example of critical research in which nurses with little or no experience of research contributed to the development of a study's philosophical and design principles. Using paint, clay and image theatre, they explored the different issues that could influence the design of their inquiry. They discovered they could draw on their professional craft knowledge (from clinical experiences) and re-contextualise it in evaluation research.

Research Questions

Research questions in interpretive and critical research are created both at the beginning of an inquiry and during it. Sometimes the data collected speak to us and suggest the question to which they are the answer. Many of the researchers with whom we work generate their initial questions, first from internal and external impulses, then through subsequent scholarship, and then through their ongoing engagement with and immersion in the data.

The Seizing the Fire (2002) collaborative set about framing the research questions in an entirely different way. As well as conducting a literature review to guide the development of research questions, collaborative members combined critical dialogue with a walk in a London park. They agreed that they would walk and talk, and then stop in places to which they felt drawn. There they would look for inspiration in the beauty of nature for their questions. Standing under trees laden with red berries and looking up into the deep contrasting blue of the sky, they distilled the essence of their conversations and formulated and debated their research questions.

Walking further, sometimes talking and sometimes in meditative or reflective silence, the group climbed a hill. At the top, the questions were re-visited and shaped through further debate and inspiration from the vista before them. At their third stop, at the bottom of the hill, they reached agreement on the questions with which they would work (Seizing the Fire, 2002).

Then they gathered berries, wood and autumn leaves to create a piece of landscape art that symbolised the questions and experience of working in this new, creative way. Thus they discovered that using creative approaches helps to get to the essence of the research and to reach consensus with stakeholders about the questions to be asked.

Philosophical Starting Points

When different world views are revealed through the surfacing of values, the creative arts can provide experiences that bring viewpoints together. For example, we find that when some people are exposed to the opportunity to draw on their creative imagination or express themselves artistically, they consider such activity a waste of time, or as diversional from the real work of rational, left-brain thinking.

However, establishing a supportive, non-judgmental culture and offering supported journeys can change their views. Such changes in world view, characterised by Jack Mezirow (1981) as perspective transformations, often occur very quickly when the creative arts are used.

The creative arts can also be used to challenge contemporary discourses that disempower and silence voices and to develop ways of working with rather than doing to. For example, they can be used to integrate the philosophical starting points of research with the practical philosophy of co-researchers who do not have research backgrounds.

By freeing up creative expression of nurses' professional craft knowledge, Brendan McCormack (in Simons & McCormack, 2007) was better able to integrate his hermeneutic starting points as an experienced researcher with the practical philosophy of the nurses with whom he was working. This meant that a philosophical starting point was created which the nurses experienced as real and relevant to them and their practice. In such situations, researchers can design studies that match the espoused values of participants.

Methodology, Methodological Principles and Methods

Methodology is shaped by the philosophical tradition(s) chosen, and creative arts media can be used to envision new methodological possibilities and principles that match that tradition (see Titchen & McCormack, 2010, for an example of how that can be done).

To show this shaping of methodology and how the methodological principles in turn shape methods, Angie presents an introspective inquiry in which she examined her professional craft knowledge (practical know-how) of doing qualitative research. She shows how using creative imagination can illuminate and capture the essence and uncertainty of experience and achieve understanding and embodiment of knowledge through artistry and creativity.

Angie: My research questions are: How do I do creative qualitative research? How do I do ontological authenticity (foreground self-in-relation)? How do I facilitate and experience the point of creativity in my research? These questions have shaped my methodology, which combines the philosophical ideas of ancient traditions and creative inquiry (through body senses, emotions, spirituality, creative imagination and artistic expression) with the raising to consciousness (for critical review) of my pre-reflective knowing, doing, being and becoming as a qualitative researcher.

I am influenced by aspects of the ancient wisdom from the traditions of Taoism (see e.g. Hill, 1997), Buddhism (see Osho, 1995), Native Americans (see Arrien, 1993) and Australian Aboriginals (see Morgan, 1994), particularly in relation to authenticity of self, balance, being in the body and precursors of creativity. Although I wanted the research product to use creative expression, I did not intend to engage in steps that were determined at the outset, as I wanted to embrace the unknown, which I regard as the distinguishing feature of creative discovery (see McNiff, 1998).

The key research method I have been using for gathering and making sense of data is authentic movement. In this process an individual can pose a question or an issue for exploration through awareness, movement and stillness of the body (Pallaro, 1999). The aim is to access the unconscious and deep embodied knowing that is difficult to express in words. The individual works in a supportive space (physically, emotionally and spiritually), witnessed by another who watches with soft, uncritical eyes. After moving, in silence, both express artistically what they have experienced and learned through accessing and watching the wisdom of the body and the heart, using paint, crayons, creative writing, etc. In this way, I have built up a collection of paintings and haiku (a form of Zen poetry that gets at the essence of experience) to interpret my painting.

Creativity

Impulse following surprise

And going with it

These data were then synthesised within a hermeneutic circle, seeking layers of interpretation and moving from the parts to the whole and back again. This was achieved by laying all the paintings on the ground. From a point of stillness and silence, I wandered through them, first with soft eyes, and then with critical eyes, looking for patterns, recurring images, themes.

I read the haiku several times, before doing some Qi Gong (part of the T'ai Chi practice within the Taoist tradition) involving the breath, movement and visualisation of energy) to clear my mind of clutter and stimulate my creative energy. I spent the rest of the day moving around the paintings, dancing them to express new connections, sitting contemplatively, making reflective notes, re-reading, scribbling.

By the end of one day of this activity, a tentative conceptual framework had formed itself through a seemingly effortless process. Over subsequent days, as I refined and tested out the framework, I took frequent walks in nature, to open my mind to new ideas that sprang into my head during the physical act of walking. I shared the framework with fellow researchers for public scrutiny and critical review before exposing aspects of it to a wider audience at a keynote presentation.

Creating and Delivering the Product

Creative forms and processes can be used to inspire and fashion the final creation or research product and then share it with others.

Tattered wisps Clouds
Archetypal imagery

Debbie: I have to move my body to be able to start writing. I walk, potter about in the garden, pulling weeds. Whatever it is, it has to be outside, I need to feel unconfined by literal man-made constructions, instead surrounded by trees, flowers, grasses and birds. I also collect words. I love the shape of them, the sound of them and the images they conjure, writing them in the back of my current note-book.

Then I dive into these words. It's a sort of haphazard, evolving approach, a collection of treasures.

Angie: Collecting words! Are they words that capture the essence of your ideas?

Debbie: No, they are words that sound perfect, look gorgeous, feel intriguing. I literally get captured by a certain word, sometimes a phrase. At the moment I'm walking around with "you wrap yourself in a clouded shadow", "tattered wisps", "shimmering" and "veils". On reflection they are often words which do capture essences, and as I look at this particular collection there are also connecting threads, but I start with my bodily response. Angie, what do you do to tap into your creativity when writing?

Angie: I also have to be outside, often walking whatever the weather! Moving in some way in nature helps a guiding or holding visual image to emerge for whatever I am about to write or create. Often this is an archetypal image like the spiral used in Figure 18.3. I then put the imagery on my desk or on the wall behind my computer. It gives me creative energy. Around me, each pile of paper and plastic folders of notes and drafts is covered by a visual image. Instead of feeling overwhelmed by huge piles of anonymous, dull-looking papers, my office is awash with colour and vibrancy that taps me effortlessly straight into the essence of the messages I wish to convey and into deeper layers of experiencing and understanding.

Debbie: I like the idea of covering folders with images. I hold the image of people I find inspirational in my mind and often literally surround myself with them – Virginia Woolf, Robin Morgan and Luce Irigaray are three of my favourites. I find words, movement and other writers inspirational.

Angie: In relation to using creative arts as ends, that is, the research product, this is a really exciting area. More and more people, including me, are overcoming a fear of using creative approaches at conferences and in publications. For example, I've done a little play, along with paintings, poetry, music, metaphor and improvisation in conference presentations. I also make my PowerPoint presentations full of colour and visual images. With my fellow researchers, we offer conference workshops and invite people to test out various theoretical and methodological frameworks by engaging with them creatively. A colleague of mine, Jenny Elliott, included a dance performance as part of her PhD thesis (Elliott, 2008).

Debbie: I wonder how much we have been imbued with the messages from our schooling about not being artistic! Most of my work in this area has been in supporting research students and in the university classroom (e.g. Horsfall, Bridges, Camden Pratt, & Salmon, 2004). A group of us have done a series of performances (e.g. Susan

Ambler et al., 2002). I was also part of a collaborative group that organised a creative conference in community development. Oh yes, and of course, various creative attempts at conference papers to avoid the talking-head syndrome (e.g. Judy Pinn & Debbie Horsfall, 1999).

Angie: And both of us know how difficult it has been when it comes to publishing paintings and so on in traditional research journals. It is getting a little easier lately but we still need to keep on challenging editors and influencing editorial panels by becoming members and facilitating cultural change from inside.

Debbie: Yes, it's so important in terms of access, equity and social change. Many people don't relate to the more traditional academic text and don't engage with academia at all. So academic text is just not useful to many people, often the very people we are working with in our research. Poetry, images (e.g. paintings and photos), language that uses a more journalistic style, data in short stories, all enable a greater variety of people to engage with research and knowledge production. Virginia Woolf wrote about the ivory tower of academia needing to lean towards the ground a bit more. I love that image.

LET'S REST A WHILE …

In this chapter we have explored, through a variety of genres, the ways in which creative imagination and artistic expression can be embodied as means and products in the qualitative research endeavour. Embodying research through the use of creative imagination and artistic expression offers a holistic view of research processes, cultures and products.

Working this way promotes a different understanding and outcome of whose knowledge and what knowledge gets to count, and of what types of knowing or researching are worth more than others, from that often encountered in research products and processes. As the field is re-imagined it becomes more expansive, more encompassing in the process.

It is also more inclusive and accessible for people, cultures and environments that are not trained in research or academic-speak, in terms of participating and embodying the research and in accessing its products. Moreover, the very nature of such research (which is often different, and sometimes shocking or surprising) facilitates creative change at personal, cultural and organisational levels.

Embodying the creative imagination and the creative act as means and ends of inquiry expands our notions of what research is and what it can do. It opens up possibilities for the creation of new methodologies to do new things, particularly in collaborative research.

In this chapter we have also gone beyond using creative arts as means and ends in research, to show how these arts can be used to involve participants as co-researchers and for team-building, generating research questions and distributing findings. Basing modes of inquiry on principles of artistic knowing will require the valuing of, and engagement in, serious and playful epistemological and ontological debate within research communities and organisations.

REFERENCES

Ambler, S., Chappelow, H., Horsfall, D., Horsfall, J., Oates, L., Pinn, J. et al. (2002). *Celebrating community work*. Performed at Celebrations for Development and Change Conference, University of Technology Sydney, March 22.

Arrien, A. (1993). *The four-fold way: Walking the paths of the warrior, teacher, healer and visionary*. New York: HarperSanFrancisco.

Boal, A. (1982). *The theatre of the oppressed*. London: Routledge.

Deacon, S. (2000). Creativity within qualitative research on families: New ideas for old methods. *The Qualitative Report, 4*(3&4). Available: http://www.nova.edu/ssss/QR/QR4-3/deacon.html30, accessed 30 November 2010.

Dewar, B. (2005). Beyond tokenistic involvement of older people in research: A framework for future development and understanding. *International Journal of Older People Nursing, 14*(3a), 48-53.

Eisner, E. (1981). On the differences between scientific and artistic approaches to qualitative research. *Educational Researcher, April*, 5-9.

Elliott, J. (2008). *Dance mirrors: Embodying, actualizing and operationalizing a dance experience in a healthcare context*. Unpublished PhD thesis, University of Ulster, Jordanstown, Northern Ireland.

Heitzman, J. (2002). Post-it notes: Social workers and research participants sticking together. *The Qualitative Report, 7*(4). Available: http://www.nova.edu/ssss/QR/QR7-4/heitzman.html, accessed 30 November 2010.

Higgs, J., & Titchen, A. (Eds.) (2001). *Professional practice in health, education and the creative arts*. Oxford: Blackwell Science.

Higgs J., Titchen A., Horsfall D., & Armstrong H. (Eds.) (2007). *Being critical and creative in qualitative research*. Sydney: Hampden Press.

Hill, S. (1997). *Reclaiming the wisdom of the body: A personal guide to Chinese medicine*. London: Constable.

Horsfall, D. (2005). Creative practices of hope. In D. Gardiner & K. Scott (Eds.), *Proceedings of international conference on engaging communities*. Brisbane, Qld: Queensland Government. Available: http://www.engagingcommunities2005.org/abstracts/Horsfall-Debbie-final.pdf

Horsfall, D., Bridges, D., Camden Pratt. C., & Sammon, L. (2004). A performance of difference. *Reflective Practice, 5*(1), 109-127.

McCormack, B., & Titchen, A. (2006). Melding, exploding, blending: Critical creativity. *Educational Action Research: An International Journal, 14*(2), 239-266.

McNiff, S. (1998). *Art-based research*. London: Jessica Kingsley.

Mezirow, J. (1981). A critical theory of adult learning and education. *Adult Education, 32*(1), 3-24.

Morgan, M. (1994). *Mutant message down under*. London: Thorsons.

Ollerton, J. M. (2010). *Rights, camera, action!: A collaborative exploration of social barriers to self-determination with people labelled with learning difficulties*. Unpublished PhD thesis, University of Western Sydney.

Osho. (1995). *Returning to the source: Talks on Zen*. Shaftesbury: Element Books.

Pallaro, P. (Ed.) (1999). *Authentic movement: Essays by Mary Starks Whitehouse, Janet Adler and Joan Chodorow*. London: Jessica Kingsley.

Pinn, J., & Horsfall, D. (1999). Creating spaces for new alliances. Presentation at XII Eco-politics Conference. Katoomba, 7-10 October.

Seizing the Fire. (2002). Nurturing creativity in health and social care and education. London: Talk at The Nuffield Trust for Research and Policy Studies in Health Services, November 27.

Simons, H., & McCormack, B. (2007). Integrating arts-based inquiry in evaluation methodology: challenges and opportunities. *Qualitative Inquiry, 13*(2), 292-311.

The concise Oxford dictionary (7th ed.) (J.B. Sykes, Ed.) (1982). Oxford: Oxford University Press.

Titchen, A., & Higgs, J. (2007). Exploring interpretive and critical philosophies. In J. Higgs, A. Titchen, D. Horsfall & H.B. Armstrong (Eds.), *Being critical and creative in qualitative research* (pp. 56-68). Sydney: Hampden Press.

Titchen, A., & Horsfall, D. (2007). Re-imaging research using creative imagination and expression. In J. Higgs, A. Titchen, D. Horsfall & H.B. Armstrong (Eds), *Being critical and creative in qualitative research* (pp. 215-229). Sydney: Hampden Press.

Titchen, A., & McCormack, B. (2010). Dancing with stones: Critical creativity as methodology for human flourishing. *Educational Action Research: An International Journal, 18*(4), 531-554.

Angie Titchen D.Phil, MSc, MCSP
Adjunct Professor
Charles Sturt University, Australia

Debbie Horsfall PhD, MA, B.Ed
Peace and Development Studies
School of Social Sciences
University of Western Sydney, Australia

JOY HIGGS

19. LIBERATING RESEARCH MENTORING

Reflecting, Re-visioning, Re-creating

Research mentoring is part of the life-cycle of research development. Early career researchers (ECRs) learn from and are supported by experienced researchers and role models and expand their horizons and capabilities, then in turn become mentors themselves. In preparing to write this chapter I reflected upon several mentoring models, projects, experiences and approaches to qualitative research mentoring that I have developed, implemented and co-created in the past, and set out to re-vision and combine them for new liberations. These include:

- A model of liberating program systems for research supervision and becoming self-directed in research and learning (Higgs, 1989, 1993)
- A 22-year history of supervising research students, providing leadership in their communities of research practice, gaining and critically appraising strategies and perspectives on research supervision (Higgs, 2003, 2006a,b,c; Higgs & Armstrong, 2007; Cohorts website1)
- A narrative inquiry project on being a qualitative researcher and doing qualitative research (Higgs & Radovich, 1999)
- An evolving series of interpretations of the value and nature of frameworks for understanding and utilising qualitative research philosophy and practice; for doing, knowing, being and becoming in qualitative research (Higgs, 2001a; Higgs, Trede, & Rothwell, 2007; Trede & Higgs, 2009; Higgs & Trede, 2010)
- A journey of reflection on bringing self and perspectives into qualitative research (Horsfall & Higgs, 2007; Patton, Higgs, & Smith, 2009; Macklin & Higgs, 2010)
- A series of projects and texts around being critical, creative, ethical and transformative in qualitative research (Byrne-Armstrong, Horsfall, & Higgs, 2001; Higgs, 2001b; Higgs & Byrne-Armstrong, 2006; Higgs & Titchen, 2007; Higgs, Titchen, Horsfall, & Armstrong, 2007; Higgs, Trede, Ajjawi, Loftus, Smith, & Paterson, 2007; Higgs, Horsfall, & Grace, 2009; Trede, Higgs, & Rothwell, 2009; Higgs, Cherry, Macklin, & Ajjawi, 2010)
- A history of learning to communicate research in multiple text forms and to help others learn about writing (Higgs, McAllister, & Rosenthal, 2008; Grace, Higgs, & Horsfall, 2009; Higgs, Cherry, & Trede 2009; Patton, Higgs, & Smith, 2009)
- An understanding of thesis writing (Higgs, 2009), book writing (Higgs & Ajjawi, 2009) and writing journal papers (Street & Higgs, 2008).

To build a picture of research mentoring from this history of experience and interpretation I have built the following pattern of arguments (see Figure 19.1).

J. Higgs et al., (eds.), Creative Spaces for
Qualitative Researching: Living Research, 191–200
© *2011 Sense Publishers. All rights reserved.*

Figure 19.1. Research mentoring

LIBERATING MENTORING

In this section I take a fresh look at a model of liberating program systems I developed many years ago (Higgs, 1989) and identify its relevance today. This model was built on the following research findings and theoretical perspectives:

– Leadership and mentoring ideally involve flexible adjustment to the novice's (here, the ECR's) learning, task performance needs, interests and capabilities.
– Research training/mentoring programs (for one or more novice researchers) need to adopt two key strategies. These are: (a) helping novices/early career researchers progress within a learning and research training environment that balances *freedom* to explore and take risks with the *control* that a scaffolding methodological and conceptual framework can provide, and (b) matching mentor approaches and support to the candidate's level of task readiness. I labelled this capability and readiness to learn/grow/advance and deal with the demands of

research and specific research development tasks at a given time "learner task maturity", recognising that it varies across the research development/project journey, from task to task, situation to situation, and time to time.

- The goal of research mentoring is to foster the novice researcher's confidence, independence and capacity for independent (meaning not sole, but self-managed) research. This is where the term liberation belongs.
- From systems theory the notion of open systems provides for interactive sub-systems or agents working interactively to achieve collaborative goals. In research mentoring situations, this involves pursuing a co-management strategy between mentor and ECR similar to collaboration among co-researchers except that, as well as co-managing the research project, the mentor and ECR co-manage the mentoring process through negotiation, communication and shared responsibilities.
- To be successful and liberating, the facilitated or co-managed system for research mentoring needs to be dynamic and individual, adapting to the changing demands of contingency factors and changing perceptions and goals of the novice.

The *liberating program system model* is a dialectical model involving a blending of freedom and control. Kolb (1984) defined a dialectic relationship as "mutually opposed and conflicting processes, the results of each of which cannot be explained by the other, but whose merger through confrontation of the conflict between them results in a higher order process that transcends and encompasses them both" (p. 29). Elements related to freedom and control occurring in research mentoring programs/relationships can be merged to develop a higher order process which can be referred to as controlled freedom or a liberating program system.

This model builds upon a situated learning and situational leadership frame of reference. There is no one optimal state for all novice researchers for all their research learning tasks and situations. Instead, the nature of the task (e.g. familiarity, difficulty, complexity, ownership), the novice's readiness, the mentor's abilities/knowledge/experience and the situation (e.g. urgency, stakeholders' interests) all impact on the levels and form of freedom and control that are needed, both for the task-moment and for the ongoing research development of the ECR. Freedom in learning can be equated with responsible learner self-direction, and control, meaning the direction and management of a learning/development support and framework, can be the role of both mentor and novice.

Extending the original research, four approaches to mentoring can be utilised to promote the learner or novice researcher's growing capability for research independence and to respond flexibly to current learning/mentoring needs. These are now illustrated through four outlines and stories. These four research mentoring approaches are summarised in Figure 19.2.

(a) Mentor-managed open-ended inquiry
Novice pursuit of guided risk-taking and experimentation

The situation:	Learner task maturity (experience and capability) is low due to lack of experience/capability/familiarity with the task.
	The task has limited structure and is open-ended, non-prescriptive.
Mentoring style	Provide guidance but promote open-ended inquiry.
Novice response	Being liberated/encouraged to take risks, comfortable to be adventurous, feeling free to experiment. Pursuing multiple ideas and strategies without pressure to find a particular answer/conclusion or reach imminent deadlines.

Jenni's Story

Never used NVivo before – but I've watched a short demo by a PhD student in a lunchtime seminar. I need to give it a go before going back to see my mentor next week. She said to enter the three interview transcripts I've done so far and start to look for key ideas and connections.

I'm actually looking forward to playing around with it. I've set aside all day Friday and my goal is to see how it works, what I can learn for my next interviews, and write down a list of questions for next week's session. I've got another 16 interviews to do, so at this stage I'm not looking for answers or great insights from the content – just getting the hang of the process. It actually looked like a lot of fun mapping things out in different ways.

(b) Mentor-managed structured challenge
Active novice pursuit of goals and quality

The situation	Learner task maturity (experience and capability) is low due to lack of experience/capability/familiarity with the difficult task.
Mentoring style	The mentor provides a clear framework to promote focus and structure, guides/assists with decision making and task framing, and encourages the novice to work independently within the boundaries/scaffold provided.
Novice response	The novice actively pursues the goals and is task-focused. The quality of the work is a particular, strong consideration. Limited risks are taken. Learners are "on-task". Deadlines are important.

Sam and the Paradigm Challenge

Today we all received topics to prepare for the ECR seminar in 3 weeks. Lucky me – (not really) – I drew the short straw. I have 15 minutes to explain the differences between the empirico-analytical, the interpretive and the critical research paradigms. So far I've heard Prof give this talk three times – and I think each time "yes, now I've got it".

Then I go away and know that the words are getting more familiar but as soon as someone asks a question, like "What's the underlying epistemological stance?" my mind goes blank again. Yes – I know it's not supposed to be easy – but it's a tough topic. Thank goodness I have a deadline, a short talk and a limit of three PowerPoint slides – that helps. And I have the handouts and the reading list. I'm planning to spend time each week to think it all through. So … time to read and hopefully putting it all in my own words will help.

(c) Novice-managed organised challenge
Novice pursuit of focused inquiry and goal pursuit/ attainment

The situation	Learner task maturity (experience and capability) is high due to greater experience/capability/familiarity and confidence with the task.
Mentoring style	Learners/novices are encouraged to identify and articulate the goals, structure and boundaries of their task and then pursue the task independently of their mentor.
Novice response	Novices rise to the (high) challenge of this task and within their clearly constructed framework actively pursue focused inquiry and goal attainment. The focus is on search for meaning.

Tom's Interview Plan of Attack

Well my ethics approval is finally through so it's time to work out a plan of action for the next 3 months so that I get the interviews all done before teaching begins again. I'm comfortable with interviewing – I enjoy it and I'm looking forward to hearing what all the participants have got to say to help me understand my topic more and answer my research questions.

I think the biggest challenge is to recruit enough people – they will all have their own list of things to do over the long break and I will have to make these interviews sound like an interesting thing to do. I've got all the equipment ready for digital recording and the consent forms are printed and ready to go. My mentor has run through the process with me and we practised an interview. And he's available on the phone if I need some help or have questions.

(d) Novice-managed open-ended inquiry
Novice pursuit of independent exploration and reflection

The situation	Learner task maturity (experience and capability) is high due to high degree of self-confidence and experience/capability/familiarity with the task. The task is non-prescriptive, open-ended and non-threatening without imminent deadlines.
Mentoring style	The mentor leaves the novice to set goals and construct boundaries independently.
Novice response	Novices pursue independent exploration and reflection in an open-ended and time-rich manner. They can adjust boundaries and timelines as they proceed in pursuit of deeper understanding and meaning making.

Shannon's Theoretical Framework

I'm really looking forward to the next 6 months. I have a mass of reading to do – which I enjoy. And I'm going into it with a really open mind. My task is to find out what key literature – research, theories, reports, discussion papers –I think is most relevant to my topic – to build up a theoretical framework for my research. I have my broad research questions, my topic area and great ideas from my mentor, my peers and from all my own experience – reading, conferences, literature searches.

I'm targeting some great books to start with, where people have already explored similar topic areas and questions – that's for background and a check for additional ideas and readings. Then I'm going to read more deeply about the work of authors or groups that interest me most. Will they be relevant? Will I enjoy them but find them not so helpful? I've got my electronic reflective journal already set up to keep the ideas and questions flowing. I know there's more focused work ahead but this exploration and reflection will be a really special time. Can't wait!

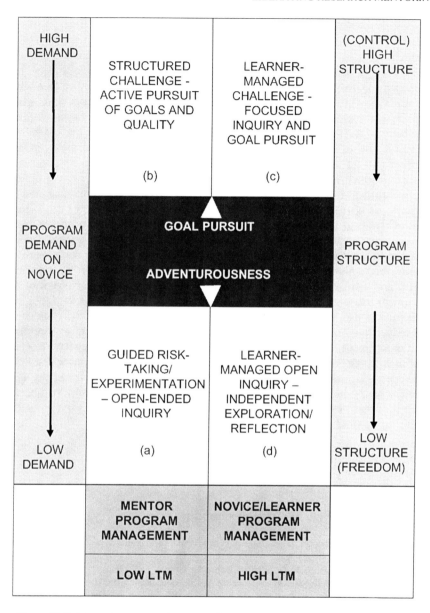

Figure 19.2. Mentoring approaches – matching program structure (freedom/control) to task/program demand and learner task maturity (LTM)

CONCLUSION

Through liberating program strategies as described here, mentors can identify when novices need a more structured program, any stages (or tasks) where students have developed a knowledge of and capacity for research program management themselves, and when they are ready for co-management systems in their research development program. Mentors continually re-appraise novice researchers' capabilities in relation to specific tasks and their readiness to embark on new tasks. Again, this leads to the need for adjustment of control/guidance and freedom parameters. For example, in early stages of novices' research development the mentor can promote the development of novices' research capacity and confidence and their willingness to explore different research strategies and goals by creating a non-directive but supportive program structure. As novices gain confidence to take on new tasks, supervisors can raise the level of challenge (for instance, asking them to make a presentation of their work), mentors can encourage novices to focus on tasks and take a greater level of independent control (e.g. in independent data collection). Emerging researchers who have reached a higher level of competence and are "on a roll" can take the initiative in inquiry and can be encouraged to follow their initiative within a framework of high mentor expectations. This could occur, for instance, in writing phases or during deep immersion in data analysis. During such phases there can be a need for restructuring and redirection. For example, novices may need a period of training in a particular analysis technique, or they could need support or time out because they have reached a dead-end, developed writer's block or feel burnt out. When early career researchers have completed tasks and are ready to identify learning and research outcomes, a time of reflection can be facilitated by creating low-demand and limited-structure programs. In each of these modes of mentor and novice behaviour there is a varying mode of controlled freedom or liberating structure.

NOTES

[1] http://www.csu.edu.au/division/landt/efp/cohorts/index.html (accessed 10/7/2011)

REFERENCES

Byrne-Armstrong, H., Horsfall, D., & Higgs, J. (Eds.) (2001). *Critical moments in qualitative research.* Oxford: Butterworth-Heinemann.

Grace, S., Higgs, J., & Horsfall, D. (2009). Celebrating writing. In J. Higgs, D. Horsfall & S. Grace (Eds.), *Writing qualitative research on practice* (pp. 323-330). Rotterdam, The Netherlands: Sense.

Higgs, J. (1989). Program structure and self-direction in independent learning programs: Towards a theory of liberating program systems for independent learning programs. Unpublished PhD thesis, The University of New South Wales, Australia.

Higgs, J. (1993). The teacher in self-directed learning: Manager or co-manager? In N. Graves (Ed.), *Learner managed learning: Practice, theory and policy* (pp. 122-131). London: World Education Fellowship.

Higgs, J. (2001a). Charting standpoints in qualitative research. In H. Byrne-Armstrong, J. Higgs & D. Horsfall (Eds.), *Critical moments in qualitative research* (pp. 44-67). Oxford: Butterworth-Heinemann.

Higgs, J. (2001b). Our collaborative inquiry. In J. Higgs & A. Titchen (Eds.), *Professional practice in health, education and the creative arts* (pp. 29-46). Oxford: Blackwell Science.

Higgs, J. (2003). Fostering cross-disciplinary qualitative research and supervision in empirico-analytical environments. In *Proceedings of the ATN WEXDEV Conference, Re-searching the Research Agenda* (p. 38). Perth, Curtin University of Technology, 25-27 June.

Higgs, J. (2006a). Challenges for qualitative research supervisors in the current research training context. In *Proceedings of the 7th International Interdisciplinary Conference – Advances in Qualitative Methods. Looking to the Future: Opportunities and Challenges for Qualitative Research* (p. 142). Surfers Paradise, 13-16 July.

Higgs, J. (2006b). Scholarship in postgraduate training: Using an interpretive research framework to facilitate quality training in pressured times. In *Fill the Gaps: Proceedings of the ANZAME Conference* (p. 21). Gold Coast, 29 June - 2 July.

Higgs, J. (2006c). Understanding the postgraduate research experience: The candidate's view. In *Proceedings of the 7th Quality in Postgraduate Research Conference: Knowledge Creation in Testing Times* (p. 18). Adelaide, SA, 20-21 April.

Higgs, J. (2009). Writing qualitative research theses. In J. Higgs, D. Horsfall & S. Grace (Eds.), *Writing qualitative research on practice* (pp. 311-322). Rotterdam, The Netherlands: Sense.

Higgs, J., & Byrne-Armstrong, H. (2006). Being creative, critical and ethical in research practice, In *Proceedings of the 7th International Interdisciplinary Conference – Advances in Qualitative Methods. Looking to the Future: Opportunities and Challenges for Qualitative Research* (p. 142). Surfers Paradise, 13-16 July.

Higgs, J., & Ajjawi, R. (2009). Writing academic books. In J. Higgs, D. Horsfall & S. Grace (Eds.), *Writing qualitative research on practice* (pp. 267-278). Rotterdam, The Netherlands: Sense.

Higgs, J., & Armstrong, H. (2007). Re-conceptualising research supervision. In J. Higgs, A. Titchen, D. Horsfall & H. Armstrong (Eds.), *Being critical and creative in qualitative research* (pp. 120-135). Sydney: Hampden Press.

Higgs, J., & Radovich, S. (1999). Narratives on qualitative research. Paper presented at AQR '99 International Conference: Issues of Rigour in Qualitative Research Melbourne, 8-10 July.

Higgs, J., & Titchen, A. (2007). Qualitative research: Journeys of meaning making through transformation, illumination, shared action and liberation. In J. Higgs, A. Titchen, D. Horsfall & H. Armstrong (Eds.), *Being critical and creative in qualitative research* (pp. 11-21). Sydney: Hampden Press.

Higgs, J., & Trede, F. (2010). Philosophical frameworks and research communities. In J. Higgs, N. Cherry, R. Macklin & R. Ajjawi (Eds.), *Researching practice: A discourse on qualitative methodologies* (pp. 31-36). Rotterdam, The Netherlands: Sense.

Higgs, J., Cherry, N., & Trede, F. (2009). Rethinking texts in qualitative research. In J. Higgs, D. Horsfall & S. Grace (Eds.), *Writing qualitative research on practice* (pp. 37-47). Rotterdam, The Netherlands: Sense.

Higgs, J., Cherry, N., Macklin, R., & Ajjawi, R. (2010). *Researching practice: A discourse on qualitative methodologies*. Rotterdam, The Netherlands: Sense.

Higgs, J., Horsfall, D., & Grace, S. (2009). *Writing qualitative research on practice*. Rotterdam, The Netherlands: Sense.

Higgs, J., McAllister, L., & Rosenthal, J. (2008). Learning to do academic writing. In J. Higgs, R. Ajjawi, L. McAllister, F. Trede & S. Loftus (Eds.), *Communicating in the health sciences* (2nd ed., pp. 41-54). Melbourne: Oxford University Press.

Higgs, J., Titchen, A., Horsfall, D., & Armstrong, H. (2007). *Being critical and creative in qualitative research*. Sydney: Hampden Press.

Higgs, J., Trede, F., Ajjawi, R., Loftus, S., Smith, M., & Paterson, M. (2007). Journeys from philosophy and theory to action and back again: Being critical and creative in research design and action. In J. Higgs, A. Titchen, D. Horsfall & H. Armstrong (Eds.), *Being critical and creative in qualitative research* (pp. 202-214). Sydney: Hampden Press.

Higgs, J., Trede, F., & Rothwell, R. (2007). Qualitative research interests and paradigms. In J. Higgs, A. Titchen, D. Horsfall & H. Armstrong (Eds.), *Being critical and creative in qualitative research* (pp. 32-42). Sydney: Hampden Press.

Horsfall, D., & Higgs, J. (2007). Boundary riding. In J. Higgs, A. Titchen, D. Horsfall & H. Armstrong (Eds.), *Being critical and creative in qualitative research* (pp. 69-77). Sydney: Hampden Press.

Kolb, D.A. (1984). *Experiential learning: Experience as the source of learning and development.* Englewood Cliffs, NJ: Prentice-Hall.

Macklin, R., & Higgs, J. (2010). Using lenses and layers. In J. Higgs, N. Cherry, R. Macklin & R. Ajjawi (Eds.), *Researching practice: A discourse on qualitative methodologies* (pp. 65-74). Rotterdam, The Netherlands: Sense.

Patton, N., Higgs, J., & Smith, M. (2009). Imagining and imaging. In J. Higgs, D. Horsfall & S. Grace (Eds.), *Writing qualitative research on practice* (pp. 183-193). Rotterdam, The Netherlands: Sense.

Street, A., & Higgs, J. (2008). Writing papers for journals. In J. Higgs, R. Ajjawi, L. McAllister, F. Trede & S. Loftus (Eds.), *Communicating in the health sciences* (2nd ed., pp. 273-280). Melbourne: Oxford University Press.

Trede, F., & Higgs, J. (2009). Framing research questions and writing philosophically. In J. Higgs, D. Horsfall & S. Grace (Eds.), *Writing qualitative research on practice* (pp. 13-25). Rotterdam, The Netherlands: Sense.

Trede, F., Higgs, J., & Rothwell, R. (2009). Critical transformative dialogues: A research method beyond the fusion of horizons. *Forum Qualitative Sozial for schung /Forum: Qualitative Social Research, 10*(1), Art. 6. Available: http://www.qualitative-research.net/index.php/fqs/article/viewArticle/1186/2602, accessed 17 July 2011.

Joy Higgs AM PhD
The Education For Practice Institute
Charles Sturt University, Australia

SUSAN GROUNDWATER-SMITH

20. LIVING ETHICAL PRACTICE
IN QUALITATIVE RESEARCH

ON "SEEING" ETHICAL PRACTICE

In her confronting and challenging book *Regarding the pain of others*, Susan
Sontag (2003) analysed images of war and asked us: When we look at the same
photographs do we feel the same things? She argued that we see through the prism
of our prejudices and expectations; that we have a capacity for both intimacy and
dissociation. The capricious viewer can choose to stay and watch, or go and forget.
Sontag's work may seem a far cry from the concept of living ethical practice in
qualitative research, but there are many invisible threads that can hold the two
together. What do we believe ethical practice to be and how can we live it in our
work? This chapter is written from the standpoint of my own experience, as one
who has retired from full-time academic work but continues to engage in
participatory action research (PAR) with field-based practitioners, more often than
not as a consultant. Thus, viewing my practice is mediated by my personal position
and what governs it.

In her vivid discussion Sontag argued that the intention of the photographer may
be to shock the viewer into taking into consideration the terror and violence of war,
but that such an assumption is often but not always overridden by a vicarious sense
of detachment which erodes empathy and instead evokes the opposite, that is apathy.
For many academic researchers the governance of the ethical conduct of their
inquiries is managed, not by *their* own ethical stance but by the determinations of the
university's human research ethics committees, whose intentions may differ from
those of the researcher. Deferring to such committees may not be a matter of choice,
but is more often than not determined by the university's policies, more concerned
with risk management than with an authentic desire for the researcher(s) to behave
ethically. Of course, I concede that not all committees function in this way. As
Gorman (2007, p. 23) explained, a human research ethics committee's work should
be designed to improve rather than inhibit the inquiry:

> If we accept that good research benefits society then it follows that the work
> of ethics committees also benefits society and researchers. ... Positively
> engaged with, the ethics review process will enhance rather than detract from
> the research.

Nonetheless, usurping the autonomy of ethical academic researchers may very well
have the effect of detaching those researchers from serious ethical considerations

J. Higgs et al., (eds.), Creative Spaces for
Qualitative Researching: Living Research, 201–210
© *2011 Sense Publishers. All rights reserved.*

of their work, instead positioning them to find ways of conforming to the requirements of the governing committee. Thus they see ethics as another bureaucratic hurdle to be satisfied.

So how do I "see" my own ethical practice when engaged in facilitating practitioner research as a form of PAR, and where I do not come under the surveillance of a university human research ethics committee? To answer that question I turn in the first instance to some work I undertook with Nicole Mockler (Groundwater-Smith & Mockler, 2008) where we argued that the most vital test of quality in action inquiry is that of the ethical principles which have underwritten the work. We proposed a series of guidelines that would inform ethical professionalism, these being (a) that the research should observe ethical protocols and processes, (b) that it should be transparent in its processes, (c) that it should be collaborative in its nature, (d) that it should be transformative in its intent and action, and (e) that it should be able to justify itself to its community of practice (pp. 85-86). In effect, my ethical position is one that seeks to be accountable to those with whom one is most directly working, ensuring that they are not left vulnerable or exploited and that they are fully appraised of the consequences of decisions they may make in the pursuit of their inquiries. One may think about it as enacting a kindness to all who participate. To make this position clear it is important first to explain more fully the nature of PAR and the ways in which I strive to live my ethical practice.

FACILITATING PARTICIPATORY ACTION RESEARCH

As its name suggests, PAR is characterised by its orientation to producing knowledge of practice in ways that can contribute to a deep understanding of that practice, so that authentic improvement can take place. Of course, we always need to be wary of what the term "improvement" implies – improvement for whom and under what conditions? After all, working within a collaborative framework itself produces many dilemmas in relation to power and authority and the expectations and rewards that go with occupying different roles. Goldstein (2000, p. 523), in her revealing discussion regarding her project to work collaboratively with an early career classroom teacher, observed:

> Any collaboration can be difficult. And when university researchers enter classrooms, some problems are bound to arise because of the issues of power and status inherent in these relations. Though the university researcher may see herself as little more than the classroom teacher she once was (as I often did), the view from the classroom is quite different.

The school-based practitioner may have been motivated by a desire to improve communication in the interests of caring for the children in her classroom in order that all may have a voice; whereas Goldstein, as the academic partner/facilitator may have shared that desire, but also was conducting the study as part of her doctoral candidature. For other academics there may be the additional pressure to conform to some kind of research selectivity exercise demanded by the university that requires them to publish in nominated journals which play little part in the communal professional debate and which arguably make little impact on practice.

Many who write of PAR emphasise its transformative and emancipatory nature, from small micro-studies through to large national investigations via social movements (see Fals Borda, 2000; Freire, 1996). Regardless of its scope and size, the work requires conditions that will allow for genuine dialogue and for social outcomes that are just and equitable. In essence it is informed by social relations whose intent is to fulfil a concern for

> doing the moral good – The emphasis is on the enhancement of ethically authentic action and the development of situated knowledge rather than on the accumulation of general (generalisable) theoretical knowledge. (Ponte & Smit, 2007, p. 3)

Those concerned with undertaking action research are familiar with the spiral of observation, reflection, theory building, planning and executing action and its study, followed by re-observation, further reflection and so on. In its most stripped-down sense, action research could be characterised as a form of systematic problem solving. But PAR has in addition a number of other key features. It has been identified by Kemmis and McTaggart (2005) as being: a social practice, participatory, practical and collaborative, emancipatory, critical, reflexive and transformative; thus it transcends any instrumental purpose based upon merely "acting".

To place these high ideals into some kind of perspective that will allow me to discuss living ethical practice it is important for me to draw attention to particular features of the context in which much of my work occurs. As a result of my appointment as Honorary Professor at the University of Sydney, over a decade ago I established, with Professor Judyth Sachs, the Centre for Practitioner Research (CPR) whose aims were to validate and value the research-based knowledge created by practitioners in the field, and to develop cross-disciplinary networks to facilitate the production and circulation of new knowledge. Its purposes were seen to be related to fostering, supporting and enhancing practitioner research in its many modes and guises.

As time went by and the University's regulatory frameworks changed, the Centre was re-designated as a Special Interest Group (SIG) and continues its work to this day. Under the umbrella of the CPR and more lately the SIG, a Coalition of Knowledge Building Schools (including government and non-government, primary and secondary, metropolitan and regional schools) was formed (see Mockler & Groundwater-Smith, 2011, for a detailed discussion of the history of the coalition, its aims and range of activities). The Coalition is affiliated with the University of Sydney, but each individual member undertakes inquiries with the support of school resources or specific project funds. Over time I have worked with each of the schools, often in association with other academic partners, as a facilitator of their PAR. In this capacity it has been my role to (a) identify and collate research discussion papers that inform the given school of recent and relevant research in the field in which it has an interest; (b) work with school-based committees (which may include students and parents) advising on qualitative research methods; (c) engage directly in the inquiry when a third party is advisable; (d) act as a critical friend in response to participant reflections; and (e) support writing and publishing the research for a broader audience such as conference delegates. It is in this context that I live my ethical practice and encounter a range of challenges and dilemmas.

ETHICAL CHALLENGES AND DILEMMAS ARISING FROM FACILITATING PARTICIPATORY ACTION RESEARCH

To give substance to my argument that living ethical practice produces very real dilemmas, not only for me but for my field-based colleagues, I narrate two case studies. One is set in a comprehensive co-educational high school in metropolitan Sydney; the other is in a facility for the support of young people requiring brief respite care.

Site A

The school is located in a community that faces challenging socioeconomic circumstances. Salaries are relatively low, few adults are engaged in ongoing training and most are in unskilled occupations. A number of the students have a Lebanese background, with some Pacific Island and a smattering of Vietnamese students, and recent refugee arrivals from West Africa, Afghanistan, Iraq and Burma. Boys outnumber girls in the ratio 2:1. The area is a well-established residential community, the school having been built some 50 years ago, with several industrial precincts and a regional airport. On the basis of its low socioeconomic status the school receives school communities partnership funding aimed to improve student engagement and attainment.

A group of teachers in the school have identified Year 9 as a pivotal point in the students' schooling, when they are in danger of becoming increasingly academically and even socially disengaged. The teachers were determined to develop a project whereby the students would have greater agency. Using partnership funding the team of teachers worked to develop a consultative model within which students would be enabled to research the conditions of their learning and make recommendations for the ways in which they could be encouraged to be active participants in learning and teaching in the classroom. The participating teachers were familiar with significant writing in the field of "student voice", such as that of Bragg and Fielding (2005) and Cook-Sather (2006); as well, they were cognisant of the need to develop pedagogies to engage students living under such challenging circumstances (Munns, 2007).

The project that was developed was designed to maximise student participation so that they might develop an informed critique of the school's practices and engage in an authentic dialogue with staff. Following a series of Year 9 meetings when all students were advised of the project and given opportunities to document their perceptions of the school, a research steering committee of 20 students was established. The team were conscious that they should not only be advised by students who generally conformed to the school's policies, but also be inclusive of students who were at times actively resistant.

Over a period of months the research steering committee met and learned something of qualitative inquiry methods ranging from focus group discussions to using visual media. As Thomson (2008, p. 4) observed:

> [Student] voice is not only about having a say, but also refers to the language emotional components and non-verbal means used to express opinions. Undertaking research which attends to voice may thus mean listening to things that are unsaid and/or not what we expect.

Add to this the argument put by Maguire (2005, p. 3):

> Children have good social radar for assessing the situations and contexts in which they find themselves. Thus children's perspectives and voices are important signifiers of their conceptualizations of the situatedness of their learning, their interests, needs and perceptions.

The steering committee's work resulted in them running a series of inquiry "stations", where all members of Year 9 recorded their responses to a number of salient prompts and questions. It is not the purpose of this case study to spell out the detail of the project, which continues to run and which the teachers themselves will be documenting, but to bring to attention a specific dilemma that has arisen and impacts upon my own sense of ethical practice and how I might best live it. In their analysis, students focused upon the many negative messages that were implicit, and sometimes explicit, in their interactions with their teachers. They perceived that their teachers did not know them and their circumstances well, that they did not encourage them in their learning, and that the classroom activities were often undemanding and thus not very engaging.

A critical stage for the project was one where the steering committee students would present their findings to the school staff at an afternoon meeting. For a number of the students this proved to be a significant challenge. After all, they were going to confront a status quo in which teachers were perceived to have the power, and they would be delivering some painful messages. Thomson (2008) cited Arnot and Reay (2007), who noted that students are already schooled in the norms and expectations of those they wish to critique. At a meeting with the students, the team and I were concerned about the students' couching of their messages in highly negative terms. Students were determined to put to staff their perceptions that teachers failed to respect them or interact with them in positive and productive ways. Here we had a paradox. The students themselves appeared to be formulating their presentations in exactly the manner that they so disliked when coming from the staff. Our shared ethical dilemma was whether to honour the students' rights to voice their negative sentiments – with the result that some harm might be done as teachers become cynical and resistant – or to appropriate their voices and have them deliver a message that would have less impact, but also produce fewer defensive reactions. The team grappled with this issue, believing that a rejection of the students' findings would reduce the potential for lasting impact. Perhaps if the students presented their idea with a "positive spin" then the hope was that the teachers would be more responsive. Students were convened in smaller groups to consider these matters, weighing up the pros and cons of the ways in which to present their idea. The consensus was that they would share with staff their school experiences as they saw them, in all their rawness and difficulty.

Our apprehensions were confirmed. While many teachers heard and understood the difficulties of the students a number were cynical and critical. An important linchpin in the subsequent proceedings, however, was that the school was formulating its Positive Behaviours Implementation Strategies (PBIS), a process that required consultation with students. The school's pastoral team saw that the steering committee's work had indeed laid the foundations for student participation, and this lent weight to the students' findings. Being on the horns of a dilemma means that we can find both costs and benefits in either direction. In this case, although we had significant concerns for the students in the longer term their persistence in the face of our caution paid off.

Site B

The setting for this case is a facility that provides respite care for young people from across the state. They may need support because there has been a death or serious illness in the family or because the family is facing challenging circumstances, either socioeconomically or as the result of an event such as a house fire or even a flood. Sometimes all factors can come into play. Along with a well-designed evening and weekend recreation program, the facility also provides schooling that needs to take account of the short-term nature of the stay. In recent years the school has moved from what had been described as a "holiday program" to an educational program with an emphasis upon emotional literacy. The program encourages students to locate and understand their emotions and the ways in which they impact on their learning potential. My role in the facility was to assist a team of teachers within the school to reflect on their professional learning and to find strategies to evaluate their practices. This was achieved by regular meetings and discussions with teachers, documenting their insights arising from critical incidents in their learning in the form of journal entries, as outlined by Tripp (1993). Critical incident analysis is an approach to identifying and managing the challenges in everyday practice in order to better understand them and find alternative ways of responding to them. They are not necessarily dramatic moments, but rather ones that present themselves, after reflection, as particular practical concerns that can arise not only from classroom practice but also, maybe, from staff interactions, or from attending a particular professional learning course. Teachers also documented their most significant change stories in a way that allowed them to use narrative and metaphor to write about changes in direction in terms of pedagogy and/or their philosophies of practice.

The school had undertaken to informally survey the home schools of the children on their return, to see what impacts the program had made. Feedback had suggested that the students returned with a more positive orientation to their learning and engagement.

However, from time to time there was pressure on the facility to provide what was seen as "harder" evidence of the impact of the program on the students. This, of course, is no easy matter. Each new cohort of young people varies in terms of its composition and the nature of the contexts from which the students have come, as well as the length of their stay. As an academic partner to the facility, I have over several years been able to work extensively with the staff and leadership within the small school and have found their commitment quite remarkable. But this personal testimony was not seen as sufficient.

The dilemma that arose for me was the result of the school seeking an acceptable measure that could be used to indicate the value that the stay had added to the lives of the young people. A measure considered by the school executive was the "Messy" or Matson Social Skills Survey, originally designed to assess social skills of students with an intellectual disability. It was later modified to have a broader social skills application. The problem with the survey, that is based upon self-report, is that it focuses on negative behaviours, for example "I threaten people or act like a bully" or "I pick on people to make them angry" or "I make fun of others" and so on. Of the 62 questions, 41 are framed in this way. My view was that the survey was inappropriate for young people who were already vulnerable and whose self-concept was fragile, to say the least. This was a view that was shared by a number of the staff. Interestingly, the school psychology literature cites the survey as a social tool, but does not develop a critique of it in terms of its consequences for those responding to the items.

Although I and others strongly expressed a view that the survey was inappropriate, it was not my prerogative to influence the final decision regarding the use of the survey. Senior management was well qualified in the field of educational measurement and believed the instrument to be appropriate to the purpose to which it was to be put. The case is included here as an instance where I, as the academic partner, faced an ethical dilemma in a context where my judgement had little impact. Although I could have chosen then to withdraw from the role as facilitator and critical friend I decided that my continuing presence could be used to create conditions where further discussions could take place. So while the survey was employed, so too did broader debates take place among the staff regarding appropriate ways to provide evidence of the impact of the facility on young people, their capabilities and their self-regard. My contribution, then, shifted from providing advice regarding the employment of an appropriate instrument to becoming the fulcrum for ongoing dialogue beyond any particular cohort of young people.

In effect, in both these case studies I found myself engaged in making particular moral judgements, in the first instance in relation to the possibility of exposing young people to the consequences of voicing their negative stance to the staff of their school. Fielding (2004, pp. 302-304) asked a series of penetrating questions to be considered when employing student voice. Among them:

- How confident are we that our research does not redescribe and reconfigure students in ways that bind them more securely into the fabric of the status quo?
- How clear are we about the use to which the depth and detail of data is likely to be put? Is our more detailed knowledge of what students think and feel largely used to help us control them more effectively?
- Are we sure that our positions of relative power and our own personal and professional interests are not blurring our judgements or shaping our advocacy?

In the second case, the judgement related to the effects on young people of engaging in a form of self-report that over-emphasized a pessimistic construction of the self. Both these case studies relate to my ethical disposition in the facilitation of PAR, and are genuine dilemmas. A crucial feature of a dilemma is that one has two choices for undertaking an action; one can do either but cannot do both. In the Year 9 case, the team and I could have intruded upon the students' decisions to present their findings in a fashion that might bring opprobrium upon their heads but failed to honour their agency and autonomy; in the second instance, I could have recognised the right of the school-based practitioner to select a strategy that would meet the needs of those asking for a particular kind of accountability by providing "rigorous" evidence but would have not done a kindness to the young people completing the survey.

Elsewhere I have discussed other examples of the kinds of ethical concern that a consultant supporting PAR faces. In a chapter concerning my professional self (Groundwater-Smith, 2006) I addressed the ways in which I was unsettled by the angry and disruptive behaviours of a number of students in the face of efforts to prepare them for mandatory state tests. I acknowledged that I could not "unknow" my own experiences or the values that infuse them, but that I could and should make my values more explicit and transparent such that they too could be challenged. This example was clearly a matter of my values, but also there are cases of actual practice. In the opening to a chapter on researching ethically (Groundwater-Smith, 2010) I outlined an instance where I had not sufficiently established the boundaries of confidentiality, with the result that information was distributed and discussed before it had been appropriately cleared by those participating in the inquiry.

Living ethical practice in the context of engaging with others in PAR is not so much a matter of being constrained by regulatory frameworks, but rather is to do with ensuring that the quality of our work is such that we can uncover and reveal the very real and complex concerns that govern social practices. As Kemmis (2007, p. 21) noted:

> The quality of practitioner research is not just a matter of the technical excellence of practitioner research as "research". It is a matter of addressing important problems in thought and action, in theory and practice – problems worth addressing in and for our times, in and for our communities, in and for our shared world. It is a matter of addressing important problems for education, for the good of each person, and for the good of our societies.

CONCLUSION – REGARDING THE WELLBEING OF OTHERS

I commenced this chapter with a reflection upon the work of Susan Sontag with regard to observing the pain of others. Here, in my conclusion I propose that living ethical practice requires of us that we put ourselves and our academic egos to one side and think instead of the wellbeing of those who are often vulnerable and lacking in power. John Stuart Mill (1806-1873) has been quoted as writing:

A person may cause evil to others not by his actions but by his inaction and in either case he is justly accountable to them for the injury. (Mill, n.d.)

In the cases that I have cited here the ethical relationships are problematic, even blurred. But they are not sundered or irreparable. To ensure that they are not injurious, ongoing dialogue and negotiation is essential. That then is my bedrock in living ethical practice: that I strive to be ever sensible to the needs and rights of those with whom I work and hold them in due regard beyond rhetoric and into action.

REFERENCES

Arnot, M., & Reay, D. (2007). A sociology of pedagogic voices. *Discourse, 28*(3), 327-342.

Bragg, S., & Fielding, M. (2005). "It's an equal thing … it's about achieving together": Student voice and the possibility of radical collegiality. In H. Street & J. Temperley (Eds.), *Improving schools through collaborative inquiry* (pp. 205-235). London: Continuum.

Cook-Sather, A. (2006). Change based on what students say: Preparing teachers for a paradoxical model of leadership. *International Journal of Leadership in Education, 9*(4), 345-358.

Fals Borda, O. (2000). People's space times in global processes: The response of the local. *Journal of World-System Research, 6*(3), 624-634.

Fielding, M. (2004). Transformative approaches to student voice: Theoretical underpinnings, recalcitrant realities. *British Educational Research Journal, 30*(2), 295-311.

Freire, P. (1996). *Pedagogy of the oppressed.* London: Penguin.

Goldstein, L. (2000). Ethical dilemmas in designing collaborative research: Lessons learned the hard way. *Qualitative Studies in Education, 13*(5), 517-530.

Gorman, S. (2007). Managing research ethics: A head-on collision? In A. Campbell & S. Groundwater-Smith (Eds.), *An ethical approach to practitioner research* (pp. 8-23). London: Routledge.

Groundwater-Smith, S. (2006). My professional self. In P. Aubusson & S. Schuck (Eds.), *Teacher learning and development* (pp. 179-194). Rotterdam: Springer.

Groundwater-Smith, S. (2010). Researching ethically? In J. Higgs, N. Cherry, R. Macklin & R. Ajjawi (Eds.), *Researching practice: A discourse on qualitative methodologies* (pp. 75-87). Rotterdam: Sense.

Groundwater-Smith, S., & Mockler, N. (2008). Ethics in practitioner research. In J. Furlong & A. Oancea (Eds.), *Assessing quality in applied and practice based research in education* (pp. 79-92). London: Routledge.

Kemmis, S. (2007). Participatory action research and the public sphere. In P. Ponte & B. Smit (Eds.), *The quality of practitioner research* (pp. 9-28). Rotterdam: Sense.

Kemmis, S., & McTaggart, R. (2005). Participatory action research: Communicative action and the public sphere. In N.K. Denzin & Y.S. Lincoln (Eds.), *The Sage handbook of qualitative research* (3rd ed., pp. 559-603). Thousand Oaks, CA: Sage.

Maguire, M.H. (2005). What if you talked to me? I could be interesting. Ethical research considerations in engaging with bilingual/multilingual child participants in human inquiry. *Forum: Qualitative*

Social Research, 6(1). Available:http://www.qualitative-research.net/index.php/fqs/article/view/530, accessed 25 January 2011

Mill, J.S. (n.d.). At BrainyQuote.com. Available:http://www.brainyquote.com/quotes/quotes/j/johnstuart118013.html, accessed August 25, 2010.

Mockler, N., & Groundwater-Smith, S. (2011) Weaving a web of professional practice: The Coalition of Knowledge Building Schools. In B. Lingard, P. Thomson & T. Wrigley (Eds.), *Changing schools: Alternative models* (pp. 294-322). London: Routledge.

Munns, G. (2007). A sense of wonder: Pedagogies to engage students who live in poverty. *International Journal of Inclusive Education*, *11*(3), 301-315.

Ponte, P., & Smit, B. (2007). Introduction: Doing research and being researched. In P. Ponte & B. Smit (Eds.), *The quality of practitioner research* (pp. 1-8). Rotterdam: Sense.

Sontag, S. (2003). *Regarding the pain of others*. New York: Farrar, Strauss and Giroux.

Thomson, P. (2008). Young people: Voices in visual research. In P. Thomson (Ed.), *Doing visual research with children and young people* (pp. 1-20). London: Routledge.

Tripp, D. (1993). *Critical incidents in teaching: Developing professional judgement*. London: Routledge.

Susan Groundwater-Smith PhD
Honorary Professor of Education
Faculty of Education and Social Work
The University of Sydney, Australia

SECTION 4: CO-CREATING QUALITATIVE RESEARCH IN CREATIVE SPACES

DONNA BRIDGES AND SHARYN MCGEE

21. COLLABORATIVE INQUIRY

Reciprocity and Authenticity

Within new paradigm research, collaborative inquiry (CI) is used as an umbrella term to encompass genres of research that are participatory, democratic and reflective in design, method and dissemination. The principles embedded in participatory methodologies emphasise inclusive participation within a mutually beneficial research project where deep interpretive processes occur and members co-construct knowledge. At the heart of CI is a call for research to be a catalyst for action and, therefore, for change.

In this chapter we argue that two significant governing principles of CI are the notions of reciprocity and authenticity. Through both these principles, individuals and communities can become empowered to understand, produce knowledge and bring about active positive change in their own lives. We describe and analyse the roles of reciprocity and authenticity in collaborative inquiry, exploring issues of power and ethics as they relate to the epistemological and methodological foundations of CI research.

COLLABORATIVE INQUIRY: PRINCIPLES AND PROCESS

The underlying principles of CI are a challenge to the central premises of positivist research and the power relations that occur within the hierarchies of academic research (Bray, Lee, Smith & Yorks, 2000; Heron & Reason, 2001). CI is an inclusive research methodology that involves participants of the research as co-inquirers. They have roles in informing and shaping research aims, are involved in the design process, and shape outcomes. Shared control in horizontal research groups focuses on the inquiry as a "joint enterprise" (Riger, 1999). Through a horizontal positioning of all co-inquirers in a democratic process, a lead researcher or principal researcher, if there is one (as in academic institutional settings) is also positioned as a co-inquirer who is no more influential or powerful than other members of the inquiry group. The principal researcher becomes a facilitator and initiator, but not a prime decision maker or authority figure. In the epistemological understanding of CI, researchers are not positioned in structured hierarchies as experts, nor are participants positioned as objects of the research. Such oppositional dichotomies are overcome in the active pursuit of CI, as "the researched" become research active and give meaning to their own lives and experience (Reason, 1994). The goals of achieving reciprocity and authenticity

J. Higgs et al., (eds.), Creative Spaces for
Qualitative Researching: Living Research, 213–222
© 2011 Sense Publishers. All rights reserved.

both strengthen and guide the co-construction research that is a shared and democratic pursuit. For instance, a keystone of understanding in CI is that informants of the research are experts about their own lives. The aim of CI is to create the conditions for co-inquirers to empower themselves through active engagement in cycles of reflection wherein participants seek understanding, produce knowledge, and endeavour to enact change (Torbert, 1983). As a research practice, CI enhances the skills of reflective practice, critical reflective dialogue, community building, strengthening communities of practice and encouraging the sharing of ideas and the negotiation of collective meaning (Cooper, 2006). The active engagement of participants in CI groups is an endeavour to be reciprocal and authentic so that participants can construct their own notions of reality, based upon their experience and their understanding of their experience, and can gain insight about the meaning of their experience. Through enhancement of knowledge and meaning the co-inquirers may become able to act in their lives for themselves and their communities.

ETHICS AND RESEARCH

Ethics is central to all research. After the slow emergence of ethical theories in the early 20th century, the ethics of research took centre stage in the period following World War Two. A number of incidents (including but not limited to the Nazi experiments) made it clear that the potential dangers of research were extensive and that global principles for guiding ethical research were needed. The Nuremberg Code in 1949 and the Helsinki Declaration in 1964 were early responses. Recent national policies and codes for ethical research with humans draw on four governing principles and obligations derived from the Nuremberg Code and the Helsinki Declaration: respect for autonomy, nonmaleficence, beneficence, and justice. Although these principles do not reflect a coherent ethical theory or bring together the work of different theorists and philosophical frames (Halse & Honey, 2007), their adoption by institutions such as universities and hospitals and at the national level has influenced the research landscape. Through the adoption of these principles ethics has expanded "from a way of thinking about research into a system of governmentality" (Halse & Honey, p. 339) which shapes the conditions of possibility of ethical research and thus research methodologies.

However, this "institutional discourse of ethical research" (Halse & Honey, 2007) has emerged from particular ways of understanding research, which are firmly based in the empiricist or positivist paradigm "where the researcher is the one in charge, keeping his [sic] distance, and using the subjects for his convenience" (Rowan, 2000, p. 103). When researchers move away from this understanding of research, as in CI, the ethical issues expand and deepen, and current ethical codes, embedded as they are in positivist research models, may not be adequate or even ethical in new paradigm research models. Rowan (2000) argued that differences in approaches oblige researchers to rethink the usual ethical codes.

Reciprocity and authenticity are concepts that have emerged in new paradigm research as part of the larger rethinking of the positivist paradigm. Both are vital in the ethical practice of the CI framework.

RECIPROCITY: ETHICS, POWER AND COLLABORATIVE INQUIRY

The concept of reciprocity has a long history in the social sciences (Bruni, Gilli, & Pelligra, 2008) and is used in a variety of discourses including anthropology, economics, social psychology, political economy, workplace relations, development studies and international relations. Ever since anthropological giants like Malinowski and Mauss focused on it in the early 20th century, reciprocity has been seen as an indispensable concept within social sciences (Narotzky & Moreno, 2002).

Reciprocity has been described as "a kind of social behaviour" (Schwandt, 2001, p. 222) and is concerned with the mutual give and take of human interactions and relationships. It is often associated with exchange theory, involving an exchange of goods or services (Schwandt, 2001). Reciprocity has also been associated with social capital, and hence is seen as "an integral social process" (Maiter, Simich, Jacobson, & Wise, 2008, p. 307) within participatory research models. Reciprocity in research is concerned with non-hierarchical, mutually beneficial relationships. Attentiveness to relationship building is at the core of reciprocity. Relationship building and "attentiveness to participants as human beings" are not easy goals to achieve. Enabling the voices of participants in research to be heard "is an ethical response to constructions of research as sterile and removed from the people being studied" (Powell & Takayoshi, 2003, p. 397). Indeed, in new paradigm research, reciprocity is seen as an important part of the research process; on the other hand, in positivist research models and the ethics codes based on them, reciprocity is not valued as fundamental to the research process. Since positivism assumes "a distanced objectivist research stance" (Boser, 2007, p. 1060) reciprocity is in fact frowned upon. Because reciprocity is part of ethical processes, and ethics is political, it is incumbent on collaborative inquirers to take account of the wider socio-political dimensions of research throughout the process, including the collaborative knowledge creation processes, the representation of that knowledge, and the related outcomes or actions as defined by the collaborators.

Reciprocity and Collaborative Inquiry: Power and Knowledge

There are challenges to achieving "strong" reciprocity (Bruni et al., 2008) in research relationships. Ultimately, CI endeavours to meet those challenges, specifically those inherent within relationships and those of power and its association with knowledge.

As introduced above, CI is a model of research that engages with participants as co-inquirers, thus challenging hierarchical models of research relationships and knowledge production. Collaborative inquirers aim for horizontal research groups in which the research becomes an endeavour carried out by a group of researchers (co-inquirers). Through this collaborative process, differences in power between co-inquirers are acknowledged and made transparent so that they may be circumvented or avoided. There are, however, challenges to this view of power in CI. Gaventa and Cornwall (2008, p.173) argued that the early understandings of power in participatory research were based on concepts of power as an attribute "that some had and others lacked, something that could be won or lost". This reflects a traditional view of power as a relationship of domination – "A over B" – which has been challenged by a number of theorists, many building on the work of Michel Foucault (Weems, 2006; Boser, 2007; Gaventa & Cornwall, 2008). According to Gaventa and Cornwall, power is socially enacted and indeed constitutes social relations. In this sense, then, power is recognised as a productive and enabling force, not simply a repressive one. Moreover, power does not exist simply in dyadic personal relationships, it "can exist in multidimensional ways ... among multiple players and in complex roles or embedded within structures" (Boser, 2007, p. 1061) or within and through discourses. Power and knowledge are inextricably linked. Thus differences in power can be challenged or resisted. Or they can be radically re-visioned, and the productive, enabling aspects of power can generate deeper understandings of the CI process and of actions within and through it, especially when reciprocity is transparently sought. Creating reciprocal relationships within CI means addressing and working with power in explicit ways (Maiter et al., 2008), for example, asking unambiguously "who does this research benefit?". Where there are benefits, there is power, and power cannot be ignored in research, nor should it be. As Gaventa and Cornwall (p.175) pointed out, "the power to act and to act in concert with others ... is fundamental to transformational social change", which is the epistemological foundation of and rationale for CI.

Reciprocity is about the give and take of human relationships and is therefore about the give and take of power-in-relationship. Reciprocal relationships in CI are not hierarchical, but neither are they totally equal. Community members can enact power within CI projects in various ways, such as redefining roles within the project and extending the give and take of reciprocity beyond the project into everyday life (Powell & Takayoshi, 2003).

Implications for CI Practice

Thus ethics and politics are inherently intertwined throughout the CI process. Human relationships are at the heart of reciprocity and in collaborative inquiry. If we are concerned about advancing knowledge from the standpoint of disadvantaged or marginalised communities, facilitating the voice of research participants' ideas, feelings, and experiences and contributing to social action taken by communities, reciprocity needs to be a governing principle of CI. At the same time it should be used as a springboard for exploring conflicts in interpretation, representation and action, not as a "landing point" or a process or tool for legitimising new paradigm forms of inquiry (Weems, 2006). This is particularly important because "collaborative relationships are not always reciprocal relationships" (Powell & Takayoshi, 2003, p. 396). CI methods that incorporate reciprocity as a springboard have the potential to "restore faith to communities who have come to view research as a bureaucratic way of avoiding social change" (Bridges & McGee, 2010, p. 258).

The sharing of power and the valuing of the expertise and contributions of the entire team are practices that ensure that research is mutually beneficial (Cooper, 2006). The participatory focus and democratic methods of CI facilitate a deep inclusivity which is potentially emancipatory. Deeply involved participant/ researchers can contribute a richness of understanding that would be difficult to access by traditional methods. For example, in a collaborative inquiry concerned with community development initiated by one of the authors, the involvement of community workers as co-inquirers enhanced the depth and richness of the data gathered through in-depth story-telling. Furthermore, the author's past experiences in the community sector and personal engagement in the collaborative process allowed deeper insights and analysis of the story-telling data throughout the four phases of the collaborative inquiry (Bridges & McGee, 2010, p. 263). In this instance personal relationships were a key part of this process.

From the academic researcher's point of view, however, this richness of understanding still needs to be contextualised within the discourse of a research community and, at times, the discourse of bureaucrats and policy makers. This means taking account of the dominant models of ascertaining "truth". Authenticity criteria (Lincoln & Guba, 1986; Guba & Lincoln, 1989) provide guidelines for us, as collaborative ethical researchers interested in reciprocity, to find a way to make our collaborative inquiries deeply ethical and ultimately reciprocal.

AUTHENTICITY

In its most general usage, authenticity in qualitative research applies to the aim to generate genuine or true understanding of the experiences, understandings and truths of respondents in the research. In this regard truth means correspondence with the facts, but also trustworthiness (see Winter, 2002). Whether the research has value and is trustworthy (validity) resides in its authenticity. The written artefacts of research are considered to be authentic, that is to have "epistemological validity and cultural authority" when the voice they represent is genuine and true to the "life-worlds" of those they are describing and analysing (Winter, 2002, p. 146).

Authenticity, as we explicate it here, builds on the authenticity criteria outlined by Lincoln and Guba (1986). Authenticity criteria are directly related to the inclusive, ethical and fair treatment of respondents, to the value of the research and its reciprocity, and to its usefulness in terms of proficiency at calling participants to action. The use of authenticity criteria in CI supports the inquiry team in its attempts to achieve principles that are deemed fundamental to CI: to democratise relations and to diminish unhelpful power imbalances; to ensure high ethical standards and respect for all members; to create knowledge and increase understanding, both within the inquiry group and outside, through reporting and dissemination; and to inspire and support action in the lives of participants or in wider social and political environs. Table 21.1 describes each authenticity criterion in turn, providing pointers to collaborative inquirers who want to determine whether their CI meets authenticity criteria within their inquiry groups and whether the research benefits co-inquirers and not only principal researchers and is, therefore, reciprocal in nature.

Table 21.1 Authenticity criteria

Fairness	This criterion reinforces the ethical basis of the research and aims to render a balanced view of all voices and perspectives represented by the inquiry. It focuses on presenting not only the construction of knowledge but also the values that underpin knowledge. – Are the views, understanding and knowledge of each individual presented, clarified and honoured? – Has there been a transparent representation of conflict over issues/values in data collection and analysis? – Does the inquiry have appeal mechanisms available to participants? – Are informed consent procedures in place? – Are member-checking processes in place? – Have recommendations regarding action arising from the study been negotiated with all stakeholders equally?
Ontological authenticity	This criterion concerns the raising of consciousness and/or uniting of divided consciousness, that can help people to understand their unstated and unconscious beliefs. – Does the research create an environment where conscious growth is nurtured, made more sophisticated, elaborated on? – Has the research improved the participants' awareness of their contexts? – Are participants enabled to understand more about themselves, in their role as co-inquirer, their experience, and their situation?
Educative authenticity	This criterion concerns the opportunity to gain understanding of all stakeholder positions. A deeper and more complex construction is facilitated through an understanding of the constructions and values of others. – Does the research create an environment where participants can understand and appreciate alternative positions regarding the questions? – Has the research increased participants' understanding of the views, assumptions and values of others in the inquiry? – Is there time and space in the inquiry for participants to share their experience, understandings and knowledge with other stakeholders?

Table 21.1 Authenticity criteria (cont.)

Catalytic authenticity	This criterion refers to whether the inquiry has prompted action and decision making, and to what degree they have been stimulated and facilitated by the inquiry. − Are participants and other stakeholders involved in the inquiry in a way that stimulates action? − Have testimonies regarding willingness and desire to participate in action been collected during earlier phases of the inquiry? − How willing are participants to use their new knowledge and understandings as a basis for action?
Tactical authenticity	This criterion is about being empowered to act. Willingness to act is not enough − participants must feel that they are able to do so. − Have all participants been involved in shaping the focus and strategies of the inquiry? − Have participants been engaged in decision making in all phases of the inquiry? − Has the inquiry provided opportunity for action? − Are participants more skilled now (in the final stages of the inquiry) than in the beginning; do they have more understanding, ability to utilise power and use negotiation techniques?

(The above questions were developed from Lincoln & Guba, 1986; Guba & Lincoln, 1989; Erlandson, Harris, Skipper, & Allen, 1993; Manning, 1997; Bray et al., 2000.)

Achieving Fairness Criteria in CI

It is understood in critical methodological paradigms that knowledge is situated, and that it is socially, culturally and historically constructed and value-based. It is therefore implicit that inquiry groups within these paradigms will generate differing constructions of reality and truth. The charge of the inquiry team or lead researcher then becomes to "expose and explicate ... possibly conflicting, constructions and value structures" (Lincoln & Guba, 1986, p. 15).

The issue of voice is therefore fundamental to fairness criteria. Voice is uncovered and communicated through dialogue and negotiation, with all participants having an equal chance to express their voices and to be heard. Issues are desirably discussed and negotiated during the initiation phase of the inquiry and the awareness of equal participation and of voice is negotiated throughout the study. Voice can be portrayed through decision making during the inquiry, and through direct quotes in written artefacts. Fairness is also achieved through informed consent regarding protection of identity, confidentiality, privacy, distribution of findings, authorship, and respondent ownership of data. Member checking, the testing of information by all members of the inquiry group reading transcripts and final reports, will to a large extent guarantee that written work is an accurate account that resonates with the co-inquirers' lives and experience "in all their complexity" (Manning, 1997, p. 3). Prolonged engagement supports the CI in intensive contact through time, or close interaction with respondents, in building understanding of a variety of complex and sometimes competing material.

Ontological Authenticity

This criterion can be achieved through providing time and space for participants to engage in dialogue about their experience, understanding and knowledge regarding the research problem in an environment where dialogue is open and non-judgmental. This space may be an interview or focus group and is a dialogical interaction/s where each party explores reality as an emergent process. Sometimes ontological awareness is reached not through reflective (cognitive) verbal dialogue but through dialogue with non-cognitive, creative imagination and expression (Titchen, 2010, personal communication). This can occur at any phase of the inquiry but should be focused on during the immersion stage, when participants can come to know their own meaning through the process of voicing it and explaining it to others. Awareness can be greatly enhanced through a focus on ontological authenticity, to grasp a broader range of issues.

Educative Authenticity

As with ontological authenticity, creating space for a dialogical exchange is fundamental for educative authenticity. This criterion supports members of the inquiry in appreciating the experience of others and the understanding and meaning that others associate with that experience. It is an opportunity to fully realise the reality of another and to understand how value systems "evoke very different solutions to issues" (Guba & Lincoln, 1989, p. 249). An inquiry group can conduct an internal audit (Manning, 1997) of written artefacts as a way of strengthening educative authenticity. In this method, a final draft of the findings is read by the group and discussed. During this close reading, findings are refined and added, and more insights crafted. The goal is not to achieve consensus but to heighten awareness and understanding of the constructions of others.

Catalytic Authentication and Tactical Authenticity

Catalytic authentication refers to the willingness of members to engage in action. To achieve this criterion in a CI it is vital that each member is involved, from the initiation phase, with decision-making power in guiding the phases of the inquiry. When action is jointly negotiated then the idea inherent in the action and the underlying political, personal and social inspirations are meaningful and personal to the participants, and they are therefore willing to carry it out (Guba & Lincoln, 1989).

Tactical authenticity refers to the level of empowerment that members have to engage in action. Negotiating action is ongoing in CI. Negotiation typically starts at the beginning of an inquiry during the initiation phase of the collaboration, and continues throughout each ensuing phase as ideas about action emerge and issues for respondents and their wider social situation are realised. The terms of the negotiation should be consistent with fairness criteria (Lincoln & Guba, 1986) they that it should be transparent, entirely inclusive of all the inquiry team, with equal access to information available to all, and with supported understanding of that information.

CONCLUDING POINTS

Authenticity criteria are important for academic researchers because they function as points of reference for scientific and policy-making communities. For inquiry groups they function as mechanisms that support the monitoring of how ethical, fair, educative and action-inducing the inquiry is. Hence they need to be included as part of a CI project from the beginning and to be negotiated throughout. At the same time, given the principles of CI as a non-hierarchical, democratic, and collaborative research process, academic researchers may feel caught between the demands of their academic community and those of their collaborators in the project. In those situations reciprocal relationships come into play. The expertise of academic participants regarding meaningful research processes and outcomes means that they can facilitate the knowledge development of the entire group. Discussion of authenticity criteria, related methodological issues and notions of reciprocity in the early stages of the project can be empowering for all collaborators and is part of the give and take of reciprocal relationships.

In this chapter we have explored the issues of reciprocity and authenticity as they relate to ethics and to power in the context of CI. Collaborative inquirers often find themselves confronting the challenges of designing research in collaboration with others, carefully negotiating research that is mutually beneficial, reciprocal and deeply ethical. Researchers who wish to forge beyond the goals of doing no harm and risk minimisation need epistemological and methodological practices to guide them in their endeavours. We hope that this chapter goes some way in providing a guide to CI groups to support them in designing research that is reciprocal and authentic in methods and dissemination.

REFERENCES

Boser, S. (2007). Power, ethics, and the IRB: Dissonance over human participant review of participatory research. *Qualitative Inquiry, 13*(8), 1060-1074.

Bray, N.J., Lee, J., Smith, L., & Yorks, L. (2000). *Collaborative inquiry in practice: Action, reflection, and making meaning.* Thousand Oaks, CA: Sage.

Bridges, D., & McGee, S. (2010). Collaborative inquiry: Process, theory and ethics. In J. Higgs, N. Cherry, R. Macklin & R. Ajjawi (Eds.), *Researching practice: A discourse on qualitative methodologies* (pp. 257-268). Rotterdam: Sense.

Bruni, L., Gilli, M., & Pelligra, V. (2008). Reciprocity: Theory and facts. *International Review of Economics, 55,* 1-11.

Cooper, C.W. (2006). Refining social justice commitments through collaborative inquiry: Key rewards and challenges for teacher educators. *Teacher Education Quarterly, Summer*, 115-132.

Erlandson, D.A., Harris, E.T., Skipper, B.L., & Allen, S.D. (1993). *Doing naturalistic inquiry: A guide to methods.* Newbury Park, CA: Sage.

Gaventa, J., & Cornwall, A. (2008). Power and knowledge. In P. Reason & H. Bradbury (Eds.), *The Sage handbook of action research: Participative inquiry and practice* (pp. 172-189). Los Angeles: Sage.

Guba, E.G., & Lincoln, Y.S. (1989). *Fourth generation evaluation.* Newbury Park, CA: Sage.

Halse, C., & Honey, A. (2007). Rethinking ethics review as institutional discourse. *Qualitative Inquiry, 13*(3), 336-352.

Heron, J., & Reason, P. (2001). The practice of cooperative inquiry: Research "with" rather than "on" people. In P. Reason & H. Bradbury (Eds.), *Handbook of action research* (pp. 179-199). London: Sage.

Lincoln, Y.S., & Guba, E.G. (1986). But is it rigorous? Trustworthiness and authenticity in naturalistic evaluation. *New Directions for Program Evaluation, 30*, 73-84.

Maiter, S., Simich, L., Jacobson, N. & Wise, J. (2008). Reciprocity: An ethic for community-based participatory action research. *Action Research, 6*(3), 305-325.

Manning, K. (1997). Authenticity in constructivist inquiry: Methodological considerations without prescription (methods for research by social scientists). *Qualitative Inquiry, 3*(1), 93-115.

Narotzky, S., & Moreno, P. (2002). Reciprocity's dark side: Negative reciprocity, morality and social reproduction. *Anthropological Theory, 2*(3), 281-301.

Powell, K.M., & Takayoshi, P. (2003). Accepting roles created for us: The ethics of reciprocity. *College Composition and Communication, 54*(3), 394-422.

Reason, P. (1994). *Participation in human inquiry.* London: Sage.

Riger, S. (1999). Working together: Challenges in collaborative research on violence against women. *Violence Against Women, 5*(10), 1099-1117.

Rowan, J. (2000). Research ethics. *International Journal of Psychotherapy, 5*(2), 103-111.

Schwandt, T.A. (2001). *Dictionary of qualitative inquiry* (2nd ed.). Thousand Oaks, CA: Sage.

Torbert, W.R. (1983). *Initiating collaborative inquiry.* In G. Morgan (Ed.), *Beyond Method* (pp. 272-291). Newbury Park, CA: Sage.

Weems, L. (2006) Unsettling politics, locating ethics: Representations of reciprocity in postpositivist inquiry. *Qualitative Inquiry, 12*(5), 994-1011.

Winter, R. (2002). Truth or fiction: Problems of validity and authenticity in narratives of action research. *Educational Action Research, 10*(1), 143-154.

Donna Bridges PhD
The Education For Practice Institute
Charles Sturt University, Australia

Sharyn McGee MA, BA (Hons), GDipComm
School of Social Sciences
University of Western Sydney, Australia

FAMKE VAN LIESHOUT AND SHAUN CARDIFF

22. INNOVATIVE WAYS OF ANALYSING DATA WITH PRACTITIONERS AS CO-RESEARCHERS

Dancing Outside the Ballroom

Figure 22.1. Symbolic and poetic expression of starting a critical creative hermeneutic data analysis

Conducting research as part of a PhD study offers students a unique opportunity to explore new methods and methodologies. Although we each based our PhD studies on a more traditional participatory action research (PAR) methodology, we also took the opportunity to experiment with a new data analysis method. Working from a critical social science paradigm (Fay, 1987) that translates into critical and collaborative research practice with an emancipatory intent, our scope of freedom as to how to process data, perform the analyses, then synthesise and report the results, became restricted. We felt that if we were to be genuine in involving practitioners in data analysis, as co-researchers, we needed to adopt approaches

J. Higgs et al., (eds.), Creative Spaces for
Qualitative Researching: Living Research, 223–234

that allowed the expression of all ways of knowing. Using the creative arts proved to be an innovative way of working and learning, facilitating the complex interpretation of narrative data, identifying patterns, themes and connections.

As in all qualitative research, in order to enhance process and outcome rigour, the (learning) strategies and methods used by researchers should be congruent with the principles characteristic of the chosen methodology. In this chapter, we want to offer you, the reader, a deeper insight into the key principles underlying this method for data analysis, before describing how we "danced" with them in each of our studies. Building on the original work of Boomer and McCormack (2010), who used the key principles of practice development, namely participation, inclusion and collaboration[1], we developed a "critical and creative data analysis framework".

This framework rests on the three main philosophical principles of hermeneutics, criticality, and creativity. Applying these principles to data analysis we have learned that multiple perspectives usually show more similarities than differences, which we express visually and poetically in Figure 22.1. The interface between two perspectives is not a juxtaposition but a fluid transition, where sky meets sea and sea meets sand. Each is separate and yet part of the whole, bigger picture.

PRINCIPLES OF CRITICAL CREATIVE HERMENEUTIC ANALYSIS (CCHA)

Qualitative research is designed to help researchers understand people as well as the social and cultural contexts within which they live, and the data collected often takes the form of loosely structured or unstructured narratives. The purpose of qualitative data analysis is to organise, provide structure to and elicit meaning from data.

Our experience is that this analysis is also an intuitive and personal journey for the researcher, which might imply that clearly agreed processes are lacking and that it is a secluded activity of the researcher. However, the analysis of qualitative data is labour-intensive, requires creativity and conceptual sensitivity, and is hard work.

Although a few standardised procedures exist for qualitative data analysis, we agree with van Manen (1990) that it is more important to consider the principles underlying the chosen methodology, the "what one should do" and "why one should do it". This explains our reference to a data analysis method, rather than technique or procedure. *Method* is charged with methodological considerations and implications of a particular philosophical perspective, in our case the use of narratives within the critical social science and critical creativity paradigms.

Hermeneutic Principles

We sought methodological guidance from the philosophical tradition of hermeneutics. Using Gadamer's (1993) perspective on hermeneutics, we tried to develop an understanding of the social world using the subjective interpretation of each individual as well as the group. Understanding arises from repetitive reading of the data; being open to the concepts being sought; being aware of one's prejudices and critiquing/allowing them to be critiqued in light of newly formulated meanings

(Boomer, 2010). Two processes key to understanding the texts are the hermeneutic circle (Heidegger, 1962), and the fusion of horizons (Gadamer, 1993).

The hermeneutic circle refers to the idea that one's understanding of the text as a whole is established by reference to the individual parts, and understanding the parts by reference to the whole. Neither the whole text nor the parts can be understood without reference to the other, and hence a circle of constant movement between the parts and the whole is established. Interpretation is never free of presupposition; what we know cognitively, pre-cognitively and feel (pre-understanding) is the frame of reference ("horizon") from which a person starts.

During dialogue with others, each starts from his or her own horizon. As researchers we wanted to explore the horizon of practitioners' (co-researchers') lived experiences, with the intention of translating this into more general findings. In doing so, our personal "horizons" were challenged, became broader and fused with theirs, resulting in a new, more encompassing understanding for us all.

Ricoeur (1976) described a methodological relationship between explanation and understanding in terms of the problem of distanciation and participation (pp. 71-88). He stated that qualitative research should be evaluated not by criteria of objectivity but by criteria of convergence: the extent to which perspectives are interwoven.

With the belief that we should fuse multiple interpretations of reality, we did not restrict ourselves only to trying to understand what the author of the narrative wanted to portray. Ricoeur called this the removal of "authorial intent" i.e. the removal of the idea that the text's meaning can reside only with its author.

Principles of Criticality

Habermas' discourse theory (1981) provides a normative base for the dialogue between researchers and practitioners. The public sphere for dialogue is a "space" open to all, providing an arena for critical discussion, contestation and debate. In the public sphere matters of public importance are discussed, and the reasoning can act as a check on one-sided interpretations, i.e. those of the researcher. As postmodernists have taught us, even within a "public sphere" we still need to be aware of power relations.

We were therefore cognisant that measures were needed to ensure that each voice was heard so that no one single perspective (driven by pre-knowledge and prejudices) overwhelmed/dominated the interpretation process. Each participant was therefore offered the opportunity to introduce and question assertions, and to express attitudes, desires and needs, verbally and creatively.

Culture and language make it possible for us to share our understandings of a situation and, through dialogue, reach intersubjective understanding that is consensual. The clarification process, where speakers and listeners define and redefine their understanding, becomes a hermeneutic movement, a recurrent testing of boundaries/horizons which enhances the trustworthiness of conclusions.

A pre-requisite for this critical dialogue is that all stakeholders have a need to understand a situation, so that the options presented for action remain relevant and valid for each participant. The intersubjective consensus was termed "mutual adequacy" by Boog (2007), and is an important validity criterion for PAR. It requires reciprocal trust, which deepens truthfulness, morality and authenticity. Although we found that reciprocal trust enhanced the researcher-participant relationship, facilitating equality in the data analysis process, it was easier said than done.

Smaling (cited in Snoek, 2008) also advocated critical dialogue and mutual adequacy, stressing the importance of intersubjectivity, communication and collaboration between (co-)researchers. However, he warned of collaboration disintegrating into competition, with overtrumping and exclusion, and too large a group resulting in conformism and pseudo-consensus.

Further, he warned of insufficient cooperation (silencing) when differences of opinion and beliefs are avoided, and debating when too much competition is present. Aware of the limitations of trying to reach unanimous consensus and working with cognitive rationale and verbal communication only, we decided to embrace ethical, aesthetic, ideological and evaluative aspects of interpretation, thereby valuing emotions and embodied experiences.

Principles of Creativity

Valuing both cognitive and pre-cognitive knowledge, our next challenge was to find ways of surfacing the pre-cognitive (i.e., pre-conscious, embodied and embedded personal/collective knowledges) into the analysis arena for critical dialogue. Verbalising the tacit is difficult, often resulting in distortions due to rationalisation (constructing logical justifications) and reasoning (looking for reasons for beliefs, conclusions, actions and feelings), or information may simply be withheld because of the negativity of rational thought.

Critical creativity states that the use of creativity and the expressive arts can aid the surfacing of these knowledges (McCormack & Titchen, 2006), potentially reducing cognitive shaping, especially when spontaneously expressed. It can reveal previously unknown aspects of self, bringing new information or embodied knowledge to the foreground, and can facilitate data interpretation by revealing patterns, themes and connections between them.

The blending of all types of knowledge can then take place, in a way the rational mind cannot perceive, offering an alternative to verbal communication (Simons & McCormack, 2007), a communal language and common discourse. Using expressive arts helps prevent the linguistic activity from becoming the object of inquiry; it prevents us becoming bogged down in discussions over semantics.

TRANSLATING PRINCIPLES INTO ACTION

Based on these principles we define CCHA as a research strategy for the analysis of texts in collaboration with practitioners and/or others. It is facilitated by the researcher/investigator who enables the movement between the parts and the whole, offering creative expression to blend cognitive and embodied knowledge/ perspectives. It aims to expand horizons for new, deeper understanding of themes arising from the texts. These (new) understandings can then be used to inform action aimed at transforming individual and/or team practice (context).

A process frequently used to derive meaning from texts is thematic analysis. However, few authors offer a step-by-step framework and none describes the use of creativity. Themes are statements of meaning that thread through most of the data (collection of texts or narratives) or can be a single meaningful account that is deemed significant to understanding the whole.

According to van Manen (1990), "theme analysis" refers to the process of recovering the theme or themes embodied and dramatised in the evolving meanings and imagery of the work. Often shortened to single words, thematic descriptions help reveal and structure the messages embedded in the data. While creating structure, thematic analysis is not a procedure, more a process of insightful invention, discovery or disclosure, a free act of "seeing" meaning (van Manen, 1990). We wanted to collate themes as they gradually emerged from the data analysis, focusing on what the texts said and how they spoke to us individually and as a group.

Examples from Dutch Healthcare Practice

We applied the principles of hermeneutics, criticality and creativity in our PhD studies to guide analysis of narrative data. Famke studied the interplay between context and facilitator characteristics in a Dutch urban hospital, and Shaun studied person-centred leadership in a different urban hospital. Although neither study was complete at the time of this publication, our aim here is to share our experience of the data analysis, not the outcomes of the respective studies.

We were inclusive, in that practitioners with little or no research background were able to engage with the narrative data and the analysis process. They were the authors of the narratives or had an affinity with the phenomenon to be analysed. This connectedness with the texts was important, as without pre-knowledge "appropriation" is difficult, one cannot understand or give meaning to the texts, or make that what is distant/belonging to "the other", one's own (van Manen, 1990).

Framework for CCHA

Based on our experiences we propose a seven-phased framework for a CCHA. The framework is intended to help researcher-practitioner teams develop themes from the data/narratives collected about the phenomenon under study.

- Phase 1: Preparation. The raw data should be prepared/re-presented as narrative texts. The primary investigator invites practitioners to participate, being mindful of interest, affinity and group dynamics.
- Phase 2: Familiarisation. When offered before the workshop, the narratives enable participants individually to get an intuitive grasp of the meanings embedded in the texts. Participants should be encouraged to be aware of and document their questions, imagery and (bodily) feelings when reading the texts.

- Phase 3: Contemplation. We advise contemplation as a warming-up exercise to help quieten the mind, enhance focus and let go of the hectic of daily practice before starting the analysis. For those who have read the narratives beforehand, contemplating the thoughts, feelings, and images they evoked, will help start "dialogue with self". Various creative arts methods such as authentic movement, contemplative walks, sculpturing, meditation and doodling can be used to facilitate the connection between the body and mind.
- Phase 4: Expression. After contemplation, participants are invited to express the "essence" of the texts, as a whole, in whatever creative way they feel comfortable. Blending embodied (pre-conscious) and cognitive (conscious) understanding into a new whole through creative expression such as collage, drawing/painting, poetry, or sculpturing, gives more depth and extends "appropriation". Merging, in silence, individual expressions into an overarching collage/creation can add a new level and create new insights not evident when the expressions were individual parts.

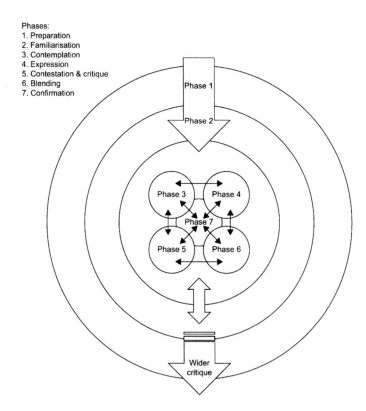

Figure 22.2. CCHA Framework

Facilitation tips:	Practical tips:
– Give clear instructions per phase. – Seek mutual adequacy in what to expect from the analysis. – Keep the group size reasonably small – Maintain an enabling stance of facilitation rather than a "doing for" stance. – Use person-centred principles of recognition, respect and trust (Kitwood, 1997). – Create sufficient time and space (2–3 hours). – Use sympathetic presence to enable distantiation and appropriation.	– Obtain consent for use of during the interview. – Code each narrative with a name/number the lines. Thus, when data supporting the themes agreed in phase 7, participants can refer using story name/number and line referencing instead of documenting citations. – Audio-record the session for later referral if needed. – Provide a variety of creative materials. – Create enough space to move freely.

- Phase 5: Contestation and critique. Collective interpretation can now start, with participants initially sharing their creatively expressed interpretation of the narratives. Critical questioning helps elicit details, creating more depth, clarity and thoroughness as participants examine the parts. Alternative interpretations can be offered and contradictions highlighted. When no collective collage has been created, participants might wish to return to their individual expressions to review them the in light of what they have heard.
- Phase 6: Blending. Stepping back to view the whole, participants can now start to seek the most apparent themes as well as those sheltered beneath the surface. This is a moment when expressed horizons meet, where participants expand their own horizons by meeting those of others, and in doing so reveal a shared understanding. The resultant collective thematic framework represents how the group is oriented meaningfully. Phases 3-6 can be iterative, allowing (co-) researchers to move back and forth, supported by the hermeneutic movement principle.
- Phase 7: Confirmation. The final phase breaks the whole back down into themed parts, but remains focused on the collective now. Still in the Habermasian "public sphere", participants now return to the original texts, retrieving the raw data that supports the thematic framework, receptive to any new themes that might emerge or themes that need rephrasing. Finally, themes will have a detailed and deep description.

The thematic framework, supported with verbatim quotes, can be used for action planning and presented to a wider audience for further critique, thereby starting a new cycle of synergistic analysis, broadening our horizons even further and deepening our understanding even more.

REFLECTION

The following dialogue reflects our experiences of using the CCHA:

Famke: When reflecting on the CCHA framework and its underlying principles, from a facilitator's perspective, what would you say are the advantages?

Shaun: This method makes clear use of the principles for practitioner research and practice development. As we have both experienced, practitioners (and management) are rarely, if ever, interested in developing research skills, considering them too difficult and irrelevant for practice. This poses challenges to researchers wanting to do participatory research.

The CCHA, however, did allow us to collaborate with practitioners. We achieved the multiple perspectives we wanted and they felt as if they were making an active and valuable contribution. They surprised themselves, as one practitioner commented: "At first I thought: 'How on earth am I going to portray what I read, as a picture?', and yet a picture quickly sprung to mind, and it meant more to me than I expected".

Famke: It's also relatively quick, very practical and efficient. Despite the high workload and the efficiency agendas that often limit the space practitioners have to engage in developmental work, people were receptive to analysis workshops of 2-3 hours at the end of an afternoon.

The use of creative expression also created a kind of new language for us to communicate with each other. We kept to the content and essence of the analysis rather than becoming stranded in discussions about words and phrases, which is then seen as a waste of time. Reading narratives in preparation for the workshop saved time and enabled authors to distance themselves from their stories.

Shaun: The whole process of creating space for each to voice their interpretations before seeking the common voice created new energies within the group. I noticed more positive regard for one another.

People were genuinely interested in each other's (interpretive) stories, more person-centredness and less power dynamics such as persuasion or overruling. A phased approach with agreed principles of recognition and respect, were key to this.

Famke: Yes, this connectedness was also reflected in an evaluation: "I think that these things [sharing narratives] are essential for our work, they should be standard, normal events, otherwise we'll never develop new insights, only work, work, work. We've talked about these issues before, but we still keep running around in circles. Now we can capture issues before they escalate.

I have also seen how some people can think completely differently about things, and that's OK".

Shaun: Placing the personal narratives "out in the open" for public scrutiny also demonstrates us valuing them. I saw how analysing these stories collectively transformed many perceptions, and how participation strengthened a feeling of ownership for the action plans that followed.

Famke: Were there any challenges working with narratives?

Shaun: Surprisingly, nurses initially found it very challenging to find and tell a story about how they experienced leadership within the unit, even though the interviews were carried out in their native language and they said they felt comfortable talking to me. I was also surprised how difficult participants found defining themes.

Apparently they were not used to thinking abstractly or in terms of "the essence" of something. Also, the themes I suggested were quickly agreed to, which challenged me in facilitating criticality. Keeping momentum and participant attention was another challenge and identifying text fragments illustrative of the themes proved challenging for participants too.

Famke: I experienced a similar situation, and was conscious of the fact that I continued the analysis alone. In order to maintain co-researcher participation I member-checked my final descriptions of the collectively identified themes. A different challenge I experienced was being the author of the narratives and then facilitating the analysis process.

It was hard to remain focused on my role of enabling others to interpret my stories, to stay connected and attentive to how participants were analysing the stories rather than what they were analysing. I believe that an enabling style of facilitation is needed, with knowledge of both the philosophical principles and group dynamics, as well as finding methods of creative expression that suit the individuals present.

Shaun: There is also a pragmatic issue related to the reading of stories beforehand. Some considered this as extra work, a burden. Spontaneity and equity may also be threatened when some people have spent a lot of time thinking about the stories, while others haven't.

As one practitioner reflected, having "coded" the narratives at home in the familiarisation phase, she felt unable to express her interpretation creatively. The lesson we can learned is that creative interpretation should precede the cognitive interpretation.

CCHA is like a tango, a dance of independent souls who connect and contest, continuously moving to and fro, illuminating a new story in the movement.

Photo by Myriam Moszkowicz

Figure 22.3. Symbolic and poetic expression of participatory, critical and creative hermeneutic data analysis

CONCLUSION

Underpinned by the principles of hermeneutics, criticality and creativity, CCHA in our experience is a practical and rigorous method for involving practitioners while, upholding the practice development principles of collaboration, inclusion and participation. Although we have only used CCHA as a collective, we see no reason why an individual cannot apply the same principles, where the "dialogue with other" becomes "dialogue with self", and multiple inner perspectives are critiqued.

Although we used narrative texts, any text can be used for analysis. As we have learned, including authors in an analysis where creative and dialogical processes are active allows distanciation without alienation. We see this *movement while remaining connected within a dialogical space* most vividly and visually expressed in the tango dance, hence our symbolic representation in Figure 22.3. Also, as in the tango, each time the dance is performed a (new) "story" unfolds.

We hope this chapter offers a methodological account and insight into CCHA as a co-creative approach to making meaning of narrative texts with practitioners in a practice context. We have examined the issues of looking at parts in relation to the whole, while remaining cognisant of prejudices. We have also shown that the identification of thematic patterns and concepts can be difficult for practitioners and so requires skilful facilitation. We hope it is clear, however, that by applying the principles of hermeneutics, criticality and creativity, a researcher can enhance rigour by synthesising multiple perspectives.

Our aim was to offer you, the reader, the necessary principles and a flexible framework to "dance" your own analysis framework, tailored to your own problem, research question and practitioner group. If this chapter helps you on your path to true participatory practitioner research, then we have performed well.

NOTES

[1] Participation = active engagement of others in a concrete activity; inclusion = holding boundaries open for others to join in an activity/process; collaboration = working together towards a common goal, but not necessarily involving participation.

REFERENCES

Boog, B. (2007). Quality of action research: Reciprocal understanding of (scientific) researchers and participating researchers. In P. Ponte & B.H.J. Smit (Eds.), *The quality of practitioner research: Reflections on the position of the researcher and the researched* (pp. 65-76). Rotterdam: Sense.

Boomer, C., & McCormack, B. (2010). Creating the conditions for growth: A collaborative practice development programme for clinical nurse leaders. *Journal of Nursing Management, 18*, 633-644.

Fay, B. (1987). *Critical social science: Liberation and its limits.* Ithaca, NY: Cornell University Press.

Gadamer, H.G. (1993). *Truth and method.* London: Sheed and Ward.

Habermas, J. (1981). *The theory of communicative action.* London: Beacon Press.

Heidegger, M. (1962). *Being and time* (J. Macquarrie & E. Robinson, Trans.). Oxford: Blackwell Science.

Kitwood, T. (1997). *Dementia reconsidered: The person comes first.* Buckingham, UK: Open University Press.

McCormack, B., & Titchen, A. (2006). Critical creativity: Melding, exploding, blending. *Educational Action Research: An International Journal, 14*(2), 239-266.

Ricoeur, P. (1976). *Interpretation theory: Discourse and the surplus of meaning.* Fort Worth, Texas: The Texas Christian University Press.

Simons, H., & McCormack, B. (2007). Integrating arts-based inquiry in evaluation methodology: Challenges and opportunities. *Qualitative Inquiry, 13*(2), 292-311.

Snoek, A. (2008). Begrijp ik u goed? Dialoog en empathie in de methodologie. Verslag van het afscheidssymposium van Adri Smaling. Do I understand you well? Dialogue and empathy in methodology. Report of farewell ceremony of Adri Smaling at the University of Humanistics, Utrecht, The Netherlands. *Kwalon, 39*(3), 53-58.

van Manen, M. (1990). *Researching lived experience: Human science for an action sensitive pedagogy.* Albany, NY: State University of New York Press.

Famke van Lieshout MPH
School of Nursing
Fontys University of Applied Sciences, The Netherlands

Shaun Cardiff MScN
School of Nursing
Fontys University of Applied Sciences, The Netherlands

23. TELLING PEOPLE'S STORIES

Creating Authentic Approaches

Angie: Debbie, we need to clarify what we mean by "stories".

Debbie: Yes, it's a rather slippery term; I find it quite hard to say what I mean. I can say that I don't mean using the actual mode and structure of the story as a research method. I don't mean any particular methodology.

Angie: Definitely not for me either, although it is for some researchers. Perhaps it would be easier if we explained how we have used stories in our research. In my thesis I used stories: first, they were a means for getting at what participants know consciously and can readily express about the phenomenon being studied or their experiences of it.

Debbie: Yes, and we have both done this, usually through in-depth interviewing of both individuals and groups. And, also using a more ethnographic approach, collecting notes during research meetings, keeping research journals.

Angie: And, second, I used these stories to uncover the unarticulated, embedded shared meanings in shared background practices that go unnoticed in the invisible coping of everyday practice. Studying the language in the stories helped me to get at both kinds of meaning; I collected data in different ways to provide distinct kinds of texts. I gathered data in situations where I could encourage reflection and deliberately push the taken-for-granted to consciousness.

Debbie: Similarly, I used purposeful listening in collaborative research, where the participants were encouraged to critically reflect on their own stories.

Angie: I also used texts in which spontaneous, natural, everyday language was used. I encouraged storytelling in interview situations and recorded naturally occurring conversations and spontaneous storytelling in the clinical setting, when the nurses and medical staff were taking coffee breaks.

Debbie: So, we are talking about seeing our raw data as stories – using story as a metaphor that enables us to relate to the data and the participants

J. Higgs et al., (eds.), Creative Spaces for Qualitative Researching: Living Research, 235–246.
© *2011 Sense Publishers. All rights reserved.*

in a particular way. And this spills over into how we analyse the data/stories.

Angie: Yes. I analysed all the stories in two completely different ways. Participants' stories were analysed to re-present their inner worlds of consciousness and their cognitions. I worked to turn their understandings or constructions (first order constructs) into more abstract ones (second order constructs), while remaining faithful to the first order constructs. In the existential hermeneutic tradition, the nurses' stories were interpreted, through dialogue with the texts within a hermeneutic circle, to uncover the transparent coping of everyday nursing practice. The uncovering occurred through a bringing-together or fusion of my interpretation and that of the nurses. So in two different ways, I was telling the story of the nurses' stories, at the same time as presenting the verbatim stories. In writing up the research, three interpretations of the same story were offered.

Debbie: And in the writing up you also became the storyteller of the whole research story. So we are talking about: what people tell us, perhaps in an interview situation, about their lived experiences; what we hear/observe when we are in the context of their everyday lives; and, what we then do with these stories when we take on the role as the research storyteller writing a report, a paper, a thesis. This is where some of those thorny issues come up, in the "what we do with the stories" bit. How we negotiate not speaking for people, not colonising their words for our purposes.

Angie: Sounds good.

Debbie: And it's important to be clear that we see this chapter as contributing to four immediate outcomes of qualitative research: illuminating phenomena, understanding experiences, foregrounding marginalised voices or those previously not heard, and appreciating differences.

Angie: Yes, and it addresses two aspects of transformation, in terms of the participants of the research (that includes us as researchers) being transformed and transforming practice. As for the thorny issues you've just mentioned, I believe we will have to address moral agency, relationships and power, and research as a political act.

In this chapter we focus on the following three aspects of narrative, or storytelling approaches to research: why we believe storytelling is a useful research tool, providing concrete examples of how we have used storytelling in research, and teasing out some of the dilemmas of using participants' voices in qualitative research. The underlying premise of this approach to research is that "experience is meaningful, and human behaviour is generated and informed by this meaningfulness" (Polkinghorne, 1988, p. 1).

Furthermore, the aspects that participants choose to tell about their experiences illuminate what they see as meaningful (White & Epston, 1990). Telling stories can be a powerful research tool in seeking to understand particular phenomena through people's experiences and the sense they make of them (van Manen, 1997).

Collecting and telling research stories is particularly effective when researchers and participants are concerned about social, political and personal change. Stories can reveal how social injustices and inequities are experienced and perpetuated. Stories can illuminate people's resistances to inequities and injustices. Although this process is undoubtedly important for researchers concerned with an emancipatory research agenda, our experiences tells us that it is full of complexities.

When we talk of stories in this chapter we mean two things. First, the data collected as part of a research undertaking can be envisioned as a collection of stories: the story of a stay in hospital, the story of becoming a social activist, the story of growing up in the country. These personal testimonials can be a way of articulating and making meaning of experiences. In *Cleaning Pam's mouth* (below), the verbatim story illustrates the researcher's second order construct and reveals hidden meaning.

Second, the resulting report can be viewed as a research story, an account of what happened, why, when, how and to whom. In constructing the final story, the researchers, and often the participants, look for connections, themes, disconnections, similarities, differences, and ways of revealing meanings (Polkinghorne, 1988; Reason, 1988). As such, research participants and the researcher can be conceived of as storytellers.

Following is a research story which begins to demonstrate some of the points above. The story takes place in a hospital setting. It was told to make a particular point and to illustrate the meaning of new challenging behaviours. It shows two things: first, that routine, unquestioned practices were beginning to be challenged in this hospital ward, and second, that nurses were pushing at the role boundaries of the ward sister and taking on decision-making responsibilities that were originally the sister's. It is an example of the kind of story, collected in the Schutzian (see Schutz, 1970) tradition, of accessing a nurse's inner world, constructions and cognitions:

> Mary [a staff nurse] decided to apply a particular dressing to a patient's pressure sore. Her colleague was not happy about this decision. When Mary pressed her for an explanation, the nurse responded, "Sister doesn't like it". Mary concluded that her colleagues were frightened to approach Sister to suggest new things. She felt their fears were unfounded because when she had presented her rationale for using the dressing, Lorraine [the sister] had accepted her argument. Mary thought that students and junior nurses expected a traditional sister to be "a bit of an ogre" and, as Lorraine was "a bit of the old school", they expected her to be fierce too. (Binnie & Titchen, 1999, p. 101)

WHY TELL STORIES?

There are many reasons why researchers would want to collect and re-tell people's stories. These reasons can be loosely grouped into three interwoven desires: to illuminate and develop understandings about phenomena, to break through the culture of silence (Freire, 1998), and to serve as a political tool which effects social change as part of the process or has social change as an explicit aim. We discuss each of these now, using examples from our research practice.

To Develop Understandings

During a reflective collaborative research project with community workers Rosie, a multicultural worker, recounted how listening to recent immigrants' experiences of being different in their new country helped her gain a greater understanding of their day-to-day lives and how they negotiated living in a new country:

> It was interesting the other day in the multicultural meeting, listening to them talking about being different and at some point saying, "Well I live here now and I have to accept that I have to let go of my [old] country" – not completely but in some ways let go – and not always be referring back to that country and having that association and talking from that experience. They had to accept their difference and move on.

> Listening to their stories of how they do feel different and having to experience that and how they work through it ... and I think their stories need to be told and heard somewhere ... I think it's like a grieving ... the experience of migration is an experience of grieving and it never ends really. It was moving to hear this and it was just a spontaneous conversation. (participant in Pinn & Horsfall, 2000, p. 371)

In relation to understanding practice in order to change it, an important first step is enabling people to engage in critical review and public scrutiny of their actions and practices and the effects of these; to begin to see where strengths and shortcomings lie and how they can build on the former and overcome the latter. Rosie's story begins to illustrate this. The people with whom she was working were publicly scrutinising their actions and reflecting upon their experiences while sharing strategies of how to negotiate their differences. This happened as Rosie provided space for people to tell their stories. A second, similar reflective cycle occurred as Rosie related her story to the collaborative research group.

In the following example it can be seen that by revealing people's hidden knowledge and unconscious assumptions, researchers can explicate invisible aspects of individual, team, institutional and community expertise and effective working practices for others to learn from. In this example, Alison believed that a lack of knowledge and understanding could induce dependence on the nurse and reduce the potential for patients and families to work effectively with her. She had, therefore, developed a number of ways of helping patients and families to take in relevant information and make it their own.

One way in which Alison helped patients to understand what was happening to them was her attempt to make the extraordinary ordinary. For example, she turned the cleaning of Pam's mouth, an extraordinary experience, into the ordinary one of cleaning her teeth (Pam was a confused and frightened patient who had been screaming almost incessantly for days in the ward and had been refusing all care from less experienced nurses):

> Cleaning Pam's mouth I knew was potentially difficult because people don't like having their mouths cleaned. It is not pleasant to have things poked in. Her mouth was a most disgusting mess, coated with medicine, sputum and God knows what.
>
> It looked quite revolting with all that running down her face. As she had a toothbrush of her own and her own teeth I thought – since the chances were that she was used to cleaning her own teeth – I would try giving her the toothbrush and she would do what came naturally with her own equipment.
>
> So that was what was in my mind: trying to get her to do what came naturally, rather than forcing anything on her, and once she got started, she would probably then allow me to help her along with it. Because actually it did need quite a lot of scrubbing ... and she didn't really have the power in her arm to do it thoroughly. Once she had got started, she didn't resent me and knew what was going on and it worked really well.

She gave clear, simple instructions and explanations to help Pam anticipate events:

> I was really trying to make clear to Pam what was going on before I did things to her. I didn't want to jump in and do things ... Then getting her up, I was trying to let her do as much of it, in her own time, as she could, taking it slowly so that she had time to realize what was happening before we moved on to the next thing. (Titchen, 2000, pp. 83–4)

This example, made public through the research reporting process, provided a clear and detailed understanding of what the nurse knew, how she felt and behaved, and how she *worked with* Pam in a mutual relationship, to enable Pam to have more control of her life, rather than *doing to* her.

To Break Through the Culture of Silence

The ethical motivations of social researchers are often strong. As Nina Simone (in Morgan, 1994, p. 1) concluded, many people feel that they suffer from a silence that feels like chains. If people could tell their stories, saying them "loud and clear", getting them heard, then they might feel free, breaking some of the social and psychological bonds of silence.

As such, telling people's stories can be a powerful experience for both the tellers and the listeners. It can widen the public debate about issues and enable social, institutional and practice change to be effected. Silencing strategies are often steeped in institutional practices which have not been questioned. Take, for example, this patient's story:

> That was the only stressful part of the day. Somehow, you always feel that the consultant is in a hurry and you've got ... I'm going to give you two minutes, madam! And if you haven't answered the questions in that time, it's

like a pound a minute or whatever. It's just that feeling, two of his doctors were with him, quite senior doctors and the three of them were looking at the X-rays, making professional judgments and in that case you do feel very small, completely overshadowed. And in danger of being rather stupid, whatever you say, you feel rather stupid. (Edwards, 2003, p. 23)

In this example the patient was effectively silenced by the power relationships operating within institutional routines that felt rushed and left her feeling unimportant and superfluous. Research which includes inviting people to tell stories of, and critically reflect on, their experiences and practices, and making these stories public, has the potential to effect change and break through some of these silencing strategies. Research in the critical paradigm does not leave this hope to chance.

In Alison Binnie and Angie Titchen's (1999) emancipatory action research to developed person-centred care, the stories of patients and relatives radiate their empowerment, in regard to making decisions about their own care in the ward and being supported by the nurses in carrying out those decisions. In another example, towards the end of a 3-year collaborative participatory action research project with community health practitioners, one of the co-researchers reported that being both an actor and researcher in the project had given her confidence and a voice, which had effected changes in institutional practices:

I have more knowledge and more power to speak … legitimized our practice in terms of primary health care and given power to fly in the face of the push from hospitals … [I have] become a lot more involved in decision making. (Horsfall, 1998, p. 155).

In effect she had begun to be more forceful at senior management meetings, had material evidence of her own and others' practices that supported her, and was able to imagine how the practices of both the health centre she managed and the local hospital could be different:

[The research] allowed us to incorporate a lot of information and know what we were doing … it changed our thinking, enabled assimilation of other research, time to think and put our ideas together. (Horsfall, 1998, p. 155).

The research project, which collected evidence of primary health care practices from practitioners, legitimised already existing practices and enabled them to be centred in terms of institutional practices, instead of remaining silently on the margins as previously. As can be seen from this example, through a process of critical reflection this participant changed relationships and work practices.

I am questioning and challenging myself and the ways I and others do things and often find myself reflecting … It has also enriched my interactions that I have with other staff … And I feel more confident in discussing and encouraging community participation. (Horsfall, 1998, p. 152).

Research can and often does break social silences (Fine, 1994). The research project *Good News Stories of Difference and Resistance*, for example, aimed to enable community workers to tell stories of their practices to each other, to theorise about these practices and to begin to work in different ways. The method was quite simple. Workers from a non-government community development organisation met with two researchers each month around a kitchen table, eating and drinking. At each meeting one person told a story about his/her practice. The others listened, using a process called purposeful listening (see Pinn & Horsfall, 2000). Any of the participants could, and did, ask critical questions, encouraging the storyteller to say more and to reflect upon what was being said. A major theme to emerge from this research was that of *new alliances/partnerships*, where old ideologies are let go and new practices emerge. The following excerpt demonstrates this:

> M. told a story about ... how this research project has freed up his thinking, moved him away from some old ideologies and helped him build an alliance with the Liberal [conservative] Party. He was part of the Grow committee, and although it was dominated by Liberal Party interests, he felt able to go there and be open, positive, and responsive and look for opportunities. This project has started attracting money into this sector because of freed up thinking. The money is linked to job creation and economic development in the Blue Mountains (Pinn & Horsfall, 2000, pp. 368-369).

This seemingly simple example is in fact extremely complex. Community development work is steeped in so-called leftist ideologies, where consumerism and capitalism are seen as the enemy (Kenny, 1994). When this particular example was opened to public debate via a conference and publication, two reactions occurred. First, there was anger from some academics who found it self-indulgent. Second, there was relief from some community workers who knew these practices were happening, indeed had been happening for a number of years, but it was difficult to speak of them. The example simply and courageously told it as it was.

To Serve as a Political Tool

Telling and re-telling how people negotiate and make sense of their worlds and making these stories public opens them to scrutiny and debate. It also adds to our options of being in the world, encouraging a practice of hope. It is encouraging to hear that people are engaged in a variety of life practices that challenge, in concrete and creative ways, the taken-for-granted assumptions of *this is the way it is*.

Stories of how people experience the institutions and practices of society can illuminate how larger social structures affect the everyday lives of people and vice versa. If researchers are going to work to change inequities and injustices they first have to understand how these are practised and experienced. In telling of their everyday experiences, people can focus on their everyday resistances to these practices. Telling participants' stories is one possible and achievable way of *doing* social change.

Change can also be achieved by not re-inscribing the dominant stories and practices of consumerism, exploitation and ethnocentrism. There is a need to tell alternative stories, to challenge the space taken up by the dominant stories and to give people alternative stories to embrace (Horsfall, 2005). As researchers communicate stories of actions, negotiations, struggles and successes they cast out threads of possibilities and hope that there is another way. As such, research using storytelling can enable researchers and the participants to:

- write different/alternative/counter histories to what has been told before, in order to show what is, and what can be possible
- make different practices possible
- resist from the margins rather than engaging in conventional political ways
- present ordinary people as historical actors by telling their collective stories.
- The action research undertaken by Alison Binnie and Angie Titchen (1999) demonstrates how different practices can be made possible through the telling of research stories. This project explored how UK nursing teams could transform their routinised, task-focused nursing care (traditional nursing) into care that was person-centred. The aim was to develop a map of the journey to help nurses in other settings make similar transitions.

The nurses' stories revealed that traditionally they expected to lack authority for decision making, either about patient care or about shaping ward life. They expected to be told what to do. The new role of team leader was introduced to begin the devolution of both kinds of decision making from the sister to the staff nurses. The nurses experienced this introduction as poorly handled, difficult and painful, causing one nurse to ask stridently, "What the hell am I supposed to be doing?"

From the nurses' stories, Angie and Alison recognised the experiences of this changing practice as forms of role ambiguity. Sharing this insight with the nursing teams, they developed collaborative strategies for clarifying and negotiating new roles (Binnie & Titchen, 1999). This strategy was tested through action research and was found by the nurses to be effective.

In another example, gathering the stories of women and children who were homeless, and the stories of the service providers struggling with this issue, and making these stories public, led to greater co-operation and collaboration of both government and non-government service providers. The local council acted by putting homelessness higher on its list of priorities in the annual social plan, and one short-term house was funded almost immediately (Horsfall & Pinn, 2000).

A collaborative action research project on community health participation led to many developments: workers establishing four community advisory committees; engaging the union to help change unsatisfactory work practices; establishing community participation as a framework for practice in three community health centres; increasing staff participation in the management of health centres; establishing a Healthy Villages Advisory Committee; and developing a new area health business plan from a community participation framework (Horsfall, 1998).

Finally, an action research study of the development of person-centred nursing resulted in multiple developments: *organisational change*, with decentralisation of decision-making about patient care and ward life to staff nurses, the development of new nursing roles, styles of clinical leadership and collegiate relationships with doctors; *cultural change*, with staff nurses shaping ward life, learning to work professionally, learning at work and caring for each other; and *practice change*, with staff nurses experiencing therapeutic relationships with the patient as person and patients and their families experiencing nursing as healing: "They make me feel I have something to live for. It's the way they talk to me, the time they take to explain" (Binnie & Titchen, 1999, p. 186).

SOME DILEMMAS OF WORKING THIS WAY

Researchers trained to analyse their findings can become paralysed as they struggle to re-present stories without speaking for participants. Researchers must seek to minimise the colonising effects of rewriting people's stories (hooks, 1984), asking whether in abstracting and conceptualising people's lived experience they are colluding with the governors of society (Harding, 1991) or providing a space for alternative voices to be heard, or both. Yet the people whose stories are told do not necessarily feel colonised.

Often re-presenting people's stories can become a liberating and joyful experience for the storyteller: "It was as if the interviewer had seen into my world more fully than my words had articulated and she had represented to me an accurate yet embellished story, with which I was delighted because it gave me new insights into my creative world" (Pinn, 2000, p. 185).

There are ways through this dilemma. Collaborating with participants in the meaning-making of their experiences and the construction of theory and knowledge, constantly verifying and checking for faithfulness and trustworthiness of what is being reported in a feedback loop, is one such way. Creatively exploring and working out ways for people to re-present themselves as much as possible is another.

This can be done by: collaborative research groups, participatory action research, dialogic research, letter-writing, sending transcripts to people to read, using creative arts processes. In our examples above we have demonstrated some of these approaches, as well as demonstrating unconventional methods of data-gathering such as Debbie Horsfall and Judy Pinn's (2000) purposeful listening around the kitchen table. Moreover, co-authoring of journal articles enables participants to retain authority (e.g. Titchen & McGinley, 2003).

There are also many ways researchers can speak with and enable participants to speak for themselves in writing up the research (e.g. using poetry, photos, written conversations, people's own words, presenting the research as a script for a play or as a performance). The struggle for researchers can be in both accepting their authority and privileged position as the writers of the research and being inclusive of the stakeholders, thus working against colonising people's words. Ideally, it is through a process of negotiation and conversation that researchers and participants create meaning from the stories told (see e.g. Karen Bridgman, 2000; Hardy, Titchen, Manley, & McCormack, 2009).

Another approach is to set up research partnerships in which participants become co-researchers who are helped by experienced researchers to engage in all aspects of the research, from formulating the research questions to communicating the results (e.g. Hardy et al., 2009).

In our experience, although we may strive to share the processes involved, for many reasons participants and researchers may resist this sharing. It may be that the researchers are the ones receiving the degrees or being paid to conduct the research. They are employed to do this work and have more time and resources to channel into it. This aspect needs to be acknowledged; time and resources for participants needs to be agreed upon. For example, to be accepted into the Expertise in Practice Project (Hardy et al., 2009), nurse participants had to demonstrate the support of senior management in their health care organisation in terms of allowing time to attend action learning sessions and to gather stories from patients and colleagues about their everyday practice.

No research is politically innocent; it is being done for a purpose. As such there is always an element of taking away people's words and some element of analysing the stories from the researchers' perspectives. Denying this is being less than honest. Accepting and foregrounding it is an ethical and challenging way forward. Making visible the political, personal and intellectual perspectives of the researchers is, therefore, essential. Below is a letter sent to possible participants of the *Good News Stories of Resistance and Difference Project* (Pinn & Horsfall, 2000). The writers tried to be reflexive as possible from the beginning:

> We are imagining this Project as a long-term partnership with you, for example 2-3 years. The Good News Stories of Difference would be a way of starting off that partnership. We would then see what emerges as we immerse ourselves in it. Perhaps a focus for these good news stories would be in the particular areas that you work in: poverty, multiculturalism and disability.

> Our interest and passion is in social change. The way we both understand social change is best described by the metaphor of many pebbles being dropped at the edges of a pool and all the ripples intersect and create disturbances and chaos, disrupting the centre (rather than the idea of social change where there is a rock thrown in the centre which trickles and ripples out to the edges). By the centre we mean the dominant stories in our western culture, for example, economic rationalism, individualism, cultural homogeneity, growth etc. By the edge, we mean resistance to that centre, such as your story of the interest-free home loans. (Pinn & Horsfall, 2000, pp. 1–2)

This reflexivity further facilitates critical analysis of the researcher's place in the interpretation and writing of the research story and the theory generation. It enables researchers to recognise and explicate their part in the process while at the same time ensuring that the theories developed are located in people's interactions with their worlds. It can ensure that theory is useful and pragmatic, and explains what is going on to the people who tell their stories.

CONCLUSION

In this chapter we have focused on some of the whys, the hows and the too often invisible practices involved in collecting and telling participants' stories as a research process. Thus we have articulated our craft knowledge of acting ethically in the re-presentation of participants' stories, sharing our power as researchers with participants and being explicit about our values, beliefs and political intentions. We are both deeply embedded in the process of re-telling stories and both deeply passionate about it. It is a process where transformation does happen, on multiple levels, where understandings occur that are often surprising, and through which creative strategies for change at many levels can emerge.

REFERENCES

Binnie, A., & Titchen, A. (1999). *Freedom to practise: The development of patient-centred nursing.* Oxford: Butterworth-Heinemann.

Bridgman, K. (2000). *Rhythms of awakening: Re-membering the her-story and mythology of women in medicine.* Unpublished PhD thesis, University of Western Sydney, Australia.

Edwards, C. (2003). Exploration of the orthopaedic patient's "need to know". *Journal of Orthopaedic Nursing, 7,* 18–25.

Fine, M. (1994). Working the hyphens: Reinventing self and other in qualitative research. In N.K. Denzin & Y.S. Lincoln (Eds.), *Handbook of qualitative research* (pp. 70-82). London: Sage.

Freire, P. (1998). *Pedagogy of the oppressed* (new revised 20th anniv. ed.). New York: Continuum.

Harding, S. (1991). *Whose science? Whose knowledge? Thinking from women's lives.* Milton Keynes: Open University Press.

Hardy, S., Titchen, A., Manley, K., & McCormack, B. (2009). *Revealing nursing expertise through practitioner inquiry.* Oxford: Wiley-Blackwell.

Hooks, b. (1984). *Feminist theory: From margin to center.* Boston: South End Press.

Horsfall, D. (1998). *The subalterns speak: A collaborative inquiry into community participation in community health care.* Unpublished PhD thesis, University of Western Sydney, Australia.

Horsfall, D. (2005). Creative practices of hope. In D. Gardiner & K. Scott (Eds.), *Proceedings of international conference on engaging communities.* Brisbane, Qld: Queensland Government. Available: http://www.engagingcommunities2005.org/abstracts/Horsfall-Debbie-final.pdf

Horsfall, D., & Pinn, J. (2000). "Where do we go?" Research report on women and homelessness in the Hawkesbury Local Government Area. Richmond, NSW: Women's Housing Information Service.

Kenny, S. (1994). *Developing communities for the future: Community development in Australia.* Melbourne, Vic: Nelson.

Morgan, R. (1994). *The anatomy of freedom* (2nd ed.). London: W. W. Norton.

Pinn, J. (2000). Crises of representation. In H. Byrne-Armstrong, J. Higgs & D, Horsfall (Eds.), *Critical moments in qualitative research* (pp. 185-198). Oxford: Butterworth-Heinemann.

Pinn, J., & Horsfall, D. (2000). Doing community differently: Ordinary resistances and new alliances. In J. Collins & S. Poynting (Eds.), *The other Sydney: Communities, identities and inequalities in Western Sydney* (pp. 360-378). Melbourne: Common Ground.

Polkinghorne, D.E. (1988). *Narrative knowing in the human sciences.* New York: State University of New York Press.

Reason, P. (Ed.) (1988). *Human inquiry in action.* London: Sage.

Schutz, A. (1970). *On phenomenology and social relations.* London: The University of Chicago Press.

Titchen, A. (2000). *Professional craft knowledge in patient-centred nursing and the facilitation of its development.* University of Oxford DPhil Thesis. Oxford: Ashdale Press.

Titchen, A., & McGinley, M. (2003). Facilitating practitioner-research through critical companionship. *NT Research, 8*(2), 115-131.

van Manen, M. (1997). From meaning to method. *Qualitative Health Research*, 7(3), 345–69.
White, M., & Epston, D. (1990). *Narrative means to therapeutic ends.* New York: W.W. Norton.

Debbie Horsfall PhD, MA, B.Ed
Peace and Development Studies
School of Social Sciences
University of Western Sydney, Australia

Angie Titchen D.Phil, MSc, MCSP
Adjunct Professor
Charles Sturt University, Australia

DEBBIE HORSFALL, KAREN BRIDGMAN, CATHERINE CAMDEN
PRATT, VIRGINIA KAUFMAN HALL AND JUDY PINN

24. PLAYING CREATIVE EDGES

Reflections from "Women Out to Lunch" 5 Years On

This chapter is an updated version of *Playing creative edges: Performing research – Women Out to Lunch* (Horsfall et al., 2007). The focus of these reflections is on motivations, desires and explanations. In updating the chapter we cut the original version nearly in half. While this was challenging, it enabled us to decide what was important, what it was we really wanted to say. This process in and of itself is a reflective one, asking us to let go of words carefully crafted years ago, and to decide what it is we now feel strongly about. Our rewriting is also informed by feedback from readers about what they found useful and interesting in the earlier version. The chapter remains a pastiche, a collection of conversations, a play script, stories and reflections on our research, our work and our writing together. Or perhaps it is a crazy quilt that the five women who comprise *Women Out to Lunch* have collectively stitched together. This chapter tells the story of our group, our writing of this chapter as a group, and shows some of our practices as we continue to play with creative edges in our personal and professional lives.

We understand that together we are practising a form of radical openness; a heart-based creative practice informed by the intellectual pursuit of embracing pluralism where "pluralism is … a response to the fact of diversity. In pluralism, we commit to engage with the other person" (Judith Simmer Brown in bell hooks, 2003, p. 47). When we talk about a heart-based practice we mean it in the sense of bell hooks' work (2003, p. 131) as "a combination of care, commitment, knowledge, responsibility, respect, and trust". When we talk about creative practices we mean using poetry, collage, painting, narrative, performance and other non-traditional teaching–research forms. Our recent collective work is about legitimising creativity as a way of accessing and representing meanings, understandings and knowings – research findings, some may say.

HOW THIS CHAPTER WAS WRITTEN

Most of us have done collaborative research which demands collaborative writing practices. In our experience this is not always a simple process. Often one or two people within the group do most of the writing, with different levels of contribution from the other collaborators. Here we have tried to do it differently – we wrote collectively – apart. At the same time we tried not to write stories of

J. Higgs et al., (eds.), Creative Spaces for
Qualitative Researching: Living Research, 247–256

smoothness "where fear, silence and difference cannot be voiced or explored" (Wendy Sweetland et al., 2004, p. 48), to pretend that tensions and differences do not exist. They do. They exist in all groups to some extent. So part of our aim is to write a single story which also speaks of differences.

Five people co-creating a book chapter is no easy task. We needed a process that was held with/in the relationships of the group. We met and talked about the overall shape of this work, what we wanted to say. One of us started, sent the writing on to the next person to add, delete, rewrite. And then back again (a relay of writing runners). We write together with permission to delete and add, not using track-change edit functions, just as we do when we work together creating a performance – taking on an idea and developing it into another. Applied principles of creativity begin with an offer, its acceptance and extension; this chapter embodies this. As a reader you are unlikely to recognise our individual voices on a page unless we name them –multiple stories become one story.

WOMEN OUT TO LUNCH – SOME HISTORY OF THE GROUP

We are a group of academics, ex-academics and recovering academics who support each other's professional and personal endeavours. More recently we have embarked on some creative research projects together. The story of our liaison over 17 years shows something of the evolution of our thinking alongside the development of our friendship and collegiality. In 1994, a group of women academics met for lunch to farewell and honour a colleague, a woman whose contract had not been renewed. This was the sixth contract that was not renewed due to fiscal restraints. All six were women. During the farewell lunch and the ensuing discussion a sense of community and support emerged, as a response to our anger with patriarchy, the bureaucracy and our sense of being marginalised. We agreed to continue meeting.

The frequency of our meetings has fluctuated over the years. The composition of the group has changed and the sense of community has increased. And our name? One colleague chose not to continue with the group, describing us pejoratively as "just women out to lunch". In claiming this name we also re-claim the pejorative criticisms that can occur in academia. Not all women support each other all the time. It is also reflective of how we each do our politics differently. If you believe there is one way of changing the world then it is easy to get frustrated when others try and act in other ways.

In practice, *Women Out to Lunch* support each other through difficult times and help each other shape our individual endeavours. Life and all its catastrophes: love affairs gone wrong; newly arrived love affairs; children growing into adults; deaths; negotiating long-term marriages; chasing income and staying solvent; shape-shifting careers and identities; breaking through menopause; completing PhDs; writing in all our genres; performing poetry and plays; exhibitions and installations; creative research and teaching practices and developing in management roles. We meet in each other's homes. We go away for weekends and discuss our roles and how we can support each other and our communities. We gather around a table, where women have always gathered, whether watching over children or weaving a rug or planning a revolution. It has been, and still is, a journey of love and laughter with a little work and lots of play thrown in. We work with humour – picking up the ridiculousness and transforming it. We are passionate about our communities, our research–teaching and our lives, but we have found that nothing of passion is produced without pain. Humour, we have found, can transform this into learning that pushes the edges of our understanding.

Our meetings are rich, complex meetings of minds and bodies. Many of our discussions have been around the politics of difference: our diversity in the group and stories from our communities. In telling our individual stories, a collective story about how we work is evolving. At this point it is a story about bringing creativity to what we do, although we still disagree about what this means to each of us. We are beginning to understand that our ability to work together well is formed by each of us having a strong creative identity that allows for collaboration. We are often hesitant, unsure and uncertain, but simultaneously we have strong values. We have each reflected deeply on our own practices – separately, together, with others. For example, we each know that everything we do in our professional and creative lives is part of our contexts, our relationships, our histories. We each know that when we say "I" there is a large group of "We" on whose shoulders we stand, or whose hands we hold. The differences emerge in the naming of this. Some of us would talk about inter-subjectivities, others about women's ways of knowing. Some of us may see ourselves as resistance workers, others would not. Some of us, who thought we could change the world, have since changed our minds! This, we think, allows us to maintain our individual and collective identities at the same time. This is important as it enables us to work together, and apart, without power struggles, competition or mistrust – so far! We also know that there is that possibility.

The following excerpts (data) from an email discussion clearly illustrate some of the conflicts we have and how they are to do with naming, language and degrees of emphasis. This discussion emerged as we were deciding whether or not to submit a creative proposal (abstract) to the 5th Biennial Regional Arts Australia national conference held in September 2006 (WOTL 2006). In having to position ourselves, publicly, it was interesting to see what positions we were happy to take:

I do not identify as an artist and I don't use art but I am happy to say "creative arts processes". I feel really strongly about this. (Debbie to WoTLs 6.9.05)

If we are alive then – aren't we artists of our own lives, and within our communities? (Virginia email to WoTLs 7.9.05)

This whole non-artist thing is interesting! ... I realise reading this draft proposal that I do identify as an artist. My WOTL difference is that personal transformation is part of it: it's an "and" ... For me transformation is a by-product that comes through using creativity. (Catherine email to WoTLs 21.10.05)

What about "Creative Edges" {as a title} – this way the artists and the non-artists are accounted for and we are talking about the edginess of bringing creativity into all kinds of environments ... In a sense we are valuing art and creativity and finding ways to bring it to the things we do. I think what we have been doing together is trying to find innovative ways to communicate and catalyse. (Judy email to WoTLs 28.10.05)

I know I stretch things – maybe bridges start with swinging ropes over deep chasms!! ... It helps me enormously to identify as a multi-faceted chameleon! ... different ways of BRIDGING that work to enable differing voices to not only be heard but impact on policy. I love it and want to enter our work as doing all of this, successfully, like a lot of other community workers, artists and even some edgy researchers! (Virginia email to WoTLs 27.10.05)

Interesting to read the discussion going on ... I'm with Debbie – let them decide. I have a feeling that we have a bit of a crisis of confidence – I really think we are far better at what we do than we think and I don't know of a lot of people who work like we do. We will always have something to offer that will be received well. (Karen email to WoTLs 24.10.05)

So we submitted the proposal below which drew heavily from our email discussions about creativity and our own identities and research work.

WALKING CREATIVE EDGES

Performed by the Women Out to Lunch

Women Out to Lunch were outed in 1992 as faux academics who used imagination, laughter and creative arts as a creative story telling. We invite people together to tell stories and show their places – environmental, personal and political. Our regional diaspora includes theatre, government policy, research, teaching, health practice, singing, writing and visual arts practice. We have written and performed a number of plays, painted and exhibited, co-created a community festival, written poetry and challenged traditional academic speak by writing articles and research reports using imagery, metaphor, photos, conversations and plays. We are interested in doing work which is heard and is useful, so we use creativity and imagination to make sure the research/policy report does not get "filed". The communities we have worked with include: women in agriculture; community workers; environmental activists; students at university; women in medicine; teenagers and adults; daughters of "mad" mothers; the older women's network. Often the issues we work with are confronting. We have found that using the creative arts can enable people to be confronted while at the same time engaging actively and collectively in imagining a "better" future. The Trembling Edgy WoTLs Show will unpick and fringe our edges while we show and explore what the hell we are doing with our various cultural community development projects. (WoTL, Regional Arts Australia National Conference 2006 Handbook)

The proposal was accepted. We performed at The Pacific Edge conference in September, 2006. The script was informed by an earlier play we had performed for the opening of the Australian Women in Agriculture Annual conference; our email conversations; our research projects and PhDs and years of reflecting on our various practices. We wanted to show how our research, teaching, community work and creativity inform each other and enable a rich and complex set of practices to both emerge and be supported (see full script in Horsfall et al., 2007).

The script began with an imagined review of a previous performance. In September 2005 Women Out to Lunch opened the Australian National Women in Agriculture conference in Orange, NSW. That performance was based on research and real events that were occurring in the agricultural and political sector in Australia at that time. We used the device of a review to introduce ourselves and our previous performance and include this scene here, slightly edited, to show how and what we did for the two performances.

Walking Creative Edges: WoTL Script for the Pacific Edge Conference 2006

[Props: chairs, a table, computer, wine bottle. Equipment: data projector, screen]

WoTL performing in Orange, NSW with members of Australian Women in Agriculture

Scene 1: Fictitious Review of the WoTL's Performance in Orange, NSW

[Various photos of the performance at Orange shown as PowerPoint images.]

Eulea:	This is ABC Radio Central West coming to you from Orange, New South Wales. I'm Elizabeth Poshingforth-Jones from the Orange Arts Council with my weekly review of arts and performance in the region.
	A troupe of players calling themselves WoTLs (Women Out to Lunch) kicked off the 2005 Australian Women in Agriculture (AWiA) Conference last week. Their play *Am I Too Outspoken?* set the stage for deliberations on the conference theme, Future Opportunities. WoTL members used the email forum as well as national and local media coverage of the Fair Food campaign to develop their play. Dr Virginia Kaufman Hall, a senior policy officer with the federal Department of Transport and Regional Services explains:
Virginia:	We used AWiA members' words – from emails, articles and media quotes. This verbatim theatre approach was mixed with invented dialogue (Faction Theatre, not documentary, partly historical, commenting upon recent herstory and current issues.)
Eulea:	The group, who come from across New South Wales and the Australian Capital Territory, rely on technology for their collaborative processes. Dr Debbie Horsfall lecturer in social research and gender relations (UWS) explains:
Debbie:	We snatch aside time to create together with a great deal of emailing and collaborative writing and editing.
Catherine:	Yes, but our creativity sparks off each other. We need to meet face to face to get that happening. We usually share a house together – lots of yummy food and wine. Just having a good time together, really.
Eulea:	With such a haphazard approach to the theatre-making process the WoTLs worked right down to the wire, says Dr Karen Bridgman, lecturer in clinical herbal medicines and vice president of the Natural Health Care Alliance.
Karen:	After one weekend meeting and 6 weeks of re-writes and edits by email, we came together 36 hours before the performance for the first rehearsal. The script kept changing up to the morning of the performance.
Eulea:	The WoTLs may be more successful academics, community developers and policymakers than they are performers. They had difficulty remembering lines; had some pitch problems among the singers and were heavily reliant on their considerable improvisational skills. However, their use of creative approaches does put the issues on show, enables discussions, shifts mindsets and develops sustainability, led by the communities affected. If you missed their show in Orange, catch them in Mackay in September 2006 with their new Walking Creative Edges Show. This reviewer can guarantee you'll not get what you expect, they're likely to stretch your mind and you won't be hurt in the process.

Reflections

Before working on this updated chapter we did what we always do, we had lunch at a local cafe. We talked about what we wanted to say 5 years on. We agreed that in this final section we would briefly talk about the "so what" of our work as Women Out to Lunch. Debbie suggested that everyone write a 500 word reflection piece about how Women Out to Lunch had informed and/or supported each of us in our work. Two months later, armed with these written reflections, we went away to finish the chapter in the Southern Highlands of NSW. Reading our five 500-word written pieces we realised that they just did not work as we had intended. Reading them one after the other was quite tedious. Below is what happened next.

Bundanoon, February 2011. The sounds of water and dishes, Debbie at the sink. Karen, Judy, Virginia and Catherine around the long wooden table. Karen's wild weeds omelette and freshly dug-up boiled potatoes digesting in our stomachs. Catherine, with laptop on the table, types the conversation, shaping it as she goes.

Debbie (back at the table): Ok, so you all gave me 500 words for this chapter about the, "so what about our work as the Women Out to Lunch?" And we didn't like what it did to our chapter; you said, Judy, the chapter got bogged down. So what do we want to say now?

Judy: I'm not particularly interested in being here and writing a chapter, but I am interested in being here with us, with the group. I don't want to abbreviate myself or ourselves into a chapter.

Debbie: Part of the knot I've got in my stomach around this is that we always feel like this about the writing and yet we still get together around the writing. How come we don't get together around say, "I'm having a rough time, let's go away for a weekend". I know you'd all come. But we don't do that.

Catherine: Maybe it's that we also want to work at the places that make a difference and do work at these areas of resistance. So making a difference in the world legitimates our coming together. Self-worth's not reason enough.

Virginia: I'm curious about articulating that spark of what happens with the WoTLs.

Debbie: The book chapter is useful because we inquire into it; we do bring our politics with us, casting our ideas out into the world.

Virginia: We compost. Bring in the shit, peelings, etcetera. And the harvest. And what we reflect back to each other about ourselves keeps me going when I'm feeling shaky because I know you women still believe in me.

Karen: Well, I get together with an amazing group of people in the market each week, all of whom want to change the world, but I wouldn't want to go away for a weekend with them! (Lots of laughter).

Catherine: I'm not questioning why I'm writing this chapter; it's a creative offer and I said yes without reservation. For me it's the belonging I experience here that's most important, not the creative work in itself, because I've been creative and transgressive most of my life. But I haven't belonged.

Judy: Well, where to after 17years? We've changed, haven't we?

Karen: I'm not interested in the big social change and activism, I know I make a difference in small ways in other's health and wellbeing. I'm comfortable in my shoes; I don't need to march in the streets any more to make a difference.

Judy: So – we're uncovering the group narrative. This group's culture has shifted from having to make a difference to..., to what? We can come here and say what we want but when we come to write about it in an academic context we have to write it against the dominant narratives.

Catherine: So who would read this chapter for pleasure if they didn't have to for their study, their research?

Virginia: So the interesting thing is the peeling away of the layers of what the WoTLs are about? What if we peel away the layers and there is no-thing there?

Judy:	Well then we'd have reached enlightenment! (Laughter).
Virginia:	I don't have to get in there and do it in that way any more AND there's still a real question for me: Is my work right livelihood?
Catherine:	I know the work I do is right livelihood and does make a difference. And I know that its co-created with the students I work with.
Virginia:	We were all activists, then we became educators, then cultural creatives, now what is it we are wanting; to be more creative about our activism?
Judy:	I think we are all different in these, anyway they are all connected. Each of us shines a spotlight on one of those areas at different times.
Debbie:	We were about making the personal political; are we taking it back now into the domestic?
Karen:	I gave up all the committees and larger political stuff. Now I know where to work, I guess it is more local, not domestic. When I go home I always understand myself better after being away with us for the weekend.
Catherine:	That's like what Virginia said about the gaze. For me it's about belonging and shaping how we are in the world. And our effectiveness.
Debbie:	You know, I feel like this is my supervision. Some professions have this and in our profession it's not seen as necessary.
Judy:	ell really that is how we formed; we came together to support each other in the face of the difficulties we were working with.
Karen:	So what is supervision, it's not support? Supervision sounds hierarchical – like power over?
Debbie:	You're right, the language is wrong. But there is some recognition in professions that some kind of talk is needed.
Judy:	So in the academic profession, this just doesn't happen; and it needs to. I don't know what the word is – it's mentoring as women in the roles we are in. The sense of it is the sisters doing it for themselves.
Debbie:	You're right, that why we started doing it. The form's changed.
Catherine:	So back to this context and our form here in this chapter. Maybe we go back to our 500 words and pull out what we think still needs to go in here?
Virginia:	I think the stories we share put the flesh on the bones of academic theorising and research.
Debbie:	How about a poem?
Judy:	Yes, the bones!
Virginia:	The bones!
Judy:	Let's make a throwing the bones poem.

Everyone took turns reading out their 500 words. The listeners silently wrote down phrases and words and ideas that resonated with them – or that they just liked. Then all the words and phrases were read out and Catherine typed them into the computer. We deleted repetitions. Catherine read out what was left. If anyone said "no" then that phrase or word was deleted – no discussion, no argument. What was left was collaboratively shaped (in 15 minutes) into a poem. We added no words.

Here, I belong.
Lineage
knowing what is possible
inside out knowing
following ancient healing paths.
No fly in – fly out research rape:
stories of our lives
restored.
Laughing at the absurdities
learning our way through
loosening our tongues
inhabiting our uncertainty together.
Democracy in action.
Sometimes to speak up is to work too hard.
Ten bottles of nail polish
WoTLs are a counterpoint.
Belonging I have with/in us.
Something happens when we're told we can't
knowledge churns through the labyrinth of our gut
naming the work
outrageously and unpublishably.
Not about why
but about why not
despite political antagonism.
Amazed ...
wait a minute ...
Why? Why not?
Breathe ...

(Self-congratulatory laughter and minor fine-tuning)

Karen: Has your knot disappeared Debbie?

Debbie: Yes it has, thank you.

Judy: I just loved writing this chapter.

Back home in Little Hartley, Debbie tidies up the punctuation, adds sentences about the process used to write the poem and breaks it into stanzas. She smiles as she realises how simple, in the end, it was to get to the essence of what we do and what it means to us. We just needed to eat lunch together and talk. Mind you, she thought, the sweating happened when we wrote our 500 words in isolation. That was the compost, the raw data which enabled our performance ethnography to take place. (And we won't mention the tears of not knowing what to do with the tedious lists and of asking her dear friends to conform to some outdated notion of academia!) As she hits Send on the email, the draft chapter goes to the Women Out to Lunch for them to make changes before it goes to the chapter editor.

THE END

REFERENCES

Hooks, B. (2003). *Teaching community*. London: Routledge.

Horsfall, D., Bridgman, K., Camden-Pratt, C., Kaufman Hall, V., & Pinn, J. (2007). Playing creative edges: Performing research – Women out to Lunch. In J. Higgs, A. Titchen, D. Horsfall & H. B. Armstrong, *Being critical and creative in qualitative research* (pp. 136-151). Hampden Press: Sydney.

Sweetland, W., Huber, J., & Wheelan, K. (2004). Narrative interlappings: Recognising difference across tension. *Reflective Practice, 3*(1), 45-74.

Women Out to Lunch (Karen Bridgman, Catherine Camden Pratt, Virginia Kaufman Hall, Debbie Horsfall, Judy Pinn). (2005). *Am I not pretty enough?* Research performance presented at Future Opportunities: National Conference of Australian Women in Agriculture Conference, Orange NSW, 1-3 Sep.

Women Out to Lunch (Karen Bridgman, Catherine Camden Pratt, Virginia Kaufman Hall, Eulea Kiraly, Debbie Horsfall, Judy Pinn). (2006). *Walking creative edges*. Research performance presented at The Pacific Edge, Fifth Biennial Regional Arts Australia National Conference, Mackay, QLD, 15-17 Sep.

Debbie Horsfall PhD
University of Western Sydney, Australia

Karen Bridgman PhD
Naturopath, University of Sydney, Australia

Catherine Camden Pratt PhD
University of Western Sydney, Australia

Virginia Kaufman Hall PhD
Research and Evaluation, Office of Indigenous Policy Coordination, Government Department of Families and Community Services and Indigenous Affairs, Australia

Judy Pinn
Writer living in the Blue Mountains of New South Wales, Australia

JOY HIGGS AND NITA CHERRY

25. CREATIVE PARTNERSHIPS IN RESEARCH DEGREE PROGRAMS

Towards Collaborative Realisations

Between the idea
And the reality
Between the motion
And the act
Falls the Shadow ...

Between the conception
And the creation
Between the emotion
And the response
Falls the Shadow ...

Between the desire
And the spasm
Between the potency
And the existence
Between the essence
And the descent
Falls the Shadow

T.S. Eliot (1925)

FROM SHADOW TO ILLUMINATION AND REALISATION

In his poem *The Hollow Men*, T. S. Eliot talks about the hollowness that arises from failing to make choices and take actions that are available and falling into the shadow, the lesser place and the lesser being. Research higher degree programs can resemble these situations and be "simply academic" if candidates are not courageous, insightful or diligent and if supervisors and systems are restrictive, unsupportive or uninterested.

In this chapter we present an alternative, positive, fruitful path in research degrees...

J. Higgs et al., (eds.), Creative Spaces for
Qualitative Researching: Living Research, 257–266

Between the idea
And the reality
Between the notion
And the act
Lies the opportunity ...
Between the conception
And the creation
Between the emotion
And the response
Lie the choices ...

Between the desire
And the pursuit
Between the potential
And the achievement
Between the vision
And the realisation
Lies the endeavour

From the opportunities
among the choices
among the endeavours
and through the partnerships
arise illuminations and realisations.

(Higgs, 2010)

TERMS

Research higher degree programs are extended and often intense journeys by students or candidates, in which various partnerships are essential to the survival and completion of the program and the success of the candidate. To focus on this journey and its inherent partnerships we adopt the following terminologies:

- While recognising the various levels of research higher degree programs (e.g. research masters degrees, PhD degrees, higher doctorates) we use the term *doctorates* to avoid clumsy repetition of many words and clarifications, and we ask readers to interpret the term collectively.
- We refer to the student, learner, or emerging researcher as the *candidate*, since this term encompasses ideas of both a mature, chosen path in search of a successful outcome and the possibility of success or failure at the final testing point. This path requires a candidate who is self-motivated and agential, in contrast to the dependent image and system that can be associated with the term "student".
- The relationship between the candidate and the supervisor/supervisors/ supervisory panel can vary through the candidature and varies considerably across different candidates and situations. Nevertheless, the relationship between the candidate and the principal supervisor is widely recognised as

being critical to the success, enjoyment and character of the journey. We refer often to the *supervisor* and at times the *supervisors* when discussing the wider group.

– Doctoral programs are inherently about the project(s) and journey of a person (the candidate) and they can be lonely and solitary, but there are others beyond the candidate and supervisors who are part of this journey or are affected by it. There are the research participants and there are the supporters: life partners, family, friends, work colleagues and fellow candidates. We see the term and completeness of the role of *friend* best fitting in this group, rather than with the supervisors who may become valued friends but who need also to take on many other roles.

RATIONALE

The setting for this revisioning is higher education, an environment facing continual change, scrutiny, changing student populations, regulation and funding constraints throughout the world. Postgraduate research programs have, in many places, become part of "research training agendas" with an emphasis on the responsibilities of supervisors and their institutions to provide relevant, timely and efficient higher degree education for their students. With the global commodification of higher education, postgraduate research students and their supervisors are challenged in many ways, particularly in relation to expediency of throughput and cost efficiency. Supervisors and candidates are under pressure to complete high quality, meaningful work within limited time and cost parameters. This pressure is compounded when candidates are mature aged, working (frequently full-time), or meeting family responsibilities at the same time as studying. The population of postgraduate research students is increasingly diverse in terms of age, sociocultural background, geographical location and distance from supervisors, and with a variety of communication technologies at their disposal.

Qualitative research further faces ongoing challenges in a funding-restricted world which more frequently understands and supports a physical science emphasis within evidence-based practice. This emphasis impacts on which research topics are more strongly supported and funded and what type of research product (e.g. experimental research journal papers) more readily attracts research credit or recognition. And yet, the research world faces many questions that require a qualitative – interpretive and critical – approach to cope with the human challenges and wicked practice problems we discussed in Chapter 2. Research students can draw upon a burgeoning variety of rich, 21st century approaches to qualitative research and an increasing liberation, legitimacy and opening-up of the scope and character of qualitative research as celebrated and examined in this book. In keeping with these new adventures in transformational qualitative research we need to transform supervisory relationships.

REALISING DOCTORAL JOURNEYS OF CHOICE AND ILLUMINATION

In this chapter we delve into the opportunities, choices, endeavours, partnerships, illuminations and realisations that can be experienced during doctoral journeys.

Lies the Opportunity

> Between the idea
> And the reality
> Between the notion
> And the act
> Lies the opportunity
> ...

Doctoral candidates arrive at the start of their research journey at various stages of previous journeys and understandings. They come with a variety of starting points, from vague ideas of research topics to detailed plans for specific research projects. One of the first challenges for supervisor and candidate is to find a working space between these ideas and the anticipated reality of the coming doctoral program. The early ideas may be too huge (several PhDs in one), too broad and need narrowing, too vague and need specifying, or completely the opposite. Whatever the case, there is a conversation to be had about the notions, the visions, the ideas that are driving the research and the reality and acts that ground and situate the research, not the least of which are the location of the research in a pass/fail candidature and in an institution with traditions, approval committees and research culture expectations. Both ideas and realities make the journey possible; both feed the ongoing directions and drive of the research; both face the challenges of realising the vision. Herein lies the opportunity to create new knowledge that does justice to ideas and actions and makes these two congruent parts of the whole (research). Many opportunities can exist in this evolving dialogue space for a candidate to take many paths and for different candidates to research similar topics differently. Such is the richness of qualitative research into human worlds and lives. Across the research journey, additional opportunities arise to think afresh about research goals and focus and to realign the strategies to match changes as the findings emerge.

Lie the Choices

> Between the conception
> And the creation
> Between the emotion
> And the response
> Lie the choices ...

The dialogue in the above section is full of choices in creating the research strategy. Choices also lie in the way the research is lived, enacted and embodied. This includes the way candidate and supervisors interact, the relationships established with participants, the authenticity the candidate adopts in being a researcher and the voices used to reflect self and others in writing the research thesis. These choices can be challenging because they sometimes involve issues that cannot be resolved in a simple, once-and-for-all fashion: they might have to be wrestled with right through the research journey. One of the key paradoxes in the supervisory relationship is how people learn to back their own judgment, to take up their own confidence and authority, to find their own voice, while at the same time being reliant on the other to guide them through the process, to appraise and give feedback on the quality of their work and to find the people who will examine their efforts. This paradox recurs right through to the very end of the supervisory relationship and it is difficult to find a recipe that will make it completely manageable or even predictable. There is always the potential for one party to surprise the other, because the reciprocal dynamics of power and authority are often unconscious for both people, for much of the time. We don't always know what really matters to us until someone else unexpectedly calls it into question. And even if we are conscious that something is happening, it is not likely that both people will always accurately read each other's intentions and needs, even if they have a good working relationship. It is inevitable that issues of power and authority are continuously worked on in supervision: that choices to take control, to comply, to collude, to challenge, to ignore, to mandate and to feel mandated, are made all the time, whether wittingly or not. And parallel processes play out between researcher and participants.

For example, there are times when the relationship between supervisor and candidate, or between researcher and participants, is genuinely collaborative, where nobody knows more than anyone else, where those involved are creating data together, making sense of things together, learning together and making decisions together. Then something happens that causes one of those involved to feel the need to exert authority or impose knowledge; or to fear loss of control of something that matters; or to take exception to the behaviour of someone else. These can be defining moments in a relationship, shaping how it will play out in what is to come. The choices made are no less choices because they are made impulsively, in a reactive way, or unconsciously. And the consequences can be significant: the voices of others can become marginalised and faint. This can mean that data are incomplete, that the perspectives brought to bear are limited and the conclusions derived are the product of a kind of domination rather than of a creative energy that finds a way to represent a deeper and wider range of human experience, especially when that experience is contrasting, different, diverse, but not wrong. Moreover, there can be important consequences for the confidence, energy and skills of others: to be dismissed from decision-making about things that matter (even if the dismissal is subtle and polite) is to be asked to leave that part of the conversation. For the supervisor, diligence is required to keep the choices open. And for the candidate, part of the journey to becoming a researcher is to recognise the need for others to make choices.

Another area of choice that can pose interesting challenges for supervisors and candidates is deciding whether to work within or across disciplines. This might occur, for instance, when the principal supervisor and the student come from different disciplinary backgrounds but choose to work together because of a shared interest in goals or methods, or perhaps for more pragmatic reasons such as availability and access. Likewise the supervisory panel might reflect different disciplinary backgrounds. Importantly, these differences are not just about content knowledge (a key consideration in providing guidance on the scope of literature coverage and existing research/theory knowledge); they can also reflect different research conceptualisations, paradigms and cultures. Table 25.1 provides an overview of key (inter-)disciplinary considerations.

Table 25.1 Comparing within- and across-discipline(s) supervision

Cross-disciplinary research

	Research Procedures	Roles	Research Goals
Challenges	To ascertain the expectations of the various disciplines and determine a product and report style that reflect the genres of the several disciplines and the school of enrolment/ examination	*Supervisor*: exploring relevant fields and resource people, providing team leadership and conflict negotiation, choosing examiners able to deal with scope and approach of study *Candidate*: diagnosing learning needs, recognising and learning to manage/access strengths of various supervisors/advisors	Choosing among different and at times contradictory procedures and/or creating a blend of procedures, making the process transparent to allow for judgment of credibility and rigour
Expectations	To generate new knowledge that crosses and is enriched by several fields	*Principal Supervisor*: resource person in own areas of strength; team manager; one of advisory group whose expertise covers the relevant fields *Candidate*: trainee, learner ++ in new fields or approaches	Constructing a path for research among the different discipline/ paradigm expectations to produce a coherent and credible research project and product

Within-discipline research

	Research Procedures	Roles	Research Goals
Challenges	To produce a research product and report (thesis) that fit the genre of the discipline and the school of enrolment/ examination	*Supervisor*: keeping on top of expanding knowledge of the field, recognising own limits and referring candidate to others for advice in content or method as needed *Candidate*: learning self-management and strategies for "managing" supervisor	Ensuring research questions and strategies are congruent with the research topic and accepted paradigms/approaches Understanding and pursuing expected standards of rigour and quality of the paradigm(s)
Expectations	To generate new knowledge in the field/discipline	*Supervisor*: mentor, guide to content and process *Candidate*: trainee, increasingly becoming an independent researcher and expert in specific topic area	Working within the dominant or accepted paradigms and approaches of the field

Lies the Endeavour

> Between the desire
> And the pursuit
> Between the potential
> And the achievement
> Between the vision
> And the realisation
> Lies the endeavour

Doctoral programs involve inspiration but they also involve toil. They are not for the faint-hearted or for those who want the pleasure but none of the pain or "graft" of research. After the first excitement of taking on the work, the realisation sets in that there are no short cuts, that this is a distinctive piece of work that no one can do for you, even though many people can help. And the reward for getting through one phase, with all its tangles and challenges, is to be confronted by the next one. Morgan (1983) has suggested that in research we meet ourselves, not primarily the world we think we are exploring. The things we discover about ourselves include the dimensions of confidence and authority just discussed, the integrity with which we conduct ourselves in the face of challenge, and the sensitivity we show to the issues and concerns of others. But the things we discover also include the way we marshal energy when things get difficult, the way we support and refresh ourselves when we feel dispirited, how resourceful we are when we have to find a way around an obstacle, how we go about involving others in problem-solving, whether we are mostly optimistic or anxious. The progress we make can be as much about how we are tackling the work as it is about what we are trying to do.

So endeavour is not just a matter of working harder or longer, but of working wisely, resourcefully, understanding our strengths and skills and not squandering the energies we bring. Those energies are not only intellectual but also creative, emotional, physical and spiritual, and it can be helpful to know when we overusing our preferred energies and failing to either replenish them or balance them with other sources of energy.

Endeavour also implies the seeming paradox of creative discipline: taking the trouble to master and use techniques and practices that keep the work moving even when greater complications seem daunting. Techniques include such things as changing writing style for a while, using a new medium, actually re-reading all those previous journal entries and notes, reading rapidly when reading slowly isn't working (or vice versa). It can mean taking time out when thinking is difficult, to do routine work like updating reference lists, or making a larger block of time after a good night's sleep to start afresh on a challenging conceptualisation.

Sometimes endeavour is assisted by going back to first principles and really immersing ourselves in the protocols of the culture of inquiry we are employing. Those protocols were often designed to keep us going when we are drowning in the detail or in danger of going into orbit because our feet are nowhere near the ground. Through endeavour our visions are shaped, challenged, tested, revisioned and realised. Ideas and experiences from previous learning and life experience are re-fashioned into researchable questions, scaffolded into research strategies, and talked through with like companions. In this way we live with our puzzles, epiphanies and irritating problems until they emerge as new understandings.

Through the Partnerships Arise Illuminations and Realisations

> From the opportunities among the choices among the endeavours and through the partnerships arise illuminations and realisations.

In doctoral training and supervision we see (at least) four partnerships, primarily between: the candidate and the research, the candidate and the supervisor, the candidate and fellow candidates, and the candidate and the other travellers in their lives. Each partnership has the potential for collaborative realisations.

a) Supervisors

In postgraduate research education programs a dynamic relationship exists between the research supervisor and the postgraduate research student. This process has special opportunities for pursuing creative research strategies and outcomes, for blending critical reflections and creative conversations and for constructing spaces and structures that liberate learning and action for supervisor and student. And these opportunities are magnified when such research journeys occur in critical, creative communities. (Higgs & Armstrong, 2007, p.120).

Traditionally, doctoral supervisors held the role of master to the student-apprentice (see Table 25.2). In such relationships and programs the supervisor-master acts as expert role model, the key guide to method and content, the program master, judge and superior. The apprentice fills the traditional role of one who works for/with the master and learns from the role model, following on the way. The key problems with this mode of learning are that if the master is neither an expert or a capable guide then the apprentice's learning is limited; if the master has narrow focus and limits, the learner's scope and depth of learning is restricted; and if the master maintains the distance between self and the apprentice then future as well as current collaboration between them is always hierarchical.

Table 25.2 Comparison between master and partner modes of supervision

Master	Role Model	Guide	Master	Critic	Senior
	A model of mastery for the apprentice to emulate	Someone who shows the way	Controller, employer, skilled artist, expert	A judge, appraiser	A leader, superior
Partner	**Muse**	**Catalyst**	**Mentor**	**Critic**	**(Emerging) Colleague**
	A guiding spirit A source of inspiration	A prompter, precipitator, stimulator	A trusted counsellor, teacher	An appraiser, judge, source of feedback	A (junior) peer, co-participant

The research supervisor is guide, mentor, communicator of standards and expectations, support person, administrator, critical friend, role model, co-researcher, learner and person. In the latter two roles ... supervisors are themselves continually learning and developing their research expertise and ... they, along with their students, face vulnerabilities, inadequacies and research dilemmas. (Higgs & Armstrong, 2007, p.121)

When a supervisor adopts the role of partner to the doctoral candidate the seeds are sown for a rich partnership where the candidate commences as a novice and becomes a colleague, often exceeding the mentor's expertise in the specific topic area of the doctorate. In this model the supervisor can serve as muse and inspiration to the novice, as stimulus, trusted counsellor and source of feedback. Through such partnerships opportunities are seized, choices are actively explored, problems are addressed and productive endeavours realise illumination (awareness, new knowledge, deeper understandings) of the research phenomenon.

b) Peers

The transition in recent years from doctoral supervision to research training programs has resulted in a greater emphasis on peer learning and group training programs. Peers play a vital role in providing inspiration to candidates, providing stimulus to consider other choices, and encouragement in times when progress is slow, when difficulties abound and when successes are shared. Peer partnerships can be vital and memorable supports for research candidates' journeys.

c) Research Partners and Participants

Research participants are important partners in doctoral research; it is their stories, conversations and experiences that provide the means for exploring the research phenomenon. In some research strategies, such as action research and collaborative inquiries, the boundary between research and research participant is blurred, with both making decisions about the research approach, interpreting data and texts collected. This blurring and co-ownership of the research can provide a real challenge to doctoral candidates who, alone, gain the research degree, are responsible for meeting university deadlines and requirements, and have to face the examiners. The institution also faces the challenge of determining whether the candidate has contributed the key intellectual property and endeavour, sufficient to warrant the award.

d) Friends and Supporters

It is sometime said jokingly that when a person enrols in a doctorate, the family enrols too. Certainly family, friends and supporters can find the pattern of their relationships changing, both in obvious ways (like time spent together and roles being renegotiated) and in less obvious ways (because one person is learning and changing and the other might or might not be learning, or might be changing in different ways). The time taken to complete a doctorate represents a significant period in an adult life, and a significant commitment by many who care about the candidate. It is no accident that most theses begin with a dedication to family members, with thanks for their practical support, their patience, or their inspiration and love. As Morgan (1983) might also have said, in research we find out who our real supporters and friends are, and most particularly we learn much about their generosity towards us.

Arguably, we can see a parallel process being played out in close relationships like those with friend/family and that with the thesis/research. The things that are known and unknown, discussable and undiscussed, negotiated and taken for granted, troublesome and delightful in the work of the thesis, upon closer inspection can have their echoes – or may be the echoes – of things playing out in the candidate's key relationships. Feelings of vulnerability and mastery, of excitement and boredom, of pleasure and pain, can all resonate in this way, for better and for worse.

IN CELEBRATION

From Hollow Men – a space of shadows and being less than one can be – to realised thesis that provides illumination and brings rewards for insightful choices, endeavour and diligence and working collaboratively in partnerships, this is the reshaping of doctoral studies we have examined in this chapter. For each candidate, topic, situation and supervise there are paths and realisations that can bring such rewards.

REFERENCES

Eliot, T.S. (1925). The Hollow Men. In Eliot T.S., *Poems: 1909-1925*. London: Faber and Gwyer.
Higgs, J., & Armstrong, H. (2007). Re-conceptualising research supervision. In J. Higgs, A. Titchen, D. Horsfall & H. Armstrong (Eds.), *Being critical and creative in qualitative research* (pp. 120-135). Sydney: Hampden Press.
Higgs, J. (2010). From hollowness to realised theses (unpublished).
Morgan, G. (Ed.) (1983). *Beyond method: Strategies for social research*. Beverley Hills, CA: Sage.

Joy Higgs AM PhD
The Education For Practice Institute
Charles Sturt University, Australia

Nita Cherry PhD
The Australian Graduate School for Entrepreneurship
Faculty of Business and Enterprise
Swinburne University of Technology, Australia

JANICE OLLERTON AND CAROLYN KELSHAW

26. INCLUSIVE PARTICIPATORY ACTION RESEARCH

Rights, Camera, Action!

Carolyn: "Rights, Camera, Action!" is a quirky title, Why did you choose it?

Janice: The international disability community has declared "Nothing about us without us", asserting people's rights to be involved in research concerning themselves (UN Chronicle, 2004). However, within the body of research and literature about people labelled with learning difficulties there is little actually undertaken by or with them. I wanted to create a research space that recognised and accommodated this right. Many research methodologies are text-based, functionally excluding non-literate researchers.

Photo-voice is a powerful camera-based research method which can bridge this gap, making the research process accessible (Wang, 1999). I chose it as one of the tools in a research project exploring social barriers to self-determination with a group of young people labelled with mild-moderate learning difficulties from Western Sydney.

Together, as the Penrith Photo-voice Project (2007-10), we undertook action causing positive social change. I should note here that disability literature often uses terms such as "mental retardation" and "intellectual disability" but I use "learning difficulties" which is preferred by many people within the self-advocacy movement (Central England People First, 2000). The slogan Rights, Camera, Action! picked up the cinematic allusion – we hoped to shed light with moving pictures. It provided a creative and effective framework for the inclusive participatory action research (IPAR) methodology developed and used in the photo-voice research project and in the dynamic outcomes achieved by the team.

Carolyn: I'm intrigued to hear about this IPAR methodology within the "Rights, Camera, Action!" framework.

J. Higgs et al., (eds.), Creative Spaces for
Qualitative Researching: Living Research, 267–278
© *2011 Sense Publishers. All rights reserved.*

RIGHTS

The Right to Inclusive Research Methodology

Janice: When it comes to research, people labelled with learning difficulties often face barriers of exclusion. I see this as a significant social injustice, indeed a violation of rights. To address these issues I sought a research approach that was genuinely collaborative. Participatory action research (PAR) was an obvious possible choice. Gaventa (1988) defined PAR as a process that attempts to break down the distinction between the researchers and the researched, the subjects and the objects of knowledge production by the participation of the people-for-them-selves in the process of gaining and creating knowledge. It is a process of creating knowledge education, development of consciousness and a mobilisation for action. I was keen to incorporate the research, education and action aspects of PAR, particularly the plan-act-review-revise reflective cycle (Reason & Bradbury, 2008). Its drawback lay in the specific standard required – I was unsure if the research team could participate as full research partners in all phases of the research.

Some team members might lack the literacy and investigative skills needed for an intensive literature review. Limited complex cognitive abilities might prevent equal participation in research design and analysis. Social skills might be insufficient for the tasks involved. I also wanted an approach that was truly inclusive. In disability studies, research specifically undertaken in partnership with people labelled with learning difficulties has been called inclusive research (IR) (Walmsley, 2001). IR does not demand the same level of shared control or explicit educational outcomes as PAR, but it does incorporate those labelled with learning difficulties, traditionally viewed as the object of research, as co-researchers. This involves a shift away from the privileged voice of the medical professional towards those with a learning difficulty, acknowledging them as the experts on what it is like to live with their difficulty.

Both PAR and IR methodologies offered significant benefits. I melded their tenets into a methodology called "inclusive participatory action research" (IPAR). The IPAR structure elevates participants to co-researchers, intrinsically involving them in the reflective PAR cycles. It also inclusively embraces the contributions of people labelled with learning difficulties to a project explicitly focused on improving their situation. In contrast to traditional disability research which positions people as objects of study, IPAR positions them as co-investigators.

The collaborative nature of IPAR partly addresses criticisms of oppressive structures within traditional disability research, which position people as inferior by denying them control over research resources and the research agenda. The term IPAR suited the research because, while maintaining elements of both PAR and IR, it differed from both, in that I facilitated the research and necessarily maintained a measure of control of the process while seeking (liberatory) educational and social action outcomes.

Therefore, although an unequal power structure within the research team was inevitable, awareness of this enabled me to make it visible and work to minimise it. Critical dialogue and shared decision-making on utilising research resources enabled distribution of power. The research team was responsible for identifying the social barriers to be explored. Team members were acutely involved in decision making on research design and data collection.

The team evaluated actions and analysed data through reflective discussion and actively disseminated our research through co-presentation at conferences and information sessions (Ollerton, Kirkwood, Boyle, & Roberts, 2009, for example). These practical strategies counteracted the inherently unequal power relations between my co-researchers and me. While not without its challenges, the IPAR approach and the use of Photo-voice allowed the research team to name (in a Freirean sense) social barriers to self-determination in their everyday lives. Further, it introduced an epistemologically different perspective to the field of disability research, dominated as it is by quantitative research.

Carolyn: Can you briefly explain this different epistemological perspective for me?

The Right to Name Their World

Janice: Certainly. The major difference lies in the way disability is understood. Traditionally, disability is regarded as a problem located within the individual. Australian legislation such as the Disability Discrimination Act (Australian Government, 1992) describes disability in terms of an individual's functional deficit. This is called the medical model of disability (Barnes, 2007). However, I used the social model of disability, which sees people as disabled by the imposition of physical, social and attitudinal barriers. The New Zealand Government also embraces the social model in its official disability strategy:

Disability is not something individuals have. What individuals have are impairments. They may be physical, sensory, neurological, psychiatric, intellectual or other impairments. Disability is the process which happens when one group of people create barriers by designing a world only for their way of living, taking no account of the impairments other people have. (New Zealand Ministry of Social Development – Office for Disability Issues, 2009)

Carolyn: OK, so how did choosing this social model of disability inform your research?

Janice: The Penrith Photo-voice Project provided team members with the opportunity to name the things in society that disable them. The social model allowed the team to expose how life was unnecessarily difficult because society is set up for able-bodied, high-functioning people. From the social model perspective, we can see that society creates barriers. These are not randomly placed, nor is social life chaotic; it is strategic and organised (Smith, 1990).

Opportunities for people labelled with learning difficulties to exercise control over their lives are often limited. I was interested to find out what these barriers were from those actually affected by them, how the barriers arose, who benefits and how they might be removed. Inevitably this led to employing institutional ethnography (IE), in conjunction with IPAR, to explicate the central issues behind identified barriers. IE helps researchers to look beyond individual perspectives to the outside forces that shape experience (Campbell & Gregor, 2004). IE asks, "How did the barriers get there and how are they socially organised?"

It has been successfully used in collaborative research undertaken with people with impairment (Campbell, Copeland, & Tate, 1998). But IE is text-based and conceptually abstract, and could therefore alienate researchers with learning difficulties and limited literacy. In the context of our research IE needed to be implemented using accessible methods. This multi-method/methodological approach allowed the co-researchers to exercise their rights, to develop their level of social awareness and to plan and execute social change in a supportive collaboration with others.

Carolyn: So, developing IPAR within the "Rights, Camera, Action!" framework opened a creative space for those with learning difficulties and limited literacy to claim their right to accessible involvement in collaborative, inclusive qualitative research. What about the issue of accessible methods that sits alongside that?

Janice: Photo-voice proved to be a flexible and accessible method by which we identified the research problematic (barriers), developed the text to be analysed (IE) and disseminated the findings. Let me explain.

CAMERA

Photo-Voice Method

Photo-voice is a research tool using photography to critically explore the world. Developed by Caroline Wang during the 1990s (Wang, 1999), it has been successfully used in inclusive research (Booth & Booth, 2003; Woolrych, 2004). Photo-voice elevates people to the status of expert in the analysis of their own lives rather than making their lives available for analysis by others. It places people in control of how they represent themselves, affording opportunity for self-determination.

Photo-voice is underpinned by three theoretical understandings: Freire's critical pedagogy, feminist theory and community-based photography (Wang & Redwood-Jones, 2001).

Carolyn: What are some of the key benefits of Photo-voice?

Janice: Photography makes the abstract concrete and is way by which people can use their own photographs to illuminate their experience of the world (Booth & Booth, 2003). Photo-voice facilitates discussions with direct stakeholders on issues that concern them. It is accessible to anyone who can learn to handle a camera, and does not require literacy skills. The technique is potent in assisting those who have difficulty articulating their thoughts. The camera enables people to creatively express themselves in their own images, words, and reflections – naming their world and photographically voicing their story. Employing Photo-voice as an IPAR method also protects against the tendency of primary researchers in participatory ethnography to negotiate participants' realities according to their own frames of reference (Manias & Street, 2001). I found it incredibly exciting!

Carolyn: I'm really keen to know how you set up your Photo-voice research project.

Loading

Janice: As the people with whom I wanted to research generally have little control in their lives, the opportunity for self-selection (rather than referral by a disability service) to participate in the Photo-voice Project was important. I promoted the project through the community and held a public information session in May 2007. I was encouraged during this meeting by the fact that many of those interested in registering for the project already seemed to have a good understanding of social barriers and were eager for action. Examples of social barriers raised by the audience at the information session included:

> You get picked on at school because you're different. It's like racism (Kathy, 23/5/2007).

> Sometimes I have control of my money, sometimes I don't. It is controlled by Mum and the carers (Alex, 23/5/2007).

> It's a barrier that I have to go to bed at 8:30pm. That's my bedtime but I'm 19 years old (William, 23/5/2007).

> By June 2007 a group of six young people (18-24 yrs) labelled with mild-moderate learning difficulties had self-selected to form an IPAR team.

Carolyn: I presume you didn't just hand everyone a camera and send them off without any preparation. How did it work out in practice?

Shooting

Janice: IPAR takes time and patience. Usually, people require time to talk through the issues in a critical dialogue of "authentic listening and speaking" (Smith, Willms, & Johnson, 1997, p. 8). We met in a neutral environment for several weeks to discuss the purpose of the research group, the concepts of self-determination and social barriers that limit self-determination, and to collaboratively establish a group code of conduct ensuring a safe and respectful environment. A professional photographer provided basic photographic technique training. During a workshop on privacy and photography ethics the Photo-voice group drafted their own participant consent form to be signed by anyone photographed. Although some of the group were unable to read the whole document, they collaboratively composed the language used, demonstrated their understanding of its purpose in discussion, and agreed on its final content and structure. All group members were issued with disposable cameras with which to name their social barriers by capturing on film those things that limited the control they could exert over their lives and that stopped them doing things other young people can choose to do. Some members preferred their own digital cameras and these were by far the better tool. They facilitated more accurate framing of the subject, were cost-effective, and enabled the group to view the photos on screen prior to printing. The group brought photos to discuss weekly. One-to-one discussions on the stories behind the photos were taped with permission of the photographer. Captions were extracted from the recorded stories and agreed upon by the group. Peer support (photographing in pairs) was used to assist those who had difficulty completing their films. Utilising local library and university computer facilities, several team members applied their information technology skills to download digital photos, develop photo files of emerging barrier themes, draft invitations to the planned photographic exhibition launch, and create a PowerPoint presentation of our work.

Downloading

Photo-voice proved to be an exciting and empowering medium for the group. All team members had the responsibility of self-determining what they would photograph. Some were invigorated by the freedom to photograph whatever they wanted and by the removal of financial considerations. One participant with a digital camera took some hundreds of photos. Many were powerful images. Photo-voice was effective in radically changing traditional research relations. It shifted power and knowledge production/distribution from "the academy" to become the shared responsibility of the research team. Charged with the responsibility of identifying the issues to be explored, the IPAR team set the research agenda.

By the end of August 2007 the group had chosen 80 photographs for enlargement and framing for the Penrith Photo-voice Project public exhibitions. Photos with captions were displayed according to the barrier themes identified by the group's photographic text analysis. Barrier themes included Government Regulations, Employment, Education, Public Transport (buses & trains), Other Transport (taxis), Communication (telephone access), No Money, Other People and Rules That Restrict/Control. The group developed strategies to choose which particular barrier(s) to investigate further, including critical group dialogue with consensus agreement and a pictorial visitor survey at the launch of their photographic exhibition The exhibition itself allowed group members to provide creative input to the project – they suggested a "lucky draw" prize to motivate visitors to do the surveys, shared the responsibility of planning and catering for the function, decorating the venue and discussing their work on the night with visitors (including the local Mayor and Member of Parliament). Public Transport was one barrier chosen for further investigation.

The first stage of the Penrith Photo-voice Project ascertained the problematic(s) to be explored and established an entry point for IE. The project gave group members freedom to expose and challenge oppressive social barriers, using inclusive and accessible research tools. As a result of the Photo-voice exhibitions, offers of advocacy were made to the group by the local Member of Parliament to speak on their behalf to the NSW Minister of Transport.

Carolyn: I was privileged to attend the exhibition. What did the group do next?

ACTION!

Janice: Our first action to explore the Public Transport barrier to self-determination was to take an excursion on Sydney's trains, buses and ferries. Photographs were taken of technology, signage and written instructions provided by the transport authorities (supposedly) to assist and inform the public. We found that some of us were unable to access/understand much of this information. The team developed and undertook a number of textual analyses of signage including the Penalty Notice shown in Figure 26.1.

Figure 26.1.
Inaccessible signage
(William, 3 October 2007)

Demonstrating considerable analytical skills and insight, they critiqued the formatting of the notice:

It has too many words and they're too little. (Andrew, 3/10/07)

You can't read across the page. It's in columns. It's boring too. The black writing on the white background. I don't even want to read that sign. (William, 3/10/07)

This is a textual analysis. The group understood the sign was textually dense:

No one is going to read all that. Who has time to read all that before they catch their train? (Bart, 3/10/07)

When asked to consider why the sign was there if people could not reasonably be expected to read all the information, Bart's insightful reply was: To cover their butts (Bart, 3/10/07).

This is a fledgling IE, examining ruling relations and institutional forces. We suspected that rather than genuinely informing the public, this sign was for the benefit of the transport authorities rather than the travelling public.

We also critiqued the Sydney Ferries sign shown in Figure 26.2. After a group discussion (critical dialogue) of this sign Bart observed,

This sign says, "Attention Sydney Ferries Customers" but it should say "who can read English", 'cause people who can't read, and visitors, and that, they can't read this sign. And that's not fair. (3/10/07)

Figure 26.2.
Inaccessible signage
(Andrew, 3 October 2007)

Bart recognised the tacit assumption that all the travelling public can access information on signs. This barrier excluded not only people who could not read, but also those who could not understand English. Bart's textual critique exposed inaccessible signage and technology rather than limited literacy as a barrier which disabled commuters. His observation that overseas visitors could be also disadvantaged displayed awareness of the breadth of the exclusivity of the text. Its inaccessibility was a disabling barrier that had nothing to do with impairment. This was a consciousness-raising experience for us all. We also analysed numerous other public transport technologies and signage including ticket machines, indicator boards and timetables. Applying institutional ethnography methods, the research team sensed the complex ruling relations behind the public transport system. Through critical discussion the team decided that safety notices were erected because of influences from authorities outside the transport department.

They also recognised that fares were set not by stationmasters or ticket inspectors but by outside influences, a "ruling relation" in IE language, with which commuters interact invisibly and unconsciously every time they buy a ticket and travel.

Carolyn: What were some of the specific outcomes from the Photo-voice Project?

Janice: Many powerful outcomes occurred as a result of our team co-creating qualitative research. I'll give you a few specific examples, others are given on our website (www.penrithphoto-voice.net). The team decided to send letters to Sydney Ferries, Hillsbus and

RailCorp. We also informed the NSW Minister for Transport of our dissatisfaction with the general public transport system. The letters included both text and photographs, the latter allowing the group's photo-voices to be heard directly by the recipients. All letters received replies, and the Minister thanked us for our input and our recommendations.

We liaised with the Independent Living Centre, making them aware of our research findings and informing their disability access report called "You're Welcome" (Evernden, 2008a) and conference paper (Evernden, 2008b). We exercised our democratic rights by meeting with our local State MP, showing our photos and raising our concerns. We exercised citizenship by contributing to the NSW Government Review of the Disability Standards for Accessible Public Transport (2008) by completing a questionnaire and sending a written submission –prepared by me but expressing the concerns of the group as articulated during our meetings – supplemented with photographic data. On behalf of the group and under its direction, I wrote to the Australian Human Rights Commissioner, Graeme Innes, who replied by thanking us for raising these civil rights issues. The team was impressed.

It's good they read our letter and wrote back. I wouldn't think they would. (Bart, 16/1/08)

It was good that we had something to say. (William, 16/1/08)

William was right. Using their *photo-voices* we named the issues. William's comment also indicated that the team members were dismantling their assumptions about themselves. The Photo-voice Project also empowered one group member to take individual social action with his local bus company to improve services. It was a great example of self-determination. The group member recognised that he had the skills and right to take action, and that proactive steps could cause positive social change.

CONCLUSION

Carolyn: Janice, thank you so much. Incorporating inclusive participatory action research with institutional ethnography is certainly challenging, especially when the collaborators have learning difficulties and are non-literate. You've shown how traditional research concepts and methods can be complex and exclusive. Photo-voice has emerged as an accessible means to articulate the problematic and make the institutional ethnographic process more accessible to people with learning difficulties. It is important to ensure that research processes and outcomes are socially just. IPAR and Photo-voice have enabled people labelled with learning difficulties to claim their rights to participate in research concerning themselves. You've employed the camera as a tool to identify the research problematic, to develop the text to be analysed, and as a means of disseminating the findings. And finally, this small innovative band of social researchers has taken action to address social barriers and has made a significant contribution to knowledge. They certainly challenge the stereotypes of people labelled with learning difficulties. Your excitement about developing IPAR and discovering its potential as a creative space for co-creating qualitative research is infectious.

ACKNOWLEDGEMENTS

Janice: It has been exciting and a great pleasure to work with my Photo-voice Project co-researchers: Andrew, Anne, Bart, Gill, James and William. I am also very grateful to Dr Debbie Horsfall for many constructive discussions.

REFERENCES

Australian Government. (1992). *Disability Discrimination Act*. Available: http://www.comlaw.gov.au/ComLaw/Legislation/ActCompilation1.nsf/0/02E50FC08E783ED7CA2 57609000288E1?OpenDocument, accessed March 23, 2010.

Barnes, C. (2007). Disability activism and the struggle for change: Disability, policy and politics in the UK. *Education, Citizenship and Social Justice, 2*(3), 203-221.

Booth, T., & Booth, W. (2003). In the frame: Photovoice and mothers with learning difficulties. *Disability & Society, 18*(4), 431-422.

Campbell, M.L., Copeland, B., & Tate, B. (1998). Taking the standpoint of people with disabilities in research: Experiences with participation. *Canadian Journal of Rehabilitation, 12*(2), 95-104.

Campbell, M.L., & Gregor, F.M. (2004). *Mapping social relations: A primer in doing institutional ethnography*. Walnut Creek, CA: Altamira Press.

Central England People First. (2000). *Who are we?* Available: http://www.peoplefirst.org.uk/whoarewe.html, accessed August 31, 2010.

Emerson, E., Hatton, C., Thompson, T., & Parmenter, T. (Eds.) (2004). *The international handbook of applied research in intellectual disabilities*. Chichester: John Wiley.

Evernden, J. (2008a). Capot, not kaput! Talking point. *Independent Living, 23*(4), 20.

Evernden, J. (2008b). The "You're Welcome" project: Designing an age-friendly public domain. Paper presented at *The International Federation on Ageing 9th Global Conference*. Available: http://www.ilcnsw.asn.au/assets/2008_DesigningAnAgeFriendlyPublicDomain.pdf,   accessed October 23, 2010.

Gaventa, J. (1988). Participatory research in North America. *Convergence, 24*(2-3), 19-28.

Manias, E., & Street, A. (2001). Rethinking ethnography: Reconstructing nursing relationships. *Journal of Advanced Nursing, 33*(2), 234-242.

New Zealand Ministry of Social Development – Office for Disability Issues (2009). *Disability in New Zealand: A changing perspective*. Available: http://www.odi.govt.nz/resources/guides-and-toolkits/disability-perspective/disability-nz.html, accessed March 10, 2009.

Ollerton, J., Kirkwood, M., Boyle, R., & Roberts, J. (2009). Rights, Camera, Action: The Penrith Photo-voice inclusive participatory action research. Paper presented at the *Disability Studies Conference*, 26 June 2009. Available: http://dsrc.arts.unsw.edu.au/news-and-events/disability-studies-conference-australia-163.html, accessed July 27, 2010.

Reason, P., & Bradbury, H. (Eds.) (2008). *The Sage handbook of action research: Participative inquiry and practice*. (2nd ed.). London: Sage.

Smith, D. (1990). *The conceptual practices of power: A feminist sociology of knowledge*. Boston: Northeastern University Press.

Smith, S., Willms, D., & Johnson, N. (Eds.) (1997). *Nurtured by knowledge: Learning to do participatory action research*. New York: The Apex Press.

UN Chronicle. (2004). "Nothing about us without us": Recognizing the rights of people with disabilities. *UN Chronicle Online Edition, 41*(4).
   Available:http://www.un.org/Pubs/chronicle/2004/issue4/0404p10.html, accessed October 23, 2010.

Walmsley, J. (2001). Normalisation, emancipatory research and inclusive research in learning disability. *Disability & Society, 16*(2), 187-205.

Wang, C. (1999). Photovoice: A participatory action research strategy applied to women's health. *Journal of Women's Health, 8*(2), 185-192.

Wang, C.C., & Redwood-Jones, Y.A. (2001). Photovoice ethics: Perspectives from Flint Photovoice. *Health Education & Behavior, 28*(5), 560-572.

Woolrych, R. (2004). Empowering images: Using Photovoice with tenants with special needs. *Housing, Care and Support, 7*(1), 31-35.

Janice M. Ollerton PhD
Social Justice Social Change Research Unit
University of Western Sydney, Australia

Carolyn R. Kelshaw MA
Fellow of Christian Educators Professional Association, Australia

SECTION 5: BECOMING TRANSFORMED THROUGH CREATIVE RESEARCH

CHRISTINE BOOMER AND DONNA FROST

27. OUR JOURNEYS OF BECOMING AUTHENTIC RESEARCHERS

Becoming Transformed through Critical Creative Research

We invite you to imagine sitting looking out at a landscape, which is surreal, fractured, showing glimpses of parallel yet linked worlds. One side is a rugged mountainous landscape, shrouded in mist. The land appears almost barren, but there are winding and perilous paths that lead out of the mist should you choose to take them. In the foreground is a fast running river, alive with white water, energised by the falling rocks that cause its path to dance and change. The other side is brighter, more vibrant and alive. Here there is sun nurturing growth and flourishing with spirals of activity as people journey through, discovering. As you take the road through this amazing landscape you encounter the fracture between the worlds, here you make a choice. Do you venture in and see where it leads? We invite you to journey with us into our transformational landscape.

We are both nurses, educators, practice developers, practitioner researchers and part-time PhD students. When we were invited to write this chapter we engaged in critical and creative ways of working (walking in nature, using creative arts media [imagery] and critical dialogue) to share our journeys and help us plan our writing. Although there were clear differences in our experiences, this initial work highlighted a number of common themes which appeared significant and which have contributed to our transformation and subsequent action as researchers. We continued to utilise both the critical and creative as we wove our writing. It is our aim in this chapter first to outline our understanding of transformation set within the context of critical creative research. Then we share our journeys of transformation by the means of individual reflective narratives, both to set the scene and to allow the reader to get to know us. Finally we explore the common themes from our journeys, outlining how we believe they have contributed to our becoming authentic in our research.

Transformation within the Context of Critical Creative Research

Put simply, to transform is to change or be changed in nature, and transformation is a marked change (Compact Oxford English Dictionary, 2005). However, this belies the complexity that has been the transformational experience for us. In illustrating our understanding of transformation we first visit Mezirow's (among others) transformative learning theory. In his early work (1981) on a critical theory

J. Higgs et al., (eds.), Creative Spaces for
Qualitative Researching: Living Research, 281–290
© *2011 Sense Publishers. All rights reserved.*

of adult learning and education, Mezirow drew from the work of Habermas, primarily in relation to knowledge constitutive interest – the emancipatory knowledge, which requires moving beyond subjective meanings to the position where action can occur (Carr & Kemmis, 1986). Mezirow (1981) explained that emancipatory action is distinctively a domain of adult learning. It can take the form of sudden insight, but is often a staged process, or "series of transitions" (p. 7) which subsequently through self-reflection facilitate the transformation. And that transformation can be viewed as a fresh way of viewing life experience and situations (Taylor, 2007). If we are to live and act as intentional researchers and practitioners we must fully understand our actions, and Mezirow (1991) challenged us to explore the values, beliefs, knowledge and personal assumptions on which our action is based. Critical reflection (often accompanied by critical discourse) is the means which enables transparency, processing of emotions, and subsequently finding self in a better position to guide future action (Matthew-Maich, Ploeg, Jack, & Dobbins, 2010). Transformative learning is not just an epistemological process where one changes for example a worldview; it is also an ontological one, where this change of view changes the way of being (Lange, 2004). Thus the process of critical (self-) reflection results in perspective transformation, which manifests as continuous development of the individual (Beeston & Higgs, 2001).

Critical creative research is still somewhat on the boundary of traditional qualitative research and it is often associated with transformational research (McCormack & Titchen, 2006; Titchen & Armstrong, 2007). We both accept and embrace the ability of research to transform both the researcher(s) and the researched phenomenon (Higgs & Titchen, 2007). For this to be a reality requires the researcher to live authentically, enabled by critique of self, values, knowledge and being. The critically creative researcher must actively engage in reflective and reflexive action.

Within Fay's (1987) complex schema of critical social science, sub-theory 4, transformative action, details what needs to be changed and an action plan for how this social transformation is to be achieved. However this still gives the impression that transformation is, although cognitively and often emotionally challenging, straightforwardly realised. The reality we and others have experienced in our practice development and research work has proved otherwise. McCormack and Titchen (2006), in critiquing and further developing the theoretical understanding of practice development, introduced the new critical creativity worldview. Critical creativity is a paradigmatic synthesis challenges Fay's (1987) accepted schema, specifically in relation to how transformative action is achieved. McCormack and Titchen argue that human flourishing is both the means and the end of transformational research and (practice) development and that creativity is the means by which transformative action is achieved. Others, too, have emphasised the importance of creativity. Freire (1970/1993) and Fals Borda and Rahman (1991), for example, considered it an essential and defining aspect of our humanity. They contended that we cannot flourish if we are restrained from exercising our creativity.

Thus although we accept much of the theoretical literature around the concept of transformation, we view achieving transformation as complex. The critical reflection and critical discourse explored in the transformation learning literature are only part of the story. We believe in the need to embrace not only our left brain (cognitive) but also our right brain (artistic) capacities to allow transformative action to occur, to achieve transformation and move towards human flourishing.

As this chapter progresses we explore our theoretical understanding of transformation in the context of our experiences. For now, however, we would like to share our individual narratives that reflect our journeys (to date), before we unravel and explore further.

INDIVIDUAL NARRATIVES

Christine's Narrative: "From Technical Undoing to Getting Going and Beyond"

Dark side playfulness
Connecting role in action
Eyes open to self

This haiku reflects unravelling, through critical creativity, my experiences of trying to get going in the field in my PhD action research study. Although from the outset I was pushed by my supervisor, I had initially avoided and then actively resisted venturing into the complex world of philosophy prior to commencing my fieldwork. Having stepped off the cliff edge (this is how it felt at the time) into the choppy waters that constituted the field I encountered a number of hurdles. This was a time of major (regional) healthcare re-structuring, resulting in an unstable context. I was very much mixed up in this and was experiencing personal job insecurity. I was attempting to recruit participants for my study at this time, which proved very slow. It was evident that this time of instability and uncertainty was affecting us all. I became disheartened and lost motivation, belief in self and in my study. At this time I elected to take a leave of absence from the university and suspend my study.

During this leave of absence I found light at the end of what had been a dark tunnel and, with the help of my supervisor, refined and revised my study to better fit with my new context. At this time I was invited to present my experiences of "getting going" at an international action research course. This required me to unravel my experiences and saw me utilising critically creative processes to gain deeper understanding. I had previously experienced difficulty trusting creativity in my research work but I found using critical creativity in this context liberating. I see this as a time of significant transformation for me, one step of many on my journey.

Undertaking this work saw me finally appreciating the need to engage with philosophy, both to further understand my experiences (technical un-doing) but ultimately to shape my "living the doing in action", that is, being an authentic intentional researcher. However, this was a world that remained challenging for me and it was not until we started to use critical creativity as a framework for my academic supervision that I found a way to process the myriad of complexities and subsequently name my theoretical and philosophical stance for the study. I see this as the next significant transformation of my journey.

Despite naming my stance, however, I had not actually embodied it, and consequently was not actively and intentionally using it in all aspects of my research. There was not congruence between my espoused values and my ways of working, I was not living the being as an intentional and authentic researcher. Coming to this realisation and ultimately taking responsibility for my future action is my current transformation space, one where I am actively working in the field with my research participants, constantly challenging self through reflection and reflexive action to be true to both myself and my theoretical and philosophical stance. I know my transformational journey will continue throughout my research career (getting going and beyond).

Donna's Narrative: "Finding My Place to Stand"

Mystery dark, deep.
Dips toes, splash, bursts through, breathes in
Turangawaewae[1]

Reasonably early in my work as a nurse I would have described "transformation of self and others" as a significant professional goal. Yet for much of my career my experience was that of having high ideals that I could never live up to. My approaches to reflection and problem solving were almost exclusively cognitive. I was unaware of the ways in which I used my body to assess situations or to process information. I was unaware of different ways of knowing – except in the limited sense of recognising that theoretical knowing needed to be augmented by practical know-how. I had read about critical theory and felt that it resonated with my values and beliefs about the world. In practice it was another of my ideals.

As a master's student, these ideas were challenged by my supervisor. I was encouraged to explore different ways of knowing, to use creative approaches to reflection and supervision. We used metaphors, for example, when re-connecting and evaluating my supervision. We walked together in nature and used our experiences on these walks as a framework for the learning points within the supervision. It was interesting and often powerful, but I wondered about my motivation for engaging in these ways of working. Was I blindly adopting my supervisor's ideas? How would these approaches be received by others?

I went on, during my master's research, to experience the enlightening and empowering consequences of using creative arts with people who lived with communication difficulties. Paintings revealed complexities of cognition and memory among participants which would have otherwise remained invisible. Furthermore, the process of painting helped me, as researcher, in the final stages of analysis. My own painting summarised the results well, representing the feelings and ideas more fluently than a written account alone. At this point I began to embrace the idea of creativity for myself, at least in terms of exploring ways of knowing and representing understandings of the world.

The transition to PhD research was enormously challenging for me. I felt unable to grasp the complexities of the philosophy and anxious about being able to facilitate the depth of involvement I would be asking from research participants.

The turning point was a supervision session in which my supervisor and I were walking by a lake. I felt completely out of my depth within our discussion about philosophy, although before we set out I had felt myself well prepared. A picnic table beside the lake provoked a strong image for me, of me sitting at the picnic table, over the years, looking out at the lake and forest before me. This represented well my engagement with the philosophical world up until this point. Over the years I had been receiving visitors at my table and hearing stories about their journeys and explorations in the philosophical landscape. I needed now to rise up, walk away from the table, take the plunge and go exploring myself. This was, in retrospect, a powerful and liberating insight.

Walking back to school afterwards we passed a child playing in a high and precarious position on a jungle gym. My supervisor asked me how I thought she'd managed to get up there. I replied that I had no idea but that I was very sure that I, as a child, would never have got there. I would not even have attempted it. I was all for playing it safe. We looked at each other and laughed. This too was a powerful metaphor, in this case of my reticence in risk-taking in terms of critical creativity and examining my way of being in the world. I was no longer content to play it safe. I wanted to be intentional and explicit about pushing my boundaries and engaging my creativity within my philosophical and wider PhD journey. And so I set out.

EXPLORING OUR JOURNEYS OF TRANSFORMATION

Our individual narratives, although clearly demonstrating unique experiences, share themes within our journeys of becoming transformed as critically creative researchers. In preparing to write about these commonalities we individually reflected on the narratives, using pictures, painting, metaphor and haiku to raise the themes. The haikus illustrate the two key themes in our narratives and journeys: our initial resistance to engagement with critical creativity, and eventual engagement with critical creativity enabling authenticity. We now explore these themes with reference both to our experience and to the literature.

Resistance to Engagement with Critical Creativity

Daunting, nebulous
Daring path of risk taking
Challenge, face shadows

When first sharing our stories with each other we were struck by our common experience of initially resisting engagement with critical creativity. Using the freedom we had been given to explore our own ways of making sense of the research "landscape" and determining a paradigm within which we would locate our research projects, we consistently turned away from or sidled around the ideas and ways of working within critical creativity, particularly those which involved the use of creative arts. What was going on here?

As nurses and research students in the Western tradition we had been powerfully socialised into a particular worldview. Worldviews, or belief systems, are typically deep-seated and refined. They include "notions about nature and reality, cause and effect, and standards for discriminating a fact from a value" (Bailey, Ford, & Raelin, 2009, p. 30). In the Western tradition, for example, propositional knowledge and cognitive ways of knowing, are traditionally respected, rewarded and privileged (Higgs & Titchen, 2001; Cowling, 2008). Belief systems can also be described as our theories-in-use (Argyris & Schön, 1974), or our mental models (Senge, 1990). Both terms give the impression that belief systems are held in our minds, but they are, of course, also carried in our bodies and given expression in our ways of being in the world. It requires effort, and McCormack and Titchen (2006) emphasised both critical and creative effort, to surface these ideas and assumptions, examine and unpick them and begin the process of transformation. Such work is by no means simple. Argyris (1991, 2003), and Argyris and Schön (1974) showed how skilled professionals are in *avoiding* the kind of learning that enables us to challenge and alter our theories-in-use. This kind of learning involves uncomfortable challenges to our self-image. It involves putting off what we think we know and setting aside that which felt certain and secure. Unsurprisingly, we protect ourselves and others from the pain and uncertainty involved in this type of transition.

In terms of our own stories, the beginning stages of this process certainly felt daunting, and the alternatives seemed nebulous and difficult to conceptualise. We had to face our own worldviews, but also the assumed worldviews of our peers and the wider research community. If we took this path, what form would our research take? Would it be rigorous and defensible? Would it be considered valid and valuable by others? What would be the nature of the challenges we would face along the way?

At some point we both reached an impasse. We could not emerge from a crisis point or continue to make meaning of our research journeys without engaging with ourselves and our work in critically creative ways. At the right times we received implicit support, or explicit permission – even urging – from our supervisors to take the plunge; "just paint it!" At this point the use of creative arts was both means and ends. Feeling able to engage our creativity and use creative arts was evidence of a transformation that had taken place for both of us. But it was also the means of surfacing and illuminating our values, different ways of knowing and (some of the) barriers to further growth.

Despite the high level of support received from our supervisors, the element of risk was felt keenly by both of us in these early stages. Embarking on a major path without knowing how to get there requires faith and belief that you will get there, even though you don't know how. A daring path of risk taking indeed. Heron (1996) described the powerful emotions that can be engendered by work of this sort, often resulting in periods of anxiety or even distress. He highlighted the spiritual nature of such transitions, as did McCormack and Titchen (2007), according to whom we call on our spiritual intelligence when being creative and moving into the unknown. They wrote further of arriving "at the boundary of order and chaos" (McCormack & Titchen, 2007, p. 51). For both of us, this boundary involved the edge of illumination and the beginning of darkness. Our willingness to enter the shadows and explore them from within was, again, both means and ends. We could not initially have visualised this terrain for ourselves, yet in exploring; we were challenging and facing our shadows, and came to experience the power of working in critical and creative ways.

Engagement with Critical Creativity Enabling Authenticity

Turbulent yet calm
Stretch self to transform, flourish
Being authentic

Navigating through the nebulous, daring to take risks and "face shadows" by embracing challenge has reaped rewards for us personally and professionally. In this new space we find ourselves being authentic. As healthcare professionals, practice that is authentic is core to our professional standards. Despite this, living authentically in practice is in reality complex. Being authentic is about reaching decisions that truly reflect all that we as individuals perceive as important, which includes values, beliefs and attitudes (McCormack, 2001). Moreover, being authentic is a core construct and value within the worldviews and frameworks that inform and guide our action as practice developers, researchers and practitioners (e.g. critical companionship, Titchen, 2000; person-centred practice, McCormack & McCance, 2006). Shaw et al. (2008) linked authenticity with ways of working that include demonstrating value and respect, integrity, transparency, love and care. McCormack (2001, p. 249) wrote, "while many aspects of an individual's reality may be shared with others so that common understandings can exist... it is the individuality of our personal meanings that determines 'who I am'". Although we had both spent time developing our "tapestry" for our professional lives as nurses, working as practice developers and subsequently researchers required us to delve much deeper into what made us tick. In exploring philosophy to inform our PhD studies we became exposed to new and complex understandings. At this time it could be easy simply to accept the beliefs of others and be swept along in the moment, thereby taking these on as one's own (Heidegger, 1990, cited by McCormack, 2001). However, at this stage we continued constantly to question what we were exploring in line with our existing values and beliefs.

As outlined earlier, living as critical creative researchers requires us to be authentic in our action; but authentic to what? Our philosophical, theoretical and methodological work has seen us gain clarity of understanding of the frameworks that guide our action and being, thereby "being true to self, and striving towards epistemological and ontological authenticity" (Higgs & Titchen, 2007, p. 5). Initially a willingness to engage and latterly authentic engagement with critical creativity enabled congruence to be achieved between the espoused and the lived. To really discover self as person and researcher, and to discover and explore incongruence in ways that were safe but powerful, enabled us to identify ways in which we could move towards authenticity.

For us, achieving authenticity in our professional lives and as researchers has been intertwined with our life journeys. It involves transitions towards intentionality, towards consciousness of and congruence between our espoused theories (about self) and our theories-in-use. Therefore it is also a story of learning how to learn about self and our way of being in the world. With this learning comes a growing capacity to change, to develop our being in the world, and to actively journey towards human flourishing. Critical creativity challenged our emotional intelligence (Goleman, 1996), as we often found our rational mind telling us one thing, and our emotions another; and when (now) utilising creativity as researchers we constantly have to manage this tension intentionally and embrace our use of creativity authentically. Thereby we are becoming more aware of our spiritual intelligence (McCormack & Titchen, 2007) as we consider challenges of value, meaning and meaning-making – aspects which become easier to identify and address when engaging our creativity and using creative methods.

Within this new space we embrace the turbulence. "Turbulent yet calm" (see the haiku above) is about us flowing with, spiralling in and embracing this turbulence, or crisis (Fay, 1987), and subsequently moving forward, growing, flourishing – "stretch[ing] self to transform, flourish". Facilitated by intentional use of critical creativity, we are able to draw from the elements of the framework to dance the praxis spiral (McCormack & Titchen, 2007). By this we mean that we draw on hermeneutic (understanding) and emancipatory (doing) praxis to frame and shape our research. Working in such a way has seen us release control and embrace the new. Theory "U" (Scharmer, 2009) describes the different levels (sensing, presencing and realising) at which we perceive reality and action. If we are to gain in-depth understanding for change we need to engage in these. It is at the *presencing* level (Senge, Scharmer, Jaworski, & Flowers, 2005) where, by giving up our need to have control, we can let go, and are free to observe, allowing something new to emerge. This leads to transformation; we act differently based on new understanding.

CONSEQUENCES FOR OUR PRACTICE

What does our transformation look like? In reality this sees us with greater self-awareness. We experience a feeling of being grounded, of knowing where we stand in the world, of being able to handle challenges and also to offer challenge, in a supportive way, to others. We are becoming aware of and learning to articulate how we use our body and our senses, and aesthetics, not only to learn about the world but also to influence the world and to be true to our axiological principles. We are no longer reliant solely on the cognitive but find ourselves willing to travel the unknown path, flow with uncertainty, and trust in the creative and the cognitive as mean for human flourishing.

How do these changes manifest themselves? We now use critical creative approaches intentionally within our own work (e.g. when reading literature, when preparing for or summarising supervision, as a framework for supervision), in work with students or groups we are facilitating, and in work with research participants. We can explicate the evidence base for such approaches and therefore, through trusting the processes we use, we can be and are intentional and authentic in our practice. We are already experiencing the consequences as both researchers and people: transformation, authenticity, intentionality and flourishing!

NOTES

[1] "Turangawaewae" is Maori for "a place to stand".

REFERENCES

Argyris, C. (1991). Teaching smart people how to learn. *Harvard Business Review, 69*(3), 99-109.
Argyris, C. (2003). A life full of learning. *Organization Studies, 24*(7), 1178-1192.
Argyris, C., & Schön, D.A. (1974). *Theory in practice: Increasing professional effectiveness.* San Francisco: Jossey-Bass.
Bailey, J.R., Ford, C.M., & Raelin, J.D. (2009). Philosophical ties that bind practice: The case of creativity. *Journal of Management Inquiry, 18*(1), 27-38.
Beeston, S., & Higgs, J. (2001). Professional practice: Artistry and connoisseurship. In J. Higgs & A. Titchen (Eds.), *Practice knowledge and expertise in the health professions* (pp. 108-117). Oxford: Butterworth Heinemann.
Carr, W., & Kemmis, S. (1986). *Becoming critical: Education, knowledge and action research.* London: RoutledgeFalmer.
Compact Oxford English Dictionary (3rd ed.) (2005). Oxford: Oxford University Press.
Cowling, W.R. (2008). An essay on women, despair, and healing: A personal narrative. *Advances in Nursing Science, 31*(3), 249-258.
Fals Borda, O., & Rahman, M.A. (Eds.) (1991). *Action and knowledge: Breaking the monopoly with participatory action-research.* New York: Apex Press.
Fay, B. (1987). *Critical social science: Liberation and its limits.* Cambridge: Polity Press.
Freire, P. (1970/1993). *Pedagogy of the oppressed.* London: Penguin (First published by Continuum).
Goleman, D. (1996). *Emotional intelligence: Why it can matter more than IQ.* London: Bloomsbury.
Heidegger, M. (1990). *Being and time.* Oxford: Basil Blackwell.
Heron, J. (1996). *Co-operative inquiry: Research into the human condition.* London: Sage.
Higgs, J., & Titchen, A. (Eds.) (2001). *Practice knowledge and expertise in the health professions.* Oxford: Butterworth-Heinemann.
Higgs, J., & Titchen, A. (2007). Becoming critical and creative in qualitative research. In J. Higgs, A. Titchen, D. Horsfall & H. Armstrong (Eds.), *Being critical and creative in qualitative research* (pp. 1-10). Sydney: Hampden Press.
Lange, E. (2004). Transformative and restorative learning: A vita dialectic for sustainable societies. *Adult Education Quarterly, 54*, 121-139.
Matthew-Maich, N., Ploeg, J., Jack, S., & Dobbins, M. (2010). Transformative learning and research utilization in nursing practice: A missing link? *Worldviews on Evidence-Based Nursing, 7*(1), 25-35.
McCormack, B. (2001). *Negotiating partnerships with older people: A person centred approach.* Aldershot: Ashgate.
McCormack, B., & McCance, T. (2006). Development of a framework for person-centred nursing. *Journal of Advanced Nursing, 56*(5), 472-479.
McCormack, B., & Titchen, A. (2006). Critical creativity: Melding, exploding, blending. *Educational Action Research: An International Journal, 14*(2), 239-266.
McCormack, B., & Titchen, A. (2007). Critical creativity: Melding, exploding, blending. In J. Higgs, A. Titchen, D. Horsfall & H. Armstrong (Eds.), *Being critical and creative in qualitative research* (pp. 43-55). Sydney: Hampden Press.
Mezirow, J. (1981). A critical theory of adult learning and education. *Adult Education, 32*(1), 3-24.

Mezirow, J. (1991). *Transformative dimensions of adult learning*. San Francisco: Jossey-Bass.

Scharmer, C.O. (2009). *Theory U: Leading from the future as it emerges*. San Francisco: Berrett-Koehler.

Senge, P.M. (1990). *The fifth discipline: The art and practice of the learning organisation*. London: Random House.

Senge, P., Scharmer, C.O., Jaworski, J., & Flowers, B.S. (2005). *Presence: Exploring profound change in people, organizations, and society*. London: Nicholas Brealey.

Shaw, T., Dewing, J., Young, R., Devlin, M., Boomer, C., & Legius, M. (2008). Enabling practice development: Delving into the concept of facilitation from a practitioner perspective. In K. Manley, B. McCormack & V. Wilson (Eds.), *International practice development in nursing and healthcare* (pp. 147-169). Oxford: Blackwell.

Taylor, E.W. (2007). An update of transformative learning theory: A critical review of the empirical research (1999-2005). *International Journal of Lifelong Education, 26*(2), 173-191.

Titchen, A., & Armstrong, H. (2007). Re-directing the vision: Dancing with light and shadows. In J. Higgs, A. Titchen, D. Horsfall & H. Armstrong (Eds.), *Being critical and creative in qualitative research* (pp. 151-163). Sydney: Hampden Press.

Titchen, A. (2000). *Professional craft knowledge in patient-centred nursing and the facilitation of its development*, University of Oxford DPhil Thesis. Oxford: Ashdale Press.

Christine Boomer RGN, MBA, PG Cert (Lifelong Learning), PhD candidate
Institute of Nursing Research/School of Nursing
University of Ulster and South Eastern Health and Social Care Trust
Belfast, Northern Ireland, UK

Donna Frost NZRN, BHSc (Nsg), MSc (Nsg), PhD candidate
Knowledge Centre for Evidence Based Practice, School of Nursing
Fontys University of Applied Sciences, The Netherlands
Institute of Nursing Research/School of Nursing, University of Ulster
Belfast, Northern Ireland, UK

DIANE TASKER, ANNETTE MCLEOD-BOYLE
AND DONNA BRIDGES

28. FROM PRACTICE TO RESEARCH AND BACK AGAIN

Living Transformations

In this chapter we follow the story of practitioners as they attempt to transition from practice to research and back to practice, working and changing their personal and professional selves in a living transformation. The phenomenon of transitioning from practice to research and back is of recent origin across all healthcare disciplines and has become part of the tertiary education experience for many postgraduate practitioners. For the purposes of convenience and access to recent experience, the personal narratives used in this chapter are those of two of the authors. References are made to other professions, and practitioners from different fields may feel resonance as they read this chapter. Transitioning through the development of a research persona can be a powerful and transformative journey for the individual. In this chapter, we explore some of the spaces and places inhabited by practitioners as they strive to become researchers and then as they integrate new skills and knowledge to transform themselves into "practitioner-researchers".

MELDING THE PRACTITIONER-RESEARCHER IDENTITY

Within the landscape of healthcare, healthcare professionals adopt a number of identities. Chan and Ng (2004) described clinical practitioners as being engaged with consumers and implementing interventions, and healthcare educators as promoting well-tested models and theories and teaching for practice. In contrast, they described researchers as those who construct and test theory and practice. Researchers obtain or generate evidence or new knowledge in a systematic and principled way in order to solve problems (Polgar & Thomas, 2000). The worlds of research and practice have previously been perceived as different communities of practice. Differences exist between the "scholarly professional", and the "professional scholar" (Gregory, 1997). Researching practitioners attempt to meld these identities.

Theoretically, practitioner-researchers possess an inherent understanding of practice through their experience of the workplace (Cusick & Lannin, 2008). They can therefore readily identify aspects of practice or the practice context that may need further investigation. The reported disconnect between knowledge generated

J. Higgs et al., (eds.), Creative Spaces for
Qualitative Researching: Living Research, 291–300

by research and knowledge used or sought in practice can potentially be addressed by practitioner-researchers (Mendenhall, 2007; Moore, 2008). "Theory needs to be articulated with practice as much as practice needs to be informed by the concepts it offers" (Edwards, 2002, p. 361, quoted by Pilkington, 2009). The integration of new knowledge into their practice enables practitioner-researchers to function as facilitators and agents of change (Foss & Moldenæs, 2007).

"Practitioner research provides a vehicle for practitioners to examine their practice and challenge the assumptions on which that practice is constructed" (Fox, Martin, & Green, 2007, p. 196). Some practitioners incorporate research into their usual practice by developing projects that address issues of relevance in a specific workplace or with a particular client group. Others enter the research arena by enrolling in higher degree programs such as Masters or Doctoral study. Because the act of researching is itself a discipline, with its own infrastructure of processes, practices and knowledge (Stewart, 2002), methodological underpinnings and correct procedures must be learned and understood. Many practitioner-researchers need to develop additional skills to successfully engage in research.

Two of the authors of this chapter (Diane and Annette) are currently undertaking doctoral studies while continuing to practise in clinical and/or teaching contexts. At the time of writing they exist within the transformation process, "betwixt and between" the worlds of practice and research (Turner, 1969; Deegan & Hill, 1991). The third author (Donna) has passed through this process and works to support doctoral students while also actively researching social and education issues. The varying nature of this experience assists consideration of the development and formation of practitioner-researchers.

A PHYSIOTHERAPIST'S TALE – DIANE

I have been a community-based physiotherapist for 30 years, working with people with chronic and complex healthcare needs in their homes, schools and workplaces. I became fascinated with the phenomenon of developing wellness for my clients and how the essential human relationship between physiotherapist, client, and family care team can influence that process. So many aspects of professional practice seem present and important but invisible and rarely spoken of, except in passing. Within physiotherapeutic practice, such implicit "craft" knowledge is considered interpretive and subjective, in contrast to more explicit evidence-based knowledge (Higgs, Richardson, & Abrandt Dahlgren, 2004).

Before considering postgraduate study I attended a professional seminar and heard some research papers, which resonated with me, offering an avenue for thinking about and acting on subliminal areas of interest within my physiotherapy practice. Postgraduate research study presented an exciting opportunity. However, I was not sure what the transition to study might mean.

Reflective Practitioner, Reflexive Researcher

Within my profession of physiotherapy, therapists have a well-deserved reputation for a "heads down, tails up" attitude to work. This attitude can occur with more quantitative evaluations of clinical work, resulting in a bypassing or sidelining of the more qualitative and humanistic aspects of work life. Dadds (2008) argued that practitioner-research can offer high levels of emotional relevance to both researchers and their audience, referring to it as *empathic validity*. Insight into the emotional aspects of practitioner research helps in understanding the cognitive and practical research outcomes and contributes to the worthwhile nature of practitioner research by its humanising effects on practitioner-researchers themselves, by its internal empathic validity and the researcher's audience, and by its external empathic validity (Dadds, 2008).

Reflection on practice and research about that practice help practitioners to locate and clarify previously veiled thought. Postgraduate research study provides opportunities to explore specific topics, to read more deeply and make connections between different areas of thought, constantly revisiting concepts to make sense and meaning. Before I embarked on this research journey there seemed nowhere for such ideas to be so carefully processed or communicated. The research process opened avenues to do so. I found a reflection journal to be a useful method of collating research thought development. This can help research practitioners to manage emotional issues arising from the research process (Arber, 2006). It is particularly important if practitioner-researchers are researching members of their own discipline effectively as insiders, as they attempt to interpret themselves as researchers (Edwards, 2002).

Although some of the skills needed for research can be compared to or drawn from clinical practice, I found that care needed to be taken not to assume that they were always the same. Pilkington (2009) and Arber (2006) discussed this tension between the different roles of practitioner and researcher, advising of the need to constantly review the way one interacts with others, depending on the role being played. I experienced an example of this when beginning to interview participants.

At first, establishing rapport and developing a conversation with research participants felt similar to a clinical situation, but I soon realised that I could not be the therapeutic "insider" that I had previously endeavoured to be for my clients. I was the researcher "outsider", both in the beginning and in the end. On the other hand, there was a generosity on the part of the research participants in sharing their feelings and experiences, which may paradoxically have been more open than the interaction they shared with their therapist in clinical situations. As the research process continued, I felt more comfortable and became able to shift my role from insider to outsider as required within interviews and focus groups.

Making room for the PhD and setting up support structures initially seemed simple but inevitably took longer than planned. Within the research setting there is an incredible multiplicity of tasks to be undertaken, but even when those tasks seem unrelated to the ongoing process their value can usually be seen after the event, adding a warp to the ongoing weave of research activities, helping me to gradually develop a woven material of new skills and knowledge with which to clothe my new endeavours for the ongoing research process.

Threshold Experiences and the Act of Writing

> " ... that private realm where self doubts
> must be confronted, where answers are
> found in the act of writing, and where the
> decision to claim a life of power must be made."
> (Deegan & Hill, 1991, p. 330)

Sociologists Deegan and Hill considered the processes that occur within doctoral candidature, describing the student researcher as a "liminal self with the structure of that self gradually being changed by the threshold experience of a rite de passage". (The word "liminal" derives from the Latin limen, meaning "threshold".) Practitioner-researchers step through a doorway from practice to research, and in doing so begin a process of self-examination in order to determine their existing assumptions in preparation for the research project ahead. Individually, such reflection necessarily has a destabilising effect on the person concerned.

A liminal journey makes the self a stranger: it stretches and sometimes severs the ties of meaning that link us with the everyday life to which we were accustomed (Deegan & Hill, 1991, p. 330).

Moving between the roles of practitioner and researcher, postgraduate students seek connections between their mind, their self and society in an effort to effect their transformation into a new identity. Such connection can be forged by the written word, making meaning and communicating that meaning to colleagues, supervisors and themselves. Just as a rough diamond is polished to reveal its facets to reflect the light as it is moved, so the development of scholarly and professional writing and its application to the area of inquiry being undertaken assist in the making of a new integrated practitioner-researcher. In the bigger picture, the empowerment of this process may assist the practitioner to bridge the gap between practice and research and enter the world of intellectual discourse. It has been suggested that it may also open up new threshold journeys for the individuals concerned, personally and professionally, every time they sit down to write (Deegan & Hill, 1991).

The Research/Practice Portal

Throughout my doctoral studies I have maintained some contact with my physiotherapy practice. Such a "research practice portal" allows my chosen research method to affect my actual day-to-day professional practice. There is mention in the literature of "knowledge portals", where networks and communities of practice can be facilitated by interactive IT processes (Van Baalen, Bloemhof-Ruwaard, & Van Heck, 2005). I see my research portal rather as an internal and personal process of role and identity changing, with obvious implications for improved knowledge sharing, networks and communities of practice for the developing practitioner-researcher.

Realisation and acknowledgment of the reciprocal effect between research and practice can be a seminal stage in deepening understanding of the interaction of the different personas needed for the doctoral journey. Criticality in relation to perceptions and assumptions is necessary for the ongoing research process. Such transformative learning involves critical appraisal and reflection, and can lead to the development of restructured and creative practice (Fenge, 2009). Research and practice may be seen as different aspects of professional practice but are also the tools of transition needed to enable the practitioner-researcher to travel back and forth through the portal between research and clinical practice. The production of knowledge within a practice context allows the dual emphasis of developing professional knowledge while also developing practice (Fenge, 2009).

Three years later, settling back from clinical work, reflecting and moving forward through the research process feels more comfortable to me now, occurring as it does from within the practitioner-researcher persona that I have been encouraged to develop, allowing me to look beyond myself as a person and as a physiotherapist. The research process seems to have allowed the development of a hiatus between my thinking spaces and the spaces I occupy with my clients and my research participants. Pilkington (2009) found that participants in his study of teacher practitioner-researchers also saw research as providing a space to think and reflect and possibly break old habits. Intellectually, there seems more "room to range" which can be a heady experience, creating excitement and joy in the process that literally wakes me early in the morning, ready to explore again. Perhaps, for me, the transformative process of my doctoral experience has opened up new worlds of possibility, rather than merely transforming me from one role to another.

A STORY FROM OCCUPATIONAL THERAPY – ANNETTE

Over the past 25 years I have enjoyed diversity, challenge and great satisfaction in my practice as an occupational therapist. Even now, my practice is characterised by an assortment of different roles and activities, namely (a) being a part-time academic teaching occupational therapy theory, assessment and professional reasoning; (b) working part-time as a clinician in a community-based programme for people with chronic illness; and (c) undergoing doctoral candidature in my spare time. While not anticipated, this is an interesting combination of roles, and I have been challenged recently by the suggestion that educator-practitioner-researchers have the responsibility of being role models by practising what we preach (Chan & Ng, 2004). This means that educators need to be competent practitioners, effective in research use and innovative in teaching and learning.

Becoming a competent practitioner has involved a journey incorporating numerous clinical jobs and interactions with many hundreds of people. Developing into an educator has also occurred over time and, seemingly, quite naturally. My greatest and most recent challenge has been the transition to the role of researcher. I have come to recognise that, as Foss and Moldenæs (2007) suggested, researchers and practitioners have different, though complementary, knowledge. To become effective as a researcher, I need to learn new skills and extend my knowledge.

Transformative Learning

Engaging in research higher degree programs often enables practitioner-researchers to develop and transform their own knowledge (Mendenhall, 2007). Working towards my Masters degree refreshed my understanding of previously rarely-considered research concepts that were introduced when I was an undergraduate. This study extended my understanding of a range of technical elements of research and also introduced me to the notion of philosophical standpoints and the critical importance of deciding which research approach was most suited to the questions being asked. Extending my knowledge in this way enabled me to be a more effective Honours supervisor, as I was able to give more appropriate direction and assistance to my students. It also enabled me to engage in formal and informal research with practitioners so that I could develop insight and understanding into what they perceived to be current trends, expectations and issues in practice in the clinical world. Such research has become a tool in my teaching practice, so that what I teach reflects what is relevant to practice and helps create a discernible link between the classroom and the clinical context. In this way I am able to directly link my transformed knowledge and skills to an area of daily practice (Burgess & Jones, 2006). My approach to practice has been transformed; I feel more confident, view topics from different perspectives, review and enhance what I teach, and help students to utilise different research methods.

Transformed Practice through Enhanced Understanding of Self

While completing my Masters degree I also came to the realisation that, for me, empirical methods often did not answer the questions I was really interested in – seeking to understand deeply the human experience of life, health and wellbeing (or lack of it), the influence of events and circumstances on living, and the impact of our practice on people's lives. So, despite performing quite well in statistics courses, I have discovered a stronger philosophical connection with qualitative research approaches and ideas. This is reflected in my chosen doctoral topic, through which I seek to understand more deeply the experience of interactions and relationships between allied health practitioners and consumers in inpatient rehabilitation settings. I can also see changes in my clinical practice, as I now consciously seek to understand more deeply the experience of daily life from my clients' perspectives, and seek to provide intervention that truly complements their specific circumstances and perceived needs.

My growing self-awareness has extended to other areas. Reflecting on the experience of doctoral study, I concur with Selby (2005, p. 1056), who wrote, "the frontiers you push back aren't just the scientific ones ... the significant ones had to do with self discipline, ... self confidence, and retaining some semblance of the idea you started with." I have learned that that I can improve my work efficiency and productivity by being more self-disciplined in planning the use of my time and energy. I have greater confidence to trial new teaching strategies in the classroom and to integrate new technology into my clinical practice. I am also more prepared to defend and pursue the development and implementation of new ideas to enhance students' experience in subjects that I teach.

Transition from Expert to Novice

The greatest development in my understanding, however, has occurred since commencing doctoral study. This has meant making a transition from the role of practitioner to that of student. Practitioners moving into research studies face transitions in relation to their identities as learners and as practitioners (Pilkington, 2009; Watts, 2009). In one community they may be confident leaders, but in 9zanother they may feel a novice. This has definitely been my experience; I have moved into the PhD student role feeling very much the novice, despite having previously completed other tertiary qualifications. This role has necessitated developing new networks that assist me to build social capital in the research environment (Pilkington, 2009) and support me in the learner role. Participating in regular research workshops with other PhD students and communicating closely with my supervisors has opened up a new world of research ideas and processes.

Transforming Insights and Understandings

Intimate engagement in the research process prompts me to challenge my assumptions about my own practice and how I understand and interpret the clinical and educational world in which I function. When I returned to part-time clinical practice three years ago I found clients' stories of their experiences of the healthcare system illuminating, as they helped me reorient myself to the clinical world. I was also troubled by some of the things I heard. I decided that my doctoral research would focus on one of the areas of concern. Of course, I have since come to realise that what might be troublesome to me may not be so for others, I have had to become far more critically reflective and reflexive, and have had to move beyond the comfortable into the unknown, questioning my motivations, actions, judgments and decisions (O'Hanlon, 1994; Fenge, 2009). Nevertheless, my hope is that the findings of my research will, in time, positively inform my own practice and that of others.

Redefinition of Self and Identity

Doctoral education has allowed transformation of my thinking, practice and professional identity. I have had to adopt new patterns of behaviour and new functions; there are new expectations to be met and new contexts that must be adapted to (Mendenhall, 2007). In joining a new community of practice, who I am as a professional, and how I see myself, are changing. Although I have always considered myself primarily a practitioner, playing dual roles of clinician and educator, I am slowly beginning to integrate the identity of researcher into my professional persona. Such redefining of professional identity appears consistent with the experience of other practitioners making the transition to the researcher role (Mendenhall, 2007). Rather than choosing one specific role, as some do, I have decided to integrate multiple professional roles into my practice. As such, I expect that in years to come, there will be continuing transformation within my professional identity. I would like to think that I will become a well-rounded, competent and ever-passionate educator-practitioner-researcher.

TRANSITIONS AND TRANSFORMATIONS

The journey of becoming a practitioner-researcher involves multiple transitions and transformations. Expert practitioners may suddenly find themselves being novice researchers. Experienced professionals undergo role transition when adopting the student role. Doctoral students or practitioner-researchers find themselves existing within two communities of practice, each requiring them to perform potentially differing activities and functions. This often requires the utilisation of new or different skills and knowledge, and therefore requires the practitioner-researcher to travel back and forth through the research-practice portal.

All practitioner-researchers will find and forge their own path into research from practice and create a unique identity for themselves. From the two stories above, it can be seen how the particular disciplines of Diane and Annette may have influenced their interpretation of the research journey. As a physiotherapist, Diane perceives the journey as a process of intellectual movement. As an occupational therapist, Annette observes and interprets the various functional and occupational aspects of her journey. Such interpretations reveal each individual's professional self, a self which is not lost in the process of learning to research but rather enhanced and transformed to form the more composite identity of a practitioner-researcher.

As well as involving multiple transitions, the metamorphosis into practitioner-researcher includes myriad transformations for the individual, many of which are ongoing. The change that occurs for practitioner-researchers may therefore be seen as a journey from *being* to *becoming*. Engaging in doctoral study transforms knowledge and skills, and can enable participation in a broader range of professional roles or novel aspects of practice. Engaging in research transforms understandings and insights into human experience and facilitates meaning-making. Transformations in self-awareness and professional identity occur, which may be demonstrated in increased confidence and changed attitudes resulting in new opportunities. Adopting a critically reflective and reflexive stance can stimulate deeper insights. All the transformative processes experienced by practitioners who enter the realms of research provide both the backdrop and the process for transformed practice. Literary gems (like cut diamonds) are forged during the journey into research to illuminate and influence the ongoing engagement with clinical practice and beyond.

For us, research and practice are indivisible.
(Groundwater-Smith & Mockler, 2007, p. 200)

REFERENCES

Arber, A. (2006). Reflexivity: A challenge for the researcher as practitioner? *Journal of Research in Nursing, 11*(2), 147-157.

Burgess, T., & Jones, A. (2006). Engaging practitioners in research: How do we meet the challenge? *Focus on Health Professional Education: A Multidisciplinary Journal, 8*(1), 25-33.

Chan, C.L.W., & Ng, S.M. (2004). The social work practitioner-researcher educator: Encouraging innovations and empowerment in the 21st century. *International Social Work, 47*, 312-320.

Cusick, A., & Lannin, N. (2008). On becoming a practitioner-researcher in remote northern Australia: Personal commitment and resources compensate for structural deterrents to research. [Rehabilitation in Practice]. *Disability and Rehabilitation, 30*(26), 1984-1998.

Dadds, M. (2008). Empathetic validity in practitioner research. *Educational Action Research, 16*(2), 279-290.

Deegan, M.J., & Hill, M.R. (1991). Doctoral dissertations as liminal journeys of the self: Betwixt and between in graduate sociology programs. *Teaching Sociology, 19*, 322-332.

Edwards, B. (2002). Deep insider research. *Qualitative Research Journal, 2*(1), 71-84.

Fenge, L. (2009). Professional doctorates–A better route for researching professionals? *Social Work Education, 28*(2), 165-176.

Foss, L., & Moldenæs, T. (2007). The engaged researcher–From translator to literary change agent. *Systemic Practice and Action Research, 20*, 27-39.

Fox, M., Martin, P., & Green, G. (2007). *Doing practitioner research.* London: Sage.

Gregory, M. (1997). Professional scholars and scholarly professionals. *The New Academic, Summer*, 19-22.

Groundwater-Smith, S., & Mockler, N. (2007). Ethics in practitioner research: An issue of quality *Research Papers in Education, 22*(2), 199-122.

Higgs, J., Richardson, B., & Abrandt Dahlgren, M. (2004). *Developing practice knowledge for health professionals.* Oxford: Elsevier Health Sciences.

Mendenhall, A. (2007). Switching hats: Transitioning from the role of clinician to the role of researcher in social work doctoral education. *Journal of Teaching in Social Work, 27*(3/4), 273–290.

Moore, J. (2008). Practitioner-researcher imaginations: Teaching social research to health science undergraduates. *Focus on Health Professional Education: A Multi-disciplinary Journal, 10*(2), 1-21.

O'Hanlon, C. (1994). Reflection and action in research: Is there a moral responsibility to act? *Educational Action Research, 2*(2), 281-289.

Pilkington, R. (2009). Practitioner research in education: The critical perspectives of doctoral students. *Studies in the Education of Adults, 41*(2), 154-174.

Polgar, S., & Thomas, S.A. (2000). *Introduction to research in the health sciences* (4th ed.). Edinburgh: Churchill Livingstone.

Selby, S. (2005). Getting started: Confessions of a novice researcher. [Viewpoints]. *Australian Family Physician, 34*(12), 1056.

Stewart, R.A. (2002). *Practice vs praxis: Modelling practitioner-based research.* Paper presented at the 31st InSEA World Congress, New York.

Turner, V. (1969). *The ritual process: Structure and anti-structure.* Chicago: Aldine.

Van Baalen, P., Bloemhof-Ruwaard, J., & Van Heck, E. (2005). Knowledge sharing in an emerging network of practice: The role of a knowledge portal. *European Management Journal, 23*(3), 300–314.

Watts, J.H. (2009). From professional to PhD student: Challenges of status transition. *Teaching in Higher Education, 14*(6), 687-691.

Diane Tasker BPhty(Qld), PhD candidate
The Research Institute For Professional Practice, Learning & Education
Mountain Mobile Physiotherapy Service
Blue Mountains, Australia

Annette McLeod-Boyle MOccThy, PhD candidate
Faculty of Science, Charles Sturt University
Northeast Health Wangaratta, Australia

Donna Bridges PhD
The Education For Practice Institute
Charles Sturt University, Australia

JOY HIGGS AND ANGIE TITCHEN

29. JOURNEYS OF MEANING MAKING

Through Transformation, Illumination, Shared Action and Liberation

This chapter examines how journeys of meaning making in the critical and the interpretive paradigms involve transformation, illumination, shared action and liberation. Such research inevitability and desirably changes researchers, as well as participants and phenomena, and involves critical and creative conversations and shared action that can transform and liberate people in life, research and practice (Higgs & Titchen, 2007a,b).

We have identified the ideas of transformation, illumination, shared action and liberation as the integrating concepts or critical essences of the experience of qualitative research as individual research episodes and as an ongoing research journey. Transformation occurs within the research process as the researcher's understanding of the phenomenon under investigation develops and as new knowledge is created through engagement with the phenomenon. The researcher(s) and fellow participants are transformed and liberated by acquiring new knowledge, through personal development, enhanced research capability, and gaining ideas for more research. The field is enhanced by knowledge illumination, critique and addition. The knowledge generated can be used by practitioners and people in society to change structures, cultures and practices. In critical paradigm research, along with knowledge creation about the phenomenon being researched, there is a clear and intentional transformation of practice and liberation of people's lives; simultaneously, researchers generate knowledge about the process of change and innovation. Such research can be characterised as a spiralling process that occurs within an environment imbued by authentic, person-centred relationships and moral agency and the interweaving of people and ideas. The result can be ever-increasing and deepening illumination of the phenomenon and transformation (learning, empowerment, emancipation) of individuals, teams, ideas, practices and other people (e.g. organisations, communities). The transformations arising from the research can prompt individuals to take on mentoring roles and to liberate and extend their research repertoires. The findings of research mirror its process and can include enabling silenced voices and practices to be heard, appreciating differences in societies, illuminating phenomena and understanding lived experiences. These outcomes can prompt further illuminative research, practice transformation and human flourishing.

J. Higgs et al., (eds.), Creative Spaces for
Qualitative Researching: Living Research, 301–310.

Meaning Making

In qualitative research we create-perform a dance that blends choreography and improvisation. We merge the being, knowing, doing and becoming of self and researcher. This research is about meaning making and illumination in terms of an increase in our understanding of phenomena or practices and our relationship to them. It is about increasing our ability to take effective shared action, informed by our increased understanding, to enhance practice. And it is about transformation and liberation in terms of freeing ourselves from inner and outer obstacles and assumptions that prevent us from pursuing informed action to transform ourselves, our infrastructures, cultures, systems, communication channels and practices to enable change to occur at multiple levels (individual, interpersonal, organisational and societal).

The relationship between illumination, transformation, shared action and liberation transcends the interpretive and critical research paradigms. Through our research journeys we have recognised the transformative effects (on ourselves, others and organisations) that can result both from interpretive paradigm research approaches such as phenomenological sociology, hermeneutics and narrative inquiry, and from critical paradigm research approaches such as collaborative inquiry and action research. We have observed the way such research can be both a tool and a process of shedding light on vital aspects of human existence that are so often ignored. We have come to see research in both these paradigms as a way of telling people's stories, of hearing and making known the words of those whose voices are silenced as well as those who shout so loudly that their messages are lost in white noise (like trying to listen to a radio announcer when the radio is not tuned in). Another core idea we identified is the importance of shared action. Sharing occurs in research collaborations, in working with people whose issues or experiences crave exploration and in enabling these people to empower themselves (and us). And shared action occurs in the transformation of individual researchers and participants into groups of co-researchers. Such collaboration we see as desirable in many forms of interpretive paradigm research and as the essence of critical paradigm research approaches.

Critical and Creative Conversations

The term "critical and creative conversations" is a core feature of meaning-making research. This term is a metaphor for qualitative research that is both transformative (through critical and shared dialogues) and illuminative (through creative discourse) (Higgs, 2006). It reflects the researchers' conversation with the phenomenon and with the research participants who have experienced that phenomenon, to explore its nature and essence. And it reflects researchers' conversations with themselves and with each other as
they plan and implement their research and learn to understand more deeply

themselves as researchers, their research strategies, and the phenomenon they are researching.

QUALITATIVE RESEARCH AS A REFLEXIVE
JOURNEY OF MEANING MAKING

The researcher's journey is ideally one of reflexivity, growth and meaning making. Here we consider the researcher as growing through development of professional artistry and a dance of research intelligences, creating an epistemology and ontology of research practice that values moral agency, wise use of power, political action, the centrality of reflexive knowing and going beyond dominant thinking.

The Self in Research

An important part of research is self-development, the enhancement of our being, doing and becoming through a rich knowing of ourselves along with the phenomenon we are investigating or the changes we are making. As the instrument of the research, the qualitative researcher needs to be self-aware, reflexive, curious, imaginative, creative, sensitive, mature, wise and knowledgeable. Being knowledgeable includes knowing (or rather seeking to know) self and the place of self in research and research relationships, as well as having philosophical, theoretical, methodological and political knowledge. Attention to ontology in qualitative research practice is as important as its epistemology in terms of producing research that is rigorous, ethical and trustworthy. By ontology, we mean our ways of being (researchers). We support an ontological perspective where researchers are moral agents who are concerned with human flourishing, respectful of power balance in their relationships, and revealers of social injustice. By epistemology, we mean what we know, how we know it and how we generate new knowledge.

Experiencing Qualitative Research: Research Intelligences

Professional artistry in research (Titchen, Higgs and Horsfall, 2007) involves the blending and interplay of, among other dimensions, a variety of research intelligences and the use of self as person, facilitator and researcher. Intelligence is taken to mean a capacity for, and quickness of, understanding or sagacity (Concise Oxford Dictionary, 1982) or the organisation of the mind (Gardner, 1993). Complementary to Gardner's theory of multiple human intelligences, we have identified four intelligences that are relevant to human being and to being human in research; these are embodied, emotional, artistic and spiritual intelligences (Titchen & Higgs, 2001). These intelligences provide the capacity and background wisdom that facilitate different ways of knowing. We hypothesise that these intelligences contribute to the rapid blending of different types of knowledge (i.e., propositional, professional, craft and personal) and the ability to switch quickly and effortlessly from one level of knowing to another (i.e., pre-cognitive,

cognitive, metacognitive and reflexive levels) as appropriate to the context and situation.

We see embodied intelligence as the wisdom of the body that enables us to engage in body-situated, reflexive analysis of our research and our research practices. We are influenced by Merleau-Ponty's (1962) view that perception has primacy over cognition and that the body holds important pre-cognitive knowing, that is, lived space, lived time, lived body and lived human relations. In our qualitative research we experience the body as holding hidden knowing or insight that is usually overshadowed by our cognitive knowing. This hidden knowing can be accessed and expressed through embodied intelligence, that is, our capacity and quickness to gain understanding of pre-cognitive knowledge of ourselves and others. Drawing on ideas from creative and ancient traditions, we have been able to develop our embodied research intelligence through enactment (role-playing), engaging the body through gesture and physical expression as critical reflection (Coats, 2001), image theatre (Boal, 1982), and authentic movement with creative expression (Titchen & McCormack, 2010). How can we develop the capacity and quickness of embodied intelligence? In our experience, it is through embodied learning and paying attention to the body and our pre-reflective bodily sense of the new arising at the edge of our thinking (cf. Gendlin, 1993). Our wordless knowing often precedes our actual thoughts and our capacity to articulate a new understanding.

Although artistic intelligence (Cowan, 2002) in research is central to the creation of an aesthetically satisfying product and expression that touches people at all levels of their being, we argue that it is also central to the process of artistic critique in critical and creative qualitative research. Building on Gardner's work (1993), we propose that artistic intelligence is the capacity to create, to perform and to appreciate artistic expression. Working synergistically with embodied intelligence, artistic intelligence facilitates the sensing of the unconscious and brings it to consciousness through artistic expression. This seems to work best when we explicitly ground and centre ourselves, let go of ego and contact our soul (Titchen & Higgs, 2001). We have found the use of creative arts media helpful not only for ourselves as qualitative researchers, but also in enabling others to surface and then critique their well-springs of knowledge and wisdom artistically, cognitively and metacognitively. What is so exciting about this way of working is that when we intentionally combine artistic with cognitive critique, the juxtaposition, or collision, potentially creates something new or articulates the previously inexpressible or unknown (see e.g., the chapter by Famke van Lieshout and Shaun Cardiff on creative hermeneutic analysis).

Synergy is created through a reiterative, reciprocal dialogue between words and art forms (McCormack & Titchen, 2006). Artistic intelligence also helps us, often in an instant, to judge whether some new thing is expressed in exactly the best way. It shows us whether the expression is satisfying and fulfilling, whether there is balance, beauty, synchronicity and interplay, when oppressed voices are truly singing, when diversity is shown, and when the blend of philosophical and methodological assumptions from different paradigms addresses the task in hand.

Emotional intelligence (Goleman, 1996) gives us awareness of, or attunement to, our own and others' feelings, facilitating empathy, compassion, motivation, caring and appropriate responses to pain or pleasure. It enables us to use our professional craft knowledge, for example, knowing the research colleague or participant as a person and knowing ourselves in relationship with them (personal knowledge). We consider that a capacity and quickness in picking up cues in ourselves and others is central to research with a concern for human flourishing and transformation. To be genuinely person-centred researchers, we must have the capacity to respond quickly to those cues and immediately engage emotionally and genuinely with others in the research, as people, with the whole of ourselves as a person. Emotional intelligence serves us well as we engage with our other research intelligences, which are likely to challenge and take us out of our comfort zones.

Spiritual intelligence (Zohar & Marshall, 2000) enables us to address and solve problems of meaning and value and to place our actions, lives and pathways in wider, richer meaning-giving contexts. It gives us our moral sense and allows us to discriminate, to aspire, to dream and to uplift ourselves. Whereas embodied and emotional intelligences allow us to work within the boundaries of our situation and context and be guided by the same, artistic and spiritual intelligences let us work with the boundaries and shape and transform the situation. However, embodied intelligence can lead to the awakening of spiritual intelligence. We also invoke spiritual intelligence when we are creative, using our deep, intuitive sense of meaning and value to guide us when we are at the boundary of order and chaos, and at the edge of our comfort zone. Thus, artistic intelligence and spiritual intelligence are very closely linked. Working reflexively and creatively at the edge can be very challenging (see Christine Boomer and Donna Frost's chapter) and it may mean that people need help to develop their spiritual intelligence. We have found that supervision and critical and creative conversations, imbued with Campbell's (1984) moderated love, enables people to develop their capacity for and understanding of artistic and spiritual intelligences.

If doing qualitative research is like dancing a choreographed piece, but with the freedom to let go, improvise and be creative, then it is the four research intelligences that give us the capacity to dance. The intelligences boogie with each other, facilitating synthesis and interplay of all aspects of self (our being, knowing, doing and becoming), and creativity emerges. Capacity and quickness develop through reflexive, creative journeying and through critical and creative conversations with others on the way. These intelligences have the potential to speed up research and all its processes and open the way for meaning making through transformation, illumination, shared action and liberation.

Moral Agency (Respect and Integrity)

Qualitative researchers often aspire towards moral agency, or acting with respect and integrity. This involves:

- researching and reporting research in a way that demonstrates a respect for the environment and living things
- recognising that relationships within research are as important as the research itself. The process and outcomes of research thus need to be congruent, respectful, compassionate, honest and supporting, as well as challenging
- pursuing transparency in all aspects of the research conduct and distribution. This includes acknowledging the ideological stances, social positioning and values of the researcher(s), stakeholders and participants
- being person-centred and working with stakeholders and participants
- asking who stands to gain and lose by implementing this research.

Relationships and Power

As with many relationships, research involves power and power differentials. Knowing that the role of researcher (and research mentor) has power, despite all attempts to share this power, it is necessary to use it respectfully, wisely and sparingly. Although researchers aspire towards equality of stakeholder participants in the research, true collaboration and equality are difficult to achieve. There are times when differences in power and role in research are desirable and should be made explicit. When there are multiple researchers, stakeholders and participants, a number of steps can be followed to facilitate agreed and empowered relationships. These include:

- clarifying terminology to ensure mutual understanding and sharing
- promoting trustworthy and trusting relationships
- using negotiation (not direction) as an inherent process in decision making
- sharing knowledge and experiences among the research participants
- advocating for vulnerable groups and using positive discrimination to foster greater equality among participants
- enabling people's own voices to be re-presented in the research product
- being aware that although we centre some practices and voices, we also need to recognise those that we consequently place in the margins.

Research as a Political Act

We see research and many other human endeavours such as education (see Freire, 1970) as political acts, reflecting Foucault's (1980) recognition of the connection between power and knowledge. Research, being political, aims to:

- reveal social injustice and work against such injustices as racism and classism
- give voice to the silenced in society, on the premise that the view from the margins in society is as important as the view from the centre
- operate with reflexivity – the circular reflection and development process that allows us to reflect on ourselves and our relations with others as we research.

As a political act, the purpose of qualitative research is to better understand practices in the widest sense, including practices of exploitation and domination, as well as practices of resistance, creativity and liberation. These practices need to be understood at the local and everyday level, as well as at institutional and societal levels. This purpose can be achieved by researching alternative practices that work against politically oppressive practices. It could mean researching how racism, sexism, ageism or other oppressive practices operate at local and everyday levels as well as at institutional and societal levels. It could include researching languaging discourses (systems of knowledge and practice sustained through language) which construct and shape these practices. Moreover, researching alternative practices can be done by creatively, courageously and compassionately engaging with people involved in the research issue, actively seeking out differences and diversity, and endeavouring to create alternative stories to pursue.

Going Beyond Current Predominant Thinking

The purposes of qualitative research outlined above (that is, increasing understanding of practices in their broadest sense, improving practice, and enhancing our own knowing, doing, being and becoming as researchers) can be gained by going beyond the traditional concepts and purposes of research. This means going beyond the straitjackets of experimental research and being open to new research strategies, at the same time as consistently pursuing quality research practices and outcomes. This can be achieved by:

- looking for complementarity among research paradigms and discipline traditions (see e.g., McCormack & Titchen, 2006)
- valuing integration of all kinds of knowledge and experience in everyday professional practice and life, including intuitive and embodied knowing about the phenomenon
- recognising that the process and outcomes of qualitative research are equally important and that both can lead to human flourishing
- seeing and enhancing realities through research (e.g. seeking difference, diversity and the unseen)
- examining the contradictions, dilemmas and the unspoken as much as (and often more than) the explicit agreements, to reveal complexity instead of consensus (which can result in silencing rather than singing up participants' voices)
- seeking innovative research approaches, particularly using creative imagination and artistic expression through the use of creative arts in qualitative research
- reclaiming but reframing rigour (e.g. as reflexive awareness of the researcher within authentic research relationships with participants and with the data)
- being our own strongest critics and looking for and explicating ways of achieving credibility and rigour relevant to our research.

Reflexive Knowing

A vital aspect of being a qualitative researcher and a phenomenologist is self-knowledge and self-awareness as researcher, and I believe that explorations in learning about phenomenological research approaches should include self-discovery. (QRP-RP11) [1]

Deep research experiences are not just about research or knowledge generation through systematic and rigorous inquiry. Instead, experienced researchers have learned to refine the process of research to an advanced level and to move beyond inquiry about the phenomenon being studied, to study themselves. In this process of reflexive knowing, they critique themselves as researchers and develop their understanding and capacity as researchers. In the following quotes from Joy's research project on the experiences of qualitative researchers, three qualitative researchers describe part of their journeys of becoming (self and researcher):

> I've just read a chapter which I wrote for a second edition of a book about two and half years ago and it's just coming out and I read it now just before it's been published, and it's so theoretical. I wouldn't present that now. It's too theoretical, it isn't related, it doesn't start off with practice and I think you have to start off with practice. But then it's very easy to say that in hindsight when you have that underpinning knowledge and critical science perspective. It's a different perception that I have than maybe somebody who is new into nursing, they wouldn't necessarily be able to make those links. I'm on my journey and they're on theirs. I do think it's very, very important. (QRP-RP2)

> I've certainly always been a very person-centred individual – I'm concerned with human being – that's why I've always been attracted to qualitative research approaches. I've learned over the years that qualitative research is extremely complex. I think that rigorous qualitative research is more difficult to do than rigorous quantitative research. I think that's partly because one is using one's self as a person and so one has to be a very mature, well-developed, sensitive individual who is very reflexive and who has undertaken a lot of personal and professional development. I think qualitative researchers have to spend a lot of time developing as people and as professional researchers. (QRP-RP1)

> For a long time I "did" research. I learned the craft of research, I honed my writing skills and I absorbed and enacted my mentors' advice. Alongside this I immersed myself in my studies and later, teaching of social ecology. My passion for my topic spilled over into my research questions and strategies. This was all smooth sailing until I attended one particular research conference where I participated in a workshop where we were asked to reflect on our research journeys. I remember being awestruck by the level of self-knowing of some of the participants and the workshop facilitator, and amazed at the little time I had spent on understanding myself. Till that time my research journey had "happened", after that I learned to be and to enjoy the bliss of being reflexive. For my own students, now, I don't leave this gem of research and self-development to chance. (QRP-RP13)

These researchers have described their reflexivity and development as researchers and people. In addition to self-knowing, such development could occur through peer feedback and collaborative review by critical friends/companions.

CONCLUSION

Our vision for the future of qualitative research is that it can contribute to the creation of healthy people spaces and conditions for the growth of individuals, teams, organisations, communities and societies that are respectful of all peoples, the land and nature. Qualitative research, we contend, can contribute to the transformation of researchers and practices both through its means – emancipation, liberation and shared action – and its research products.

Meaning making in qualitative research commonly involves seeking to understand and interpret lived practice and personal experience, and theorising from this knowledge. This is the approach we have taken to produce this book. We have adopted an experiential and scholarly approach to re-searching our own research practice. In doing so we offer our theorisations in the form of discussions of illuminative and transformative qualitative research grounded in shared practice and liberation. We offer our experiences and practice wisdom as a contribution to understanding the practices of qualitative research.

NOTES

[1] This quote and others similarly labelled are derived from Joy's "Research on Research" Project, a narrative inquiry to explore the experiences of qualitative researchers from several countries working in tertiary education contexts. This project is referred to as the Qualitative Research Project (QRP). The research was first reported by Higgs and Radovich (1999). The participants were grouped into two categories. The first group were entering their research journey and coming to grips with the nature and strategies of qualitative research; much of their focus was on direct research approaches. The second group were experienced researchers and qualitative research artists.

REFERENCES

Boal, A. (1982). *The theatre of the oppressed*. London: Routledge.
Campbell, A.V. (1984). *Moderated love: a theology of professional care*. London: SPCK.
Coats, E. (2001). Weaving the body, the creative unconscious, imagination and the arts into practice development. In J. Higgs & A. Titchen (Eds.), *Professional Practice in Health, Education and the Creative Arts* (pp. 251-263). Oxford: Blackwell Science.
Concise Oxford Dictionary (1982) (Eds. A.L. Hayward & J.J. Sparkes). London: Omega.
Cowan, D. (2002). Artistic intelligence and leadership framing: Employing the wisdom of envisioning, improvisation, introspection and inclusion. Paper presented at The Art of Management and Organization Conference, King's College, London.
Foucault, M. (1980). *Power/knowledge: Selected interviews and writings by Michel Foucault* (Ed. C. Gordon). Brighton: Harvester Press.
Freire, P. (1970). *Cultural action for freedom*. Cambridge, MA: Harvard Educational Review, Monograph Series, 1.
Gardner, H. (1993). *Multiple intelligences: The theory in practice*. New York: Basic Books.

Gendlin, E.T. (1993). Three assertions about the body. *The Folio 12*(1), 21-33. Available: http://www.focusing.org/gendlin/docs/gol_2064.html, accessed March 31 2009.

Goleman, D. (1996). *Emotional intelligence: Why it can matter more than IQ*. London: Bloomsbury.

Higgs, J. (2006). Realising hermeneutic dialogues: Creating spaces for critical, creative conversations in learning, research, clinical decision making and practice advancement. CPEA Occasional Paper 5. Collaborations in Practice and Education Advancement, The University of Sydney, Australia.

Higgs, J., & Radovich, S. (1999). Narratives on qualitative research. Paper presented at AQR '99 International Conference: Issues of Rigour in Qualitative Research, 8–10 July, Melbourne.

Higgs, J., & Titchen, A. (2007a). Becoming critical and creative in qualitative research. In J. Higgs, A. Titchen, D. Horsfall & H. Armstrong (Eds.), *Being critical and creative in qualitative research* (pp. 1-10). Sydney: Hampden Press.

Higgs, J., & Titchen, A. (2007b). Qualitative research: Journeys of meaning making through transformation, illumination, shared action and liberation. In J. Higgs, A. Titchen, D. Horsfall & H. Armstrong (Eds.), *Being critical and creative in qualitative research* (pp. 11-21). Sydney: Hampden Press.

McCormack, B., & Titchen, A. (2006). Critical creativity: Melding, exploding, blending, *Educational Action Research: An International Journal, 14*(2), 239-266.

Merleau-Ponty, M. (1962). *Phenomenology of perception* (C. Smith, Trans.). London: Routledge.

Titchen, A., & Higgs, J. (2001). Towards professional artistry and creativity in practice. In J. Higgs & A. Titchen (Eds.), *Professional practice in health, education and the creative arts* (pp. 273-290). Oxford: Blackwell Science.

Titchen, A., Higgs, J., & Horsfall, D. (2007). Research artistry: Dancing the praxis spiral in critical-creative qualitative research. In J. Higgs, A. Titchen, D. Horsfall & H. Armstrong (Eds.), *Being critical and creative in qualitative research* (pp. 282-297). Sydney: Hampden Press.

Titchen, A., & McCormack, B. (2010). Dancing with stones: Critical creativity as methodology for human flourishing. *Educational Action Research: An International Journal, 18*(4), 531-554.

Zohar, D., & Marshall, I. (2000). *SQ: Spiritual intelligence the ultimate intelligence*, London: Bloomsbury.

Joy Higgs AM PhD
The Education For Practice Institute
Charles Sturt University, Australia

Angie Titchen PhD
Knowledge Centre for Person-Centred, Evidence-Based Practice
Fontys University of Applied Sciences, The Netherlands

CONTRIBUTORS

Christine Boomer RGN, MBA, PG Cert, PhD candidate
Institute of Nursing Research/School of Nursing
University of Ulster and South Eastern Health and Social Care Trust, UK

Karen Bridgman PhD
Naturopath, The University of Sydney, Australia

Donna Bridges PhD
The Education For Practice Institute
Charles Sturt University, Australia

Catherine Camden Pratt PhD
University of Western Sydney, Australia

Shaun Cardiff MScN
School of Nursing
Fontys University of Applied Sciences, The Netherlands

Nita Cherry PhD
The Australian Graduate School for Entrepreneurship
Faculty of Business and Enterprise
Swinburne University of Technology, Australia
Adjunct Professor, Charles Sturt University, Australia

Julia Coyle PhD
School of Community Health
Charles Sturt University, Australia

Anne Croker PhD Candidate
School of Community Health
Charles Sturt University, Australia

Sally Denshire PhD
Faculty of Science
Charles Sturt University, Australia

Jan Dewing PhD, MN, BSc, RN, RNT, Dip Nurs Ed, Dip Nurs
East Sussex Healthcare NHS Trust
Canterbury Christ Church University, Kent, England

Jan Fook PhD
Interprofessional Institute, South West London Academic Network, UK

Adjunct Professor, Charles Sturt University, Australia
Donna Frost NZRN, BHSc (Nsg), MSc (Nsg), PhD candidate
Knowledge Centre for Evidence Based Practice, School of Nursing
Fontys University of Applied Sciences, Eindhoven, The Netherlands
Institute of Nursing Research/School of Nursing, University of Ulster
Belfast, Northern Ireland, UK

Susan Groundwater-Smith PhD
Faculty of Education and Social Work
The University of Sydney, Australia
Adjunct Professor, Charles Sturt University, Australia

Joy Higgs AM PhD
The Education For Practice Institute
Charles Sturt University, Australia

Debbie Horsfall PhD
Peace and Development Studies
School of Social Sciences
University of Western Sydney, Australia
Adjunct Research Associate, Charles Sturt University, Australia

Virginia Kaufman Hall PhD
Research and Evaluation, Office of Indigenous Policy Coordination
Government Department of Families and Community Services and Indigenous
Affairs, Australia

Carolyn R. Kelshaw MA
Fellow of Christian Educators Professional Association, Australia

Elizabeth Anne Kinsella PhD
School of Occupational Therapy & Occupational Science Field
Faculty of Health Sciences
University of Western Ontario, Canada
Adjunct Professor, Charles Sturt University, Australia

Stephen Loftus BDS MSc PhD
The Education For Practice Institute
Charles Sturt University, Australia

Sharyn McGee MA, BA (Hons), GDipComm
The School of Social Sciences
The University of Western Sydney, Australia

Paul McIntosh PhD, MSc, PGCE, BSc (Hons), RNMH
Research Fellow, Institute for Health Sciences Education
Barts and The London School of Medicine and Dentistry
Queen Mary University London, UK

Annette McLeod-Boyle MOccThy, PhD candidate
Faculty of Science, Charles Sturt University
Northeast Health Wangaratta, Australia

Nicole Mockler PhD
School of Education
University of Newcastle, Australia

Theo Niessen PhD, MSc, RN
Fontys University of Applied Sciences, The Netherlands

Janice M Ollerton PhD
Social Justice Social Change Research Unit
University of Western Sydney, Australia

Marissa Olsen MSc (Nutr/Diet) APD PhD Candidate
School of Dentistry and Health Sciences
Charles Sturt University, Australia

Anna Park Lala MSc (OT) PhD Candidate
Health & Rehabilitation Sciences
University of Western Ontario, Canada

Narelle Patton BAppSc(Phty) MHSc, PhD Candidate
School of Community Health
Charles Sturt University, Australia

Shanon Phelan MSc (OT) PhD Candidate
Health & Rehabilitation Sciences, Occupational Science Field
University of Western Ontario, Canada

Judy Pinn
Writer living in the Blue Mountains of New South Wales

Megan Smith PhD
School of Community Health
Charles Sturt University, Australia

Diane Tasker BPhty, PhD candidate
The Research Institute For Professional Practice, Learning & Education
Charles Sturt University, Australia

Angie Titchen D.Phil, MSc, MCSP
Independent Research & Practice Development Consultant
Fontys University of Applied Sciences, The Netherlands
University of Ulster, Northern Ireland
University of Warwick, England
Adjunct Professor, Charles Sturt University, Australia

Julie-Anne Tooth PhD Candidate
The Education For Practice Institute
Charles Sturt University, Australia

Franziska Trede PhD
The Education For Practice Institute
Charles Sturt University, Australia

Famke van Lieshout MPH
School of Nursing
Fontys University of Applied Sciences, The Netherlands